Comparative Legislative Behavior:
Frontiers of Research

Comparative Studies in Behavioral Science:

A WILEY SERIES

Robert T. Holt and John E. Turner, *Editors*
Department of Political Science
University of Minnesota

The Logic of Comparative Social Inquiry
by Adam Przeworski and Henry Teune

The Analysis of Subjective Culture
by Harry C. Triandis

Comparative Legislative Behavior: Frontiers of Research
edited by Samuel C. Patterson and John C. Wahlke

Comparative Legislative Behavior: Frontiers of Research

Edited by

SAMUEL C. PATTERSON

JOHN C. WAHLKE

University of Iowa

WILEY-INTERSCIENCE

a Division of John Wiley & Sons, Inc.

NEW YORK · LONDON · SYDNEY · TORONTO

Library of Congress Cataloging in Publication Data:

Shambaugh Conference on Comparative Legislative
  Behavior Research, University of Iowa, 1969.
  Comparative legislative behavior.

  (Comparative studies in behavioral science)
  Sponsored by the Dept. of Political Science,
University of Iowa and held May 1969.
    1. Legislative bodies—Congresses. 2. Comparative
  Includes bibliographical references.
government—Congresses. I. Patterson, Samuel Charles,
1931–   ed. II. Wahlke, John C., ed. III. Iowa.
University. Dept. of Political Science.

JF501.S5 1969   328'.3   72-3387
ISBN 0-471-67020-0

AUTHORS

JOHN A. BRAND is Senior Lecturer in Politics at the University of Strathclyde, Glasgow, Scotland.

HANS DAALDER is Professor of Political Science at the University of Leiden. He has taught at the University of Amsterdam and in the Institute of Social Studies at The Hague, and has been a Fellow at the Center for Advanced Study in the Behavioral Sciences, a British Council Scholar at the London School of Economics and Political Science, and a Rockefeller Foundation Fellow at Harvard University and the University of California at Berkeley.

HEINZ EULAU is Professor and Chairman of the Department of Political Science at Stanford University. He has taught at Antioch College, at the University of California (Berkeley), and at the Institute for Advanced Studies in Vienna, and has been a Fellow at the Center for Advanced Studies in the Behavioral Sciences. During 1971–1972 he was President of the American Political Science Association.

PETER GERLICH is head assistant in the Department of Political Science of the Institute for Advanced Studies in Vienna. He holds a Master of Comparative Law degree from Columbia University and a doctorate in Law and Political Science from the University of Vienna.

JOHN G. GRUMM is Professor of Political Science at Wesleyan University. He has been Research Director of the Citizen's Conference on State Legislatures, Staff Director of the Federal Advisory Committee on Higher Education, and Book Review Editor of the *Midwest Journal of Political Science,* and has taught at the University of Kansas and the University of California.

GEOFFREY LAMBERT is Assistant Professor of Political Science at the University of Manitoba, Winnipeg, Canada.

GERHARD LOEWENBERG is Professor of Political Science at the University of Iowa. He has taught at Mount Holyoke College, Columbia University,

v

the University of California, Cornell University, and in the Bologna Program of the University of Massachusetts.

SAMUEL C. PATTERSON is Professor of Political Science at the University of Iowa. He has taught at the University of Wisconsin and the University of Essex, England, and has been editor of the *Midwest Journal of Political Science.*

MOGENS PEDERSEN is Associate Professor of Political Science at the University of Aarhus, Denmark. He has been Ford Foundation Fellow at Stanford University, engaging in a major collection of historical data on Danish Folketing members.

PERTTI PESONEN is Professor of Political Science at the University of Helsinki, Finland, and at the State University of New York at Stony Brook. He has served as Dean of the Faculty of Social Sciences at the University of Tampere and as a member of the University Council of the Government of Finland. In 1970, he was elected a member of the Finnish Academy of Sciences. He has been a research fellow at the University of Michigan, a Visiting Professor at the University of New Hampshire, and served from 1967 to 1971 as Regular Visiting Distinguished Professor at the University of Iowa. He has been editor both of *Politiikka* and *Scandinavian Political Studies.*

JERROLD G. RUSK is Associate Professor of Political Science at Purdue University. He has been associated with the Survey Research Center of the University of Michigan as a Study Director, and served as Visiting Research Scholar at Tilburg University, The Netherlands, during 1969–1971.

JOHN E. SCHWARZ is Associate Professor of Government at the University of Arizona. He also taught at the University of Minnesota.

JOHN C. WAHLKE is Professor of Political Science at the University of Iowa. He has also taught at Amherst College, the University of California, Vanderbilt University, and the State University of New York at Buffalo, the State University of New York at Stony Brook, and served as President of the Midwest Political Science Association.

The last decade has witnessed the burgeoning of comparative studies in the behavioral sciences. Scholars in specific disciplines have come to realize that they share much with experts in other fields who face similar theoretical and methodological problems and whose research findings are often related. Moreover, specialists in a given geographic area have felt the need to look beyond the limited confines of their region and to seek new meaning in their research results by comparing them with studies that have been made elsewhere.

This series is designed to meet the needs of the growing cadre of scholars in comparative research. The emphasis is on cross-disciplinary studies, although works within the perspective of a single discipline are included. In its scope, the series includes books of theoretical and methodological interest, as well as studies that are based on empirical research. The books in the series are addressed to scholars in the various behavioral science disciplines, to graduate students, and to undergraduates in advanced standing.

Robert T. Holt
John E. Turner

University of Minnesota
Minneapolis, Minnesota

Preface

While parliamentary bodies lie at the heart of democratic representative government, and while there exists an enormous descriptive literature about legislative politics in Western countries, especially the United States, the systematic analysis of parliamentary institutions on a cross-national comparative basis is in its infancy. This book is a contribution to the emerging study of comparative legislative behavior.

The chapters were, with one exception, presented in preliminary form at the Shambaugh Conference on Comparative Legislative Behavior Research, held at the University of Iowa in May 1969. For a number of years the Department of Political Science at the University of Iowa has been able to present lecture and conference programs because of a fund created in memory of Benjamin F. Shambaugh, who for many years was Chairman of the Department of Political Science at the University of Iowa and Superintendent of the State Historical Society. The first department executive officer, he served for about 40 years, including service as President of the American Political Science Association. Under the aegis of the Shambaugh fund, a series of distinguished lectures has been possible, including presentations by Karl Deutsch, Herman Finer, Charles S. Hyneman, Dayton D. McKean, Arnold Rogow, and Sheldon Wolin. In 1967, the first Shambaugh Conference was held—a Conference on Judicial Research. The papers from that conference, *Frontiers of Judicial Research,* edited by Joel B. Grossman and Joseph Tanenhaus, were published by Wiley in 1969. Thus the present book constitutes the second set of research papers from a continuing series of research conferences.

With the exception of the chapter by John Schwarz and Geoffrey Lambert, all the chapters in this book were presented in preliminary drafts at the research conference. John E. Schwarz was a conference participant, and some of his work was discussed at the conference, although his paper was done later with Geoffrey Lambert. Although their research efforts are not represented by chapters in this book, major presentations were made at the conference of Mattei Dogan of the *Centre National de la Recherche Scientifique* in Paris, Henry Valen of the University of Oslo, and Jens Christophersen of the University of Oslo. Other participants in conference discussions included Allan Kornberg (Duke University), Andrew Milnor (Cornell University), Malcolm E. Jewell (University of Kentucky), Thomas Flinn (Cleveland State University), Marvin G. Weinbaum (University of Illinois), Donald R. Matthews (Brookings Institution), Richard Fenno, Jr. (University of Rochester), Chong Lim Kim (University of Iowa), and G. Robert Boynton (University of Iowa).

The conference in Iowa City provided a vitally important setting for the extended discussion of research interests, findings, and problems in legislative analysis by investigators from a number of countries. We all are indebted to Phillip G. Hubbard, now Vice-Provost for Academic Affairs of the University of Iowa, Brooks Booker, Director of the Center for Conferences and Institutes, and Allin W. Dakin, Administrative Dean of the University. For financial support of the conference, we are grateful to the Trustees of the Shambaugh Fund, and to the National Science Foundation (GS-2990). We are especially indebted to Dr. Howard Hines, Director of the Division of Social Sciences of the National Science Foundation, who encouraged us to develop an international conference of this kind, who helped to fund the project, and who attended the conference sessions and was an active and contributive participant in them.

Samuel C. Patterson
John C. Wahlke

Iowa City, Iowa
March 1972

CONTENTS

xi

Comparative Legislative Behavior:
Frontiers of Research

PART ONE

Introduction

CHAPTER ONE

Comparative Legislative Research

GERHARD LOEWENBERG

UNIVERSITY OF IOWA

Recent Tendencies in Legislative Research

"Research on legislative behavior has been more sensitive to problems of technique than to problems of conceptual clarification."[1] This assessment, made by Wahlke and Eulau in 1959, still accurately describes the state of legislative behavior research over a decade later, despite the prodigious amount of work on legislatures published in the intervening years. An inventory of legislative research in the 1960s reveals both an impressive accumulation of data and the development of increasingly sophisticated analytical techniques. While Meller, in his survey of American research in 1960, complained that "legislative behavior studies . . . have failed to furnish anything resembling understanding" because they are "too scattered" and because "conflicting findings have not served as stimuli for further clarifying research,"[2] his reassessment 5 years later attributed to subsequent studies "breadth, diversity, focus, replication, detailing of methodology, (and) concern for explicit theoretical formulation."[3] Meller warned, however, that "the attempt to formulate a theory of legislative behavior" threatens "to be completely submerged in a tor-

[1] John C. Wahlke and Heinz Eulau, *Legislative Behavior; A Reader in Theory and Research* (Glencoe, Ill., 1959), p. 535.

[2] Norman Meller, "Legislative Behavior Research," *The Western Political Quarterly,* **13** (1960), p. 152.

[3] Norman Meller, " 'Legislative Behavior Research' Revisited: A Review of Five Years' Publications," *The Western Political Quarterly,* **18** (1965), p. 792.

3

rent of print."[4] The inventory by Eulau and Hinckley a year later concluded that "we know a good deal about legislatures and the men who people them" but "the next step toward maturity must be accelerated theoretical advance."[5]

A parallel development took place during the 1960s in research on non-American legislatures. At the beginning of the decade Meynaud wrote of the "inequality in political knowledge" about different legislative systems, complained that "in the United States . . . the formation of any general picture is impeded by the great number of separate research projects," that "the results of observations relating to the American system cannot be applied, lock, stock and barrel, to other countries," and observed "confusion and incompleteness . . . aggravated by major hesitations as to theory."[6] Seven years later Patterson recorded "a sizeable increase . . . in the level and intensity of research on parliamentary institutions in other countries, mostly in other western countries." But while he found that "we have made great leaps ahead in our knowledge about legislative institutions outside the United States," he concluded that "it is largely descriptive knowledge. Almost all of the new research has been on a country-by-country basis, and there still are very few attempts to test hypotheses cross-nationally."[7]

The very tendency to take stock of legislative research at regular intervals indicates a self-conscious and deliberate effort to develop systematic knowledge about legislatures on the part of a group of political scientists pursuing a recognized subspecialty. An analysis of first-choice fields of specialization of members listed in the 1967 Biographical Directory of the American Political Science Association places the study of legislatures eighth among 27 specialties for the youngest half of the profession; it stands twenty fourth for the middle-age group, and seventeenth for the oldest.[8]

The reasons for the apparent growth of interest in legislative research are themselves interesting. Until the 1960s, executive institutions and bureaucracies had attracted the chief attention of students of political

[4] *Ibid*, p. 793.

[5] Heinz Eulau and Katherine Hinckley, "Legislative Institutions and Processes," in James A. Robinson Ed., *Political Science Annual, An International Review,* Vol. 1—1966 (Indianapolis, 1966), p. 179.

[6] Jean Meynaud, "General Study of Parliamentarians," *International Social Science Journal,* **XIII** (1961), p. 515.

[7] Samuel C. Patterson, "Comparative Legislative Behavior: A Review Essay," *Midwest Journal of Political Science,* **XII** (1968), pp. 599–600.

[8] Heinz Eulau, "Quo Vadimus?," *Political Science,* Newsletter of The American Political Science Association, **II** (1969), p. 13.

institutions for at least 30 years. Bryce's observation on "the decline of legislatures" had become a dictum, and a reason for avoiding legislative research, although Bryce offered it as an interim analysis of an institution which he believed "must remain the vital centre of . . . government."[9] "American political scientists," David Truman wrote in 1966, "have carried on a love affair with the presidency and with the administrative side of government and only recently have begun to show reduced ardor."[10] While an emphasis on the executive overshadowed scholarly interest in the legislature, the behavioral approach in political science diminished attention to institutions altogether, as behavioralism sought at first to distinguish itself from "descriptive-institutional approaches."[11] However, by the beginning of the 1960s, there was a growing "recognition of the institutional context of most behavior which is relevant to government."[12] Furthermore, scholars interested in employing sophisticated statistical techniques, such as factor analysis and Guttman scaling, found in legislative votes and appropriations decisions a ready source of data for analysis. For these reasons, legislative institutions, once the center of scholarly attention, attracted renewed attention after a lapse of several decades.

The consequent accumulation of new findings, and the development of new research methods, has, however, failed to produce a cumulative explanation of legislative behavior. Although the most recent research exhibits some consolidation of approaches, work in the field continues to be highly individualistic. Eulau and Hinckley used a dozen categories in their attempt to classify work published between 1961 and 1964. No common theory or set of concepts is accepted in legislative research, and despite repeated appeals for "accelerated theoretical advance," little effort has been devoted to that end.

It is not surprising that the most sustained attempt to develop a theoretical framework for legislative research was undertaken by the authors of the comparative study of four American state legislatures.[13] Comparative research imposes a concern with theory, because comparison can take place only within a common analytical framework. The failure to

---

[9] James Bryce, *Modern Democracies* (New York, 1929), Vol. II, p. 344.

[10] David Truman, "The Representative Function in Western Systems," in Edward H. Buehrig Ed., *Essays in Political Science* (Bloomington, Ind., 1966), p. 85.

[11] Robert A. Dahl, "The Behavioral Approach in Political Science: Epitaph for a Monument to a Successful Protest," *The American Political Science Review*, **LV** (1961), p. 766.

[12] John C. Wahlke et al., *The Legislative System, Explorations in Legislative Behavior* (New York, 1962), p. 4.

[13] *Ibid.*, ch. 1.

undertake extensive comparative research has permitted the neglect of theory. The few existing comparative studies have analyzed legislative institutions within the American political system. Studies have been undertaken comparing not only state legislatures, but municipal councils, as well as substructures such as committees and party organizations within legislative bodies.

Comparisons within the United States system, however, leave many varieties of legislative behavior out of any account, and legislative theory resulting from research exclusively in the United States risks being parochial. The very term "legislature," with its allusion to the lawmaking function, derives from the United States experience, in contrast to the term "parliament," which calls to mind the deliberative function of the medieval assemblies of Europe. Both terms connote functions, when the function of the institution should be an empirical question. Likewise, any definition of legislatures that includes election as the basis of membership leaves out of the account many nonelected representative bodies that, even in democratic states, share structural characteristics with elected legislatures. Furthermore the emphasis on the analysis of legislative roll calls in United States research clearly reflects the frequency of public voting and its importance as an index of decision-making in United States legislative bodies, but the utility of this type of analysis is at best dubious in the many non-American systems where public votes are either rarely taken or have an entirely different significance.

The development of broadly comparative research and the development of theory in this important field of political science are, therefore, mutually dependent. The boundaries of the subject should certainly not be drawn along any geographical lines. The first question, then, concerns the appropriate delimitation of the subject.

Definition of the Subject

As soon as comparative study is undertaken, the identification of the phenomena to be compared poses problems. What do we mean by "legislatures"? Are they, as Wahlke and Eulau suggested in one admittedly restricted context, "those elected bodies in political systems of the Western culture that engage in the functions of proposing, deliberating, and deciding about public policy"?[14] This definition would exclude not only the House of Lords and the Bundesrat, but probably the House of Commons and the National Assembly as well. Since comparisons can be made only against the background of uniformities, what

[14] John C. Wahlke and Heinz Eulau, *Legislative Behavior, op. cit.,* p. 3.

are the defining uniformities of the subject? Are they to be found in a particular method of selecting members? Or in the performance of particular political functions? Or in a particular institutional context of behavior? Any one of these patterns could, of course, provide a focus for comparative study. However, legislative behavior is presumably behavior taking place within a particular institutional structure, regardless of the functions that this behavior performs for the system, or the method by which the actors are selected. If we can agree on this, then the uniformities which delimit the field are, by definition, structural and organizational, and the functions performed, as well as the method of selecting the actors, are variables for empirical investigation.

There are indeed remarkable structural uniformities among the bodies variously called legislatures, parliaments, councils, chambers, assemblies, or diets in different political systems and at different times. These uniformities are due to the common historical origin of this institution in medieval Europe and the strong influence of the development of the British and French models on other parliaments. A common history, a common source of formal rules and organization, and an exceptional dependence upon informal norms of behavior sanctioned by relatively stable customs have contributed to the structural similarity of these bodies over time and space.

It is not difficult to identify the common elements of these bodies. A legislature consists of a collection of members who are formally equal to each other in status and whose authority derives from the belief that they represent the other members of the community—in some sense of that protean concept, representation. The decisions of legislatures are, therefore, taken collectively by their members. The rules governing members characteristically consist of precedents, folkways, and habits, backed by the expectations of the group rather than by externally imposed sanctions. The selection of members of the legislature takes place by a process that the community believes to assure its representation. In these respects legislatures are clearly distinguishable from hierarchically organized institutions and from bodies whose members are recruited for their specialized skills. However, legislatures vary considerably in age, size, and jurisdiction; in their decisional structures; and in the consequences of their activity for the political system of which they are a part. These variables are the subjects for study.

Conceptualization of the Study

As a result of the behavioral persuasion of U.S. political scientists, with their focus on the actions of individuals, the concept of "role" has become an important unit of study in legislative behavior research, for "role theory . . . pinpoints those aspects of legislators' behavior which make the legislature an institution."[15] Under the influence of systems theory, United States scholarship has regarded the legislature as a subsystem of the political system that performs "functions" for the system as a whole. Since the concepts of "role" and "function" have been most widely used in recent legislative behavior research, it seems necessary to examine them more closely to determine whether they might provide the terms in which a theory of legislative behavior suitable for comparative research could be formulated.

The Use of Role Concepts. Since in its original sociological sense, a "role" consists of expectations regarding the relevant behavior of a particular actor, legislative roles consist of expectations regarding the relevant behavior of those holding positions in legislative structures, both in their relations with each other and with outsiders. The set of all legislative roles may be regarded as the behavioral aspect of the legislative structure.

United States research, guided by the familiar techniques of attitude surveys based on interviews, has gathered considerable data on legislators' own expectations regarding legislative behavior. The unproblematic definition of the respondent group as all members of the legislature, the relative accessibility of the respondents, and the sophistication of interview schedules, all have facilitated research. Uniformities of expectations among members of the same legislature have been clearly established.[16] Research on U.S. legislators has been replicated in separate studies of the roles of Canadian, French, German, Austrian, and Japanese representatives.[17] This approach has led to the identification of various patterns of informal norms of behavior in different legislative institutions. Although in the State Legislative Research Project the attempt

[15] John C. Wahlke et al., *The Legislative System, op. cit.,* p. 9.

[16] *Ibid.,* Chap. 7, especially pp. 144–152.

[17] Cf. Allan Kornberg, *Canadian Legislative Behavior; A Study of the 25th Parliament* (New York, 1967); William H. Hunt, "Legislative Roles and Ideological Orientations of French Deputies," paper delivered at the 65th Annual Meeting of the American Political Science Association, September 2–6, 1969; Arthur B. Gunlicks, "Representative Role Perceptions Among Local Councillors in Western Germany," *The Journal of Politics,* **31** (1969), pp. 443–464; Peter Gerlich and Helmut Kramer, *Abgeordnete in der Parteiendemokratie* (Vienna: Verlag für Geschichte und Politik, 1969); Chong Lim Kim, "Consensus on Legislative Roles Among Japanese Prefectural Assemblymen," in Allan Kornberg, Ed., *Legislatures in Comparative Perspective* (New York, 1972). An English language summary of the research on the Vienna City Council is contained in Peter Gerlich, "Legislators and Legislatures: Roles and Functions," *infra,* pp. 87–106.

was made to interview all legislators,[18] an arduous and expensive undertaking, more recent work has used stratified samples.[19] There is evidence that members of non-U.S. legislatures are as accessible, candid, and cooperative respondents as U.S. legislators have been.[20]

The use of role concepts raises three questions: (1) Whose expectations define the legislative role? (2) How are expectations, which are normative, related to actual behavior, which is presumably the subject of the inquiry? (3) Among all the relationships between legislators and others, which are relevant to the legislative role and which are not?

We cannot assume that roles are defined by legislators alone. The expectations of interested outsiders, such as staff members, journalists, lobbyists, and constituents, must also be examined, despite the difficulty of determining the relevant group of respondents. Furthermore, we cannot assume agreement among the expectations of all respondents, whether legislators or outsiders. Distinctions between the expectations of experienced and inexperienced members, between leaders and back-benchers, and between constituents and their representatives may distinguish stable from temporary norms, may give clues to the process of socialization by which legislators are inducted into their roles, and may indicate sources of role conflict. Studies comparing the behavioral expectations of different groups of respondents may yield explanations of some of the most distinctive behavioral patterns within legislatures, such as bargaining, and give insight into the informal hierarchies that generally exist within these bodies, since these may well be the mechanisms for dealing with role conflict.[21] A model of the role system that constitutes a stable legislature has yet to be developed.

Roles, which are normative, presumably guide actual behavior, and behavior presumably modifies expectations. But the link between role and role behavior must be established by investigation. Research can conceivably begin at either end, studying roles and relating them to behavior or studying behavioral patterns in order to identify roles. The use of the role concept, therefore, does not limit the student to interview techniques, but may well include the use of documentary and newspaper sources of data on behavior.

[18] John C. Wahlke et al., *The Legislative System, op. cit.,* p. 31.

[19] Roger H. Davidson, *The Role of the Congressman* (New York, New York, 1969), Appendix.

[20] William H. Hunt, Wilder W. Crane, and John C. Wahlke, "Interviewing Political Elites in Cross-Cultural Comparative Research," *The American Journal of Sociology,* **70** (1964), pp. 59–68.

[21] Malcolm E. Jewell and Samuel C. Patterson, *The Legislative Process in the United States* (New York, 1966), pp. 19–20.

The use of role concepts requires the capacity to distinguish between legislative and nonlegislative roles. Even a legislator plays nonlegislative roles, and many nonlegislators, such as lobbyists and constituents, play some legislative roles. The role concept does not solve the problem of delimiting legislative research but, on the contrary, raises it in a new form. The State Legislative Research Project drew a distinction between core roles, consisting of those norms that guide the behavior of all legislators with each other; specialized subroles, comprising norms for occupants of particular positions within the legislature; clientele roles, guiding the behavior of legislators with their various constituent groups; and incidental roles, setting norms governing the relevant personal relationships of legislators.[22] This classification seems sufficiently comprehensive for the study of a wide variety of legislative bodies, though in place of a clear boundary between legislative and nonlegislative roles it suggests a gradual shading-off from the core to the periphery. Furthermore, it does not take account of all the relevant legislative roles of nonlegislators.

While the concept of role has demonstrated its descriptive utility, it has hardly been used for explanatory purposes. Some studies have regarded role as a dependent variable and have sought the correlates of particular role orientations in the socioeconomic or political environment of the legislature. So far, however, the influence of the legislative role system on the output of the legislature has not been explored. The establishment of connections between legislative roles and other variables of legislative behavior, therefore, seems necessary if this concept is to be employed profitably in the formulation of theory for comparative research.

The Use of The Concept of Function. By the use of the concept of legislative "function," attempts have been made to study the consequences of legislative actions for the political system. The logic of functional analysis, however, raises empirical problems that legislative research is nowhere near solving. Strictly speaking, to determine the consequence of any political activity for a political system it is necessary first of all to identify those functions that are both necessary and sufficient for the persistence of certain measurable traits of the system.[23] As long as a legislative function, for example, cannot be shown to be both necessary and sufficient for the persistence of any system character-

---

[22] John C. Wahlke et al., *The Legislative System, op. cit.,* pp. 11–14.

[23] For an excellent critique of the state of functional analysis in political science, see Jerone Stephens, "The Logic of Functional and Systems Analysis in Political Science," *Midwest Journal of Political Science,* **XIII** (1969), pp. 367–394.

istic, neither its presence nor its absence can have demonstrable consequences for the system. Furthermore, unless the functional requisites
of political systems are defined in operational terms which are equivalent
cross-nationally, the concept cannot be used in comparative research.
For these reasons, we stand a long way from a rigorous use of functional
analysis in comparative legislative research.

Nevertheless, it seems unlikely that functional analysis will be
abandoned, because it does contain the promise of providing links between parts of political systems, like the legislature, and the system
itself. Early approaches to the functional analysis of legislatures employed a scheme of classifying functions which was largely a derivation
of American separation of powers doctrine. Among three basic governmental functions, lawmaking was regarded as the function of the legislature and became the focus of inquiry into legislative activity and its
system relevant consequences. The functional approach of Almond and
Powell began with the premise that an identifiable set of activities
was common to all political systems. It stipulated a division of these
activities into ten or twelve separate functions and proposed that variation in the manner in which these functions were performed by different
structures in different political systems be the central subject for comparative research.[24] However, no common set of measures of the functions that Almond and Powell defined has been developed. Furthermore,
whether any set of functions is performed in all political systems is
itself an empirical question, which has hardly been raised, let alone
answered.

Most structural-functional analyses of legislatures have in the last
decade employed their own typologies. Jewell and Patterson, for example, suggest that "conflict management" and "integration" are the
most general functions of legislatures, with deliberative, decisional, ad-
judicative, and cathartic functions as specifications of the first general
function and authorization, legitimation, and representation as specifications of the second.[25] These are thoughtful and thought-provoking terms,
but they cannot be employed in comparative analysis until they have
been operationalized and measured. Decisional functions, for example,
must be further specified and equivalent indicators for them found before they can be observed. A definition of lawmaking, which is an obviously important and apparently observable form of decisional activity,

[24] Gabriel A. Almond and G. Bingham Powell, *Comparative Politics; A Developmental Approach* (Boston, 1966) pp. 27–30.
[25] Malcolm E. Jewell and Samuel C. Patterson, *op. cit.*, pp. 8–15.

has so far eluded legal scholarship. Most accepted definitions of law are purely formal: law is defined as a rule enacted by the legislature.[26] In comparing lawmaking activities of legislatures, however, we need a definition of law independent of the institution being studied.[27]

Representational functions are similarly difficult to observe. Representation, like lawmaking, is an ill-defined concept that has acquired conflicting meanings through long use. It may be employed to denote any relationship between rulers and ruled or it may connote responsiveness, authorization, legitimation, or accountability. It may be used so broadly that any political institution performs representative functions or so narrowly that only an elected legislature can do so. To a surprising extent, the Burkean conceptualization of the representative function is still in use, and Eulau's call for a concept adequate to modern concerns about the relationship between legislators and their constituencies has not been answered.[28]

The obstacles to a functional analysis of legislatures that would link their activities to the political system are, therefore, formidable. Both operational concepts of legislative functions and a theory of the functional requirements of the political system are needed before significant progress is possible. To realize this, however, is to be alert to the possible relevance of theories and measures developed in other subspecialties of political science to problems of legislative research.

The refinement of the concept of communication, for example, opens the possibility of studying the communications functions of legislatures. Grumm has employed this concept in his test of the "feedback effect" in legislative systems.[29] Legislatures have undoubtedly lost the preeminence they once held as media of communications between the attentive public and the government. Modern means of mass communications and the specialized channels of communcations developed by interest groups naturally compete with the legislature in this respect. Nevertheless, it is plausible to expect that legislatures do perform some part

---

[26] Benjamin Akzin, "The Concept of Legislation," *Iowa Law Review*, 21 (1936), pp. 713–750, reprinted in John C. Wahlke and Heinz Eulau eds., *Legislative Behavior, op. cit.*, pp. 9–22.

[27] For one of the first serious attempts to measure the decisional outcomes of legislatures, see Jean Blondel et al., "Legislative Behavior: Some Steps Toward Cross-National Measurement," *Government and Opposition*, 5 (1969–70), pp. 67–85.

[28] Heinz Eulau, "Changing Views of Representation," in Ithiel deSola Pool, Ed., *Contemporary Political Science; Toward Empirical Theory* (New York, 1968). See also Hanna Fenichel Pitkin, *The Concept of Representation* (Berkeley, Calif., 1967), *passim.*

[29] John G. Grumm, "A Test for the 'Feedback Effect' in Legislative Systems," *infra*, pp. 267–285.

of the communications functions that take place in political systems, and an examination of legislative activities from this functional perspective seems promising.

The concept of recruitment, to take another example, is applicable to the study of those activities of legislatures that affect the selection of political personnel for the courts or the executive agencies. The concept of politicization, furthermore, may prove useful in studying the effect of the activity of legislators on their constituents, the reverse of the influence of constituents on their representatives that has so far preempted the study of the representative relationship. It seems possible that the legislature, because of its centrality as a political institution, influences the formation of political demands and supports among the members of the political system.[30] Finally, the concept of demand, and the indices of demand that have been developed in comparative studies of policy making, opens the possibility of investigating the functions of legislatures in converting preferences, interests, and wants of various kinds into binding policies.[31]

If functional concepts can be specified and operationalized, the way is open for testing hypotheses concerning the relationship between the activities of the legislature and particular traits of the political system. By these means we may begin to understand the functional requisites of system persistence.

Although both "role" and "function" are thus problematic concepts requiring further refinement, they guided a considerable portion of empirical research on legislatures during the 1960s. We are not yet at the point in legislative research where any one set of concepts has proven so useful that others are likely to be discarded. A decision-making model of legislatures, employing roll-call votes as the chief measures of decision-making, promises to increase our understanding of the decisional process, at least in American legislatures.[32] The concepts of bargaining and exchange may be particularly useful in the study of coalition forma-

---

[30] John C. Wahlke, "Representation Theory and Policy Research," *British Journal of Political Science,* **1** (1971), pp. 271–290.

[31] Recent research on the relationship between demands and policy outputs in the American states suggests the need to reintroduce political variables into the equation. See, for example, Ira Sharkansky and Richard I. Hofferbert, "Dimensions of State Politics, Economics, and Public Policy," *American Political Science Review,* **LXIII** (1969), pp. 867–879.

[32] Donald R. Matthews and James A. Stimson, "Decision-Making by U.S. Representatives: A Preliminary Model," in S. Sidney Ulmer, Ed., *Political Decision-Making,"* (New York, 1970), pp. 14–43.

tion in multiparty legislatures.[33] The concept of the professionalization of the legislature appears capable of explaining some of the variance in policy outputs among the legislatures of the United States and perhaps elsewhere. It would be premature to disparage these or other conceptualizations, but it is possible to observe some consolidation in the catalog of research concepts, to indicate the value of conceptual order, and to suggest the need to develop theory formulated in terms of the concepts which are guiding current research.

Independent Variables

The legislature is a central institution in the political system. Much of its activity takes place in public. Its members tie voters to decision-makers. The centrality of the legislature permits, and indeed requires, research to seek explanations of legislative behavior from a wide variety of independent variables at different levels of analysis.

Political culture is often the residual variable in attempts to explain legislative activity. Few attempts have been made to specify how the cultural environment affects the legislature or to overcome the difficulty of controlling for variations in political culture in comparative research. Comparisons of similar legislative bodies within a single political system. such as comparative state legislative research in the United States, offers one way to solve the problem of control, on the assumption that a relatively common political culture pervades the United States at any given moment. Comparative research on the parliaments of the German *Länder,* or of any subnational councils, has similar advantages. Likewise, comparisons within a single system over time permits control of the cultural variable, on the assumption that the political culture changes relatively slowly compared with other variables. When the value of this type of longitudinal comparison is fully recognized, the price in terms of the relative inadequacy of data may not seem prohibitive.

Much attention has been devoted to the social background of legislators. European scholarship in particular, influenced by a pervasive class consciousness, has amassed a large body of information on the social, economic, religious, and occupational background of members of legislatures.[34] Unfortunately, these background data have often not

[33] Timothy Hennessey and Jeanne Martin, "Exchange Theory: A Conceptual Link Between Legislative and Electoral Coalitions," paper delivered at the Conference on the Concepts and Methods of Comparative Legislative Research, Quail Roost, North Carolina, February 24–27, 1970.

[34] See particularly the work of Mattei Dogan on France, Giovanni Sartori on Italy, W. L. Guttsman and J. F. S. Ross on Great Britain, Henry Valen on Norway,

been related to performance data. They have usually not been employed as an independent variable to explain legislative behavior.[35] Furthermore, the categories employed for research in different countries have varied.[36] Nevertheless, the sophistication of European studies in this area provides a strong basis for testing hypotheses regarding social background as a determinant of legislative performance.

While social background has been emphasized in European research, constituency background has been frequently studied in the United States, under the influence of the apparent importance of the local attachments of members of the U.S. House of Representatives. The availability of census data by congressional constituencies has facilitated this kind of research in the United States; its general unavailability until recently in Great Britain has been an obstacle to parallel work there. Furthermore, this research depends on the existence of single-member constituencies having some stability over time, a condition not met in France or Germany, for example, or wherever electoral systems are subject to frequent change. The work of Miller and Stokes has added data on the beliefs of constituents to the archive of information on the background of legislators and has provided a model for relating constituency variables to legislative behavior measured in terms of roll-call votes.[37]

The difference between European and United States research on legislators' backgrounds reflects not only differences in the availability of data and the propensity of scholars, but also assumed contrasts in voting behavior. The presumed class consciousness of European voters, in comparison with the localism of United States voters, has reinforced the tendency to regard social background as the most interesting variable explaining legislative behavior in Europe, and constituency factors as the variables promising the greatest explanatory power in the United States. However, these presumed contrasts in voting behavior have not

---

Martti Noponen and Pertti Pesonen on Finland, Frederick Frey on Turkey, and the symposium edited by Jean Meynaud, "The Parliamentary Profession," *International Social Science Journal,* **XIII** (1961). I have tried to use some of the existing data, together with my own data on Germany, comparatively, in *Parliament in the German Political System* (Ithaca, N.Y., 1967), pp. 84–130.

[35] For exceptions, see Allan Kornberg, *Canadian Legislative Behavior,* and Gordon J. DiRenzo, *Personality, Power and Politics: A Social Psychological Analysis of the Italian Deputy and His parliamentary System* (Notre Dame, Ind., 1967), which deals with personality variables and their influence on parliamentary behavior.

[36] The ambiguities of the occupational category "lawyer" in cross-national research is explored by Mogens N. Pedersen, "Lawyers in Politics: The Deviant Case of the Danish Folketing," *infra,* pp. 25–63.

[37] "Constituency Influence in Congress," *The American Political Science Review,* **LVII** (1963), pp. 45–56.

themselves been subject to stringent comparative tests. Electoral behavior deserves separate study as an independent variable affecting legislative behavior because of its possible consequences for the composition and rate of turnover in the membership of legislatures.[38]

Party organization appears as an independent variable in much legislative research, but relatively little work has been done on party organization at its closest point to legislative behavior: within the legislature itself. Truman's work in *The Congressional Party*[39] is a notable pioneering study in this regard, but it depends on roll-call analysis to an extent that cannot be duplicated in most legislatures outside the United States; France and Finland are exceptions, as the works of MacRae and Pesonen indicate.[40] Elsewhere, the study of legislative party organization meets obstacles in the secrecy of party caucuses and the loyalty to party in the public activity of legislators. However, newspaper coverage of parliamentary party meetings has greatly expanded in Great Britain and Germany in recent years and now provides a significant source of data in these countries. Furthermore, it is likely that interview data can be obtained in many places.

Political culture, the socioeconomic background of legislators, constituency influences, and the party organization of the legislature in no sense exhaust the list of relevant variables in the legislature's environment. A brief review of research on these variables does, however, suggest the fragmentary manner in which these variables are generally linked to the pattern of legislative behavior they are presumably designed to explain. The neglect of linkages is another indication of the inadequacy of theory to guide legislative behavior research.

Measurement

If the first prerequisite of comparative legislative research is the further development of theory, the second condition is the attainment of cross-national equivalence in the measurement of those concepts which the theory employs.[41] Some concepts now used in comparative

[38] The problem is being explored in the Norwegian Storting by Henry Valen.

[39] (New York, 1959).

[40] Ducan MacRae, Jr., *Parliament, Parties, and Society in France, 1946–1958* (New York, 1967). See also Pertti Pesonen, "Political Parties and the Finnish Eduskunta: Voters' Perspectives, Party Nominations, and Legislative Behavior," *infra*, pp. 199–233.

[41] The following discussion of cross-national equivalence in measurement owes a great deal to Adam Przeworski and Henry Teune, *The Logic of Comparative Social Inquiry* (New York, 1970), especially Part Two.

research, such as role orientations, have been defined in terms of the operations used to measure them. The purposive role of legislators, for example, is defined as the response given by legislators to interview items asking them about their views of their job. Interview findings are by definition valid measures of the concept. When concepts are thus given an operational definition permitting them to be measured directly, problems of cross-national validity do not arise.

However, it may prove difficult to employ a standard for interpreting and coding interview responses that is consistent across nations. In replicating the U.S. State Legislative Research Project in Austria, for example, Gerlich found no members of the Vienna City Council preoccupied with parliamentary routine and procedure, as were the legislators whom Wahlke and Eulau had called "ritualists" in their United States study. Gerlich attributed this to the "restricted freedom of action of representatives subject to strict party discipline."[42] Nevertheless, he concluded that over half of the members of the Council were "ritualists" in the sense of regarding attendance at committee meetings and the study of Council documents as their primary obligation. By employing a different standard for assigning legislators to the category of "ritualists" from that used by Wahlke and Eulau, Gerlich retained the category, at the expense of its reliability as a cross-national measure. The narrowness of operationally defined concepts often restricts their utility in cross-national research.

The more general, and theoretically more interesting concepts, however, cannot usually be measured directly. Such concepts as decision-making, representation, communication, or recruitment can only be measured indirectly by observing specific phenomena, such as roll-call votes, appropriations, or cabinet appointments, and by treating these as indicators of the variables to be measured. Inferences must be drawn from the observation to the variable. But an inference which is valid in one political system is not necessarily valid in another. The roll-call vote, for example, has been regarded as a measure of the decisional behavior of individual legislators in the United States.[43] In Great Britain or in Germany, however, where party discipline in voting is nearly perfect, the roll-call vote is usually only a measure of the aggregate decisional behavior of a party group. Or, the ability of members of Congress

---

[42] Peter Gerlich and Helmut Kramer, *op. cit.,* p. 147. Cf. John C. Wahlke et al., *The Legislative System, op. cit.* Chap. 11 and p. 467.

[43] The validity of roll-call analysis has seldom been questioned. For a rare critique, see Fred I. Greenstein and Alton F. Jackson, "A Second Look at the Validity of Roll-Call Analysis," *Midwest Journal, of Political Science,* **7** (1963), pp. 156–166.

to get their bills or appropriations measures enacted has been used as a measure of the members' "legislative effectiveness."[44] In a parliamentary system, however, "bill success" cannot be regarded as an index of the effectiveness of individual legislators, since the budget and most successful bills are government projects for which particular members may be assigned tactical responsibility. Membership on a particular congressional committee may indicate the legislative specialization chosen by a United States senator, because of the clear specialization of Senate committees and the seniority system of appointments; but where committees are less important, less specialized, or more susceptible to party control, membership may indicate party standing or role orientation rather than subject-matter specialization. Indirect measures, in short, raise problems of validity in cross-national research, because the inferences drawn from them are relative to the context of particular political systems. The same measure may not exist in all systems, or it may measure different concepts in different systems.

In order to obtain cross-national equivalence in indirect measurement, in the sense of valid measures of the same concept across nations, it may be necessary to use different indicators for the same concept in different systems. For example, the equivalent of roll-call votes in Congress as a measure of individual decisional behavior may be votes in the parliamentary party in the House of Commons; the equivalent of "bill success" as an indicator of legislative effectiveness in Congress may be career ladders in the Bundestag, by which the movement of members from the backbenches to committee, cabinet, or party leadership may be traced; content analysis of parliamentary speeches in some systems may be the valid counterpart of committee membership in others as an index of subject-matter specialization.

But how can we be sure that different indicators will measure the same concepts so that valid comparisons can be made? Ideally, we must try to discover multiple indicators for each concept in each system. If some indicators are then common to all systems being studied, they will provide a standard for estimating the validity of system-specific indicators. Even in the absence of common indicators, however, a similar structure within each set of system-specific indicators, in the sense of a similar pattern of correlations among the indices, permits the inference that each set measures the same concept.

[44] For the use of such indices in the study of Congress, see Donald R. Matthews, *U.S. Senators and Their World,* (Chapel Hill, N.C., 1960), p. 278–279; and Richard F. Fenno, Jr., *The Power of the Purse; Appropriations Politics in Congress* (Boston, 1966), Chap. 8 and pp. 572–590.

In attempting to develop additional indicators of legislative behavior, we may find it useful to consider data both older and newer than that recently emphasized. Procedural precedents, for example, may permit inferences about legislative roles; content analysis of oral questions in parliamentary debate may allow measurement of political cleavages among members; attendance lists may provide data distinguishing professional from amateur politicians.

Once we realize that common indicators do not guarantee cross-national validity in measurement, the opportunities for comparative research are actually expanded. The absence, outside of the United States, of those measures widely employed in American legislative research should no longer be regarded as an obstacle to comparative research. Instead, efforts should be made to expand the variety of indicators used in all legislative research, with the aim of finding sets of multiple indices for theoretically relevant concepts in all systems. To be sure, comparative research depends on progress in the development of measurements. The need, however, is not for measures which are identical, but rather for ones which are equivalent across nations. The premium is on imaginative use of varieties of data rather than on the replication of United States data.

Although we must look for variety among indicators, we need uniformity in conceptualization. Rule-making must mean as nearly as possible the same thing from one system to another, while indices for measuring rule-making behavior may well vary; constituency influence must have the same meaning across systems, but the measure of constituency expectations may need to be adapted to different social and electoral systems. Comparison depends on the existence of a common standard. That standard must consist of theory and concepts; among measures and indices what we need is equivalence.

Conclusions

Legislative research has recently exhibited some consolidation of approaches, concepts, and methods, but cumulative knowledge about legislative behavior has been slow to develop. This seems to be due to the failure to pursue comparative research that is guided by explicit theory. The desire to employ particular analytical techniques, rather than to solve problems of theoretical relevance, seems often to have determined the choice of subjects for inquiry. Commitment to a particular type of data has preceded conceptualization of the study. Enthusiasm for factor analysis and Guttman scaling, for example, has directed attention to subjects for which interval data were available and has led to the evasion of work in other areas. The accessibility of United States legislators for purposes of interview, the availability of reliable United States census data, and the existence of endless series of roll-call votes for United States legislative bodies has produced parochialism in the choice of research sites.

With many varieties of legislative behavior left out of account, research findings have done little to stimulate the formulation of theory. An implicit theory of United States legislative behavior has sufficed for most research, with the notable exception only of those comparative studies conducted within the United States system. Narrowness in the selection of research topics and the poverty of theory have reinforced each other.

As a result, the prospects of comparative research are impaired. The concepts and measures established in the field of legislative research are the product of the study of United States political phenomena. They are not usually suitable for research on other systems without adaptation to a higher level of generality. When these concepts have nevertheless been used in work on non-United States legislatures, the results are not necessarily comparable to United States findings because of the problems of reliability and validity in cross-system measurement. Most research on non-United States legislatures has employed its own concepts, making all attempts at comparison futile. Therefore, instead of discovering cross-national uniformities or explaining differences among legislative systems, there has been a complacent tendency to regard each system as unique. Generalizations about legislative behavior have been limited to the narrow field of United States experience, and cross-national variation remains not only unexplained but unexplainable.

Although a discouraging gap thus appears to exist between prodigious research efforts and limited results, it does seem possible, on the basis of the work done so far, to develop the broadly conceived comparative research which is needed to expand our understanding of legislative behavior. The prerequisite is the formulation of theory, based on present findings, but containing implications to be tested by the observation of legislatures in unfamiliar settings. This means that students of legislative behavior would have to expand their horizons to include the investigation of legislatures under the most varying possible conditions, even where access to data is difficult, allowing theoretical considerations to guide the selection of subjects, and employing a set of common concepts and equivalent measures. By studying legislatures at all levels of government, at all stages of historical development, and within dissimilar political systems, the number of units for analysis could be greatly increased, the amount of variance observed could be multiplied, and evidence could be obtained for increasingly accurate and parsimonious explanations of legislative behavior and its systemic consequences. Although this research direction poses many risks and obstacles, it is the only way of achieving what has so far eluded legislative research: a cumulative understanding of one of the central institutions of politics.

PART TWO

Legislators and Legislative Decision-Making

Introductory Note

In this part, authors deal with the composition of legislative bodies and the climates of decision-making within them. Mogens Pedersen presents a detailed comparative analysis of the composition of legislative bodies in terms of the presence of lawyers among their membership and makes an assessment of various explanations for the importance of lawyers as members of legislatures. Pedersen submits United States research to the test of comparison with the role of lawyers in a northern European system, the Danish Folketing. His analysis points up the importance of breaking out of ethnocentric, United States conceptions of the role of lawyers in legislative politics and constructing theories of legislative recruitment and behavior in the light of the different roles of legislators with legal training in non–United States systems.

John E. Schwarz and Geoffrey Lambert attempt to explain the internal cohesion of the Conservative Parliamentary Party in the British House of Commons. By assessing the effects of the constraints of potential career vulnerability, career enhancement aspirations, and feelings of party identity, they are able to account for variations in the predispositions of Conservative backbenchers to join rebellions against party whips. Their analysis points up the importance of both career objectives and party attachments in understanding the behavior of legislators in the British system.

Research on the role orientations of legislators has been conducted for a number of American legislatures, but Peter Gerlich's analysis of the members of the Vienna City Council represents one of the few systematic attempts to analyze legislative roles in a non–United States legislative set-

23

ting. Gerlich's investigation makes it possible to see some of the effects of a highly partisan legislative chamber on the character and distribution of role orientations which legislators exhibit. While the existence of relatively strong party discipline in the Vienna Diet significantly constrains options among representational roles for legislators, Gerlich did find that Austrian provincial representatives could exercise considerable role flexibility in their purposive, or instrumental, role orientations.

California city councils provide the research site for Heinz Eulau's detailed analysis of decision-making structures in legislative bodies. He distinguishes among unipolar, bipolar, and nonpolar decisional structures for small legislative groups and then elucidates the variations in decision-making climates, styles, and practices that develop as properties of these varying decisional structures. These group properties suggest the context in which public policy and symbolic output may be supplied by legislative bodies.

In sum, we have in Part II exemplifications of four specific kinds of constraints that the legislative context may present for political representation: the composition of the legislative body, orientations toward political careers held by legislators, conceptions of the representative's role, and the decisional properties of legislative bodies as wholes.

CHAPTER TWO

Lawyers in Politics: The Danish Folketing and United States Legislatures.

MOGENS N. PEDERSEN

UNIVERSITY OF AARHUS, DENMARK

Introduction

It is proverbial that United States Congressmen are lawyers. Several studies have demonstrated that in almost 60 percent of all cases the occupational background of representatives and senators is that of the legal profession. Furthermore, it is a well-established fact that lawyers are active at all levels of United States politics and that they have been so since the Declaration of Independence. The legal profession is and has always been the most substantial reservoir of political personnel. Lawyers have become "the high priests of United States politics."

Since the days of de Tocqueville the disparity between the microcosm, Congress, with its 50 to 60 percent of lawyers, and the macrocosm, the whole population of the United States with its 0.15 percent of lawyers, has attracted scholars. Many hypotheses have been forwarded in order to explain the affinity of law and politics, but only in the last decade has the problem been seriously discussed.[1]

This discussion among United States political scientists is of interest not only for specialists in United States government, but is equally relevant

[1] Joseph A. Schlesinger, "Lawyers and American Politics: A clarified view," *Midwest Journal of Political Science*, **1** (1957), pp. 26–39, who started the discussion, remarked that "many reasons have been proposed for this phenomenon, but for the most part they have been unrefined and untested inferences based upon the original observation."

25

for all, inside and outside the United States, who are doing research in the field of legislative behavior and especially in the field of recruitment of political elites. This is true, first, because an affinity of law and politics is a widespread phenomenon, visible in most European political systems and outside Europe as well. If it becomes possible to explain the phenomenon in the United States context, we should also be able to explain the same phenomenon when observed outside the United States. Second, it is evident that an explanation of the pronounced dominance of lawyers in one system would bring us a long step towards a middle-range theory of political recruitment. A "lawyers-in-politics theory" in sufficiently general terms might enable us to explain all kinds of deviances from a much-used ideal type of representation, that of parliament as the mirror of the represented.[2] The problem has become more complex and the solutions more sophisticated during the last decade, but legislative research has not yet arrived at any definitive or even preliminary conclusion. The most generally formulated attempt to build a middle-range theory of all the relationships between law and politics has been the "convergence theory," put forward by Heinz Eulau and John D. Sprague,[3] which has not yet been accepted as *the* explanation.[4] In a recent review article the status has been summed up by Samuel C. Patterson: "for American legislative systems, we have no adequate explanation for the extraordinary over-representation of lawyers."[5]

The most conspicuous result of a decade of discussion has been the discarding of a series of single-factor explanations that provide neither necessary nor sufficient bases for inferences about the affinity of law and politics. The conclusion to be drawn is that, for the present, a theory of lawyers in politics will have to be a weak structure consisting of a list of factors, together forming a multivariate, probabilistic explanation.

---

[2] For discussions of the mirroring theory of representation and its adequacy as value theory, and as a requisite in empirical research, see, e.g., Giovanni Sartori, "Representational Systems," in *International Encyclopedia of the Social Sciences,* **13** (1968), pp. 465–73; Heinz Eulau, "Changing Views of Representation," in Ithiel de Sola Pool, Ed., *Contemporary Political Science: Toward Empirical Theory,* (New York, 1967), pp. 53–85. An advocacy for a strategy of research, which uses this ideal type, is a main theme in Jean Meynaud, "Introduction: General Study of Parliamentarians," in *International Social Science Journal,* **13** (1961), pp. 513–43.

[3] Heinz Eulau and John D. Sprague, *Lawyers in Politics: A Study in Professional Convergence,* (Indianapolis, 1961).

[4] See, e.g., reviews by William L. Day and Joel B. Grossman in *Midwest Journal of Political Science,* **9** (1965), pp. 314–18, and *American Political Science Review,* **59** (1965), pp. 161–62, respectively.

[5] Samuel C. Patterson, "Comparative Legislative Behavior: A Review Essay," *Midwest Journal of Political Science,* **12** (1968), p. 606.

Three characteristics of the discussion are interesting when the topic is observed from a European view. First, that the investigation was started by Europeans, by none less than Alexis de Tocqueville and Max Weber, but that the modern discussion has been an entirely United States enterprise. Second, although the data used and the factors singled out are almost exclusively American, the problem is regarded as a general problem and its solution, at least implicitly, as one which should be relevant beyond the United States context. Finally, it is astonishing that the phenomenon has not yet been scrutinized as a problem in comparative politics; the explanatory sketches, which are the results of the analysis of United States data, have not been tested against European data.[6]

It is tempting for European political scientists to take over the explanations from the United States literature. Especially the fact that one of the most-used arguments was formed in the context of European politics 50 years ago makes uncritical acceptance understandable. The inequality in political knowledge between the United States and the rest of the Western world, and the still more pronounced inequalities in academic status of political science within Europe, really present the political scientists from the more backward areas with daily temptations to use—and misuse—the huge mass of knowledge which is collected and systematized in the United States.

Jean Meynaud has warned us, however, that "the results of observations relating to the American system cannot be applied, lock, stock and barrel, to other countries."[7] This statement can be given a more positive formulation: European political scientists might help their United States colleagues by testing their hypotheses and by discussing the limits and the possibilities of their findings in a comparative context. The affinity of law and politics and the theoretical reasoning around this phenomenon in American literature provide a basis for such a discussion.

Lawyers in Legislatures

It is often asserted that a special affinity exists between law and politics in every representative democracy. "In all the Western democracies the law has been the dominant occupation of politicians and the lawyer's importance has reached its highest point in the United States," remarked Joseph A. Schlesinger.[8] When Frederich W. Frey found 27 percent of the

[6] But see the discussions in Patterson, *op. cit.*, and in Dankwart A. Rustow, "The Study of Elites: Who's Who, When and How," in *World Politics*, **18** (1965–66), pp. 690–717, especially pp. 705–07.

[7] Meynaud, *op. cit.*, p. 515.

[8] Schlesinger, *op. cit.*, p. 26.

members were lawyers in the Turkish legislature, he compared this finding with the more familiar knowledge: "Though there are a few striking exceptions, such as Germany, and though most national legislatures are not so heavily populated by lawyers as those of the United States and some of the British Commonwealth nations, the fact that lawyers tend to be the largest single occupational group in parliament after parliament all over

Table 2.1   Lawyers in Parliament

Country	Legislative Body	Year	Percent Lawyers
United States	House of Representatives	1957	56
Canada	House of Commons	1962	33
Lebanon	Chamber of Deputies	1960–1964	28
Turkey	National Assembly	1954	27
Ceylon	House of Representatives	1964	26
India	House of the People	1952	25
Belgium	House of Representatives	1964	25
Italy	Chamber of Deputies	1958	21
United Kingdom	House of Commons	1959	20
Switzerland	National Council	1959	11
Eire	Lower House (Dáil)	1965	10
Israel	Parliament (Knesset)	1957	10
France	National Assembly	1967	10
Finland	Parliament (Eduskunta)	1962	10
West Germany	Chamber of Deputies (Bundestag)	1961	8
Japan	House of Representatives	1963	8
Iceland	Parliament (Alting)	1952	8
The Netherlands	Second Chamber	1967	7
Denmark	Parliament (Folketing)	1968	4
Austria	Parliament (Nationalrat)	1966	3
Norway	Parliament (Storting)	1965–1969	3
Sweden	Lower House	1964	2

SOURCES: Based upon a similar but smaller table in Patterson, *op. cit.* Supplemented and revised for Ceylon, by Marshall R. Singer, *The Emerging Elite: A Study of Political Leadership in Ceylon* (Cambridge, Mass., 1964), p. 171; for India, by W. H. Morris-Jones, *Parliament in India*, (London, 1957), p. 120; for Switzerland, by G. A. Codding, Jr., *The Federal Government of Switzerland*, (Boston, 1965), p. 75; for France, by Philip M. Williams, *The French Parliament 1958–67*, (London, 1968), p. 34; for Iceland, by *Svensk Juristtidning*, 37, (1952), p. 872; for the Netherlands, by *Statistiek der verkiezingen 1967,—Tweede Kamer der Staten-Generaal, 15 februari*, (The Hague, 1967), p. 25; for Austria, Heinz Fischer, "Struktur einer Volksvertretung," *Die Zukunst*, 4 (1948), 15–18; for Denmark, by author's own data calculated from *Folketinget 1968*, (København, 1968); for Norway, calculated from O. C. Torp, *Stortinget 1965/66-1968/69*, (Oslo, 1966); for Sweden, by *Sveriges Officiella Statistik: Riksdagsmannavalen 1961–64*, *II*, (Stockholm, 1965), pp. 56–57; for Eire, Basil Chubb, *The Government and Politics of Ireland* (Stanford, Calif., 1970), p. 210.

the world is certainly one of the outstanding facts to emerge from the existing body of social background studies."[9]

Lawyers are over-represented in all parliaments, no doubt about that. The lawyers' share of the populations varies, but hardly exceeds 0.2 percent anywhere. Their share of seats in the national legislatures is far higher. Nevertheless, very crude calculation of lawyer-legislator percentages for various countries shows that the extent of over-representation varies tremendously—from 2 to 56 percent (Table 2.1).

These figures are hardly consistent with the above-mentioned generalizations, which we are therefore compelled to modify. Is it really appropriate to consider the United States especially representative of a typical trend? Ought we not conclude that more balanced statements are necessary? Is it not more in accordance with the facts to say that the United States as well as the three Scandinavian countries represent deviant cases, and that the "typical" parliament is one in which lawyers form a considerable, but not necessarily the largest occupational group? In 12 of the 22 countries ranked in Table 2.1 the share of lawyers does not exceed 10 percent.

With so wide a range of variation, and with a set of hypotheses specially fitted to explain the affinity of law and politics in the United States, the need for a test of these hypotheses is apparent. In the existing United States literature the method used in validating hypotheses has been that of comparison of the background, career, and behavior of lawyer-legislators and other legislators within a single legislature or group of legislatures. Crossnational comparisons might serve the same purposes. At this moment, though we cannot expect to find really comparable data but will have to rely upon a secondary analysis of whatever kinds of data we can find, still it might be profitable to compare the position of the lawyer in United States legislatures with that of his colleague in a country at the other extreme.

In this paper I treat Denmark as a deviant case. My point will be that a deviant case ought not to be regarded as a deplorable phenomenon, but instead as a chance to refine the analysis. If an explanation of the lawyer's ubiquity in politics requires a multivariate approach, then a deviant-case analysis might serve some useful purposes.[10] By means of an observation of the deviant case we sometimes become able to supply the explanatory

---

[9] Frederick W. Frey, *The Turkish Political Elite,* (Cambridge, Mass., 1965), p. 395.

[10] Concerning deviant case analsis, see Patricia L. Kendall and Katherine M. Wolf, "The Two Purposes of Deviant Case Analysis," in Paul F. Lazarsfeld and Morris Rosenberg, Eds., *The Language of Social Research,* (New York, 1955), pp. 167–74; also William J. Goode and Paul K. Hatt, *Methods in Social Research,* (New York, 1952,) pp. 88–89.

scheme with additional variables, hitherto disregarded. Another function of this kind of analysis is to weaken some of the already-used variables and perhaps thereby give some other variables a more central position in the scheme.

Compactly formulated, the train of thought in this chapter is the following: In the United States political system there is a pronounced affinity between the legal profession and politics; in the Danish system, no such affinity, or at least only a very modest affinity, can be observed. *If* most of all the factors used to explain the former coincidence are also operating in the Danish system, *then* this finding calls at least for refinement of the theoretical structure which has been constructed for the United States case.

The method has its obvious limitations. First, in order not to complicate the discussion, in this chapter only those factors will be discussed that hitherto have been regarded as explanatory variables in the United States literature. Consequently, I have not attempted to find entirely new variables. The strategy instead is an exercise in the use of John Stuart Mill's *"method of difference,"* stated negatively: "Nothing can be the cause of a phenomenon, if the phenomenon does not take place, when the supposed cause does."[11] If it is possible to make probable that factors, *a, b, c, . . . n*, which are supposed to produce outcome Z in the American system, are also operative in the Danish system, except, say, factors *m* and *n*, but that the outcome in the latter system is non-Z, then we have at least put a questionmark behind factors *a, b, . . .* as causal factors and have strengthened the position of factors *m* and *n* in the explanatory scheme.

Another limitation ought to be stressed from the very beginning. While the United States literature on various aspects of the legal profession is huge and the study of legislative behavior is far advanced in the United States, the Danish literature on the legal profession, in contrast, is scarce, and legislative research has made only a modest beginning. There is as yet no relevant survey research, and studies making use of the rich mass of biographical data are only in their preparatory phase. In fact, this inequality in data and theory makes comparison a hazardous affair. One is forced to use the scattered observations and the unsubstantiated generalizations provided by Danish legal historians and to rely upon the sparse contributions of political scientists proper. Nevertheless, even though results must be considered incomplete and highly provisional, they might contribute to the step-by-step progress which is a characteristic of the whole literature on the lawyer-legislator.

[11] Morris R. Cohen and Ernest Nagel, *An Introduction to Logic and Scientific Method,* (New York, 1934), p. 259; see also Goode and Hatt, *op. cit.,* chapter 7.

The "Classic" Explanations

Many of the explanations given in the United States literature are presented or can be interpreted as explanations of a general ubiquity of lawyers in politics and not as statements about the United States lawyers.

When de Tocqueville remarked that "the government of democracy is favourable to the political power of lawyers,"[12] and when later on Max Weber stressed the economic independence and the economic dispensability of the lawyer in contrast to most other professional men, both of them gave explanations in general terms. The foundations for their generalizations were general, too. Max Weber's analysis was made in the context of European politics. It must be remembered that his aim was to demonstrate that "some very trivial preconditions must exist in order for a person to be able to live 'for' politics"[13]—as contrasted to living 'off' politics—and that he found lawyers in an optimal position in this respect. He himself was decidely in favor of the professional parliamentarian, who was able to live "for" rather than "off" politics. Although Max Weber's analysis has evaluative overtones, his statement was primarily intended as a generally valid explanation, if not the only one. De Tocqueville arrived at his explanation by means of truly comparative, crossnational reasoning, clearly visible in his conclusion that "in America there are no nobles or men of letters, and the people is apt to mistrust the wealthy; lawyers consequently form the highest political class, and the most cultivated circle of society."[14] The structure of these arguments is typical of many modern explanations, which are in fact often derivatives and refinements of the classical statements.

We can lump together some of the traditional explanations into a few categories that, although not exhaustive, cover the main themes. First we have the "social status arguments,"[15] which was introduced by de Tocqueville and restated by Donald Matthews. It ascribes the dominance of lawyers in American politics to the fact that "lawyers meet what seems to be the first prerequisite of top-level political leadership: they are in a high-prestige occupation."[16] Another set of explanations can be traced back to Max Weber. The "economic independence/dispensability argu-

---

[12] Alexis de Tocqueville, *Democracy in America,* (New York, 1947), p. 172.

[13] Max Weber, "Politics as a Vocation," in H. H. Gerth and C. Wright Mills, Eds., *From Max Weber: Essays in Sociology,* (New York, 1946), p. 85.

[14] De Tocqueville, *op. cit.,* p. 175.

[15] This term is from Eulau and Sprague, *op. cit.,* p. 34.

[16] Donald R. Matthews, *The Social Background of Political Decision-Makers,* (New York, 1954), p. 30.

ment" ascribes the affinity of law and politics to some characteristics that, it is argued, are rather unique for the legal profession—the lawyer is able to leave the profession for a time while pursuing a political career without doing damage to his future career as a lawyer; often he is able to proceed in his practice while in politics; a legal education is "the best hedge against the ever-present possibility of failure in politics."[17] A third set of explanations is based upon a "skill argument." Already Max Weber asserted that "the craft of the trained lawyer is to plead effectively the cause of interested clients," both when the case is good and when it is bad. "To an outstanding degree, politics today is in fact conducted by means of the spoken or written word. To weigh the effect of the word properly falls within the range of the lawyer's tasks . . . ," he said, and this notion still forms the hard core in this argument, which in its various shapes states that the legal profession is made up of men who develop special skills and qualities which are useful and indispensable in a political career.[18] Training in interpersonal mediation and conciliation, facility in the use of words, training in consultation, and drafting work form the nucleus of skills that give the lawyer an advantage in the race for all kinds of political office and make him the favorite choice for representative.[19]

These explanations have been heavily criticized. They may sound plausible, but even upon the United States premises they have to be modified or outrightly rejected as satisfactory explanations. When confronted with the Danish situation their value diminishes further. Whatever the advantage ascribed to the United States lawyer in the competition for political office, his Danish colleague seems to be in the same position—yet he is almost absent from the Folketing.

Notice, first, that Danish lawyers are definitely in a *high-prestige occupation*. Although lawyers in all societies are criticized by the public—and in this case Denmark is no exception—they are nevertheless positioned

[17] Schlesinger, *op. cit.,* p. 2.

[18] Weber, *op. cit.,* pp. 94–95.

[19] The "skill-argument" is possibly the most frequently used explanation of the affinity of law and politics. For a sample of elaborations, see James Bryce, *The American Commonwealth,* (New York, 1911), vol. II, pp. 306–07; David Gold, "Lawyers in Politics: An Empirical Exploration of Biographical Data on State Legislators," in *Pacific Sociological Review,* 4 (1961), pp. 84–86; Charles S. Hyneman, "Who Makes Our Laws?" in *Political Science Quarterly,* 55 (1940), pp. 556–81; Harold D. Lasswell, "The Elite Concept," in H. D. Lasswell, Daniel Lerner, and C. Easton Rothwell, *The Comparative Study of Elites,* (Stanford, 1952), p. 18; Harold D. Lasswell and Myres S. McDougal, "Legal Education and Public Policy: Professional Training in the Public Interest," in H. D. Lasswell, *The Analysis of Political Behavior: An Empirical Approach,* (London, 1948), p. 27; Donald R. Matthews, *op. cit.*

among the occupations ranking high on sociologists' measures of occupational prestige. Comparison of the occupational prestige of lawyers in the United States and Denmark indicates that in both systems the legal profession is a high-prestige occupation, although there is some difference between the relative positions of lawyers and legislators in the two societies (*Table 2.2*). Another characterization of the position of lawyers in the

Table 2.2   Occupational Prestige Rating of National Legislators and Lawyers

	Rank Number	Number of Occupations Rated	Score/ Mean Prestige	Empirical Range
U.S. Representative	7		89	Highest: 96 (U.S. Supreme Court Justice)
		90		
U.S. Lawyer	15		86	Lowest: 33 (shoeshiner)
Danish M. F.	21		2.51	Highest: 1.20 (ambassador)
		75		
Danish attorney, High Court (LRS)	14		2.20	Lowest: 4.79 (shoeshiner)

SOURCES: United States: Albert J. Reiss, Jr., et al., *Occupations and Social Status*, (New York, 1961), p. 54; Denmark: Kaare Svalastoga, *Prestige, Class, and Mobility*, (København, 1959), p. 75.

society can be obtained by a comparison of the incomes in the profession (*Table 2.3*).

Here we also observe that lawyers in both societies, Danish lawyers in particular, are situated at a high level of the economic structure. The legal profession is the occupation figuring highest in the Danish statistics of taxable income. We can safely say at last that Danish lawyers do not fall behind their United States colleagues as far as relative income is concerned. The data available further indicate a greater amount of homogeneity in the social status position of Danish lawyers.

Are United States lawyers more independent and *dispensable* than the Danish? Among other explanations of the absence of lawyers from the Folketing, Danish legal historians have used a reversed "dispensability argument": in connection with the withdrawal of lawyers from politics in the nineteenth century (see the following) it has been mentioned that lawyers could not combine the requirements of their legal practice and their

Table 2.3   Income Distributions of American and Danish Lawyers in
Private Practice

U.S.: 1954		Denmark: 1964	
Net Income Level ($)	% of All Independent Lawyers	% of All Independent Lawyers	Income Assessment level (D.kr.)
Below 0	1.1	1.1	0
0–1,999	9.4	1.5	0–9,999
2,000–3,999	14.8	7.2	10,000–19,999
4,000–5,999	15.0	15.0	20,000–29,999
6,000–9,999	22.9	34.8	30,000–49,999
10,000–19,999	25.7	31.7	50,000–99,999
20,000–39,999	9.2	7.3	100,000–199,999
40,000 and over	1.9	1.4	200,000 and over
N = 7234 (sample)	100.3	100.0	N = 2126 (all assessments)

SOURCES: United States: Maurice Liebenberg, "Income of Lawyers in the Postwar Period," in *Survey of Current Business*, 36, (December, 1956), p. 28; Denmark: *Statistik Årbog 1968*, pp. 414–15. The intervals in the two tables are equivalent: Danish = American × 5.

political activities.[20] In a modern context it is nevertheless difficult to imagine any significant difference. Membership both of the Congress and of the Folketing has become a fulltime job in the twentieth century. Under such conditions it is almost impossible to live "for" politics in the Weberian sense, and the opportunities of lawyers are not definitely better than the opportunities of members of other occupations. Only lawyers in the capital are able to remain active without special arrangements; most lawyers will have either to quit their practice or to carry it on by means of partners.

This brings us to a structural difference between the two legal professions. In the United States the "legal factory," the big firm with, say, 50 partners and numerous associated attorneys, is a reality in the big cities. Smaller firms with from 3 to 20 lawyers are abundant in the urban areas. At the bottom of the hierarchy are the vast majority of lawyers who are practicing alone or in partnership with another lawyer. In Denmark law firms in the United States sense are nonexistent. Most of the lawyers practice alone or in small partnerships, and only a few firms, situated in Copen-

[20] Palle Rosenkrantz, *Prokuratorerne i Danmark i det 19. Aarhundrede*, (København, 1928), pp. 143–44; H. Hjort Nielson, "Af den Danske Sagførestands Historie 1736–1936," in E. Reitzel-Nielsen and Carl Popp-Madsen, Eds., *Festskrift i Anledning af Tohundrede Aars Dagen for Indførelsen af Juridisk Eksamen ved Københavns Universitet*, (København, 1936), p. 382; Svend Heltberg, "Sagførerlovgivningen og Organisationsarbejdet i det 19. Aarhundrede," in *Sagførerbladet*, 17, (1938), p. 85.

hagen, exceed 10 partners. This difference should be taken into consideration, especially if it is possible to observe a more pronounced inclination for political careers among United States lawyers in big firms than among solo practitioners, which might be interpreted as indicating a different degree of dispensability in the two systems. At this point evidence is ambiguous.[21]

Apart from the different structure of the two professions in this respect, there is no evidence pointing in the direction of dissimilarities between the dispensability or indispensability of the United States and the Danish lawyer. It is tempting to conclude that the "dispensability argument" cannot function as a central explanatory factor.

The "skill argument," according to which the lawyer develops some indispensable political skills during his education and in his practice, may sound convincing, but is nevertheless a dubious explanation. We are able to call attention to a series of generalized political skills that are traditionally ascribed to the lawyer, but they can be ascribed to lawyers as well in Denmark as in the United States.

The Danish system of legal education differs from that of the United States, and as methods of legal training undoubtedly affect the skills and perspectives that lawyers bring to their practice, we should discuss briefly some of these differences.

In contrast to the Danish, legal education in the United States is characterized by its heterogeneity.[22] The requirements for admission to the bar

---

[21] Max Weber based his dispensability-argument upon the possibility of association with other lawyers, the use of proxies, the lack of capital risks, and the possession of an organized secretarial assistance. See Max Weber, *Gesammelte Politische Schriften,* 2nd ed., (Tübingen, 1958, pp. 260 and 378. Eulau and Sprague, (*op. cit.,* p. 44), mention that a few lawyer-legislators were "sent" to the state legislature as "agents" of their firm. In general, however, corporation lawyers are reported to be more or less absent from local and state politics. Wardwell and Wood found in one large southern city that 56 percent of the solo practitioners, against 28 percent of the firm lawyers, had been active in politics. See Walter I. Wardwell and Arthus L. Wood, "The Extra-Professional Role of the Lawyer," in *American Journal of Sociology,* **61** (1956), pp. 304–07. Cf. also Herbert Jacob, *Justice in America: Courts, Lawyers, and the Judicial Process,* (New York, 1965), pp. 59–64; James David Barber, *The Lawmakers: Recruitment and Adaptation to Legislative Life,* (New Haven, 1965), pp. 67–68. Most of the findings are related to the state legislature, and their relevancy for a discussion of the "dispensability-argument" in connection with national legislatures are in doubt.

[22] See Albert P. Blaustein and Charles O. Porter, *The American Lawyer: A Summary of the Survey of the Legal Profession,* (Chicago, 1954), chapter VI; C. Ray Jeffery et al., "The Legal Profession," and Henry H. Foster, Jr., and C. Ray Jeffery, "Legal Education," chapters 9–10 in F. James Davis, et al., *Society and the Law: New Meanings for an Old Profession,* (New York, 1962).

changed from period to period in the United States, and the development of modern legal educational standards is described as a "long, slow process opposed at every turn,"[23] in which "attempts to raise educational standards of admission to the bar have met only limited success."[24] The transition from apprenticeship training to a standardized academic training was delayed by a widespread disrespect for formal education as a prerequisite for admission to the bar. It was only in the beginning of this century that the bar associations took an initiative in order to harmonize and strengthen the professional education and standardize the law curriculum.

The still existing wide range in United States legal education is reflected in surveys that have been conducted in the profession. By 1951, 80 percent of all lawyers had received a law degree, and about 95 percent had attended some kind of law school, be it a high-prestige, internationally renowned national school, an unapproved school offering part-time evening instruction, or even a correspondence school giving only the minimum education necessary for the prospective lawyer to pass the bar examination; furthermore, there is little uniformity in the demands on knowledge and procedural skills at the bar examinations throughout the United States.

In contrast to the United States pattern Danish legal education is highly standardized and has been so for centuries. Since 1736 there has existed a law degree, and the universities have had complete monopoly in legal education. The curriculum has been almost uniform for all students,[25] and its aim has been to provide a high-quality training in the various fields of law, but first and foremost in those fields that are specially relevant to the prospective judicial officer and the attorney. The law degree is obtained after approximately 6 years' studies, which corresponds to the duration of most other Danish university studies. The law graduate who wants to become a practicing lawyer is required to have a further 3 years' apprenticeship training in a private practice before he is allowed to start on his own. The bar examinations of the United States legal system have no equivalent in Denmark, where the young graduate is simply admitted to the bar by means of a practicing certificate given by the Ministry of Justice.

One of the speculative comments made by Danish legal historians on

---

[23] A. A. Berle, Jr., "Modern Legal Profession," in *Encyclopedia of the Social Sciences,* **IX** (1933), p. 343.

[24] Philippe Nonet and Jerome E. Karlin, "The Legal Profession," in *International Encyclopedia of the Social Sciences,* **9** (1968), p. 68.

[25] Until 1936 there existed two degrees: a "Latin" degree and a "Danish," the latter a sort of bachelors' degree open for persons without the matriculation examination. As it was not able to compete with the former degree, it was finally abolished, and after its abolition the legal profession and the organizations have fought against a restoration of a bachelors degree.

the relative absence of lawyers in Danish politics has to do with the nature of legal training in Denmark. It is argued that at the Danish universities jurists are trained primarily in the classic disciplines of civil law and that this onesidedness, which becomes more and more pronounced as the tasks of the lawyer change from "citizen versus citizen" to "citizen versus state" cases, has had profound influence upon the whole legal profession, in which it is a "very wide-spread view that the proper mission of the jurist in the state is to devote himself to the problems concerning the legal status of the individual."[26]

Exactly the same points have been made in debates on legal education in the United States. Charges of onesidedness, of overspecialization, and of educating "technicians of law," have been abundant. Since the days of Thomas Jefferson attempts have been made to widen legal education and to make it an adequate training for policy-making. In this respect the Danish and the United States legal professions show remarkable similarities.[27]

To compare the politically significant qualities ascribed to the two professions, we must proceed from formal education to the working conditions of the practicing lawyer. Do they differ? With more than 200,000 lawyers in the United States as against approximately 2000 in Denmark, we should expect to find some differences. Most conspicuous is the marked tendency toward specialization in the United States profession. This inclination is most pronounced in the large law firms, but it is also typical for smaller firms. Many lawyers restrict their practice to a narrow specialty in the total field of law, or they specialize functionally as counsels to business or as trial lawyers. In these firms another kind of specialization can be observed too—one of the partners can serve as the public partner or "business-getter," his function being to make the right kind of contacts with potential clients, for example, in the political circles of the community. Although specialization is a growing phenomenon, the solo practitioners, who still comprise the bulk of the lawyers in private practice, are still unable to specialize to any great extent.

Danish lawyers do not specialize. A few of them try to concentrate their business, but the great majority have to act as the "family doctor" who is supposed to know something about everything. They all have to appear

---

[26] Kai Fr. Hammerich, "Juristerne og Embedslivet," in Reitzel-Nielsen and Popp-Madsen, *op cit.,* p. 306. Questions about the adequacy of the legal education in Denmark are continuously debated in the journal *Juristen,* published by the Association of Danish Jurists—see especially *Juristen,* **48** (1966), pp. F. 227–253.

[27] See Blaustein and Porter, *op. cit.,* chapter VI; Davis et al., *op. cit.,* chapter 10, and Lasswell and McDougal, *op. cit.*

in court, and they are all trained in oral procedure, but they all also act as counsels to individual clients and to business.

We do find one differentiation in the Danish legal profession that is absent in the United States. In the Danish judicial structure there are three kinds of courts: 108 lower courts, two high courts, and the Supreme Court. From 1869, when the occupation of lawyer became a free trade, there has existed a kind of quality-grading of Danish lawyers. All have been given the right to appear in the lower courts, but in order to appear in courts at higher levels a lawyer is obliged to pass examinations and to have demonstrated some procedural experience. This division into three categories has tended to produce a sort of specialization in the whole profession, because it promotes the view among clients that there are differences between the quality of work done by members of the three categories. Supreme Court lawyers were long considered the most qualified, and accordingly, this category of lawyers got a disproportionate share of the best-paid business. In 1958 this strict split-up was softened, but there still exists some differentiation within the profession.

Although it is easy to see differences in the working conditions of the two professions, nevertheless none of them seem to support the "skill argument." If we restrict ourselves to an observation of lawyers in private practice, there are no signs that the United States lawyer should have, develop, or monopolize qualities which his Danish colleague misses. The education and the practical training of the Danish lawyer give him at least the same opportunities to "develop ability in interpersonal mediation and conciliation and skill in verbal manipulation."[28]

The three explanations reviewed have all been rejected as satisfactory explanations by most United States authors. The conclusion to be drawn from a comparison of the United States and the Danish legal professions is that these explanations are further weakened, because apparently the two professions do not differ in such ways as might be relevant for the social status, the dispensability, or the general skills of the members of the profession. However, to state that these explanations are not satisfactory means only that they cannot stand alone. They may very well function as components in a broader theoretical structure.

The Theory of Professional Convergence

By far the most elaborate and profound analysis of the lawyer's prominence in United States politics has been given by Heinz Eulau and John

---

[28] Donald R. Matthews, "United States Senators: A Collective Portrait," in *International Social Science Journal,* **13** (1961), p. 628.

D. Sprague.[29] Their starting point is a paradox, namely, that "though lawyers are clearly a distinct occupational group that is more visible, more ubiquitous, more prominent, and even more dominant in American political life than in any other, their private profession does not seem to affect a great deal of their political behaviour."[30] Earlier attempts to explain the dominant position of lawyers in United States politics in general and in the legislatures in particular paid no attention to this fact.

The solution of this paradox is simple and elegant, if only for the reason that it makes it possible at the same time to explain the affinity of law and politics as vocations, to explain why many lawyers begin participating in politics before starting their legal career, to explain the absence of differences between the behavior of lawyers and nonlawyers in the legislature, and yet to maintain the general hypothesis that a man's occupation influences his political behavior. Eulau and Sprague introduce the notion of *professional convergence,* a purely theoretical construct signifying a special relationship between two professions; if the two professions have common characteristics that are especially relevant to the performance of those roles which make up the professions, then they are said to be convergent. The connection between the alleged convergence of the legal and the political profession and the often-demonstrated affinity of law and politics is that "it may be said that lawyers tend to become politicians more than members of other professions do, or that politicians tend to choose law rather than another career, *because* law and politics are convergent professions."[31]

The fact that the two professions show a certain structural isomorphism, enabling us to describe them as being in the process of converging, is demonstrated by Eulau and Sprague, who introduce three criteria that, taken together, define the concept "profession" and that are at the same time relevant to explication of the alleged convergence of law and politics. On the following pages, I follow the line of arguments of these authors and try to show that the conditions of convergence are present to at least the same degree in Denmark as in the United States.

First, all professions are set apart from other occupations by their *independence* of control from outside. The members feel proud of this independence, which is regarded as the hallmark of the profession and which is very often strengthened by institutionalized safeguards. A comparison

---

[29] Eulau and Sprague, *op. cit.,* especially chapter 5.

[30] Eulau and Sprague, *op. cit.,* p. 3. David R. Derge, "The Lawyer as Decision Maker in the American State Legislature," *The Journal of Politics,* **21** (1959), pp. 408–33, apparently the first to discover that the legislative behavior of lawyers does not differ significantly from that of nonlawyers.

[31] Eulau and Sprague, *op. cit.,* p. 144.

of the two legal professions indicates that the demands for independence are similar. In both cases it is obvious that the role of *the lawyer* has to be described as that of a trustee; the code of ethics of the legal professions demands that the lawyer shall be free from outside pressures, his relationship with the clientele shall be fiduciary, in short, the risks of captivity ought to be minimized.

In Denmark the definition of the professional role of lawyers began very early. Already in 1638 an ordinance stated that "no public authority was allowed to make lawyers odious."[32] The professional secrecy of lawyers was later made part of Danish legislation, and thereby an important guarantee against outside pressures was secured for the profession.[33] Also, the relationship with the clientele has been extensively regulated by legislation, first and foremost by the profession's own code of ethics. It is explicitly stated that "a lawyer has solely to act in the interests of the client,"[34] and this obligation is surrounded by a series of rights and duties for the client and the lawyer himself. The client may dismiss the lawyer if he is dissatisfied with his conduct of the case, but apart from regular complaints to the courts or the bar organization, dismissal is the only sanction the client has at his disposal. The lawyer is warned against identification with the client and against instructions or orders from him. "The lawyer must be free and independent in his relationship with the client. A state of dependence, regardless its form, hinders a free formation of standpoints," as a Danish lawyer summarizes the position of the legal profession.[35] His United States colleague would not disagree.

In Denmark as well as in the United States *the legislator* takes a role which is partly isomorphic with that of the lawyer. Just as was the case with the lawyer, he is dependent on his "clients" in the sense that the voters at least in principle are able to dismiss him at election day, but independent in the sense that the voters are unable to bind him in his daily work. The dominant view in United States legislative research describes the U.S. legislator as predominantly a "free agent," and his role as a trustee role. Without methodologically similar research in Denmark, it is of course hazardous to describe the role orientations of Danish legislators, but from the

---

[32] Axel H. Pedersen, *Indledning til advokatgerningen, II* (København, 1963, 2nd ed.), p. 38.

[33] Axel H. Pedersen, *Indledning til advokatgerningen, I,* (København, 1962, 2nd ed.), pp. 89 ff. See also Axel H. Pedersen, *Det Danske Advokatsamfund 1919–1969,* (København, 1969), pp. 23–24.

[34] See Lov om Rettens Pleje, (*Lovbekendtgørelse, 1. juli, 1963*), Kap. 13; "Regler for god sagførerskik og kollegialitet, vedtaget af sagførerrådet d. 7. september 1956," in *Sagførerbladet,* 35 (1956), pp. 265–69.

[35] Axel H. Pedersen, *op. cit.* (*1962*), pp. 115 ff.

sparse evidence at hand the picture of the trustee appears, nevertheless. Since 1849 the Danish constitution has established that "members of the Folketing shall be bound solely by their own consciences and not by any directions given by their electors." In the latter half of the nineteenth century the members in several constituencies were exposed to subsequent control from their voters, and especially their voting behavior in the chamber was scrutinized; it rather often happened that an incumbent was rejected after a conflict with the voters in his single-member constituency. The process of party formation was rather slow. Shifting coalitions among the members in the chamber, especially among the representatives of rural Denmark, were a characteristic of the first decades after 1849. Several members survived shifts in party orientation—indeed a few kept their mandate although they "crossed the floor" from the left to the right side of the party spectrum.[36] Despite a bewildering variety of fates, we are entitled to argue that Danish MF construed their role as to represent at the same time a constituency and the whole country, without submitting to voters or to other members of the Folketing.

Three events tended to transform this role: first, the rise of mass parties in the last decades of the nineteenth century, second, the change from a simple-majority electoral system to proportional representation, which occurred 1915–1920, and finally, a universal tendency that made the questions with which the legislators deal more and more complex, so that they are beyond the comprehension of the ordinary citizen. These events have changed both the relationship between the MF and his voters and between him and his party colleagues in the Folketing.

In this century it has become more and more seldom that an incumbent is refused renomination. Today the MF is secured reelection as long as his mandate is kept by the party. Furthermore his reelection in the proportional representation system is dependent not only upon the reactions of the voters in his own constituency, but upon the fate of the party in the country in its entirety as well. In his relation with the voters in the constituency, the MF has become more independent. He still functions as an "errand-boy," who brings the small and the great problems of the voters to the attention of public authorities, but his role has developed into a fiduciary role, which is comparable to that of the lawyer vis-à-vis his clients.

On the other hand, the relationship between the single legislator and his party group in the Folketing, the other central focus of representation, has changed profoundly. From a low degree of cohesion in the nineteenth

[36] See, e.g., Per Salomonsson, ed, *Den politiske magtkamp 1866–1901*, (København, 1968), pp. 40–41.

century, a very strong cohesion has developed in most of the Danish party groups.[37] It has been argued that this development has involved a violation of the freedom and independence of the members. "Folketing members are more to be regarded as a kind of party functionnairies than as bearers of individual convictions," says a leading expert on public law.[38] It is evident that loyalty to the party is very highly valued in Denmark, but decision-making in Danish party groups is not describable as a "master-servant relation." The position of the party is laid down at the meetings of the group, and in these meetings all members may advance their opinions. If it should happen that a deep disagreement comes out, which the members are not able to reconcile by means of a compromise, then the opinion of the majority becomes the standpoint of the party. The minority yields, and this acceptance of the majority view is normally not conceived by politicians as a deprivation of their independence: loyalty to the party is simply conceived as one among several premises for a decision. Furthermore, in most cases the party groups tolerate deviant behavior if the member has informed his colleagues beforehand, and there do exist shared, unwritten norms which make some divisions "free."[39]

Although we lack data directly comparable with the United States data, we are permitted to view the representational roles of Danish lawyers and Danish politicians at least in a restricted sense as structurally isomorphic. The crucial test of this isomorphism and its relevance for the recruitment of lawyers into politics in the two systems has, however, to include, not only an investigation of the roles of lawyers and politicians as seen by themselves, but, equally important, an investigation of how the lawyers in general see the representational role of politicians; this kind of survey has been conducted neither in the United States nor in Denmark.

The second criterion of a profession is the existence of *a code of ethics* that regulates the relations of the profession with the societal environment and the mutual relations among the members themselves. In this respect lawyers in the two countries form professions, and in a way the professional trait is more pronounced in Denmark. Both in the United States and in Denmark very elaborate codes of ethics have developed; their ob-

---

[37] Mogens N. Pedersen, "Consensus and Conflict in the Danish Folketing 1945–65," in *Scandinavian Political Studies,* 2, (Helsinki, 1967), pp. 143–66.

[38] Alf Ross, *Dansk Statsforfatningsret,* (1st ed., København, 1959), I, p. 309; but see Poul Meyer, *Politiske Partier,* (København, 1965), p. 51. Ross has modified his point of view considerably in the 2nd edition (København, 1966), p. 359.

[39] See further Erik Vagn Jensen, ed, *De politiske partier,* (København, 1964), pp. 120–39; Poul Meyer, *op. cit.,* pp. 51–56; Erik Rasmussen, *Komparativ Politik,* (København, 1968), I, pp. 204–08; Mogens N. Pedersen, *op. cit.*

servance is rather strictly controlled, and deviators are censured, penalized, suspended, or possibly disbarred.[40]

Canons of legal ethics are an international phenomenon, in many respects mere sublimations and applications of generally accepted ethical standards. Many of the rules in the Danish and the United States codes are almost completely identical, and the outline of problems covered by them is a common one. In both countries these codes express the ideals of the profession. They are faithfully observed by the overwhelming majority of the lawyers, and the professional organizations are eager to see that these rules are kept by the lawyers, also, because unethical behavior in the general sense does great damage to the public image and reputation of the profession. The bar organizations play an important role in the maintenance of the discipline. Not only are they active in the formulation and interpretation of the ethical standards, but they serve as prosecutors and investigators as well. While in the United States the organized bar primarily carries out the preliminary investigations, before the complaints are brought before the courts, the Danish Council of the Bar acts both as an investigating and as a direct disciplinary authority, endowed by the Administration of Justice Act with judicial power over its members alongside the judicial power of the courts, which handle the most serious complaints against lawyers. The Danish Bar Association, the membership of which is compulsory, is recognized in this Act as the "community of all lawyers" and as a self-governing profession.

The theory of professional convergence argues that a political profession exists in the same sense as a legal profession. As regards a specific code of conduct for *politicians,* we are unable to grasp it in the same literal sense as the code of legal ethics, but the requirements are also considerably lower. In the formulation of Eulau and Sprague we should be satisfied if we find that what is proper political behavior in the legislatures is determined by "rules of the game," or "folkways," which are not necessarily written, nor even spoken, but about which there exists nevertheless consensus among politicians. The most conspicuous legislative norms in Denmark are the highly formalized, written Rules of Procedure and the rulings of the chairman,[41] but of course there exist many informal norms of con-

---

[40] See Blaustein and Porter, *op. cit.,* chapter VIII for the United States legal ethics. For Denmark, see first and foremost Axel H. Pedersen, *op. cit.,* (*1962–63*), which is a codification and interpretation of Danish legal ethics. Axel H. Pedersen, *op. cit.,* (*1969*), gives an up-to-date description of the organization of the Danish legal profession and its history.

[41] *Folketingets Forretningsorden,* (latest ed., København, 1966). Rulings and precedents have recently been codified in Johs. Thorborg, *Kommentarer til Folketingets Forretningsorden,* (mimeographed, Folketingets Sekretariat, København, 1969).

duct in the Folketing too. Typical United States legislative norms, like the seniority rule, the apprenticeship norm, norms of specialization, interpersonal courtesy and reciprocity, have their more or less similar counterparts in Danish politics. The fact that, while the "folkways" of the United States national and state legislatures have been thoroughly investigated, those of the Danish Folketing are yet to be mapped out should not prevent us from speaking about politics as a profession in the sense that term is used in the theory of convergence.

The third and final criterion of professional status of an occupation is the profession's alleged orientation to *public service* rather than to private gain. As far as the *politician* is concerned, he is a "public servant" in a very literal sense. He is expected to serve the public, and the standards of proper political conduct forbid him to use his position in his own favor or in favor of narrow specific interests.

While United States legislators in general tend to view lobbyists and interest groups as playing a functional role in the political system, and in accordance with this view maintain friendly and relaxed relations with lobbyists, the Danish politicians in contrast seem to take a more cautious attitude. The interest groups get access to the Folketing through MFs with overlapping memberships or through the "official channels." Direct personal contacts with single members are of minor importance, and the "social lobby" is virtually nonexistent. United States observers have stressed the absence of serious ethical problems in the relations between interest groups and Danish politicians, and whatever evidence we have indicates that MFs are not in any sense less "public servants" than their United States colleagues in their attitude towards the organizations.[42]

Both United States and Danish legislators are required by their voters to act unselfishly as agents or errand boys vis-à-vis the public authorities in the capital. In Denmark this kind of "public service" has always been regarded as part of the representational role, and it still takes up much of the time of the MF, especially if he is elected in the provinces. "Many members of Parliament act as a kind of unofficial lawyers," an experienced observer of Danish MFs once remarked.[43]

The fact that *lawyers* are public servants in their own judgment as well

---

[42] See William E. Laux, *Interest Groups in Danish Politics*, (Ann Arbor; University Microfilms, 1963), especially chapter 5. Kenneth E. Miller, *Government and Politics in Denmark*, (Boston, 1968), pp. 116–23, with references to the scanty Danish literature.

[43] Svend Thorsen, *Danmarks Rigsdag*, (København, 1949), p. 141. Cf. Vagn Bro, "Rigsdagsmændenes rettigheder og forpligtelser," in *Den danske Rigsdag*, IV, (København, 1949), especially pp. 301–03.

as in the estimation of the public is evident in Denmark, perhaps more clearly so than in the United States. Roscoe Pound has defined the concept "profession" with special reference to the legal profession in the United States as "a group of men pursuing a learned art as a common calling in the spirit of a public service—no less a public service because it may incidentally be a means of livelihood. Pursuit of the learned art in the spirit of public service is the primary purpose . . . ."[44] Talcott Parsons has stressed the same characteristic of the United States lawyer, who "by virtue of his admission to the bar becomes in a limited and qualified sense a public official, as an 'officer of the court.' The profession is thus an entity which, as it were, penetrates the boundary between public and private capabilities and responsibilities. Its members act in both capacities, and the profession has major anchorages in both."[45]

The Danish legal profession is described in exactly the same terms. When lawyers characterize their role, they stress that they are, along with the judges, "bearers of the concept of justice" and as such "have a vocation to protect the rights of citizens both against other citizens and against the public authorities"; in short, they form a "very important profession."[46]

Conceptions like these have been a professional creed for a very long time, having their root in the early history of the legal profession.[47] From the beginning of the seventeenth century, but especially after the introduction of the law degree in 1736, a practice was formed according to which admission to the bar was given by a license signed by the King, and as a consequence attorneys were considered a special kind of public servant with rights and duties like all other public servants. In one of its paragraphs, the Constitution of 1849 promised the abolition of "any restraints of the free and equal access to trade, which is not based on the public weal," and in accordance with this promise the occupation as lawyer became a

---

[44] Roscoe Pound, *The Lawyer from Antiquity to Modern Times,* (St. Paul, Minn. 1953), quoted from Blaustein and Porter, *op. cit.,* p. 283.

[45] Talcott Parsons, "A Sociologist Looks at the Legal Profession," in *Essays in Sociological Theory,* (rev. ed., New York, 1964), p. 378.

[46] These quotations are taken from an "Introduction to the Study of Law," written as a primer for beginning law students, Stig Juul, Alf Ross and Jørgen Trolle, *Indledning til retsstudiet,* (3d ed., København, 1967), p. 42.

[47] To the following, see Axel H. Pedersen, *op. cit. (1962),* pp. 11–38; Axel H. Pedersen, *op. cit. (1963),* pp. 40–41; H. Hjort-Nielsen and Svend Heltberg, "Sagførerstanden gennem 300 Aar," in *Sagførerbladet,* **17** (1938), pp. 75–91; Tage Holmboe, et al., "Advokaterne, herunder deres rekruttering m. v.," in Poul Bagge, Jep Lauesen Frost, and Bernt Hjejle, Eds., *Højesteret 1661–1961,* (København, 1961), II, pp. 231–56.

free trade in 1869. In the future, attorneys were not to be appointed by the King, but instead to be admitted to the bar by the Minister of Justice, and this admission was only dependant upon the before-mentioned law degree, 3 years of apprenticeship training, and a documented "honourable character."[48] In spite of this reform the conception of the lawyer as a public official survived for a long time, and the lawyer's special public responsibility is still a reality in the minds of the members of the profession.

Fitting the legal profession into the modern legal system as a whole was a major result of the Administration of Justice Act of 1919, in which the profession got its final recognition. It is beyond doubt that today most lawyers would endorse the professional creed put forward by a former chairman of the Danish Council of the Bar: "We ought never forget our connexion with the society at large and our position as the servants of Justice. It is in that capacity that the society has given us the freedom to govern and to judge ourselves. Our freedom in this respect will only last if unceasingly we take a social point of view and are prepared to accept our responsibility . . . ."[49]

So far I have tried to show, through an examination of selected professional role components, that the legal and the political professions in Denmark are partly isomorphic, and therefore they can be described as being in a state of convergence. Furthermore, we have seen that the United States and Danish legal and political professions share the relevant characteristics to a considerable extent. The conclusion that flows from these comparisons is that if "convergence is the conceptual tool through which the affinity of law and politics may be explained,"[50] then we should find a far greater share of lawyers in the Danish legislature than is actually observed. The theory of professional convergence may be satisfying, if we want to explain the absence of significant differences between the legislative behavior of lawyer-legislators and other legislators, but as a sufficient explanation of the ubiquity of lawyers in politics the theory comes down when confronted with Danish data.

The Lawyer-Concept

Until now the mode of reasoning has been purely destructive, tending to show that some of the factors used to explain the affinity of law and

---

[48] *Lov om Adgang til Sagførervirksomheden,* May, 26, 1868, §1. In order to become High Court Attorney or Supreme Court Attorney, the demands in terms of experience and legal skills were considerably higher.

[49] Bernt Hjejle, "En sagfører ser på sit virke," in *Norsk Sakførerblad,* (1951), p. 131.

[50] Eulau and Sprague, *op. cit.,* p. 144.

politics in the United States are operative in the Danish political system too, without producing a similar effect. It is necessary at this point, however, to note that the occupational categories that have been characterized as "lawyers" or the "legal profession" are, on the one hand, those United States lawyers who are in private practice, and, on the other hand, that part of the Danish law graduates who are in a similar practice as *"advokater."* This limitation was justified because both the classical and some of the newer analyses treat this subcategory only and not the legal profession *in toto.* The classical arguments, those of both de Toqueville and Max Weber, tried to explain why the *private practitioners* of law were so numerous in politics, and the convergence theory apparently makes the same limitation.

This usage raises a serious conceptual problem, which easily becomes a source of semantic confusion in a comparative study of lawyers in politics. While in the United States "lawyer" is the generic term, not depending upon subsequent career, for all those persons who, on basis of a certain legal education and as a rule through a more or less rigorous bar examination, have obtained admission to the bar, the European vocabulary, including the Danish, is more differentiated, using different terms according to the post-graduate career, and reserving the generic term as an indication of educational level.[51] Some United States authors use the term "lawyer" in the broad sense, others in a narrow sense equivalent to "practicing lawyer," and others again apparently use the broad and the narrow term simultaneously in the same study.[52] In a comparative study the temptation to generalize about "lawyers in politics" without precise definition is obviously great. Perhaps this fallacy has been committed in the first sections of this chapter, for it was not always possible to discern the definition used

[51] This dissimilarity in usage makes translations a rather difficult enterprise. As a relevant example of a distorted translation, Gerth and Mills' translation of Max Weber's "Politik als Beruf" should be mentioned, (Gerth and Mills, *op. cit.,* pp. 77–128). In the original German text [in Max Weber, *Gesammelte Politische Schriften,* (Munich, 1920), pp. 396–450] Weber makes a distinction between *"die universitätsgeschulten Juristen"* and a subcategory, *"die Advokaten."* It is men from the latter category who, in Weber's opinion, are dispensable and possessing superior political skills. This distinction is maintained in the English translation, but as a distinction between *"university-trained jurists"* and *"lawyers"*—which is not *necessarily* the same distinction! Cf., e.g., the lawyer concept in Gold, *op. cit.,* p. 85: ". . . I have classified as lawyers all who, it could be determined, had completed law school or who listed themselves as lawyers or for whom there existed other fairly definite evidences that he is a lawyer, such as, for example, membership in a bar association or service as city attorney."

[52] Examples of the three usages are Gold, *op. cit.,* Schlesinger, *op. cit.,* and Eulau and Sprague, *op. cit.,* (pp. 36–37, 39–50, and 135–36).

by those authors and institutions upon whose calculations Table 2.1 was based.[53]

In order to cope with this problem a more detailed picture is drawn in Table 2.4. In all those countries for which we have data, the share of

Table 2.4   Legislators with a Law Degree and Lawyers in Private Practice in Selected European Countries. (% of Total Membership)[a]

Country	Year	Law Degree	Lawyers in Private Practice
Italy	1948–1963	38	27
The Netherlands	1967	29	7
Iceland	1952	24	8
United Kingdom	1953	20	17
France	1958	20	16
West Germany	1957	19	8
Austria	1966	14	3
Norway	1957	11	4
Finland	1951	11	2
Denmark	1966	10	4
Sweden	1952	3	1

[a] Neither in *Table 2.4*, nor in *Table 2.1* has it been possible to make a distinction between "occupation at first entrance" and "present occupation."
SOURCES: Italy: G. Sartori, "Italy: Members of Parliament," in *Decisions and decisionmakers in the modern state*, (UNESCO: Paris, 1967), pp. 156–73; United Kingdom, France, and West Germany: Gerhard Loewenberg, *Parliament in the German Political System*, (New York, 1967), p. 109; Iceland, Finland, and Sweden: *Svensk Juristtidning*, 37 (1952), pp. 872–73; Norway: Henry Valen, "The Recruitment of Parliamentary Nominees in Norway," in *Scandinavian Political Studies*, I, (Helsinki, 1966), pp. 121–66; The Netherlands, Austria, and Denmark: as in *Table 2.1 supra*.

jurists is considerably higher than the percentage of lawyers in private practice. At the same time we find that the ranking of the countries in the table above does not differ much from that of Table 2.1.

Thus it is ascertained that in many European countries the legislature

[53] In the Finnish case the percentage in *Table 2.1* was the percentage of legislators with a law degree [Martti Noponen and Pertti Pesonen, "The Legislative Career in Finland," in E. Allardt and Y. Littunen, Eds., *Cleavages, Ideologies, and Party Systems. Contributions to Comparative Sociology.*, (Helsinki, 1964), p. 455]. The Belgian percentage included judges [F. Debuyst, *La Fonction Parlementaire en Belgique: Mécanismes d'Accès et Images*, (Bruxelles, 1967), p. 95]. However, these and similar errors do not violate the argument in the second section above.

is equipped with legal expertise and acquaintance with law through the membership of other categories of lawyers rather than those in private practice. In order to investigate the presence or absence of lawyers in the legislatures as a problem in comparative politics, we must consequently take into consideration all subcategories of the legal profession, primarily because the nearest European equivalent to the American *lawyer* in politics is the university-trained *jurist*. In short, it is the relationship between the whole legal profession and politics that ought to occupy our interest, and accordingly, the explanatory scheme should be able to encompass all components of the profession.

On the following pages I discuss some differences between the American and the Danish legal professions and between the two political systems. Taken together they may furnish us with a better understanding of the affinity of law and politics in the United States.

The Disappearance of Jurists from Danish Politics

A conspicuous difference between the Congress of the United States and the Danish Folketing is the presence in the latter of legislators who combine a political career with a judgeship or a position as a civil servant. While the separation-of-powers doctrine makes employment in the government service or as a judicial officer a disqualification for membership in the United States legislature, no one at all is excluded from the Folketing by virtue of the holding of office. In fact it is expressly stated in the Danish Constitution that "any person who has the right to vote at Folketing elections shall be eligible for membership of the Folketing . . . ," and further that "civil servants who are elected Members of the Folketing shall not require permission from the Government to accept their election." According to this provision nothing can hinder the election of public employees from the highest to the lowest echelons of the administrative hierarchy, nor can judges be prevented from pursuing a political career. When a civil servant or a judge is elected, he is entitled to a leave of absence without loss of pension rights, and his salary is at worst reduced by one-third. It is evident that these provisions tend to make public employees highly dispensable, and especially the higher civil servants have a favorable position.[54]

---

[54] This problem is discussed in *Betænkning afgivet af Tjenestemandskommissionen af 1965*, I, (Bet. nr. 483/1969), p. 119. A member of this commission, the former Social Democratic member of the Folketing Holger Eriksen, has remarked that if these provisions are not changed "the end of it will be that the Folketing will mainly be composed of public employees," *Jyllandsposten*, January 27, 1967.

In United States literature this difference in eligibility has formed the basis of a new, sketchy explanatory hypothesis. When Dankwart A. Rustow found very few lawyers in private practice among the members of the Swedish *Riksdag* and at the same time found rules of eligibility similar to the Danish, he advanced as a hypothesis that in Sweden the political parties were able to draw on nominees from the reservoir of public employees, and consequently they did not require the services of the lawyers, whereas "in countries where public employees are barred from active politics, lawyers fill the vacuum—not perhaps because they are adept at law-making, but rather because a law practice that can be dropped or resumed almost at will offers a refuge from the uncertainties of periodic election."[55]

This is of course a sort of "dispensability argument," although more sophisticated than the one reviewed earlier in this chapter. It is of particular interest because this tentative explanation apparently makes it possible in a modified form to save at least parts of the traditional explanations, in case it is possible to show that the Danish Folketing counts among its members a considerable amount of relatively high-prestige judges and civil servants with a legal education.

In the first years after the introduction of democratic government, these categories were in fact abundant in the Folketing, and their political activities were considered an obvious consequence of their position in Danish society. In 1821, during the period of royal absolutism, jurists had been given monopoly of the higher posts in the administrative hierarchy, and earlier, in the eighteenth century, they had gradually monopolized the judiciary. The jurists held a leading position, and they were very much conscious of their own worth. They were the "really reigning class," it has been said.[56]

In the Constituent Assembly of 1848 they had a strong representation. Out of 152 members, 40 had a legal education, and only 8 of these 40 were lawyers in private practice. Most of the ministers were high civil servants, and jurists dominated the debates and the drafting work in the committees.

No one in the Assembly did in fact challenge the eligibility of civil servants or judicial officers, so obvious was their position. "It is undesirable to remove the civil servants from Parliament, particularly so long as the

---

[55] Rustow, *op. cit.,* pp. 705–07.
[56] Hammerich, in Reitzel-Nielsen and Popp-Madsen, *op. cit.,* p. 260. See further Holmboe et al. in Bagge, Frost and Hjejle, *op. cit.,* II, pp. 231–56; Rosenkrantz, *op. cit.*; Ebba Waaben, "Træk af Embedsstandens Stilling 1848–1948," in *Central-administrationen 1848–1948,* (København, 1948), pp. 105–43.

Intelligentsia in this country is not more extensive," one of the members declared.[57]

In the first decade after 1849 the jurists still occupied a central position in Danish politics. Lawyers in private practice did not seek election in great numbers, but civil servants, law professors, and judges, including Supreme Court Justices, were members of the Folketing during the first sessions, as were a considerable number of landowners and journalists with a background in legal education. The greatest share of jurists was, however, not to be found in the Folketing, but in the other chamber, the Landsting, and particularly in the Cabinet. The position of minister was still looked upon as the culmination of the administrative career, and accordingly many of the ministers were former civil servants.[58]

But then the jurists began disappearing from the political scene. This change in the recruitment pattern occurred simultaneously with the rise of modern political parties; in Danish historical literature the disappearance of jurists is in fact seen as a consequence of the formation of class-oriented parties, particularly as a consequence of the constitutional struggle that dominated Danish politics in the last 30 years of the century, terminating in 1901 with the royal recognition of the principle of government responsibility.[59]

This political conflict had many dimensions. It was a conflict between "the haves" and "the have-nots," a conflict between urban and rural Denmark and between the exponents of Danish absolutist tradition and populist reformers. At an early time the civil servants, and therefore the jurists, became scapegoats in this struggle. Already in the 1850s the representatives of rural Denmark (*Bondevennerne*) had opened an attack on the civil servants, who were considered a closed circle of Mandarins, bearers of the absolutist values. They tried in vain to break the jurists' monopoly as civil servants—even the law degree as such was criticized as a source of the alleged evil. When the party system unfolded in the 1870s with the organization of the farmers and a little later the manual workers, the attacks became even more furious. Because the civil servants and most other jurists were identified with, or at least were considered the allies of, the Conservative governments in the period after 1870, they, and to a high degree the whole legal profession, came under fire from the majority

---

[57] *Beretning om Forhandlingerne på Rigsdagen 1848–49*, sp. 2823.

[58] Of 22 ministers in the cabinets between 1856 and 1865, 7 were recruited from the Central Administration, and of the remainder 13 were government employees at other levels; see Waaben, *op. cit.*, p. 124.

[59] About this period in Danish History, see, e.g., Miller, *op. cit.*

parties in the Folketing.[60] The argument in Danish legal history runs that under this pressure the jurists were either forced out of politics, because their party stronghold in the Folketing crumbled away, or they withdrew themselves, and since then they have been reluctant to take up a political career. "The more public life has widened, the more jurists have locked themselves up behind one thing or another, behind the bar of the courtroom, behind the doors of the bureau, behind the desks of the university," a Danish legal historian has characterized the fate of jurists in Danish politics.[61]

This very rough outline of a genetic explanation of the relative absence of jurists from Danish politics is difficult to test. Biographies and contemporary data are scarce or silent. If, however, we cannot say for certain, *why* jurists disappeared, we are at least able to demonstrate fairly well that they *did* disappear. An inspection of a sample of Folketing sessions indicates fragmentarily that a profound change took place in the last

---

[60] As the vote was open in Denmark until 1901, and a number of electoral registers are still at hand in the archives, it is at least in principle possible to scrutinize the voting behavior of Danish jurists in the latter half of the nineteenth century. In Vagn Dybdahl, et al., *Sagførere i Aarhus: Undersøgelser og aktstykker tilegnede Carl Holst-Knudsen,* (Aarhus, 1956), pp. 32, and 49–52, the authors have analyzed the political activity of the lawyers in private practice in a large Danish town; they found that lawyers did not participate much in political activities, but that they voted frequently, and almost exclusively cast their votes for the Conservative candidates.

[61] Hammerich, in Reitzel-Nielsen and Popp-Madsen, *op. cit.,* p. 306; cf. Axel H. Pedersen, *op. cit. (1963),* pp. 46–47.

Table 2.5   Jurists in the Danish Folketing, Occupations at First
Entrance, Selected Sessions

	Session						
Occupation	1855	1887	1901	1920	1935	1950	1966
Private practice (attorneys)	5	8	5	7	4	4	7
Central administration	—	—	—	—	—	3	6
Judiciary	4	2	—	3	1	2	2
Other occupations	12	7	4	1	1	2	3
Total number of jurists	21	17	9	11	6	11	18
Percentage of all MF	21	17	8	7	4	7	10

SOURCES: Data from pilot study of recruitment patterns of the Danish Folketing, cf. Mogens N. Pedersen, *"Rekrutteringen af danske folketingsmænd,"* paper delivered at the 2nd Nordic Conference of Political Science, Helsinki, August 1968, (mimeographed, Institute of Political Science, University of Aarhus).

decades of the nineteenth century (Table 2.5); the jurists' share of the seats shrank.[62]

A far better visualization of the trend can be obtained from an analysis of the social background of the nominees during and immediately after the constitutional conflict (Table 2.6). The withdrawal of civil servants[63]

Table 2.6 Attorneys and Civil Servants among Candidates 1876–1913: Percentages of Candidates in the Three Main Party Groupings

Party	Occupation	Elections			
		1876–1881 (4 elections)	1884–1892 (4 elections)	1895–1903 (4 elections)	1906–1913 (4 elections)
Conservatives	attorneys	2.7	6.2	3.4	7.4
	civil servants	11.6	8.6	4.7	0.4
	all candidates (N)	292	304	232	250
Liberals	attorneys	5.4	6.8	2.4	3.7
	civil servants	2.3	2.3	2.1	3.3
	all candidates (N)	386	443	533	630
Social Democrats	attorneys	0	0	3.8	1.2
	civil servants	0	0	0	0
	all candidates (N)	14	31	133	256
All three parties	attorneys	4.2	6.3	2.9	3.9
	civil servants	6.2	4.6	2.4	1.9
	all candidates (N)	692	778	898	1142

SOURCE: Calculated from data in Vagn Dybdahl, *Partier og Erhverv. Studier i partiorganisation og byerhvervenes politiske aktivitet 1880–1913*, (Århus 1969), vol. 2, pp. 72–79.

took place primarily in the Conservative Party along with a general withdrawal of this party from the electoral contests, while in the growing Liberal Party the previously small share of jurists was diminished further as attorneys gradually disappeared from the nominations. By far the most

[62] Cf. also Victor Elberling, "Rigsdagsmændenes livsstilling, milieu og uddannelse," *Den danske Rigsdag 1849–1949*, IV, pp. 382–83; in Table 2.5 the category "Private Practice" includes apprentices, "Central Administration" comprises employees in departments and directorates, "Judiciary" includes judges and deputy judges, and the residual category contains one student of law.

[63] While the category "attorneys" includes only jurists, the "civil servant" category may contain members of other academic professions, but the majority has graduated in law. See further Vagn Dybdahl, *op. cit.* (1969), I, chapter II,1.

remarkable phenomenon to be envisaged in this table is, however, the almost complete absence of jurists in the emerging Social Democratic Party.

This tendency makes it seem at least probable that during this period the whole profession developed an apolitical orientation, often admitted by the jurists themselves. And it is probable that the differing inclinations among the parties toward nominations of jurists is a byproduct of the bitter and long-winded constitutional struggle.

In Denmark lawyers were not replaced in the Folketing by civil servants with a legal education. Neither did other categories of public employees get a foothold in politics comparable with that of the United States lawyer.

Open versus Closed Patterns of Political Recruitment

In the last section we saw that the rise of political parties in Denmark and the subsequent party struggles had important consequences for the position of lawyers in general and for their political opportunities. A second conspicuous difference between the United States and Danish political systems is to be found in their party structure, and this dissimilarity strongly affects the opportunities of jurists/lawyers.

Many features set the United States party system distinctly apart from most others, including the Danish. A few of those traits are especially relevant in this context. First and foremost, United States lawyers have an almost equal opportunity to get nominated and elected whether they are Republicans or Democrats and whether they seek nomination in rural or in urban constituencies. The reliance upon lawyers as legislators is spread uniformly all over the country. Especially it ought to be stressed that there are no particular idiosyncrasies or particularly favorable attitudes about lawyers in any of the parties.[64]

In contrast the opportunities of jurists differ in the Danish system from party to party. As party strength earlier varied markedly from region to region and still does to a certain extent,[65] the opportunities for successful nomination vary regionally too (Table 2.7).

The already-mentioned total absence of jurists in the Social Democratic Party and the relative stronghold of jurists among the Conservatives are partly historically determined, but do certainly reflect the surviving class structure, too. Danish party organizations are guided during the nominations by the class orientation of the party, and, inasmuch as the Social Democrats in particular have considered the jurists representatives of the

---

[64] Hyneman, *op. cit.*
[65] Ole Borre and Jan Stehouwer, *Partistyrke og social struktur 1960,* (Aarhus, 1968).

Table 2.7   Jurists in the Danish Folketing: Party and Occupation at First
Entrance, Selected Sessions[a]

	Session					
Party	1887	1901	1920	1935	1950	1966
Social Democrats	(1)	(14)	(48)	(68)	(59)	(59)
Attorneys	—	—	—	1	2	1
Other jurists	—	—	—	—	2	1
Radical Liberals	+	+	(18)	(14)	(12)	(13)
Attorneys	+	+	3	—	—	—
Other jurists	+	+	—	—	—	2
Conservatives	(27)	(8)	(27)	(26)	(27)	(34)
Attorneys	2	1	4	3	1	3
Other jurists	5	1	2	2	3	2
Liberals	(72)	(91)	(51)	(28)	(32)	(35)
Attorneys	6	4	—	—	1	3
Other jurists	4	3	2	—	2	3
Other parties	+	+	(5)	(13)	(21)	(28)
Attorneys	+	+	—	—	—	—
Other jurists	+	+	—	—	—	3
Total	17	9	11	6	11	18

[a] The numbers in parentheses indicate the total number of seats; + indicates party/parties
not represented.
SOURCE: Data from pilot study of recruitment patterns of the Danish Folketing, Mogens
N. Pedersen, *op. cit.* (1968).

"haves," we should not be surprised to find that the largest party has at
times lacked legally trained politicians in its parliamentary group.[66]

It has recently been hypothesized that lawyers are more likely to be
recruited to political office in "open" systems of recruitment than in systems where political parties set up distinct channels and where parties in
general try to control nominations. In other words, the more politicized
in party terms a legislative system becomes, the more lawyers and other

[66] This is a general phenomenon of the Danish labor movement. In the trade
unions, lawyers have until recently been absent as employees. The legal procedure
in the Labor Court is conducted by elected trade union officials, while the Employers'
Association always uses trained lawyers for this job. See further Walter Galenson,
The Danish System of Labor Relations, (Cambridge, Massachusetts, 1952), p. 214.
In the collective bargaining process the trade unions are exclusively represented by
elected officials too, and the present chairman of the Danish Federation of Trade
Unions has even deplored the use of "economists, jurists, and other experts" by the
Employers' Association in the negotiations. See *Danske Økonomer*, **14**, (1967),
p. 552.

professionals are likely to be displaced by party, governmental, or interest-group organization men.[67]

In the Danish Folketing election in 1968 only 5 candidates of a total of 1156 were put up outside the parties. The remainder, at least in the older parties where election chances exist, were predominantly candidates with a long experience as active party workers. The self-starter is an unknown phenomenon in modern Danish politics. While it often happened in the first years after 1849 that a candidate suddenly appeared on the political scene, was elected without organized support, and often disappeared again at the next turn, this is unheard of today. Parliamentary turnover rates have declined, party affiliation is a must, and as a rule a long period of work in the party organizations, including the youth organizations, is required before an aspiring politician gets an opportunity to be nominated in a "safe" constituency. Half of the members—among Social Democrats, even two-thirds—have had a previous career in municipal politics. Very often the prospective candidate will have to move from constituency to constituency in order to get elected—so to speak "advancing" in the hierarchy. Only 42 percent of members of the 1966 Folketing were elected the first time they were put up as candidates, against 75 percent in 1855.[68]

In the two largest parties, the Social Democratic Party and the Liberals, at least for long periods, the occupational distribution of members was very uneven. A few categories (e.g., journalists, trade union officials among the Social Democrats, and farmers and teachers among the Liberals) dominated the party groups in the Folketing. During this century the occupational bases of recruitment in the Danish parties have tended toward increasing homogeneity. A career as professional party politician or functionary has become a steppingstone to the Folketing in several parties, but as a whole the "mirroring function" of the Danish legislature has been accentuated. As professionalization seems to have speeded up, while homogenization has been rather slow, the system of recruitment nevertheless looks still more closed than 50 years ago. Proportional representation has had far-reaching consequences for the recruitment patterns, because it has in a way made the country one big constituency: the election chances in one constituency have become dependent upon the fate of the party as a whole, and accordingly nominations in the relatively "safe" as well as in the "marginal" constituencies have become a matter of concern for the party. A political career in this system in most cases follows a regular series of steps, leading from local party work, through involvement in local

---

[67] Patterson, *op. cit.,* p. 606. Cf. Loewenberg, *op. cit.,* pp. 107–111.
[68] Mogens N. Pedersen, *op. cit.* (1968).

politics or in organizations at the national level, and finally terminating in a seat in the Folketing. The Folketing is first entered by the average MF at the age of 44.

If it is true that lawyers are displaced by other categories in party-politicized legislative systems, we should expect to find that this displacement occurs at a rather early stage in the process of selection. A comparison of the two sets of nominees and incumbents confirms this hypothesis: the inclination of Danish lawyers in private practice to get nominated is small (Table 2.8). The lawyer in private practice is almost absent among

Table 2.8   Lawyers in Private Practice as Candidates and Members, by Party, Folketing Election 1968

Party	Candidates		Members	
	Number	% of Party's Candidates	Number	% of Party's Members
Social Democrats	1	0.8	0	0
Radical Liberals	2	1.7	1	3.7
Conservatives	6	4.2	4	10.8
Liberals	5	3.9	2	5.9
People's Socialists	0	0	0	0
Left Socialists	0	0	0	0
Other parties (without representation)	7	1.6	—	—
Lawyer-candidates	21	1.8	—	—
Lawyer members	—	—	7	4.0

SOURCE: Calculated from "Folketingsvalget den 23. januar 1968," *Statistiske Meddelelser, 1968:8,* (København, 1968).

the nominees. Only 1.8 percent out of 1151 candidates nominated for the last election were practicing lawyers before election day. Although the before-mentioned differences among the parties are reflected in Table 2.8 too, it is also the case that in all parties, election chances are better for the lawyers than for the average candidate. This suggests that lawyers tend to seek nomination and are relatively highly appreciated in the safe constituencies.

It is beyond doubt that the United States lawyer in private practice may feel some temptations to enter politics, which his Danish colleague never will come to feel. In the United States running for political office can be seen as a convenient way of "self-advertising" for the young and ambitious lawyer.[69] Both the campaign itself and the tenure of office may give the

---

[69] Blaustein and Porter, *op. cit.,* p. 98; Eulau and Sprague, *op. cit.,* pp. 43 ff.

lawyer a publicity that can be used for several ends. In Denmark a political career is an insecure investment on the long view, not a short-range opportunity. In order to get nominated, the prospective politician has to be at the right place at the right time, and still more energy, patience, and luck are required for the successful nominee. In a party system like this few, if any, ambitious men will say with Woodrow Wilson that "the profession I chose was politics, the profession I entered was the law. I entered one because I thought it would lead to the other."[70]

Two Judicial Career Patterns

Among the most suggestive explanations of the ubiquity of lawyers in politics is one originally put forward by Harold D. Lasswell: "Possessing a practical monopoly in the West of one type of administration—the courts—the lawyers have another foothold on the political ladder."[71] This monopoly gives the lawyer a competitive advantage in the recruitment processes, the argument runs in its more extended form. Because it is so easy to change from a position in the law-enforcement hierarchy to a position in the political hierarchy and vice versa, this monopolistic advantage of the lawyer "leaves the occupational market for politicians in a state of imperfect competition."[72]

Although the relations between the judicial and the political career in the United States have not been mapped out in detail, it is a well-established fact that these two career patterns are tightly interwoven. Seats in the legislatures are considered natural springboards for lawyers who aim at State or Federal Courts and for the lawyers who go for a post in the legal enforcement hierarchy. Inversely, legislators and other politicians are often recruited from the judiciary and from among law-enforcement officers. The relationships between political office and judicial office in its widest sense are so complex that they defy short descriptions, but the continuous interchange of personnel has been demonstrated in several studies; especially studies of the legislative career have revealed that lawyer-legislators depend upon judicial positions as means of initiating their own careers and that post-legislative advancement into public attorneyships and judgeships is usual among lawyer-legislators.[73]

The selection procedures used in the United States judicial system reflect

---

[70] Quotation from Eulau and Sprague, *op. cit.,* p. 1.

[71] Lasswell, "The Elite Concept," in Lasswell, et al., *op. cit.,* (1952), p. 18.

[72] Schlesinger, *op. cit.* p. 32.

[73] See, e.g., Leonard J. Ruchelman, "Lawyers in the New York Legislature. The Urban Factor," in *Midwest Journal of Political Science,* **10,** (1966), pp. 484–97, and Eulau and Sprague, *op. cit.,* pp. 50–53, and 79 ff.

this intertwining of law and politics. The involvement of political considerations is heavy, whether the judges are directly elected or appointed by
the executive. Especially in the Federal Courts judges have been appointed through a highly complex bargaining process, in which the President, the Attorney General and his staff, the White House Staff, the Senate
and its Judicial Committee, plus several interest organizations, including
the American Bar Association are deeply involved. Even the few "nonpartisan" appointments are frequently the result of "package-deals" among
the political actors.[74]

This politicization of the judicial career in the United States has its opponents, but the overwhelming opinion seems to be that the interplay of
law and politics in the selection of judicial officers at all levels in the United
States judicial system is a natural, even a functional, phenomenon. Speaking about the U.S. Supreme Court, John R. Schmidhauser emphasizes the
intimate relationship between law and politics: "Since the most important
function of the Supreme Court is the settlement of fundamentally political
issues, the political background of the justices undoubtedly represents a
very necessary and valuable source of experience and training."[75] The process of recruiting judges is described as a "fascinating aspect of our political life," and the federal judgeship as "an index of political success," as
a "reward for political activity (which) can attract able and ambitious lawyers to the ranks of party workers."[76]

The relationship between the Danish judiciary and the Folketing could
not be described in these terms. We have already seen (Table 2.5) that
although it is permitted by the constitution to combine a position as judge
with that of MF, very few judges have ever been members of the Folketing. It is rare to find politicians with an occupational background in the
judiciary, and it is still more seldom that a judge at the moment of his

---

[74] The literature on judicial appointment and the judicial process is huge. See
among others Sheldon Goldman, "Judicial Appointments to the United States Courts
of Appeals," *Wisconsin Law Review,* (1967), pp. 186–214; Harold W. Chase,
"Federal Judges: The Appointing Process," *Minnesota Law Review,* **51** (1966), pp.
185 ff.; Joel B. Grossman, *Lawyers and Judges: The ABA and the Politics of
Judicial Selection,* (New York, 1965); and Richard A. Watson and Rondal G.
Downing, *The Politics of the Bench and the Bar,* (New York, 1969).

[75] John R. Schmidhauser, "The Justices of the Supreme Court: A Collective
Portrait," *Midwest Journal of Political Science,* **3** (1959), pp. 1–57.

[76] Grossman, *op. cit.,* p. 7; but confront these opinions with the harsh remark by
David Riesman, that lawyers "will move heaven and earth to get on the bench
themselves (which is the source of much dirt in our political system, since many
congressmen have partners who itch to be judges . . .)," David Riesman, "Toward
an Anthropological Science of Law and the Legal Profession," in *Individualism
Reconsidered,* (New York, 1954), p. 441.

first appointment or his promotion to higher legal office has a political career behind him. Political positions simply do not form a step in the Danish judicial career or vice versa.

Apart from what has already been said about the jurists' position in the Danish society, this lack of overlap between the two elites can best be rendered understandable by a reference to the Danish judicial career pattern itself.[77]

The young jurist who aims at a judicial career can follow one of a limited number of narrow avenues, which may lead to appointment to the bench. A career as deputy judge, as prosecutor, or as a civil servant in the Ministry of Justice are the three most promising routes, the last one being the most preferred by those ambitious and talented jurists who aim at the bench of the High Courts or the Supreme Court. Promotion in each of these careers is bureaucratically regulated and strictly determined by seniority. Only a limited number of all those who start at the bottom of the escalator are raised to the bench. The appointment as a judge is normally obtained at the age of approximately 50, and the careerist who has passed this critical age without being appointed has missed the chance for good. It is also important to note that the careerist who leaves the career halfway as a rule drops out of the crowded waiting list, and, as is the case with most Danish public employees, loses the accumulated pensions rights. Inversely, it is normally impossible to board the career at any of the higher levels. A judicial career in Denmark demands patience and faithfulness to the judiciary.

This means that the prospective Danish judge does not get any promotional rewards at all from a political career. If he stays firmly in the bureaucratic judicial career, his chances of appointment to a judgeship are optimalized. Still more decisive, the Danish political system will punish severely careerists who try to advance their judicial career by means of political activity. Although appointments are made formally by the King, but in reality by the government through the responsible Minister of Justice, every precaution is taken to secure a politically neutral recruitment to the various benches. The courts themselves are heard before the appointment takes place. When judges are appointed for the Lower Courts and the High Courts, the presidents of the High Courts and the president of the Supreme Court are consulted first, and then the Minister of Justice makes his decision. Before a Supreme Court justice is called to the bench he is even required to serve in at least four cases and give his opinions in a manner that the Court finds satisfying. Departure from this firmly

---

[77] The education and career patterns of Danish judges are described in *Betænkning vedrørende Dommeres Uddannelse,* (København, 1951).

established practice of neutrality would be considered a grave abuse of the Minister's powers, and it is certainly no overstatement to predict that a charge of favoring political friends would produce a major cabinet crisis, and possibly, if well founded, it would cost the Minister of Justice his office.[78]

If prior political involvement can be seen as a desirable prerequisite for an American judicial career, and the judgeship as a reward for political services, the same is certainly not true in Denmark. There the interplay of law and politics is considered a bogey by all politicians and judges. In a leading text on constitutional law the author firmly declares that "appointment of judges is made without any political considerations at all," and he no doubt expounds a widespread fear in Denmark in this passage: "If *appointment* of judges, including *promotion* to office at higher levels . . . is made by the Government, this may involve the danger that political and other non-objective aspects come into play. This phenomenon is not unknown in other countries. It is for example common knowledge that in the United States political considerations have been of importance not only at appointment of popularly elected judges, but also at appointments even to the U.S. Supreme Court . . . ."[79]

Although this comparison of the two judicial career patterns is brief, it nevertheless makes plausible the claim in United States literature that the interchange of personnel between the law-enforcement hierarchy and the political world gives the United States lawyer a competitive advantage in the political career. Political activities by prospective judges are not penalized in the United States—perhaps unless the judicial careerist belongs to the "wrong" party—while in Denmark and several other European countries firmly established norms prohibit advancement in the judicial hierarchy by means of political activities.[80]

[78] Some appointments of Supreme Court Justices in the nineteenth century have been discussed in the literature, but none of them has been classified as "pure" examples of political appointments. See Holmboe, et al., in Bagge, Frost and Hjejle, *op. cit.,* II, pp. 217 ff.; Bent Christensen, *ibid.,* I, pp. 349 ff.; Troels G. Jørgensen, *Bidrag til Højesterets Historie,* (København, 1939), pp. 160 ff.

[79] Alf Ross, *op. cit.,* (2nd ed., 1966), II, pp. 543–45. In a recent discussion in the Folketing on the autonomy of the judiciary, provoked by a proposal made by the small party "De Uafhængige" for a further protection of the independent status of Danish judges, none at all of the spokesmen from the political parties contested the political neutrality of the appointment of judges. See *Folketingstidende,* 1964–65, cols. 1959–64, and cols. 2373–2404.

[80] In retrospect it ought at this place to be mentioned that the theory of professional convergence may get new impetus, if the relevant roles are defined broadly enough to encompass those norms which are related to the careers in the legal profession, i.e., stretched beyond the three distinct criteria used by Eulau and Sprague, *op. cit.,* chapter 5.

Conclusion

The difficulties of a comparison such as the one attempted here are obvious. Comparison of segments of two political systems raises many methodological problems, to which as yet there are no easy solutions. When the systems compared are the big and complex United States and the small and relatively simple Danish ones, the task easily becomes an exercise in the impossible. Furthermore, the comparison has had to be performed, on the one hand, by means of a huge and sometimes sophisticated literature covering several fields of knowledge and including both institutional and behavioral data and, on the other hand, by use of a scanty and scattered Danish literature comprising some political institutional data and mainly the legal historians' untested, and indeed often untestable, allegations.

What comes out of this comparison is not definitive. Without a quasi-experimental research design it is impossible to reach beyond the speculative.[81] Deviant case analysis in itself cannot give any proofs. It is primarily able to weaken or strengthen existing hypotheses and to attract attention to new variables.

What is then the result of this analysis of two sets of lawyer-politician relations, both of which, in a broad comparative perspective, look atypical?

First, it has been demonstrated once more that an explanation of the affinity of law and politics has to be multivariate. None of the existing single-factor explanations is able to account for the dominance of lawyers in politics in the United States and at the same time for the relative absence of jurists and practicing lawyers in Danish politics.

This does not necessarily mean that these factors are irrelevant. The high-status position of the legal profession, the dispensability of lawyers, the skills developed by lawyers, and the professional convergence of the lawyer role and the legislator role are apparently features common to a number of countries. These factors may facilitate ambitious lawyers who aim at a political career as an end in itself or as a means to intraprofessional ends, primarily by making them more visible to those who control nominations and by making it easier and less risky for them to enter politics.

On the positive side the comparison has indicated that in some systems of the Danish type effective barriers are set up, which discourage or even hinder lawyers and other jurists from pursuing a political career.[82] The

---

[81] This shortcoming characterizes the entire literature on lawyer-legislators. A control group, consisting of lawyers without political commitments, has never been introduced in these studies, cf. the remarks in Eulau and Sprague, *op. cit.,* pp. 3–4.

[82] Ulf Torgersen, "The Role of the Supreme Court in the Norwegian Political System," in Glendon Schubert, Ed., *Judicial Decision-Making,* (New York, 1963), pp. 221–44, discusses partly similar problems in the Norwegian context.

class orientation of Danish parties in the past resulted in the formation of hostile attitudes toward lawyers in some of the parties. Furthermore, distinct channels of recruitment were set up which are not favorable to lawyers. Equally important, the selection procedures and the prevailing norms of proper behavior in the Danish judicial system have effectively hampered an interplay of judicial and political careers.

The absence of these barriers in the United States may explain why legislatures there represent a deviant case at the other extreme. The fact that these phenomena are "phenomena of absence" may further explain why they have not hitherto had a more prominent position in the United States literature.

What has been accomplished here is to make clear the necessity of devising a multivariate theory of lawyers in politics, and to suggest as major variables in it the party system, the internal life of the legal profession, and especially the relations between the judicial and the political career patterns. Cross-national comparisons in a larger universe of countries will make it possible to evaluate the power of this crude sketch of a theory of lawyers in politics.

CHAPTER THREE

The Voting Behavior of British Conservative Backbenchers*

JOHN E. SCHWARZ, UNIVERSITY OF ARIZONA

and

GEOFFREY LAMBERT, UNIVERSITY OF MANITOBA

Voting cohesion has been of central concern to students of legislative politics at least since Lowell and Rice. Research on legislative party voting behavior has grown rapidly in recent years both within and outside the United States. One significantly neglected field of inquiry, however, has been the British Conservative party. The parliamentary group of the Conservative party has a high degree of voting cohesion, and an analysis of its voting patterns can help to illuminate the bases upon which its voting cohesion has been built.

The cohesion of the British Conservative Parliamentary party is remarkably high. For the whole of the 1959–68 period, deviation from the leadership on two- or three-line whips was greater than 10 percent of the backbenchers on only six divisions. This corresponds to a ratio of one vote out of approximately 300 votes, while the ratio was 1 to 30 for the French

* This chapter was published, under the title "Career Objectives, Group Feeling, and Legislative Party Cohesion: The British Conservatives, 1959–1968," in *The Journal of Politics* **33** (1971) pp. 399–421. The authors would like to thank Professors David E. RePass of the Department of Political Science at the University of Connecticut and Charles E. Walcott of the Department of Political Science at the University of Minnesota for their helpful comments and criticisms. A somewhat altered version of this paper was presented at the Annual Convention of the American Political Science Association, Los Angeles, 1970.

SFIO, 1 to 6 for the German CDU/CSU, 1 to 5 for the French Radical Party and 1 to 3 for the United States parties.[1]

What has led to such a high degree of voting cohesion? Speaking of Canadian parties, Epstein and Kornberg each postulate that the cohesion of these parties is a function of both the members' self-interest and the interest of the members' party.[2] The member remains loyal to his party's leadership because it is in the interest of his political career to do so and because his attachment to his party makes him want to do so. It is also thought that similar constraints are important to British MPs and that their operation is responsible for the high degree of cohesion exhibited by the British Parliamentary parties.[3] Briefly stated, these constraints are potential career vulnerability (checks imposed on deviant behavior by a member's local party), career enhancement aspirations (checks imposed by the Parliamentary party leaders through their control of higher offices), and feelings of group or party identity.

Despite the acknowledged operation of these constraints in the Conservative Parliamentary party, rebellions have occurred among Conservative backbenchers. In addition to the six most widespread rebellions referred to above, there were a number of other important rebellions joined by less than 10 percent of the backbenchers.[4] To what extent is the theory that the three constraints determine backbench behavior consistent with the occurrence of these rebellions? It should be possible to demonstrate the significance of the constraints by showing that the MPs most likely to join these rebellions were the MPs least affected by each of the constraints. This is the hypothesis we shall examine in this chapter. Our find-

[1] Figures for France are based on Duncan MacRae, *Parliament, Parties, and Society in France, 1946–1958* (New York, 1967), p. 56. Figures for the United States are based on a yearly analysis of all votes and the 20 closest votes from 1948–68. Figures for West Germany are based on all votes in each of the three Bundestags, 1953–65.

[2] Leon Epstein, "A Comparative Study of Canadian Parties," *American Political Science Review,* **58** (March 1964) pp. 46–60 and Allan Kornberg, "Caucus and Cohesion in Canadian Parliamentary Parties," *American Political Science Review,* **60** (March 1966), pp. 83–92.

[3] Leon Epstein, "Cohesion of British Parliamentary Parties," *American Political Science Review,* **50** June 1956), pp. 360–377, and Robert Jackson, *Rebels and Whips: Dissension, Discipline, and Cohesion in British Political Parties Since 1945* (London, 1968), pp. 245–252. See also Kornberg, *op. cit.,* p. 83 and p. 91.

[4] Ronald Butt, *The Power of Parliament,* (New York, 1967), and Robert Jackson, *Rebels and Whips: Dissension Discipline, and Cohesion in British Political Parties Since 1945,* (London, 1968). For an excellent review of major Conservative rebellions from 1951–57, see James J. Lynskey, "The Role of British Backbenchers in the Modification of Government Policy" (unpublished Ph.D. dissertation, University of Minnesota, 1966).

ings and conclusions will be based on an analysis of the voting behavior of all Conservative backbench MPs on all rebellions between 1959 and 1968 in which 5 percent or more of the backbenchers deviated.

Conservative Backbench Loyalty

Our hypothesis is that variations is loyalty to the leadership within the Conservative backbench are a function of variations in the effect of the three constraints on individual backbench MPs. Before examining this relation, however, we must first demonstrate that variations in career vulnerability, career aspirations, and group feeling exist within the Conservative backbench population and establish indicators by which these differences can be detected.

To see how backbenchers could be affected differently by the constraints, let us look first at potential career vulnerability. To survive, an MP must be renominated (readopted) by his local constituency association. At times, renomination challenges have been employed by local associations to support the party leadership against a rebellious MP. In the period 1956–1964, local associations seriously challenged the candidatures of at least 11 Conservative MPs who had opposed the parliamentary party leadership in speeches and voting. Seven of these MPs failed to be renominated. Yet, there was no case in which the renomination of a Conservative MP was challenged successfully on the grounds that he had *supported* the party leadership.

While a Conservative MP might thus have found himself in some difficulty with his local association if he persistently rebelled, not all rebellious MPs faced these difficulties to the same degree. It is known that MPs in marginal seats were less vulnerable to renomination challenges because infighting could cause the loss of the seat.[5] Local associations in marginal constituencies were less likely to proceed against a rebellious MP than were local associations in safe constituencies. In fact, six of the seven rebellious MPs who were not renominated held safe seats (the sole Labour MP purged during the period also held a safe seat). The only Conservative exception was Dr. Johnson, whom Rasmussen considers so atypical as to defy generalization.[6]

The fact that some MPs were less likely than others to face renomination challenges because they came from marginal constituencies meant that they were on the whole potentially less vulnerable than other MPs. We would thus expect MPs from marginal seats to have been among those most likely

[5] Leon Epstein, *British Politics in the Suez Crisis,* (Urbana, 1964).
[6] Jorgen S. Rasmussen, *The Relations of the Profumo Rebels with Their Local Parties* (Tucson, 1966), p. 47.

to join the backbench rebellions. Conversely, MPs from safe seats should have been the least likely to join the backbench rebellions.[7]

Of the three constraints considered in this study, potential career vulnerability is the only one to have been the subject of previous testing. Divisions on two issues were used with results that supported the importance of this constraint.[8] This study will go beyond earlier research both by using nine additional divisions and by assessing the relative importance of this particular constraint in light of our findings for the other two constraints.

A second constraint that can operate unequally on backbenchers is career enhancement aspirations. The Conservative leadership, when in power, has many rewards at its disposal. There are more than 75 governmental rewards composed of ministerial, junior ministerial, and Whip offices. There is also the Honors' List. Loyalty to the Parliamentary party leadership was certainly not the sole criterion for the distribution of these rewards. But, it was a significant criterion. To quote Jackson: "There is little doubt that a Member's former loyalty to his party and especially to the person who is Prime Minister are important factors . . . Several Chief Whips have reported in interviews that they were consulted about all appointments of junior ministers and that the main question they were asked was whether or not the MPs had been loyal supporters".[9] Martin Redmayne, Chief Conservative Whip during much of the period under discussion, said that, "a regular rebel . . . is by definition not suitable for office. He can't be. It isn't a sensible attitude."[10]

The importance of loyalty as a criterion for gaining ministerial rewards in the Conservative Party can also be observed in the behavior of the Party. During the seven major rebellions from 1959 to 1964, a total of 58 MPs rebelled more than once. Only two of them were subsequently given a governmental post. Whereas these rebels made up 20 percent of the backbenchers who served during the entire 1959–64 Parliament, they accounted for only 6 percent of the backbenchers who were subsequently advanced to governmental rank.

Thus the Conservative backbencher found that moving upward to governmental rank was to an important extent dependent upon voting loyalty. Yet, we need not assume that all backbenchers had exactly the same career enhancement aspirations. Some MPs would presumably not aspire as strongly to governmental office as would others and we would expect those

---

[7] Our operational definition of safeness of seat was whether or not the candidate had won his previous contest by at least a 10 percent plurality.

[8] Epstein, *Suez Crisis,* and Rasmussen, *op. cit.*

[9] Jackson, *op. cit.,* pp. 245–246.

[10] Martin Redmayne, "The Commons in Action," reprinted in Anthony King, *British Politics: People, Parties, and Parliament* (Boston, 1966), p. 145.

with lower career enhancement aspirations to be among the most likely to join backbench rebellions and those with higher aspirations to be among the least likely to join these rebellions.

Our indicator of a high level of career aspirations was either (1) if an MP had already been rewarded with higher office *or* (2) if that MP had served less than 5 years in the Commons without a reward and was not over the age of 50. Our indicator of a low level of career aspirations was if an MP had not been rewarded with higher office and either had served more than 5 years in the Commons or was over the age of 50. The use of years of service in the Commons and age as an indicator of career aspirations may seen surprising. It was chosen because very few MPs gained a first reward after reaching 50 years of age or after serving 5 or more years in the House of Commons.[11] This is shown in Table 3.1, in which

Table 3.1   The Conservative Backbench: Age, Number of Years in the Commons Without a First Reward, and Promotions to Governmental Office (in %)[a]

	1959–1963		1959–1964	
	Backbench (*N* = 268)	Promotees (*N* = 17)	Backbench (*N* = 269)	Promotees (*N* = 31)
Age: Over 50	42.5	5.9	43.0	9.7
Five years or more in the commons without a first reward	40.0	11.8	40.5	19.3

[a] Number of backbenchers is based on all backbench MPs, excluding former ministers, who served during the period under consideration. Backbench promotions considered were to any ministerial office or any Whip office. Since promotions were made starting in 1960, both age and years in the Parliament were calculated as of 1960.

one can observe the considerable difference between the percentage of all backbenchers and the percentage of backbench promotees that these MPs constituted. Since they had a considerably lower probability of gaining future rewards even if they remained loyal, we inferred that these MPs might look upon rebellion as less costly than would other MPs. Hence, we concluded that career aspirations would not act to constrain these MPS as greatly as they would the other MPs. Thus these MPs should have been among the most likely to join the major backbench rebellions.

A final constraint we shall consider is the sense of group feeling or group

[11] For an historical account of the relation between age and ministerial rewards see Phillip W. Buck, *Amateurs and Professionals in British Politics* (Chicago, 1963), p. 117.

loyalty. Epstein and Kornberg argue that the cohesiveness of Canadian Parliamentary parties is heavily dependent upon legislators' perceptions of party distinctiveness and upon group orientations. Because MPs view their party as being different from other parties and because they believe they ought to act in unison with their group, they are not likely to want to rebel. Kornberg points out that, in holding these views, MPs tend to look upon the party's policies as their own.

Since there are a number of perceptible differences between the two major British parties and because the significance of group orientations runs deep in British culture,[12] it is likely that almost all British Conservative MPs hold these attitudes to a significant degree. It is also possible, however, that these attitudes are held more strongly by some MPs than by others.

It is reasonable to assume that differences in attitudes can be created by differences in early socialization experiences. Particularly significant in this regard may be the place of a Conservative backbencher's educational background. The most prestigious educational institutions in Britain are two of the Clarendon public schools (Eton and Harrow) and the Oxbridge universities (Oxford and Cambridge). Conservative MPs who have attended these prestigious institutions also have generally come from a social atmosphere in which a "natural" identity as Tories is quite often strongly inbred even before schooling begins. Moreover, a strong network of cross-cutting family and social ties form both in these institutions and in the Conservative Party. Pursuing them through school and beyond, these friendship networks act to reinforce a sense of group identity. There is considerable evidence indicating that the life experiences of persons who have attended one of these institutions intensifies their sense of group feeling and their Conservative identity.[13]

It is possible, then, that Conservative MPs who have *not* attended any one of the four most prestigious educational institutions would share a sense of group identity with somewhat less intensity than would their colleagues who have attended these schools. If voting loyalty is a function of group feelings, our inference about the importance of educational background would lead us to conclude that MPs who have not attended any one of the four educational institutions would have been more likely than the other MPs to join the backbench rebellions.

Thus far in our analysis we have discussed indicators that denote varia-

---

[12] Samuel H. Beer, *British Politics in the Collectivist Age* (New York, 1966).

[13] This observation is found in numerous studies about Great Britain, as well as in many biographies and autobiographies. See, for example, Anthony Sampson, *Anatomy of Britain,* (London 1965), especially Chaps. 4, 5, 12, and 13; and Hugh Thomas, Ed., *The Establishment* (London, 1962).

tions in three constraints thought to be significant for voting behavior. The three constraints are career vulnerability, career aspirations, and prior socialization into group feeling or party orientation. We shall employ these indicators to differentiate backbenchers most strongly affected by each constraint from backbenchers who are less affected. Application of the indicators shows that Conservative backbench MPs differed considerably in regard to how many and which combination of constraints affected them most strongly. Table 3.2 presents these data for Conservative backbenchers who served during the 1959–64 Parliament. This table is useful for more than descriptive purposes. It also delineates both the various configurations of the three constraints and the number of MPs in each configuration; these data are then used as the basis of our analysis of backbench voting behavior in the following section.

Table 3.2 Configurations of the Constraints and Conservative Backbenchers, 1959–1964

Career Vulnerability	Prior Socialization	Career Aspirations	N	Number of Constraints	Total N	Percent
+	+	+	73	Three high	73	22.5
−	+	+	25			
+	−	+	31	Two high	117	36.0
+	+	−	61			
−	−	+	22			
−	+	−	14	One high	107	33.0
+	−	−	71	Zero high	28	8.5
−	−	−	28			
					325	100

Before turning to an analysis of backbench voting behavior, we should like to remind the reader that inferences were required in order to use the indicators we selected. The arguments presented above suggest that these inferences generally appear to be warranted. Moreover, we find that the hypothesis yielded by these inferences are strongly corroborated by the data. Finally, our position is supported by an analysis of some potential alternative variables and factors which we feared these indicators might have been tapping. This analysis, which produced negative results, can be found in the appended Methodological Note.

Constraints and Voting Behavior

We shall begin our examination of the effects of variations of the three constraints on cohesion and rebellion by looking at each of the constraints alone, without holding the others constant. We shall then turn to an examination of the separate effects of each constraint by holding the others constant. Following this, we shall examine the combined effect of the constraints. These analyses will be based on the seven largest Conservative rebellions that occurred from 1959 to 1964, when the Conservatives were in power. Finally, we shall examine the predictive accuracy of the three constraints for major rebellions when the Whips were on and when they were off. This analysis will proceed from the three major Conservative rebellions that took place after 1964 when the Conservatives were no longer in power.

There were seven major rebellions among Conservative backbenchers on two- or three-line Whips during the 1959–64 Parliament. In each of these cases, 5 percent or more of the backbenchers rebelled.[14] The votes were on corporal punishment (1961), The Wedgwood Benn issue (2 votes—1961), the Common Market (1961), the Profumo affair (1963), and resale price maintenance (2 votes—1964). A total of 123 different Conservative MPs rebelled on at least one of these seven votes. This accounts for 38 percent of the backbench population.

The largest backbench rebellion during the 1959 period of Conservative rule took place in 1961 over the issue of whether to reinstate corporal punishment for young offenders. A total of 69 right-wing Conservatives[15] jumped a Government two-line Whip that would have required Conservative backbench MPs to vote against reinstating corporal punishment.[16] This rebellion was followed shortly thereafter by two more over whether Mr. Anthony Wedgwood Benn, a Labour MP, should be allowed to sit in the House of Commons. A special committee set up by the Conservative Government had recommended that (in accord with long established practice) Wedgwood Benn be required to succeed his father as Viscount Stansgate, which would have prevented him from sitting in the House. The Government put on a two-line Whip, but even so, major backbench rebellions took place on two separate votes. On a Labour motion that Wedgwood Benn be allowed to address the House, 14 Conservative backbenchers voted with the Opposition. A total of 15 Conservative backbenchers rebelled on a later vote to require the Government to facilitate the renun-

---

[14] Rebellion was taken to mean cross-voting or, where it could be ascertained, deliberate abstention. Earlier debates, newspapers, and commentaries were used to calculate deliberate abstentions. The method is similar to that used by Rasmussen, *op. cit.*

[15] Our operational definition of "left," "center," and "right" is found in the "Methodological Note."

[16] See 638 H. C. Deb., Col. 57 and 145, April 11, 1961; *Manchester Guardian,* April 12, 1961; and *Daily Telegraph,* April 12, 1961.

ciation of peerages.[17] Although some of the rebels were from the center and the right, these were predominantly left wing rebellions.

The fourth major rebellion occurred during 1961. This rebellion took place over the question whether Britain should apply for membership in the Common Market. The Government asked the House to approve its application and backed it with a three-line Whip. Still, 22 Conservative backbenchers rebelled.[18] The rebels were from the Party's right wing.

Another serious rebellion occurred over the Profumo affair in 1963. John Profumo, the War Minister, resigned while admitting that his previous denial of illicit relations with Miss Christine Keeler was a lie. Not only did some people see this as a serious moral issue, but the fact that another of Miss Keeler's affairs had been with an attache at the Soviet embassy raised grave fears about the country's security. Macmillan, already under fire for his party's declining popularity, was held responsible for the breach in the nation's security system and for his incompetence in dealing with Profumo's original denial. As a result, the Labour Party tabled an adjournment motion that implied no confidence in the Government. A total of 27 MPs from all sections of the Conservative backbench disregarded their leaders' three-line Whip and abstained.[19]

The final two major revolts in the 1959–64 Parliament were over the abolition of resale price maintenance in 1964. This bill, upon which the Government placed a two-line Whip, was designed to end informal and formal price controls on retail goods. Many persons from both outside the Commons and within, however, felt that the abolition of R.P.M. would ruin small shopkeepers. On the Bill's second reading, 21 Conservative backbenchers from the center and right voted no, with an additional 17 abstaining. A little later, during the grueling committee stage of the bill, an amendment to exempt medicine and drugs from the act nearly defeated the government. The Labour Party, joined by 31 Tory cross-voters, cut the Government's majority to one.[20]

Most of these rebellions appear to have been significant in their political

[17] See 638 H. C. Deb, Col. 561 and 635, April 13, 1961, and *Manchester Guardian*, April 14, 1961.

[18] See 645 H. C. Deb., Col. 1777–1884, August 3, 1961, *Manchester Guardian*, August 4 and 5, 1961; and Anthony Sampson, *Macmillan* (New York, 1967), pp. 214–215.

[19] See 679 H. C. Deb., Col. 169, June 17, 1963; *Manchester Guardian* June 18 and 19, 1963; *Daily Telegraph,* June 18 and 19, 1963; Randolph Churchill, *Fight for the Tory Leadership* (Boston, 1964), p. 76.

[20] See 691 H. C. Deb., Col. 377–380, March 11, 1964; *Times,* March 11 and 12, 1964; *Sunday Times,* March 15, 1964; and 692 H. C. Deb., Col. 399–404, March 24, 1964, and Ronald Butt, *The Power of Parliament* (New York, 1967), pp. 251–274.

consequences. Ronald Butt, for example, argues that the rebelliousness of Conservative backbenchers over the entry into the Common Market helped force Macmillan to attach to the British application several significant amendments that eventually led to the French veto.[21] Butt also points out that backbench opinion against the elimination of R.P.M. was a central reason the government waited almost a decade to introduce the 1964 bill.[22] In addition, the two Wedgwood Benn rebellions apparently gave added impetus to the pressure for reform of the peerage, which eventually resulted in legislation supporting the rebels' position.[23] Finally, the Profumo rebellion, which is thought by some to have been the most serious challenge to the leadership during this period,[24] appears to have made matters considerably more uncomfortable than they already were for Harold Macmillan.[25] Macmillan resigned as Prime Minister less than 4 months later.

We suggest that the voting behavior of the backbenchers on these rebellions was a function of variations in career aspirations, prior socialization, and potential career vulnerability. Each of these constraints is examined individually, without holding the others constant, in Tables 3.3, 3.4, and 3.5. One can see that the degree of voting loyalty among MPs was related

Table 3.3   Conservative Backbenchers: Career Aspirations and
Voting Behavior, 1959–1964

	Consistently Loyal	One Rebellion	More than one Rebellion
Higher career aspirations ($N = 151$)	72.2	17.2	10.6
Lower career aspirations ($N = 174$)	53.4	22.5	24.1
$p < .001$			

to the strength of their career aspirations and prior socialization.[26] Those MPs with lower career aspirations or with less prior socialization were more likely than other MPs to rebel. Those consistently loyal accounted

[21] Ronald Butt, *op. cit.*, pp. 233–240.
[22] Ronald Butt, *op. cit.*, Chapter 9.
[23] Bernard Crick, *The Reform of Parliament* (London, 1965), pp. 134–144.
[24] Robert Jackson, *op. cit.*, p. 169.
[25] Robert McKenzie, *British Political Parties,* (London, 1963), p. 594a, and Randolph Churchill, *op. cit.*, pp. 76–77.
[26] The exact measure of aspiration was calculated on the basis of the month and year of the first major rebellion following a general election. These were April, 1961 for the 1959–64 Parliament, December, 1965 for the 1964–66 Parliament, and May, 1967 for the 1966 Parliament.

for 72 percent of the MPs with higher career aspirations and only 53 percent of the MPs with lower career aspirations; they accounted for 71 percent of the most intensely socialized MPs and 53 percent of those who were not as strongly socialized.

Table 3.4 Conservative Backbenchers: Prior Socialization and Voting Behavior, 1959–1964

	Consistently Loyal	One Rebellion	More than one Rebellion
More strongly Socialized ($N = 173$)	70.5	17.9	11.6
Less strongly socialized ($N = 152$)	52.6	22.4	25.0
$p < .001$			

Table 3.5 Conservative Backbenchers: Potential Career Vulnerability and Voting Behavior, 1959–1964

	Consistently Loyal	One Rebellion	More than One Rebellion
Higher potential vulnerability ($N = 236$)	63.6	21.6	14.8
Lower potential vulnerability ($N = 89$)	58.5	15.7	25.8
$.001 < p < .01$			

Less impressive are the figures pertaining to career survival. Although the pattern is in the expected direction, the difference in consistent voting loyalty between those MPs who were potentially vulnerable and those who were less vulnerable was only 5 percent. Even so, those who rebelled on more than one vote accounted for 26 percent of the potentially vulnerable group of MPs and only 15 percent of the potentially more vulnerable group.

From Table 3.6 one can examine whether variations in each of the three constraints had an effect on loyalty independently of variations in the other constraints. The table is based on the configurations presented in Table 3.2, and the values represent the percentages of MPs within each configuration who remained consistently loyal. The eight marginals of the table show that the percentages of these consistently loyal declined whenever *either* career aspirations or prior socialization was reduced to a lower level, regardless of the levels of the other two constraints. This decline occurred in every instance. The rates of decline shown in the table ranged from a minimum decline in percentage of 11 for each constraint to a maximum decline in percentage of 21 for prior socialization and 28 for career aspirations. The conclusion these results warrant is that career aspirations and prior socialization *each* had a marked effect on loyalty and rebellion among Conservative backbenchers, an effect that cannot be accounted for by variations in the other two constraints. Although the effect of each constraint on backbench loyalty was very similar, the marginals indicate that variations in career aspirations consistently had a modestly greater effect on voting loyalty than did prior socialization (−11.4−−10.8, −13.8−−13.2, −22.9−−16.4, and −27.8−−21.3).[27]

Table 3.6 The Impact of Career Aspirations, Prior Socialization, and Potential Career Vulnerability Independently on the Voting Behavior of Conservative Backbenchers, 1959–1964
(in % of those consistently loyal)[a]

	Higher Prior Socialization	Lower Prior Socialization	Effect of Socialization[b]
Higher Career Vulnerability			
Higher career aspirations	(a) 75.3	(b) 64.5	−10.8
Lower career aspirations	(c) 63.9	(d) 50.7	−13.2
Effect of aspirations[a]	−11.4	−13.8	
Lower Career Vulnerability			
Higher career aspirations	(a) 80.0	(b) 63.6	−16.4
Lower career aspirations	(c) 57.1	(d) 35.8	−21.3
Effect of aspirations[a]	−22.9	−27.8	

[a] *N* for each cell is shown in Table 3.2.
[b] The marginals reflect difference in percentages.

Since the effect of career aspirations on voting behavior was subject to change over time, it can also be treated in a longitudinal fashion. Significantly, a considerably higher degree of rebellion was noted among the *same* MPs as their career aspirations diminished over time. There were 70 high

[27] The independent impact of each constraint became greater as MPs became decreasingly subject to the other two constraints. This can be demonstrated by examining the marginals once again. Doing so for career aspirations shows that the effect of career aspirations on loyalty rose from 11.4 percent when both of the other constraints were high to 27.8 percent when neither of the other constraints was high. The intermediate points indicate differences in rates of loyalty of 13.8 percent and 22.9 percent. The same procedure applied to prior socialization shows that its influence also increased as MPs were less subject to the other two constraints—from 10.8 percent to 21.3 percent with intermediate points of 13.2 percent and 16.4 percent.

aspirants in the 1955–59 Parliament who by virtue of length of stay in the Commons or change in age became low aspirants in the 1959–64 Parliament. Comparing the eight 1955–59 divisions upon which backbench rebellion was most widespread[28] with the seven 1959–64 divisions, rebellion within this group of MPs grew by a factor of three. Only 13 percent of these MPs rebelled on any of the eight divisions during the earlier period, whereas after their career aspirations had diminished, rebellion within this group increased to 39 percent. In combination with the findings reported above, this finding lends strong support to the hypothesis that differences in the level of career aspirations had an important effect on the loyalty and dissidence of Conservative backbench MPs. The finding also appears to lend support to our assumption that *the causal relation is in most cases from disappointed career aspirations to rebellion rather than the reverse.*

The third constraint, potential career vulnerability, appears to have had an effect considerably weaker than that of either of the other two constraints. One can see this by comparing the cells of the upper half of Table 3.6 with their counterpart cells on the lower half of that table. The comparison shows that when potential career vulnerability was reduced to a lower level the largest decline in the number of those who were consistently loyal was 14.9 percent (comparison of cells (d)). No other decrease in loyalty amounted to more than 5 percent, since the effect of career vulnerability apparently became consistently weaker as MPs became increasingly subject to the other two constraints. The effect of potential career vulnerability was thus considerably less than that of either of the other two constraints.[29]

While it appears that the effect of potential career vulnerability was at most a modest one, its influence in combination with the more consistent and sizeable effects of the other two constraints suggests a total effect on backbench voting behavior which should be considerable. Table 3.7 shows this to be the case. In this table we examine the effect of the three constraints by the number of constraints acting on each MP. The table is also constructed to distinguish those MPs who rebelled only once from

[28] The votes were on rents, Suez (3), Cyprus, coal, NATO, and the economic situation. Rebellions on the whitefish and cotton industry divisions were not included because they were regional in nature.

[29] Although the renomination of some MPs was publicly challenged, the fact that local associations did not generally challenge the renominations of their MPs for joining major rebellions probably explains why this was the weakest of the three constraints. The relative lack of challenges may be due to the fact that most rebels were from the right wing and were therefor less susceptible to local challenge (i.e., they did not join the enemy).

the MPs who rebelled more than once, as well as to distinguish the unswervingly loyal from the rebels.

The results reported in Table 3.7 show the marked relation between variations in the operation of the three constraints and Conservative backbench rebellion from 1959 to 1964. Backbench rebellion consistently increased as the number of constraints operating strongly on backbenchers diminished. Indeed, the voting behavior of MPs upon whom all three con-

Table 3.7   Conservative Backbenchers: Variation in the Operation
of the Number of Constraints and the Voting Behavior,
1959–1964 (in %)

Number of Constraints	Consistently Loyal	One Rebellion	Multiple Rebellion
Three constraints high (N = 73)	75.3	19.2	5.5
Two constraints high (N = 117)	67.5	20.6	11.9
One constraint high (N = 107)	54.3	16.8	28.9
No constraint high (N = 28)	35.8	32.1	32.1

straints were operating strongly was almost the polar opposite of the voting behavior of MPs upon whom none of the three constraints was operating as strongly. The former group of backbenchers approached almost complete support for the leadership on these seven highly divisive votes, with 94 percent remaining loyal on at least six of the seven divisions and 75 percent remaining loyal on all seven divisions. The latter group of backbenchers, on the other hand, were about as likely as not to rebel against the leadership. Over 30 percent of these MPs rebelled on two or more of the seven divisions and 64 percent rebelled at least once.[30]

Whips On and Whips Off

The above findings, which establish a close relation between the constraints and backbench behavior on votes subject to the whip raise the question of what effect the removal of discipline might have on backbench voting. In such a situation, one would not necessarily expect variations in the operation of these party-oriented constraints to be as striking (although occasionally they might be) since removal of the Whip at least partially transforms the question so that it becomes less a party issue.

[30] Comparing MPs who rebelled on more than one issue with those who were consistently loyal and with those who rebelled on a single issue yields a Gamma of .47 (see Table 3.7).

For this reason a comparison of the three major backbench rebellions from 1964 to 1968, when the Conservative were in opposition, is especially interesting. These rebellions were over Rhodesia (1965) and the Common Market (1967—two votes). Each vote dealt with a matter of foreign policy closely related to the question of sovereignty, and the Conservative leadership took a clear public position on each vote. An important difference between the votes, however, was that no Whip was applied in the Rhodesia case, whereas the Whips were applied on the Common Market votes.

An examination of the Rhodesia vote shows that the effect of the constraints practically disappeared. A total of 81 backbenchers rebelled on this vote against their party leadership's united and public position of abstention.[31] But there was on this vote only a slight difference in the degree of voting loyalty and rebellion among backbenchers regardless of the configurations of any number of constraints. These points are demonstrated in Tables 3.8 and 3.9. Approximately 30 percent of the MPs with two or more constraints operating at their highest levels rebelled, whereas 34 percent of the backbenchers with either none or one of the constraints operating at their highest level rebelled.[32]

While the Whips were off in the Rhodesia case, they were on once again during the two Common Market divisions in 1967. It is therefore significant that voting behavior on these two divisions once again followed in almost every respect the pattern of the seven major rebellions of the 1959–64 Parliament. A total of 26 MPs rebelled on the two Common Market votes.[33] Variations within each of the constraints again had an effect on voting behavior (with potential career vulnerability, as usual, having lesser influence than the other two constraints). This is demonstrated in Table 3.8. Table 3.9 shows, moreover, that as the number of constraints operating at highest levels decreased, voting rebellion constantly increased from a low of 2 percent to a high of 29 percent.

[31] See 722 H. C. Deb., Col. 2053–2058, December 21, 1965; *Manchester Guardian,* December 23, 1965; and *Daily Telegraph,* December 23, 1965. The right wing had 50 rebels and precipitated the vote.

[32] It should be noted that the Conservatives do not appear to apply discipline as much when they are in opposition as they do when in power. Other examples in addition to the Rhodesia case were the primarily left-wing Kenya and race-relations rebellions of 1968, which occured outside the period covered in our study. In these cases, discipline was so relaxed that two members of the Conservative shadow cabinet joined the rebellion (these members went unpunished). Cursory examination of the rebels suggests that, in these rebellions as in the Rhodesia question, the three constraints were not predictive of backbench voting behavior.

[33] See 746 H. C. Deb., May 11, 1967; *Daily Telegraph,* May 12, 1967; and *The Guardian,* May 12 and 13, 1968. The 26 rebels were the same for both votes.

The Common Market votes and the Rhodesia vote thus add further support to our earlier findings on the importance of the three constraints. First, the effect of these constraints on backbench cohesion and rebellion was the same in virtually every respect for the 1967 Common Market votes as it was for the earlier 1959–64 votes. Second, when there was reason to believe that a division was not entirely regarded as a party vote, as was the case in the Rhodesia issue, backbench voting behavior changed, and the effect of the constraints diminished.

Table 3.8   Conservative Backbenchers: Level of Constraints and Voting Behavior on Rhodesia and the Common Market, 1965–1967 (% rebels)

	Rhodesia		Common Market	
	High Constraint	Low Constraint	High Constraint	Low Constraint
Career aspirations	31.5	30.5	5.4	17.7
Prior socialization	29.7	32.5	5.1	22.1
Career vulnerability	30.2	32.2	9.9	14.1

Table 3.9   Conservative Backbenchers: Number of Constraints and Voting Behavior on Rhodesia and the Common Market, 1965–1967 (% rebels)

	Rhodesia	Common Market
Three constraints high	32.4	2.1
Two constraints high	27.2	6.8
One constraint high	34.3	18.0
No constraint high	33.3	29.3

Conclusion

Other scholars have hypothesized that the cohesion of the British Conservative Parliamentary Party depends in particular on the operation of three constraints. These constraints are (1) the control of offices by the Parliamentary party leaders and their distribution on the basis of loyalty, which keeps in check those backbench MPs who aspire to higher office; (2) checks imposed on deviant behavior by a member's local party; and (3) group loyalty and Conservative identities.

Our study has demonstrated the significance of these constraints by showing the close relation between variations in the operation of these constraints and backbench voting behavior. We established this relation mainly through an examination of the ten largest rebellions to face the Parliamentary party between 1959 and 1968. When major rebellions occurred within the Conservative backbench, the backbenchers who were most likely to join them were those who had lower career aspirations, weaker socialization into Conservative identities and group orientations, and lower vulnerability to renomination challenges.

The seven major rebellions from 1959 to 1964 revealed that variation in each constraint had an effect on the loyalty and dissidence of backbench MPs. This was true even when the other constraints were held constant.[34] In addition, the constraint most subject to change over time (career aspirations) was examined longtitudinally, by use of the major 1955–59 rebellions, and was again found to have a considerable effect on backbench rebellion.

When the three constraints were examined in combination, their effect on the voting behavior of backbenchers was substantial. Thus, only about 25 percent of those MPs for whom the three constraints operated strongly rebelled on any of the seven 1959–64 votes, while 64 percent of the MPs for whom none of the three constraints operated as strongly rebelled. The operation of the three constraints also had a marked effect on the propensity of MPs to dissent on more than one issue.

The pattern of voting behavior in the three major rebellions after the conservatives left power also indicates the influence of the constraints. Although the leadership took a united position of all three votes, the whip was not applied on the first vote but it was applied on the latter two. Backbench behavior on the votes with the whip on exhibited the same pattern in virtually every respect as it did on the seven votes from 1959 to 1964, whereas the effect of the three constraints diminished considerably when the Whip was off.

Finally, the ability of the three constraints to retrodict voting patterns for each individual roll-call was relatively accurate. Using eight divisions, there were 24 possible retrodictions in adjacent categories.[35] The retrodictions of the hypotheses were correct on 18 occasions, or 75 percent of

---

[34] Recall that potential career vulnerability had decidedly the least effect of the three constraints.

[35] The eight divisions exclude Rhodesia and count the two 1967 Common Market votes as one, since the same 26 MPs rebelled on both votes. Passing from three constraints to two, from two to one, and from one to zero constitutes three adjacent categories of MPs for each division. Thus, by examining only adjacent categories, we find a total of three possible retrodictions for each vote, or twenty-four for eight votes.

the time. Overall, there was a total of 48 possible retrodictions in which the hypotheses were correct on 39 occasions, or just over 81 percent of the time.

The study thus supports in a number of ways the centrality of career objectives and party orientations to the Conservative backbencher and the close relation between these factors and his voting behavior. Even so, more exact work could undoubtedly be accomplished in examining this relationship through interviews. It would be possible through interviews both to measure the effect of the constraints more accurately and to examine the question of which particular MPs have taken the lead in organizing voting rebellions. In addition, the extent to which the constraints affect the MPs' other behavior patterns in Parliament still requires study. In examining this question, it may prove useful to employ signatures on Early Day Motions as an indicator of policy rebelliousness at other stages of the parliamentary process and to use certain written and oral questions as indicators of backbench supervision over the administration.

Although we have focused our study on the Conservative backbencher, the theoretical basis of our findings can also be applied on a comparative level. We have already referred to the work of Kornberg and Epstein on Canadian Parliamentary parties. The cohesion of legislative parties in the United States Congress has been profitably examined from the perspective of career objectives and party identities, as well. It would not be particularly difficult in applying the same variables to the behavior of legislators either in other developed areas, such as Western Germany or France, or in the less developed areas, such as India. Past success in employing these variables to explain legislative behavior and also the findings of the present study lend support to the notion that these variables provide one axis around which comparative legislative theory can be developed.

Methodological Note

The indicators we have selected are subject to the criticism that they may in fact measure other variables. This is especially true for indicators of career aspirations (age and length of service in the Commons without a reward) and of early socialization (educational background).

Use of educational background, for example, might be criticized because of its apparent association with career aspirations. It could be argued that an MP's attendance at one of the four most prominent educational institutions and his subsequent voting loyalty is a function of career aspirations rather than of stronger prior socialization into group orientations and Conservative identities. Although MPs who attended one of the four educational institutions mentioned comprise only 58 percent of the backbench, they constitute approximately 75 percent of the MPs who attained governmental office from October 1959 through October 1964. Still it is important to note that MPs attending one of the four institutions were likely to attain governmental office, whether or not they were loyal. Only two MPs who rebelled on more than one vote were advanced to governmental rank after 1959. Both of these MPs had attended at least one of the institutions. Indeed, only 11 percent of the group of MPs having gone to at least one of the four institutions was promoted to governmental rank after 1959 (they represented 67 percent of all MPs promoted). Yet 13 percent of this group who rebelled on more than one vote were subsequently promoted. In addition, of the 28 rebels on the well-known Suez votes, only 2 were subsequently elevated to governmental rank. Again, both of these MPs had attended at least one of the four institutions. It would thus seem that rewards given to this group of MPs were less contingent on voting loyalty than rewards for other MPs. Hence, if education had been an indicator of career aspirations instead of prior socialization, one could not have retrodicted correctly that voting loyalty among these MPs would have been higher than it was among other MPs.

It is also possible that length of service in the Commons without rewards is as much an indicator of an MP's propensity to rebel as it is of his career aspirations. It could be argued consistently with our hypotheses that those MPs who rebelled did not get rewarded. The failure of certain MPs to receive rewards over a 5-year period in the Commons might thus have been only because of their tendency to rebel. If that were so we should no longer require the notion of a reduction in career aspirations to explain the rebelliousness of these MPs.

Our earlier longitudinal analysis of the effect of a change in career aspirations on voting loyalty provides an answer to this criticism. It was found in that analysis that as the career aspirations of the same MPs diminished over time, the rate of their rebellion increased by a factor of three. Moreover, while these MPs had high career aspirations (1955–59), rebellion among them was remarkably low (12 percent). Thus it does not appear that our indicator for career aspirations denotes either similar or high rates of rebelliousness by the MPs prior to the 1959–68 period.

Finally, one could argue that our indicators of aspirations and prior socialization may be revealing ideological orientations instead and that rebellion is a function of ideology. It is of course possible that the older MPs have ideological orientations that differ from those of the younger MPs, or that ideological tendencies of MPs varied according to educational background.

To deal with this problem, it was necessary to develop a measure of ideological orientation. Our measure was based on each member's record of signing Early Day Motions in the 1959–1964 Parliament.[36] If a member signed a motion criticizing his leader's policy, he was given a criticizing score of plus one if the motion was to the left and minus one if it was to the right. If the motion applauded or maintained the leader's policy, it was scored zero. A motion was considered to be to the left if it criticized the leadership by favoring a greater role for the government in social welfare or economic management, disengagement from imperial or colonial postures, a pro-European stance, or greater penal liberalization. A motion which criticized the leaders by favoring policies toward the opposite pole was considered to be to the right.

Using these criteria, each backbench MP was accorded a net score computed from the number of motions signed and character of the motions. The score furthest to the left totaled +8 and the score furthest to the right totaled —48. We divided the backbench according to ideological tendency into two wings as equal as possible, and those MPs tending toward the left had scores of +8 to —1, while those MPs tending toward the right had scores of —2 to —48.

Table 3.10   Career Aspirations and Prior Socialization as Indicators of Leftist Ideological Tendencies

	Career Aspirations	Prior Socialization
Left and center ($N = 166$)	—04	+20
Left without center ($N = 72$)	+12	+38
Right ($N = 159$)	+10	+08

The application of this measure of ideological orientation suggests that the indicators of career aspirations and of prior socialization are *not* good indicators of ideology. About 48 percent of the left (80 of 166) and about 45 percent of the right (71 of 159) had high career aspirations. About 60 percent of the left (100 of 166) and 46 percent of the right (73 of 159) were educated at Eton or Harrow or Oxford or Cambridge. If one excludes the center (score of +1, 0, or —1) about 56 percent of the left (40 of 72) and 45 percent of the right had high career aspirations. Sixtynine percent of the left (50 of 72) and 46 percent of the right were subject to stronger prior socialization. While these figures suggest a modest tendency for Conservative MPs on the left to have higher career aspirations

---

[36] For an earlier application of Early Day Motions to the study of backbench thinking, see S. E. Finer *et al., Backbench Opinion in the House of Commons,* (Oxford, 1961).

and to have been subject to stronger prior socialization, both these factors would obviously contain considerable error as *indicators* of leftist tendencies. Table 3.10 summarizes the situation. A value approaching $+100$ suggests a perfect direct relation and -100 a perfect inverse relation. Values closer to 0 suggest no value as an indicator.[37]

We can conclude from this table that the relations we found between career aspirations and prior socialization on the one hand and backbench voting behavior on the other are apparently not vulnerable to the criticism that the indicators of the former two variables may instead have been denoting differences in ideological orientation.

---

[37] We employed our measure of ideological orientations to examine whether differences in such orientations affected the relations between the constraints and voting behavior reported in the base of the paper. This examination revealed that the relationships reported above were substantially the same for the left, center, right, and far right MPs in the party. The results are tenuous, however, and are not reported at length because the number of cases in the cells was generally very small. Voting percentages in half of the cells had to be based on less than twenty cases. There were less than ten cases in four of the cells. The problem of the effects of ideological orientation and intensity on voting behavior certainly merits further research. This research might best be accomplished through interviews and through an analysis of more Parliaments than were considered in the present study.

CHAPTER FOUR

Orientations to Decision-Making in the Vienna City Council*

PETER GERLICH

INSTITUTE FOR ADVANCED STUDY, VIENNA

Introduction

The aims of comparative legislative research are description and explanation of variations in legislative actions. Both tasks, but especially the second one—identifying those characteristics of different legislatures and their political environments that make for such variations—should lead us toward a more general theory of legislative behavior. Comparative, especially crossnational analysis will most likely identify two kinds of variables influencing such variations: specific forms of institutional settings and specific patterns of cultural norms. Differences of behavior within and between legislative systems will, for example, be caused by constitutional structures and arrangements, as well as by elite or general attitudes towards the political process. On these assumptions the present study puts the re-

* This paper is based on the Vienna City Council Research Project sponsored by the Institute for Advanced Studies in Vienna. It expands some of the results and interpretations included in the general project report, P. Gerlich and H. Kramer, *Abgeordnete in der Parteiendemokratie* (Vienna, 1969). I want to express my thanks to Helmut Kramer, with whom I wrote that report, for his critical help in drawing up this chapter.

sults of research on one particular legislative system into comparative perspective.[1]

In this connection a specification of the rather vaguely conceptualized dependent variable of legislative behavior seems necessary. To limit one's definition, as is implicitly or explicitly quite frequently done, to those attitudes, actions, and interpersonal processes which affect legislation and legislative decision-making in its more narrow sense, seems insufficient. Legislatures are concerned with a great variety of actions and perform quite a number of distinct tasks different from mere lawmaking in its technical form. The multifunctionality of legislative structures has been frequently noted, changes in the functions of representative bodies have been often described, and it has not infrequently been concluded that parliamentary influence on the process of lawmaking is declining. Therefore, the question as to what parliamentary assemblies actually do becomes quite important when establishing dimensions of individual legislative behavior that can be used as equivalent areas for comparison.[2] The actual legislative functions, that is, the fields and kinds of legislative activity prevalent in a certain political environment, may thus be considered intervening factors specifying or modifying the influence of institutional and cultural factors upon legislative behavior.

For this reason, the determination and categorization of legislative functions may be looked upon as an important intermittent task of legislative theory building. Note that the term legislative function is used here in a nontechnical sense, simply describing actual operations of the legislature, and that it must be distinguished from the concept of function within the framework of structural-functional theories of the polity.[3]

The relevance for legislative behavior of institutional and cultural pat-

[1] The comparative framework outlined here corresponds to a large extent to the one developed by Robert Dahl for the analysis of the comparable phenomenon of political opposition. See his *Opposition in Western Democracies* (New Haven, 1966), pp. 348 ff. See also J. C. Wahlke, H. Eulau, W. Buchanan, and L. C. Ferguson, *The Legislative System* (New York, 1962), pp. 4 ff.

[2] For the question of legislative functions see J. C. Wahlke, "Behavioral Analysis of Representative Bodies," in S. C. Patterson, Ed., *American Legislative Behavior* (Princeton, 1968), pp. 391 ff.; for the problem of operational equivalence, M. E. Jewell and S. C. Patterson, *The Legislative Process in the United States* (New York, 1966) pp. 543 ff.

[3] For the different meanings of the term function in general, see R. K. Merton, *Social Theory and Social Structure*, Rev. ed. (Glencoe, Illinois, 1957), pp. 19 ff. The term has been retained following general usage. Its explicit use under a meaning which does not imply certain purposes to the actions analyzed seems preferable for a descriptive analysis. This does not, however, exclude an evaluation of legislative activity in functional (in its more usual meaning) terms. Interpretations of the latter kind can be found in Jewell and Patterson, *op. cit.*, pp. 8 ff.

terns, on the one hand, and, on the other, the kinds of legislative functions actually performed may possibly be underestimated in research carried out in one national setting, where their specific forms may be taken for granted. Even if it cannot immediately lead to a general legislative theory, comparative research on legislatures therefore should have at least the secondary effect of making us aware of the characteristics and conditions of our own particular research setting.

This was the kind of experience encountered in the Vienna City Council Research Project. In it a set of questions developed for the study of legislatures in one cultural sitting was applied to a formally quite comparable assembly in another. While certain similarities could be found, the differences were considerable, a fact that seems to have largely frustrated similar research attempts in comparable environments.[4]

In the Vienna study we attempted to turn these difficulties into an advantage by making the basic differences of the legislative settings explicit. With the use of the theoretically intermediate position of roles between behavior (interpretable as role behavior) and institutions (interpretable as clusters of role norms), role orientations were used as indicators for individual behavior, on the one hand, and for institutional functions on the other.[5]

The study of the Vienna City Council was undertaken in 1965 as a graduate-seminar project by Heinz Eulau, then visiting professor at the Institute for Advanced Studies, in an effort to replicate some of the research reported in *The Legislative System*. The study utilized a questionnaire that followed the general design and covered the same subject areas as did the American study, but with some modifications to take into account the different national setting. As was its model, the Vienna study was conceived as mainly exploratory and descriptive in character. The main areas of interest were the composition of the legislature, recollections of socialization, recruitment and career patterns, and especially the role orientations of the legislators.[6]

The Vienna City Council and its setting are briefly described here. Vienna is, of course, both the capital city and one of the provinces of the Republic of Austria. Its political system mirrors some of the most characteristic features of Austrian national politics: a "grand coalition" govern-

---

[4] See W. H. Hunt, W. W. Crane, and J. C. Wahlke, "Interviewing Elites in Cross-Cultural Comparative Research," in Patterson, *op. cit.,* pp. 412–423, especially p. 420; and especially W. Crane, *The Legislature of Lower Austria* (London, 1961).

[5] For the concepts of legislative role, legislative role-orientation, and their operational implications, see Wahlke, et al., *op. cit.,* pp. 7–24.

[6] Final results of the study are reported in P. Gerlich and H. Kramer, *Abgeordnete in der Parteiendemokratie* (Vienna, 1969).

ment (still practiced in Vienna, although recently given up on the national level); strong politico-social cleavage; high degrees of formal political participation and party membership; and a varied history of successes and failures of the parliamentary system of government.[7] In many respects it is the most important political subentity in Austria: more than a quarter of all Austrians live in the capital; constitutionally, a great many matters fall within the city's competence; in contrast with the national level, the city has always been dominated by the Socialist party, leading observers to stress the contrast between "red" Vienna and "black" national politics; and, of course, the City Council (*Gemeinderat*) serves also as a provincial diet (*Landtag*).

The constitutional model of government is more or less a parliamentary one. Of special note are the rather strong positions in it of the government (the City Senate, *Stadtsenat*) and the City Council's committees. The City Senate deliberates all matters that go into the assembly beforehand. The Council is usually presided over by the mayor, and the Council's committees are given administrative oversight tasks that they perform independently from the Council itself. The assembly consists of 100 members elected by a system of proportional representation. At the time of the study, 60 of them belonged to the Socialist Party (SPOe), 35 to its coalition partner, the Conservative People's Party (OeVP), 3 to the Liberal (FPOe) and 2 to the Communist (KPOe) opposition parties. The two big parties maintain large and very active membership organizations: every third Socialist and every fifth Conservative voter is a card-carrying party member. In the Council, strict voting discipline is observed practically without exception. The decision process is characterized by a method of centralized bargaining between the two leadership groups. These procedures typical of a grand coalition are even formally institutionalized by a contract between the parties.

Role Orientations in the Vienna City Council

The conception of role orientations, the questions used to elicit data about them, and the techniques of coding and analyzing responses were

[7] For an introduction into the specifics of Austrian politics, see F. C. Engelmann, "Austria: The Pooling of Opposition," in Dahl, *op. cit.,* pp. 260–283; F. Pinner, "On the Structure of Organizations and Beliefs: *Lagerdenken* in Austria," a paper presented at the annual meeting of the American Political Science Association, Chicago, 1967. The parliamentary experiences in Austria are described for the national level by B. Skottsberg, *Der Österreichische Parlamentarismus* (Göteberg, 1940); and F. Koja, "Parlamentarismus in Österreich," *Zeitschrift für Politik* (Munich, 1967), pp. 333–351; for the Viennese Legislature by F. Patzer, *Der Wiener Gemeinderat 1918–1934* (Vienna, 1961).

in general drawn from earlier studies of such matters,[8] but the Vienna study distinguished two broad areas of legislative role orientations: those that could be called *representational,* concerned with more general attitudes of the legislator toward his tasks and positions as a representative, and those that may be termed *instrumental,* directed toward more specific and concrete tasks and activities that councillors felt obliged to perform. Each of these two dimensions comprises several analytically distinct sectors. The representational dimension includes a sector directed toward party and caucus as predominantly important settings of the legislator's activity, a sector concerned with the "style," and another sector concerned with the "focus" of representation. The instrumental dimension includes a general-purposive sector, comparable to the similarly named sector in the United States study's role definitions, an executive-oriented sector, and a clientele-oriented sector, the last made up of those activities concerned with individuals and groups of supporters among the electorate with whom the legislator actually has contact.

We turn now to a brief description of how these role orientations were distributed among the Vienna City Councillors.

Representational Role Orientations. In any political system characterized by disciplined parties, the party, especially its legislative party caucus (*Fraktion*), must hold a pivotal position among the legislator's role conceptions. In such a system the legislator is able to act only within the framework of his party organization and caucus. Any independent activity of the sort implied by the liberal parliamentary tradition's "free mandate" doctrine is beyond him. Decision-making in the legislature concerns the processes within the caucus, where those party stands that later bind the legislator are decided on by majority vote. Taking into consideration these intracaucus aspects of legislative activity and the contrast between the formal fiction of free mandate still embodied in the constitution and the reality of strictest voting discipline observed in practice, we can distinguish two types of role orientations in the caucus-oriented sector: that of *Loyalists,* who consider conflict and disagreement within the party inconceivable, and that of *Independents,* who, although remaining firm party supporters, think disagreement and difference of opinions and conflict within the caucus is

---

[8] Cf. Wahlke, et al., *op. cit.,* pp. 7 ff, especially p. 16, and for the following, pp. 237–376. Role orientations were operationalized through a careful content analysis of several very general open-ended questions eliciting descriptions of legislative duties and activities. A list of a large number of typical role items (specific duties considered obligatory) was drawn up and all interviews coded according to this list. Items that seemed related were then drawn together into the different role orientations, which in turn were combined into role sectors. See Gerlich and Kramer, *op. cit.,* pp. 15–20.

Table 4.1   Party-Sector Representational Role Orientations of Vienna City
Councillors, by Party Affiliation and Party Status (in %)

Role Orientation	Total $N = 98$	Status (SP and VP only[1]) FB $N = 15$	BB $N = 78$	Party SP $N = 58$	VP $N = 35$	OP $N = 5$
Individualist	50	71	44	48	51	60
Loyalist	46	29	51	50	40	40
No mention	4	0	5	2	9	0
Total	100	100	100	100	100	100

[1] The following abbreviations are used in this and in following tables: FB = Frontbencher. BB = Backbencher. SP = Socialist Party. VP = Volkspartei (Conservative Party). OP = Opposition parties (Liberal and Communist).

possible and acceptable. The distribution of these two types of orientation among the Vienna City Councillors is shown in Table 4.1.

Representational "style" is also modified by the conditions and possibilities of a disciplined party system. The Burkean role of a trustee, who makes up his mind and acts independently in the interest of the common good of the whole electorate, obviously cannot be performed. A legislator nominated, elected, and acting within the organizational framework of his party has first of all to represent the interests of the party and of those parts of the electorate that support it. However he can also take broader interests into account, even if only in a supplementary way. Instead of distinguishing the representational style role orientations of trustees and delegates, (as did the four-state United States study), therefore, it seemed more appropriate in the Vienna City Council to distinguish between *Partymen,* who represent *only* the narrower interests of party and of party supporters in the electorate, and *Generalists,* who consider not only those party interests but also the interests of nonparty groups and persons. The distribution of these role orientations in the Vienna City Council is shown in Table 4.2.

With regard to the areal focus of their role orientations, Vienna City Councillors were classified into those who considered themselves to be representative primarily of their own district, that is, *district oriented;* those who sought to represent simultaneously both their own district and the whole city, that is, *district and city oriented,* and, finally, those thinking only in terms of whole-city interests, that is, *city oriented.* This classification is, of course, quite similar to that made in the United States four-state and other studies of legislative role. One should note, however, the local

Table 4.2　Style-Sector Representational Role Orientations of
Vienna City Councillors (in %)

		Status		Party		
		(SP and VP only)				
Role	Total	FB	BB	SP	VP	OP
Orientation	$N = 98$	$N = 15$	$N = 78$	$N = 58$	$N = 35$	$N = 5$
Generalist	40	65	37	40	42	20
Partyman	47	35	50	48	45	40
No mention	13	0	13	12	13	40
Total	100	100	100	100	100	100

Table 4.3　Areal-Focus Representational Role Orientations of
Vienna City Councillors (in %)

| Role | | FB | BB | SP | VP | OP[a] |
Orientation	$N = 98$	$N = 15$	$N = 78$	$N = 58$	$N = 35$	$N = 5$
District oriented	24	12	29	24	29	0
District-city oriented	16	12	17	21	9	0
City oriented	24	59	18	29	20	0
No mention	36	17	36	26	42	100
Total	100	100	100	100	100	100

[a] The members of the opposition parties are elected on a city-wide ticket and a priori do not represent any district; they are therefore all not codable in the representational "focus" sector.

circumstances of the council districts, of which there are 23. The character of party organization as well as the electoral arrangements put much weight on these districts, and there are certain local traditions in most of them. Nevertheless, they play a rather subordinate role in the overall structure of city government. The city of Vienna is much more an integrated political entity, with certain categoric divisions cross-cutting the whole—as, say, urban-rural or class differences cut across provincial politics—than a loose collection of geographically autonomous wards, regions, and legally distinct towns and villages, like many United States cities. Table 4.3 shows the distribution of these focus-sector representational role orientations among the Vienna City Councillors.

The three tables show that, in general, over the council as a whole, the different types of orientation in each of the three representational role sectors are more or less equally represented. But both party affiliation and party status markedly affect the distribution, with the legislator's status within his own party being the more influential factor: the tendency of frontbenchers to be individualists, generalists, and city oriented is pronounced; the Socialists show some propensity for the loyalist and city-oriented category, and the Opposition Party councillors some for the individualist. This may reflect not merely greater discipline in the left-wing party but also the fact that the SPOe, as senior partner within the great coalition, carries the main responsibility for administering the city and therefore stresses general goals. The prime importance of the individual councillor's relationship to his own party in shaping his role orientations is indicated not merely by the influence of his status (front- or backbench) within the chamber but also by the influence of his position in the extra-legislative party hierarchy. Table 4.4 shows that for both big parties, the higher the individual's party status, the greater the tendency to assume individualist rather than loyalist party-sector role orientations.

Table 4.4   Party-Sector Representational Role Orientations of Vienna City Councillors in Various Extra-Legislative Party Statuses (in %)

Role Orientations	Lower Officials $N = 22$	District Officials $N = 33$	District Chiefs $N = 20$	Top Officials $N = 17$
Individualist	29	55	47	76
Loyalist	71	45	53	24
Total	100	100	100	100

Instrumental Role Orientations. Within the broad area of role orientations we have described as instrumental, a purposive sector comprises the legislator's general attitudes toward the legislative decision-making processes. The orientations included here in the Vienna study closely resemble those discussed in the United States four-state study. As in the United States scene, *Tribunes* see themselves mainly as representatives of the wishes and complaints of the voters. *Initiators,* who closely resemble the innovators described in the United States study, are councillors whose primary goal is to start getting things done and to get decisions made. *Coordinators,* who correspond to the United States study's brokers, see their main legislative tasks as one of coordinating proposals and actions over related problem areas and of bargaining between opposing political interest. *Ritualists* in the Vienna City Council resemble the similarly described legislators of *The Legislative System,* but there is less emphasis in their conceptions than in the United States legislators' on procedural finesse, and more emphasis on the more passive attitude of fulfilling one's duties by being present at legislative sessions, doing one's legislative homework, and so on. Of course these four orientations are not mutually exclusive; a given councillor might well switch from one to another as appropriate to him for different kinds of legislative situations. Table 4.5 displays the distribution of these role orientations in the Vienna City Council.

Table 4.5   Purposive-Sector Instrumental Role Orientations of Vienna City Councillors by Party Affiliation and Party Status (%)

Role Orientation	Total $N = 98$	Status (SP and VP only)		Party		
		FB $N = 15$	BB $N = 78$	SP $N = 58$	VP $N = 35$	OP $N = 5$
Ritualist	59	47	58	53	66	100
Tribune	57	33	59	57	60	60
Initiator	33	47	29	31	34	60
Coordinator	42	71	37	34	60	20

Note: Columns can total more than 100% since categories are not mutually exclusive. Every respondent mentioned at least one.

Another important sector of instrumental role orientations is that directed toward the executive. The City Senators (*Stadträte*), who are more or less the local equivalents of the ministers in national parliamentary systems, it must be noted, are themselves members of the House. We are therefore particularly concerned here with attitudes of councillors toward the bureaucracy and civil servants. Two principal types of role orientation in this sector seem to emerge from the descriptions given in the interviews with the Vienna City Councillors. One we have called the orientation of *administrator.* An administrator is a legislator who considers it his job, when dealing with civil servants and the bureaucracy, to collaborate with the administrative officials and to help them execute or apply administrative decisions. The occasion for such collaboration is of course provided in council committees, which make independent administrative decisions on some minor matters. *Controllers,* in contrast to administrators, see their main job as one of checking, controlling, and criticizing the bureaucratic apparatus. Again, these are not mutually exclusive orientations, but analytically distinguishable tendencies, either of which might be controlling or preponderant in a given situation. The distribution of these orientations is shown in Table 4.6.

The final sector to be considered includes those orientations which guide the legislator in his dealings with supporters, party members, voters, ordinary citizens, and other persons with whom he comes into actual personal contact in the course of doing his legislative business. All these people

Table 4.6   Executive-Sector Instrumental Role Orientations of Vienna City Councillors, by Party Affiliation and Party Status (in %)

Role Orientation	Total $N = 98$	Status		Party		
		(SP and VP only)				
		FB $N = 15$	BB $N = 78$	SP $N = 58$	VP $N = 35$	OP $N = 5$
Administrator	40	65	38	57	20	0
Controller	44	23	46	41	43	100
No mention	31	23	34	24	46	0

Note: Columns can total more than 100% since categories are not mutually exclusive.

constitute the councillor's "constituency," however imprecisely delineated that group might be and however fluid and changing its composition. A substantial proportion of the Vienna City Councillor's time and energy is expended in activities involving these relationships. Two principal types of orientation are revealed by the data in this sector. The *errandboy* (*Intervent*) concerns himself primarily with performing services and promoting interests of individuals and groups such as those just described. The *communicator* (*Mittler*) is the councillor who thinks of his task in this sector as one of establishing communication between the city administration and politically interested parts of the citizenry. This task can include conveying both suggestions and grievances from below and explanations and information from above. Again, these two orientations are not mutually exclusive. Their distribution in the Vienna City Council is shown in Table 4.7.

The distribution in all three instrumental role sectors is relatively symmetrical. However, it was not possible to classify a number of respondents in both the executive and the clientele sectors, principally because the classification was based on coding of open-ended, rather general questions. Our experience, as well as that of other researchers, suggest that closed-type, more focused questions would undoubtedly yield a far higher response rate. For example, Wilder Crane found when posing specific questions that all Austrian legislators seemed to be engaged in considerable errand-running activity.[9] While difficult to interpret, it is interesting to note that two-thirds of the councillors displayed the two more-abstract purposive role orientations (ritualist, tribune), while not much more than one-third of them seemed to show the more concrete, action-oriented orientations (initiator, coordinator).

Table 4.7   Clientele-Sector Instrumental Role Orientations of Vienna City Councillors, by Party Affiliation and Party Status (in %)

Role Orientation	Total $N = 98$	Status (SP & VP Only)		Party		
		FB $N = 15$	BB $N = 78$	SP $N = 58$	VP $N = 35$	OP $N = 5$
Errand-boy	39	29	42	36	46	40
Communicator	37	41	37	43	29	40
No mention	37	47	33	38	31	60

Note: Columns can total more than 100% since categories are not mutually exclusive.

There is again, in the instrumental as in the representational area, a rather decided influence of party status. Frontbenchers tend to be initiators, coordinators, and administrators; backbenchers tend rather to be ritualists, controllers, and errand-boys. Status in the legislative party does not, however, seem to affect councillors' proclivity for tribune or communicator orientations. On the whole, the distribution seems to reflect the different action potentialities and capabilities, and the different responsibilities and tasks of frontbenchers and backbenchers, more specifically, the higher influence of frontbenchers as members of the executive.

With respect to the influence of party affiliation, the conservative legislators seem to tend strongly toward the communicator orientation and somewhat less strongly toward the errand-boy orientation. As members of the minority element in the coalition they are, one may suppose, especially concerned with bargaining for their interests and the wishes of their supporters, vis-a-vis a city administration dominated mainly by the other party.[10] Socialist councillors show a certain preference for the administrator orientation. This may likewise indicate their closer identification with

[9] W. W. Crane, "The Errand-Running Function of Austrian Legislators," *Parliamentary Affairs* (1962), pp. 160 ff.

[10] The very similar positions and strategies of minority parties in American cities are described and theoretically analyzed by J. Q. Wilson, "The Economy of Patronage," *Journal of Political Economy* (1961), pp. 369 ff.

the city administration. Socialist ranks also include a considerable number of controllers, however. It would therefore seem that close identification with the city administration does not suppress tendencies toward critical or suspicious attitudes toward a bureaucracy, even if it is dominated by the legislators' own party. It should be noted in this connection that the opposition legislators all display the controller orientation.

A further clue concerning the mechanisms of opposition and control is provided by the influence of committee membership on role-taking in the executive-oriented sector. In the Vienna City Council each committee corresponds to a department of the city administration, and each department is headed by a City Senator. The 12 departments are divided among the coalition partners in the ratio 8:4. In their committee work, therefore, some Vienna City Councillors deal with administrative agencies headed by City Senators of their own party, whereas others are confronted with agencies headed by officials of another party. Most councillors are members of more than one committee. We can differentiate those legislators who serve only on committees dominated by their own party and those who serve on at least one committee dominated by some other party. Table

Table 4.8   Executive-Role Orientations of Vienna City Councillors, by Type of Councillor's Committee Membership (in %)

Role Orientation	Members of Committees Dominated by Own Party N = 37	Members of at Least One Committee Dominated by Another Party N = 53
Administrator	65	26
Controller	27	51

Note: SP and VP members only.

4.8 shows that the former tend strongly to the administrator, the latter to the controller orientation. This association appears to be a rather striking illustration of the phenomenon of *Bereichsopposition,* opposition within the coalition, that has been described impressionistically as a characteristic of grand coalition governments, particularly the Austrian national system, but not yet related to specific behavioral data.[11]

In general, then, this necessarily sketchy survey of the distribution of role orientations within the Vienna City Council yields findings very similar to those of research in the United States of similar nature. Not only do

[11] See O. Kirchheimer, "The Waning of Opposition in Parliamentary Regimes," *Social Research* (1957), pp. 127 ff.

Vienna legislators, like those of U.S. states and cities, appear to be readily classifiable in terms of major differences in role differentiation, but, as in the United States, what role orientations they assume appears to be related not so much to differences in their background, career, and other personal characteristics (we have not shown the data for Vienna on this point) as to institutional variables, such as status within the legislative hierarchy, caucus and committee membership.[12]

Comparison of Vienna and Other Legislative Systems

As has often been noted, there has so far been relatively little genuinely comparative legislative research. Even comparison of one study with another is made difficult by the very general lack of comparability in terms of questions asked, indicators used, variables examined, results produced, and all other respects.[13] We may nonetheless note briefly how these findings concerning the Vienna City Council seem to compare with some others.

We have already noted, of course, that the high degree of party discipline and its associated role-orientation effects in Vienna constitutes a basic difference from United States legislatures in general. Given these cultural conditions, debate and vote in the legislative plenary session takes on quite different form and meaning in the Vienna legislative body—and, we might add, in most European assemblies as well—from that taken on in most United States legislatures. Where decisions are taken beforehand, usually in the majority-party caucus, and where legislators' formal floor activities are primarily compliant with those decisions, the roll-call and other formal floor behavior obviously becomes a rather ritualistic demonstration of party discipline. Roll-call analysis, therefore, which has been usefully applied in many American studies, cannot tell us very much about legislative behavior in most European systems.[14]

Role analysis of the Vienna City Council does, however, permit us to make some observations about legislative behavior in a disciplined party type of legislative arena. It seems, for example, to support the hypothesis that party discipline is greater in left-wing parties than in others.[15] More

---

[12] See K. Prewitt, H. Eulau and B. Zisk, "Political Socialization and Political Roles," *Public Opinion Quarterly* (1966), pp. 569 ff.

[13] Cf. S. C. Patterson, "Comparative Legislative Behavior: A Review Essay," *Midwest Journal of Political Science* (1968), pp. 599 ff, especially 608 ff. See also N. Meller, "Legislative Behavior Research Revisited: A Review of Five Years Publications," *The Western Political Quarterly* (1965), p. 792.

[14] See, e.g., M. N. Pedersen, "Consensus and Conflict in the Danish Folketing 1945–1965," *Scandinavian Political Studies* (1967), pp. 143 ff.

generally, analysis of representational style orientations reveals the influence of a disciplined party system on the decision-making and choice-making behavior of the representative. The relative decline in importance of the Burkean "trustee" orientation among Canadian legislators, for example, has been attributed to the disciplined character of the Canadian party system, as compared with that in the United States.[16] As the authors of *The Legislative System* noted, "in a political system where party discipline is very strict . . . the legislator's party orientation is so intense that he is unlikely to have much leeway in assuming a representational role other than that of a delegate."[17] Our findings with respect to the Vienna City Councillors confirm this assumption. While the inadequacies of our data make it difficult to draw conclusions with respect to the representational focus of Vienna City Councillors, the trend of disciplined party systems toward community-wide rather than segmental focus which has been observed in some other systems does seem to be confirmed in the Vienna setting.[18]

Table 4.9   Purposive-Sector Role Orientations in Vienna City Council
and Four American State Legislatures (in %)

Role Orientation	N.J. $N = 79$	Ohio $N = 162$	Calif. $N = 113$	Tenn. $N = 120$	U.S. Average $N = 474$	Vienna $N = 98$
Ritualist	70	67	58	72	66	60
Tribune	63	40	55	58	52	58
Initiator (innovator)	49	33	36	30	36	34
Coordinator (broker)	33	48	27	15	33	43

Note: The U.S. data are from Wahlke, et al., *op. cit.*, p. 259n.

Whereas the impact of party discipline leads to rather great differences in representational role orientation patterns between disciplined-party legislative systems like that of Vienna and loose-disciplined U.S.-style systems, there are some striking similarities in the patterns of instrumental role orientations, at least in the important purposive sector. Table 4.9 com-

[15] See H. Valen and D. Katz, *Political Parties in Norway* (Olso, 1964), pp. 219 ff.

[16] A. Kornberg, *Some Differences in Role Perceptions Among Canadian Legislators* (unpublished Ph.D. dissertation, University of Michigan, 1964) p. 89.

[17] Wahlke, et al., *op. cit.*, pp. 393 ff.

[18] For examples of areal role-orientations and some comparative implications, see Wahlke, et al., *op. cit.*, pp. 292 ff, Jewell and Patterson, *op. cit.*, p. 388, Kornberg, *op. cit.*, p. 63, and Patterson, *op. cit.*, p. 611.

pares the Vienna and the U.S. four-state study findings on this point. As the table shows, the only noticeable departure of the Viennese from the United States pattern is the relatively larger proportion of coordinators in Vienna than of brokers in the United States. This difference can perhaps be explained by the noncompetitive character of the political process in the Austrian grand-coalition system as compared with the more competitive political culture of the United States systems. Even though elections in Austria may be competitive, legislative decisions rarely are. Rather, they emerge from a long process of bargaining and rarely are taken by majority vote. This form of decision-making not only was characteristic of the national grand coalition system, as of the Viennese local one, but also seems to persist since its dissolution. While this kind of mutually adjustive mode of decision-making may thus appear to be a culturally rooted characteristic of Austrian politics, it is to be found also in other countries. This pattern, which has been labeled *Konkordanzdemokratie* or consociational democracy, may be viewed as an alternative model to the traditional and more familiar competitive model of democracy.[19] It is instructive to note, in this connection, that Austrian legislators frequently label decision-making by simple majority vote "undemocratic," a usage which startles some Americans.[20]

It has often been noted that relations with the executive branch and bureaucracy constitute perhaps the most salient and frequent set of legislator's activities and bulk large in the concern of representatives almost everywhere.[21] It is therefore surprising that almost no empirical analyses of this relationship have yet appeared.[22] The Vienna data tend to confirm the impression that controlling the bureaucracy is an important role orientation of a substantial number of representatives in most systems, and that friendly, cooperative attitudes may nonetheless also be prevalent.[23] But the absence of genuinely comparative data, as well as the limited character of our own, make it very difficult to reach any general conclusions here.

Much the same must be said with respect to clientele-oriented roles and activities. Errand-running and service functions for constituents seem to be a time-consuming part of legislators' tasks almost everywhere. The

[19] For the analysis of this model referring especially to Austrian politics see G. Lehmbruch, *Proporzdemokratie* (Tübingen, 1967). See also Arend Lijphardt, "Typologies of Democratic Systems," *Comparative Political Studies* (1968), pp. 3 ff.

[20] See Crane *op. cit.,* p. 14.

[21] Jewell and Patterson, *op. cit.,* pp. 394, 484; C. J. Friedrich, *Constitutional Government and Democracy* (Waltham, Mass., 1968), pp. 327 ff.

[22] In the *Legislative System* this area of the legislative role was explicitly excluded from the analysis. Wahlke, et al., *op. cit.,* p. 13.

[23] See Jewell and Patterson, *op. cit.,* pp. 496 ff, and S. Scher, "Conditions for legislative control," in Patterson, Ed., *op. cit.,* pp. 264 ff; for cooperative attitudes toward the executive, Jewell and Patterson, *op. cit.,* p. 394.

amount of such activity probably increases with the expansion of government administration and especially with the increase of governmental welfare services.[24] It is possible, thus, that the high incidence of errand-boy orientations and the high salience of errand-boy activities among Austrian legislators reflect the high degree of bureaucratization of everday life in Austria.[25] Neither our data nor other available studies, however, permit very confident hypotheses here.

While we have no data dealing directly with the question, the Vienna findings do inferentially link up with the conclusions and findings of other studies relevant to legislators' clientele role orientations. It has often been noted that citizens are poorly informed about and take little interest in legislative business and therefore read little and listen to little news about it. Our study, like others, also has found that legislators do have personal contact with numerous individuals and groups of individuals. It seems likely, therefore, that the kind of communicative activity—relaying information and explanation downward and demands and requests as well as political intelligence upwards—is a very important general aspect of legislative work in every system.[26] Perhaps it is especially important in a political system like Austria's, where there is a very high degree of organizational mobilization of the electorate by membership parties. More research on this general problem seems especially desirable, since it would relate very closely to the problem of "support," which is becoming increasingly central to theorizing about political representation.[27]

---

[24] Compare for the United States: Wahlke, et al., *op. cit.*, pp. 304 ff; Jewell and Patterson, *op. cit.*, pp. 353 ff. For Britain: P. G. Richards, *Honourable Members* (London, 1959), p. 171; B. Crick, *The Reform of Parliament*, rev. ed. (London, 1968), pp. 72 ff; and R. E. Douse, "The MP and his Surgery," *Political Studies* (1963), pp. 333 ff. For France: J. Meynaud, "The Parliamentary Profession," *International Social Science Journal* (1961), p. 533. For Germany: G. Loewenberg, *Parliament in the German Political System* (Ithaca, N.Y., 1966), p. 427. For Belgium: F. Debuyst, *La Fonction Parlementaire en Belgique: Mécanismes d'Accès et Images* (Bruxelles: 1966), pp. 41 ff. For Austria: Crane, *op. cit.* Similar activities may also be one of the main tasks of representatives in non-western systems. See, e.g., D. Scott, *Russian Political Institutions* (London, 1958), pp. 100 ff.

[25] See Crane, *op. cit.*

[26] See for example Jewell and Patterson, *op. cit.*, p. 343; Debuyst, *op. cit.*, p. 398; and S. C. Patterson and G. R. Boynton, "The Missing Links in Legislative Politics: Constituency Influentials" (Paper presented at the annual meeting of the Midwest Political Science Association, Chicago, Ill., 1968, mimeo).

[27] See J. C. Wahlke, "Public Policy and Representative Government: The Role of the Represented" (Paper presented at the VIIth world Congress of the International Political Science Association, Brussels, 1967, mimeo), and S. H. Beer, "The British Legislature and the Problem of Mobilizing Consent," in E. Frank, Ed., *Lawmakers in a Changing World* (Englewood Cliffs, N. J., 1966), pp. 30 ff.

Role Orientations and Legislative Functions

Formal constitutions and traditional political science recognize three main parliamentary functions: lawmaking, control of the executive branch, and (in parliamentary systems) selection of the personnel of the Government. Later observers have recognized other equally important though perhaps less formal ones. Walter Bagehot described the "lyrical functions" of expression by plenary debate.[28] And Hans Kelsen, himself an Austrian, and other continental theorists have stressed "adaptive functions," which seem particularly relevant to the *Konkordanzdemokratie* model of decision-making described above: meetings and interpersonal contacts to limit and restrain cleavages, to permit minority wishes to influence majority positions, and to formulate and promote political compromises.[29] Max Weber and others have viewed the legislative assembly as a place of leadership training and recruitment.[30]

Empirical analysis in many systems seems to show that most of these functions, which in following Robert Merton's well-known terminology may be termed "manifest," are modified today, while certain other activities, which one might call "latent" functions, become apparent. The constitutional functions of lawmaking, control, and election of the government have tended to turn into rather ritualistic activities, more so while the executive is getting more powerful and where the majority party identifies itself with their leadership holding government positions. This decline of primary activities remains true even if one considers the possibilities of intraparty democracy within the parliamentary parties and caucuses. In the Vienna study the situation is illustrated by the prevalence of the activity-oriented role definitions with frontbenchers mostly government members, as compared with relatively vague passive role definitions of the backbenchers.

Control, one of the few reserved areas of substantial back-bench activity, is not exercised in its constitutional forms of vote of confidence or impeachment, functions almost totally atrophied, but rather in personalized engagement, criticism, and conflict with the bureaucracy. The symbolic meaning of parliamentary debate is rather reduced in a time of general information explosion and may be in part supplemented by more subtle

[28] W. Bagehot, *The British Constitution,* Ed. by R. H. S. Crossmann (London, 1963), p. 150. See also how Bagehot's editor interprets these observations from a modern standpoint, pp. 9 ff, 39 ff. For more recent views, see Friedrich, *op. cit.,* pp. 306 ff, and Jewell and Patterson, *op. cit.,* pp. 28 ff.

[29] H. Kelsen, *Vom Wesen und Wert der Demokratie,* reprint ed. (Aalen, 1963), pp. 54 ff.

[30] M. Weber, *Gesammelte Politische Schriften,* rev. ed., (Tübingen, 1958), p. 352.

forms of legislator-constituency communication. The adaptive function may be still more realistic. It finds expression in Vienna in the frequency of the orientation of coordinator. The recruiting and schooling activities of parliaments also seem to be still important.

The manifest functions of representative bodies, especially in lawmaking and other decision areas, therefore, do generally seem rather ineffective vis-a-vis an executive that is more powerful, able to act faster and more efficiently. The Vienna study suggests that a parliamentary assembly nonetheless may fulfill important representative tasks in its latent functions: specific control and critique of executive and civil service, representation of the citizens confronted with the bureaucracy, and linking government and active groups communicatively. If one considers the steady increase in bureaucratic tasks and therefore influence, the prevailing tendency of depoliticization of the citizenry, and the growing distance between it and the government, these latent functions do appear at least possible avenues for the realization of important democratic values like popular participation in as well as control of the political process.

It has to be stressed in conclusion both that the typologies presented are probably not exhaustive on either the manifest or latent sides, and that it is not possible to measure through an analysis of subjective role orientations whether and how much any of the functions are actually fulfilled. To answer these questions a more thorough analysis of actual behavior and decision processes within the larger legislative systems would be necessary. In spite of this the results of this study may show that analysis of legislative functions has to be considered an important precondition for the comparative study of legislative behavior.

Conclusion

Returning to the initially outlined framework we may conclude that the results of the Vienna study support the assumptions proposed. Effects of institutional and constitutional parameters on legislative behavior are evident, first, in the predominance of front benchers caused by the strong position of the executive in a parliamentary system, which is especially stressed in the Viennese constitution; second, in the high incidence of administrators caused by the special constitutional situation of the City Council committees; and third, in the special importance of errand-running, which may be effected by the great amount of welfare and other citizen-oriented activity the Vienna administration is engaged in. Cultural conditions are evident, first in the specific forms of the representational role orientations strongly influenced by the norms of a disciplined party system; second, in the importance of the role of coordinator; and, finally, in the phenomenon of opposition within the coalition, the last two being consequences of the specific political cultures of a *"Konkordanzdemokratie."*

Moreover, it has been demonstrated that the kinds of activities (functions) a legislature is actually engaged in do constitute intervening factors modifying the effects of institutional and cultural variables and do, at the same time, point out areas of equivalence for comparative behavior-oriented research. In this latter respect it should have become clear that a necessary precondition of such research, more so if it is to be truly comparative, would consist in close scrutiny of actual functions, influences, and outputs of legislatures in all or at least a large sample of those political systems in which legislative bodies do exist.[31]

More general and still more tentative propositions concerning legislative functions may be suggested by way of conclusion. If one looks at the spread of legislative institutions in the world today—including quite a number of cases in which assemblies can hardly be assumed *prima facie* to be engaged in decisions but nevertheless are maintained and exist as behavioral systems—it seems justifiable to assume that the prevalence of latent functions of representative bodies might be a rather general phenomenon.[32] At the same time the existence of an assembly exercising just these reduced functions of representing, controlling, and communicating in the interest of a larger constituency may appear to be an almost universal precondition for the maintenance of a political system of any but the most primitive kind.

In terms of the structural functional model of the polity[33] (the term function being no longer used only descriptively) the functional consequences of legislative performance may then quite generally be interpreted in the following way: representative assemblies, contrary to common doctrine, tend to be structures that are not engaged in rule making, a function which tends to be performed by the government and the bureaucratic hierarchies. They play an important role, however, in the performance of the input functions of interest articulation and support mobilization and of the output function of rule-application, the latter by controlling the executive

---

[31] Cf. J. Blondel, *An Introduction to Comparative Government* (London, 1969).

[32] A survey taken at the end of 1968 showed that in 116 of the 138 larger countries and independent territories in the world, that is, in more than 80 percent, legislative bodies did exist. The 25 systems without parliamentary assemblies include mostly Arab and African countries with a very low stage of socioeconomic development as well as a number of authoritarian systems both of the socialist (Cuba, Burma) and conservative varieties (Argentina, Peru). Information taken from Blondel, *op. cit.,* Appendix.

[33] See, e.g., G. Almond and B. Powell, *Comparative Politics, A Developmental Approach* (Boston, 1966), pp. 25 ff.

and by providing services for the constituency. Moreover, they do perform functions of communication and feedback, by their symbolic, adaptive, and constituency-oriented communication activities.[34] Elaboration and testing of this kind of model in a number of national cases would seem a useful starting point for comparative legislative analysis.

[34] See Blondel, *op. cit.*, pp. 304 ff, 355 ff.

CHAPTER FIVE

Decisional Structures in Small Legislative Bodies*

HEINZ EULAU

STANFORD UNIVERSITY

All legislative bodies, large or small, have characteristic decision-making structures. By decisional structure is meant the structure of relationships among the legislature's members at the stage in the legislative process when the votes are counted. For instance, where, as in England, a strong two-party system guarantees disciplined legislative behavior, the parliamentary structure is bifurcated. Where, as in France or Italy, majority rule requires the formation of parliamentary coalitions among several parties, the decisional structure is fragmented. In the one-party legislatures of Communist states the decisional structure is centrist. By way of contrast, in the congressional regimes of the United States, the decisional structure is relatively fluid, often exhibiting different patterns that give it a certain kaleidoscopic quality. As a result, the decisional structure of any particular American legislature is difficult to identify and name. Some legislatures have what may be called a bipolar structure; others have a unipolar structure; and still others a nonpolar structure.

Its decisional structure is one of a legislature's most pervasive and enduring properties. The party balance may change, coalitions may be reformed, or individual members may come and go, but the decisional structure itself will generally remain stable. There is something definitive and

* The larger project of which this analysis is a part, the City Council Research Project, is sponsored by the Institute of Political Studies, Stanford University and is supported by the National Science Foundation under contracts GS 496 and GS 1898. The author is indebted to his chief collaborator, Kenneth Prewitt, University of Chicago, for comments on an earlier draft of the chapter.

final in the voting stage of the legislative process that sets it off from preceding stages. The voting stage is the point of no return, the point at which the legislature's collective choice emerges from the individual choices of its members.

Finding one's way through the labyrinth of United States legislative decisional structures is a continuing preoccupation of scholars. Their main guide in this task has been analysis of legislative roll-call votes. A variety of techniques—indices of cohesion and likeness, unidimensional scaling, or sociometric methods—have been used to identify the legislature's partisan alignments, ideological groupings, leadership patterns, and power structure.[1] All these studies assume that alignment patterns evident in the legislative vote are more or less stable and regular, so that valid inferences can be made from manifest outcomes recorded in the call of the roll about latent behavioral aspects of the legislative process.

While roll-call analysis is a powerful method to identify important dimensions of the decisional structure, it is not adequate to discovering other correlate attributes of a legislature's decisional structure. For instance, there are such emergent properties as the legislature's "atmosphere," its "governing style," or its "decision-making practices," that cannot be inferred from voting patterns.

The task of this chapter is a modest if intricate one. It is to *describe*, if only partially, the anatomy of small legislative bodies in terms of three types of decisional structure and certain emergent group properties. As is readily evident, even a small legislative body's decisional structure is highly complex. Because it is complex, a relatively large number of small legislative groups were chosen for analysis. Small institutionalized groups can be inspected with a degree of attention to detail that is difficult in large legislatures, and the logistic feasibility of inspecting many such groups facilitates statistical analysis that is precluded when dealing with a limited number of large legislatures. The task of this chapter, then, is to describe patterns of relationship among some of the legislative group's multiple properties, not to test hypotheses about the cause of the relationships that may be found.

The analysis attempted here is in many respects simplified by the fact

[1] See Stuart A. Rice, "The Identification of Blocs in Small Legislative Bodies," *American Political Science Review,* **21** (August 1927), pp. 619–27; or John G. Grumm, "The Systematic Analysis of Blocs in the Study of Legislative Behavior," *Western Political Quarterly,* **18** (June 1965), pp. 350–62; Duncan MacRae, Jr., *Dimensions of Congressional Voting* (Berkeley, Calif., 1958); David B. Truman, *The Congressional Party: A Case Study* (New York, 1959); Duncan MacRae, Jr. and Hugh D. Price, "Scale Positions and 'Power' in the Senate," *Behavioral Science,* **4** (1959), pp. 212–18.

that the legislatures—82 city councils in the greater San Francisco Bay region[2]—are formally nonpartisan.[3] Nonpartisanship, at least in intent, emphasizes the independence of members who are elected at large and who are assumed to be uncommitted to a political party or to other easily identifiable groupings of voters.[4] In other words, the presumption is that the selection process of the legislative group leaves it basically unstructured in comparison with legislatures elected by party ballot or proportional methods in specified jurisdictional units. If this is so, the patterns of relationship among the group's members and other group attributes may be more readily considered undisturbed by extraneous variables. While this assumption may be questionable, the analysis will proceed as if it were valid.[5]

Identification of Decisional Structures

Although the data base of this study is interviews with individual city councilmen, the description of council properties and their interrelations

[2] Interviews were conducted in 1966 and 1967 in 87 of the 90 Bay Area cities then in existence. San Francisco was omitted because its county-city type of council—called Board of Supervisors—is more professional than, and very different from, the councils in the other cities. In two cities, Emeryville and Millbrae, the whole council refused to be interviewed (for reasons well known to us: both cities were at the time involved in controversies with the state and/or county). In five cities— Brisbane, Hercules, Corte Madera, Pittsburgh, and Suisan—analysis at the group level could not be performed because only three or fewer councilmen were interviewed. That is, group analysis was attempted only if, for instance, four out of five men had been interviewed. Of the 82 councils in this analysis, 67 had five members, 11 had seven members, 3 had nine members, and one, Palo Alto, had 13 members.

[3] That partisan considerations seem to intrude into council elections was tentatively explored in Heinz Eulau, Kenneth Prewitt and Betty H. Zisk, "Latent Partisanship in Nonpartisan Elections: Effects of Political Milieu and Mobilization," in Harmon Zeigler and Kent Jennings, ed., *The Electoral Process* (Englewood Cliffs, N.J., 1966), pp. 208–37.

[4] See Eugene C. Lee, *The Politics of Nonpartisanship* (Berkeley and Los Angeles, 1960). See also Oliver P. Williams and Charles R. Adrian, "The Insulation of Local Politics under the Nonpartisan Ballot," *American Political Science Review,* 53 (December 1959), pp. 1052–63.

[5] For instance, we know from our data that certain types of decisional structure— especially those we call unipolar and nonpolar—are strongly related to both city size and the stage of city policy development. Interestingly, this is not true of bipolar (conflictual) structures; they are found in equal proportions in small and large cities and in cities in various stages of development. For the notion of "policy development," see Heinz Eulau and Robert E. Eyestone, "Policy Maps of City Councils and Policy Outcomes: A Developmental Analysis," *American Political Science Review,* 62 (March 1968), pp. 124–43.

proceeds at the group level of analysis. To permit description at this level, the individual data are transformed into grouped data by various coding techniques. These techniques differ, depending on the nature of the original data and the particular group property constructed out of them. The major techniques are only briefly described here, while illustrations of the concepts referring to the properties and relevant procedural points are introduced at appropriate places in the analysis.

The council's "decisional structure" was constructed from sociometric questions in the interview that asked each councilman with whom he votes on controversial issues and with whom other councilmen vote.[6] The questions assumed, of course, that councilmen line up with each other more or less regularly regardless of the content of specific issues. This procedure had to be followed because conventional bloc analysis based on roll-calls was impossible due to the fact that in many councils either votes are not recorded or, if recorded, names are not given in council minutes.

The use of sociometric questions proved to be highly successful.[7] The procedure produced data patterns that permitted the construction of three decisional structures. In some councils, the questions about voting patterns are seen as irrelevant; no line-ups ever occur in the council, and all respondents agree that this is the case. These councils have a *unipolar* decisional structure: all members always vote together, although there may be an occasional deviant on a given vote. In other councils the question yielded the response that there are no reoccurring line-ups and that though the council often splits on controversial issues, different members vote with each other depending on the issues involved. These councils have a *nonpolar* decisional structure: there is no regular voting pattern, although there may be minority cliques that at times vote together. The voting pattern of the nonpolar council is best viewed not as one which is irregular but as one in which no regular alignments persist from issue to issue or from meeting to meeting. Finally, in the third type of council, the responses to the questions on voting reveal clear factional line-ups: members of one

---

[6] The question: "When the Council is in disagreement on an issue, would you say there is more or less the same line-up of votes here in (city)? I mean, do some members seem to vote together on controversial issues? If YES: With whom do *you* usually vote on controversial matters? Now, what about the others? Are they united or split? IF SPLIT: Who would you say votes most often together when the others are split?"

[7] The procedure is more fully explained in Heinz Eulau and Peter Lupsha, "Decisional Structures and Coalition Formation in Small Legislative Bodies," in Elke Frank, Ed., *Lawmakers in a Changing World* (Englewood Cliffs, N.J., 1966), pp. 150–86. It should be mentioned that what we now term "nonpolar" was called "multipolar" in this article. Theoretical reconsideration of what was there called multipolar suggested that nonpolar is the empirically more appropriate designation.

faction named themselves as voting together and identified those voting against them, and members of the other faction did likewise. These councils have a *bipolar* decisional structure: the council is divided by a permanent split into two factions, although there may be "swing voters" who from time to time shift, without, however, disturbing the basic pattern. Here, in a nutshell, are some comments from interview protocols:

Unipolar: "By the grace of God we've never brought that in there. The five of us are Republicans; the five of us are Protestants."

Nonpolar: "I think that's healthy—to be diverse. A five-to-nothing council shows a lack of preparation or thinking—or they are all alike. There's bound to be controversy among five different individuals."

Bipolar: "Some of us are on the power team and some of us are not. The three want the power and they have it. Jones and I are not concerned about the power we can control."

Although the typology was constructed without making any assumptions about an inherent ordering, it may be treated as an ordinal scale if certain theoretical assumptions are accepted. For instance, as will become clear later on, if one assumes that from a political standpoint bipolar structures are the most conflictual and unipolar structures are the least so, the typology may be ordered as a continuum from a unipolar end (most harmonious, least conflictual) through a nonpolar middle to a bipolar end (least harmonious, most conflictual). This is the ordering adopted in the following analysis.[8]

While sociometry is essentially a computational method, other council properties, such as governing style and decision-making practices, were constructed by imputational coding. That is, individual respondents in the council were treated as informants about the council as a whole; a council property was imputed on the basis of the strength of the total evidence rather than aggregated from individual respondents. The coding technique was as follows: two investigators jointly read through all responses to relevant questions from all members of a given council and then came to agreement on how the council was to be classified. This coding technique stresses the quality of the evidence rather than simply depending on the number of times a particular bit of information appears in the interviews. For instance, councils were dichotomized with respect to whether bargaining went on. A detailed statement by a single councilman describing and

[8] For further discussion of alternate theoretical dimensions that can be imputed to the decisional structure typology, making for different orderings, see Heinz Eulau, "The Informal Organization of Decisional Structures in Small Legislative Bodies," *Midwest Journal of Political Science,* **13** (August 1969), pp. 341–66.

illustrating situations of bargaining in the council, corroborated by less complete evidence from one or two of his colleagues, was accepted as information sufficient for coding the presence of bargaining activity. In this case, the single councilman is an informant; his colleagues either confirm his information or do not deny it.

While these ways of constructing analytic attributes and coding councils are admittedly more judgmental and subjective than aggregating individual data or establishing modal distributions, they are appropriate in the case of properties that are neither distributive (such as average policy view) nor relational (such as decisional structure). They are emergent properties that have no direct analogue at the level of the individual. Because comparison of institutionalized groups requires comparative analysis at the group's own level, to overlook properties that can be derived from imputational coding is to preclude important group properties from analysis.

The rest of the chapter is in three parts: first, an explication of the decisional structures as these are accounted for by the councils themselves; second, analysis of various group properties and their association with different decisional structures; finally, an attempt is made to construct at least partial models of different council structures.

Explication of Decisional Structure Typology

To elucidate more fully the meaning of the three types of decisional structure we draw on councilmen's own accounts of the sources of or reasons for the occurrence or nonoccurrence of various kinds of voting patterns.[9] These accounts tend to confirm the theoretical assumption that at least one dimension of the decisional structure can be thought of as a harmony-conflict continuum. As Table 5.1 shows, councilmen's explanations of prevailing voting patterns are strongly ordered by the decisional structure typology.[10] In turn, these accounts deepen our understanding of the three types of decisional structure.

Bipolar Structure. The bipolar or most conflictual structure seems to

---

[9] Individual councilmen were asked: "How do you account for the fact that the Council divides as it does?" The procedure for coding a council as a whole was imputational: a council was classified into a response category when one respondent's *detailed* account was *corroborated* by at least one supportive statement (usually there was more than one such corroboration). In regard to "personal differences" several unfavorable remarks by one councilman about another was accepted as sufficient evidence for classifying the council, though in most cases more than one respondent made such remarks. "Idiosyncratic behavior" was treated similarly.

[10] These codings were, of course, made independently of prior knowledge of the council's decisional structure.

Table 5.1   Council Accounts of Voting Patterns in Three Types of
Decisional Structure (in %)

	Decisional Structure		
	Harmonious ←——————→		Conflictual
	Unipolar	Nonpolar	Bipolar
Sources of Voting Patterns[a]	N = 33	N = 29	N = 20
Split is due to basic ideological or policy differences	0	14	65
Split is due to differences in background or experience	0	17	60
Split is due to personal differences and difficulties	0	17	45
Split is due to partisan division	0	7	20
Split is due to differences of opinion on particular issues	0	48	25
Split is due to individual members thinking independently and differently	0	31	0
Split does not generally occur; if it occurs, is due to idiosyncratic behavior	48	10	10
Split simply does not occur	52	0	0

[a] Cell entries may total more than 100 because a council could be coded in more than one category. The entries represent codings obtained by the imputational method described more fully in the text. In the case of the data presented in this table, a council is coded in one or more of the categories if there is a detailed statement about the sources of voting patterns made by one respondent that was corroborated by another or several others.

be strongly rooted either in differences stemming from disagreements over basic policy issues or in differences stemming from different backgrounds or experiences of the membership. Policy differences often have a strong ideological component, involving the role of government, planning, development, taxation, private enterprise, and so on. For instance:[11]

"It's the progressive against the nonprogressives. We (progressives) are for civil rights, planning, recreation, and the view of the city. Our minds reach the same conclusions. We have seen the same facts. We do disagree over labor and the budget among the progressives, though."

Almost equally significant sources of conflict are differences in councilmen's social backgrounds and experiences. Age differences, differences in length of residence, differences in ethnic origin or occupation, and differ-

[11] All names appearing in the quotations from interview protocols are pseudonyms, used to protect the anonymity of the informants. Similarly, all references to a particular city have been omitted.

ences in political experiences appear to be sources of continuing voting splits. For instance:

"Maybe their backgrounds and outlooks are related—e.g. Bonham and Eldridge have lived all their lives here—from well-known families and farming people. Sabbatini and myself both have kicked around the country quite a bit before settling down here—both now in business here."

Personal differences and resulting difficulties, rooted in mutual dislikes, suspicions, distrust, and personality clashes, are somewhat less frequent sources of conflict, but they too distinguish bipolar from nonpolar structures. For instance:

"An underlying personality conflict between Parsons and Nisbet who both want to be mayor. Also, Parsons and Pearl have been feuding for years. All agree that we should have a city manager, though. There is an underlying conflict between Nisbet and Rudolfo. They seem to respect me for having no personal animosity."

Voting splits due to partisanship account for decisional structuring in only six councils, four of them bipolar and two of them nonpolar. The following is typical of the comments offering this explanation:

"The groups have different political philosophies entirely. The majority of seven are conservative Republicans. The rest are left-wing Democrats."

"It's a difference primarily in philosophies. Steward and Lotti are hard-core Democrats. Their ideas are different. Young and Bryce are Republicans."

Nonpolar Structure. There is a clear shift in the pattern of Table 5.1 at the point where voting splits are accounted for in terms of differences of opinion on particular, nonoverlapping issues. In almost half of the nonpolar structures (48%), but only a fourth of the bipolar, is this explanation offered. It is quite clear that these occasional and nonrepetitive situations make for less pervasive conflict on the council than do basic policy issues, differences in backgrounds, or personal difficulties. Some typical accounts:

"We all vote that way. We all shift. Bock, for example, was against gambling but then he shifted to the anti-ministerial position . . . an absolute switch. We were all flabbergasted. It was just that some woman really irritated him and he got at her this way. We respond to pressure: political, personal, financial. It's brought on an individual from a number of sources."

"Some of the councilmen go along with the staff and let staff thinking influence their common sense. It happens on lots of items. For example, Mechan and I voted against participation in the county library system, but the rest went along with the staff recommendation to get the "free money." There isn't any one person really because the lineup is not consistent from item to item. We may have six 4–3 votes in a night, but not the same lineup each time."

Similarly, councils stressing group members' independent thinking as the source of voting splits tend to be nonpolar. These accounts occurred in almost a third of the nonpolar but in none of the bipolar councils. Typical remarks were:

"All I can think is that each of us takes each item as it comes up and votes according to how we think it should be voted upon. As it comes up."

"No one pressures any of us into a decision, and no one expects we'll all vote the same way, unless we come to our individual conclusions by ourselves and they happen to be the same."

Unipolar Structure. Although unipolar councils, by definition and construction, are not characterized by voting splits, they are not always unanimous; dissenting votes may be cast. These dissenting votes do not disturb the council's basic decisional structure. For instance:

"There is a four to one split because of Robinson. He doesn't figure into much of what we do. I have an absolute conviction that whatever decision Robinson makes is based on purely personal advantage. My colleagues agree with me on this, and that's why we split as we do in general."

Unipolarity in the decisional structure need not mean that the council has not disagreed before the voting takes place. Some comments suggest that it is often the social pressure inherent in the functioning of small-face-to-face groups that makes a dissenting member abandon his opposition and accede to the wishes of the others.[12] For instance:

"Sorenson was the protege of the vociferous minority for a long time. Since being on the Council he has more or less moved away from that. First, he used to be for whatever they wanted. He realizes now they're a minority. On apartment zoning, they opposed just to oppose and opposed the freeway. He was their champion but not anymore. All they have to do is get elected to the Council and see the facts first, then it changes."

"There is really no split. I guess this is because we have such similar points of view as to what the people of the town want in the way of government. It is also because we are small and if this in itself does not lead to unanimity on most decisions, then we try to achieve a unanimous vote by persuading dissenters, because we don't want to appear wishy-washy. We want complete agreement on the issues."

Other instances of what was coded as idiosyncratic behavior (which may

[12] This is not the sole reason for unanimity, of course, either in unipolar or nonpolar and bipolar councils. It should be pointed out that unanimity may be the outcome in 90 percent or more of voting even in nonpolar and bipolar councils. But see Heinz Eulau, "Logics of Rationality in Unanimous Decision-Making," in Carl J. Friedrich, Ed., *Rational Decision* (New York, 1964), pp. 26–54.

occur also in nonpolar and bipolar councils) are accounted for by lack of information, outside pressures, or personal indecision. For instance:

"Sometimes they don't understand an issue, then get more information and change their vote. The floor influences the vote a great deal. For example: there is a respected doctor's wife on the floor who protests something or takes a public stand. This will make us think more and *be very careful how we vote.*"

"I guess different people figure differently. I'm more conservative, and will generally vote with the other two conservatives. The other two will switch around since one is more liberal and one middle of the road. We may not all be in agreement on how to do something—but in general, we are in principle. It may be at times that *they cannot be able to make up their minds.* Perhaps they're convinced by the applicant that this is the way they should vote."

Legislative Atmosphere

No sensitive observer of a city council in session can fail to sense a characteristic something that may be labeled its "legislative atmosphere." The notion is admittedly intangible, but it is nonetheless evident that councils differ in the solemnity of this proceedings, in the degree of camaraderie that is expressed in words or deeds, in the level of tension that seems to pervade the legislative business, and in other "atmospheric" respects. In some councils, members address each other only by surnames, while in others first names are freely used. In some councils, the proceedings rigidly follow Roberts' Rules; in others discussion and voting are informal and relaxed. In some councils, all members are listened to carefully; in other councils, members interrupt each other incessantly. In some councils, the language of discourse is polite and deferential, in others, harsh and abrupt. In some councils, members pay little heed to the audience; in other councils, they vie for attention from the floor. In some councils a member's lack of information leads to patient explanation of facts and circumstances; in others the uninformed member is ridiculed. In some councils an individual's strong feelings in a matter of controversy are assuaged by tabling or concessions, while in other councils he is simply outvoted.

Direct observation of behavioral patterns that give rise to a council's legislative atmosphere is extraordinarily difficult, and to pursue it in a large number of legislative groups, even though they may be small in size, is costly. Interviews may therefore yield information that is impractical to seek through direct observation. For it is plausible that a councilman who refers to his colleagues by their first names on the council floor is likely to do the same when referring to them during an interview. If members of a council collectively exhibit cooperative and friendly attitudes while doing their council business with one another, it is reasonable to expect they will verbally manifest similar sentiments when describing their colleagues and activities to an interviewer. Reading the interviews council by council, some 200 pages of open-ended material for each council, it becomes readily apparent that remarks and comments of this kind are not random: if they occur in one respondent's protocol they are likely to be echoed in another's.

Holistic coding was therefore used to categorize the 82 councils on two dimensions labeled "collegiality" and "tension."[13] Collegiality refers to the spirit of cooperation, teamwork, mutual deference, friendship, and appreciation that pervades the group as a whole. For instance:

"We all express ourselves and try to reach agreement satisfactory to everyone . . . In a body of people not paid, like we are, we feel quite independent, yet we want to work as a team. We are all interested in what is best for the city, and no one has a particular axe to grind."

"We pretty much agree on things as it stands. We are all buddies, first name friends, and when one of us has something on his mind, we just go to each other and discuss it to see how the other feels. If I discover that several feel the matter is important, I will bring the matter up in a meeting."

On the other hand, tension refers to the presence of a competitive struggle for status, power, prestige, or influence among council members. For instance:

"Marconi is very wealthy and feels his primary responsibility is to those who got him where he is. He's more business oriented. He feels the businessman does everything, he should have more privileges. Sartori usually sides with whoever is putting the pressure on. The rest of us, when we want to know how he's going to vote, say "Well, who talked to him last." He agrees with everybody. The most you can say about him is that he is a nice guy. Funny thing is I used to be known as Edward's man. He was the one who encouraged me to run and it was said that I was his

---

[13] For a council to be coded as "collegial" or "tense," there had to be pervasive evidence that the property in question was actually present. For instance, if all or most respondents referred to each other by first name and if there was other evidence of mutual deference, the council was coded as collegial. If there was pervasive evidence of an internal power struggle, competition for status and frequent negative references to other members, the council was coded as tense. Collegiality and tension are emergent properties that cannot be either computed from individual data or imputed from direct information by one or a few individual respondents. We term the method "holistic" because what we are coding is a configuration of many aspects of legislative behavior that seem to characterize the group as a whole.

man, but I wasn't. He was powerful on the council at that time, and now he doesn't like me so much. I guess it's because now I'm more powerful than he is and he kind of resents it."

However, it should be emphasized that collegiality and tension are not dichotomized poles of a single continuum but rather separate aspects of the legislative atmosphere. While a collegial council can never be tense, the absence of collegiality does not mean that the legislative atmosphere is necessarily tense or even hostile. In other words, some councils may have an atmosphere that is neither particularly collegial nor tense. In such councils business is transacted in a businesslike and impersonal manner with a minimum of interpersonal affect. The group is, above all, task oriented, and the relationships among councilmen are free of emotional ties, whether these ties are warm and indulgent or competitive and deprivational.

From what we know about the three types of decisional structure, we would expect unipolar councils, characterized as they are by harmonious voting patterns, also to have a collegial atmosphere, while bipolar councils, characterized by conflictual patterns, are most likely to have a tense legislative atmosphere. As Table 5.2 shows, these expectations are born out by

Table 5.2 Collegiality and Tension in Decisional Structures (in %)

	Decisional Structure		
	Harmonious ←	→	Conflictual
	Unipolar	Nonpolar	Bipolar
Legislative Atmosphere	$N = 33$	$N = 29$	$N = 20$
Collegial ($N = 40$)	70	41	25
Neither collegial nor tense ($N = 20$)	24	34	10
Tense ($N = 22$)	6	24	65
Total	100	100	100

the data. Moreover, the relationship between council decisional structure and legislative atmosphere is highly monotonic: not only are there spectacular differences in legislative atmosphere between the unipolar and the bipolar structures, but the nonpolar structures—more conflictual than the unipolar but less so than the bipolar councils—clearly fall in the middle of the polar continuum and, in addition, include more councils whose legislative atmosphere is neither collegial nor tense.

The distribution of the councils in terms of legislative atmosphere also gives some clues about how the three types of decisional structure may solve what is sometimes called the "problem of integration."[14] In the case of the five bipolar, collegial councils we can assume that the basic conflict inherent in the bipolar decisional structure is resolved through the workings of a high degree of affect; whatever issues might divide the members into majority and minority factions, the disagreement does not spill over into interpersonal relationships, so that the council atmosphere can be collegial. On the other hand, the two unipolar, tense councils may represent cases of "antagonistic cooperation."[15] But only deviant case analysis can confirm or disconfirm these speculations. In general, it seems that decisional structures generate their own characteristic legislative atmospheres that, in turn, may be associated with other council properties.

Governing Styles

A council's legislative atmosphere is an emergent property set by the mood of its members' interpersonal relations. Whether a council is collegial or not, tense or not, depends on the attitudes councilmen entertain toward one another, the evaluations they make of each other's behavior, the standards they live by, and their competitive aspirations or expectations. But the presence of collegiality or the absence of tension does not automatically guarantee that the council is a well-functioning governing group. A council overly committed to maintaining "internal peace" may immobilize itself for governmental action as readily as a group that is profoundly split. In other words, both collegial and tense councils face the problem of becoming effective working groups. How do councils cope with this problem, and how is it dealt with in different decisional structures?

There are two possibilities. One is that the council develops decision-making practices that countervail malfunctionings stemming from its structural form and legislative atmosphere. This possibility is treated in the next section. The other possibility is that the council has developed a characteristic "governing style"—a set of basic premises as to how the legislative business is or should be transacted. By governing style is meant what is sometimes called "operational code"[16]—latent general beliefs, values, and norms that the governing group itself only vaguely recognizes, because it

---

[14] See Richard F. Fenno, Jr., "The House Appropriations Committee as a Political System: The Problem of Integration," *American Political Science Review,* **56** (June 1962), pp. 310–24.

[15] For the notion of "antagonistic cooperation," see David Riesman, *The Lonely Crowd* (New Haven, 1950), p. 104.

[16] See Alexander L. George, *The "Operational Code": A Neglected Approach to the Study of Political Leaders and Decision-Making* (Santa Monica, Calif., 1967, Rand Corporation Memorandum RM-5427-PR).

lives by them, or customary procedures so widely approved that alternatives are rarely contemplated. Governing style refers to the council's approach to its decision-making tasks and is likely to influence its more deliberate choice of decision-making practices.

Like the dimensions of legislative atmosphere, particular governing styles are easier to identify than to name. But three distinct styles seem to be characteristic properties of councils. Giving these styles names involves some hazards, for such naming has evaluative overtones that may be misleading. Yet, there seems to be no alternative but doing so.

The Benevolent Style. This style comes perhaps closest to the "city father" image so idealized in the textbooks on local government. Witness the following from a recent text:[17]

"Despite all possible divergencies of opinion, and even on the occasions when there is mutual dislike, the council and mayor sitting together as a legislative body possess a special type of unity. They are bound together as those who have survived the election battles and represent the people's choice; by possession of a body of common knowledge about city problems far more thorough than that of the best informed private citizen; by common pressures from the outside; by a common sense of responsibility; by a common awareness that they no longer possess the luxury of criticism without responsibility but that they must ultimately vote—and be accountable for that vote."

In some respects, the benevolent style is residual in the sense that it is probably so pervasive in the culture of nonpartisan politics that, when it is articulated, it is expressed sparingly if not banally. The council works for the good of the city and its citizens; its work is a public service, and serving on the council is not a matter of self-interest; the council is open to suggestions from its members, the city staff, and citizens, but though responsive it leaves the initiative to others. Some statements from the interview protocols will illustrate.[18]

"General willingness to work for the good of the city. There is no undue pressure. They must all feel like I do—a sense of satisfaction in performing an underpaid job."

"The council is objective and all five councilmen are independent in

[17] Robert L. Morlan and Leroy C. Hardy, *Politics in California* (Belmont, Calif., 1968), p. 107.

[18] These quotations are responses to the following question in the interview schedule: "Overall, just what makes the Council tick? I mean, *besides* the manager, the staff, or charter prescriptions, who decides what the Council should do, and how does it work?" It is interesting to note that the responses elicited by this question were not what it was designed to elicit. That it yielded the responses it did emphasizes the pervasiveness of "benevolence" as a governing style.

thinking with the best interests of the city at stake. Their decisions are based on this."

The Pragmatic Style. Just as every benevolent council probably has a pragmatic component in its governing style, so every pragmatic council probably has a benevolent component. The difference from council to council is one of emphasis and degree. In general, a council has a pragmatic governing style when the emphasis is placed on knowledge, facts, expertise, or the substantive merits of a proposal in proceeding with council business. The pragmatic style stresses planning, meeting problems before they arise, following external standards, and coming to efficient, economically sound, and technically competent decisions. As some councilmen put it:

"In the normal course of events, we have a planning consultant, the city administrator, and the planning commission. These three are the ones who recognize conditions that are supposed to keep us attuned to the trends and the times and working with the Chamber of Commerce. We know they need parking, and they know we know they need it—we work together. This comes to us. We just have to be alert to things that will make this a better place to live."

"It all comes about from just daily things that occur—as a problem arises, the council meets it. I would like to see more planning for the future like rapid transit, parking, expectations of the Public Works Dept., etc. There is a need for more advance planning—there is some thinking on this—but we need an administrative man to handle these future problems so we can work things out before they get to the point where they are very difficult to handle."

The Political Style. This style differs markedly from the benevolent and pragmatic styles. This is not to say that the other two styles are altogether absent in councils chiefly characterized by the political style. But the council is seen as primarily an arena in which a political game is played, where advantages may be derived from going along or obstructing, where differences in status and power are seen as important, where there is more emphasis on policy payoffs that may benefit the individual councilman or his particular clientele. Here, for instance, are statements by two councilmen from a "rural" council in a city of about 27,000 that is a fruit-and-wine processing center with growing residential sections:

My views are closely aligned with those of two members. I am more aggressive, I will fight for principles. The old boy (mayor) is too slow, doesn't understand. I have a majority, and so I don't feel a need for compromise. There are variations and degrees—Jones will only vote with me four times in a row and that is the end."

"He has the force. He's a hard, dedicated party worker, the voice of

Decisional Structures

the party. The others have to follow or they get in trouble with the party. . . . The council doesn't weigh both sides of problems. There are too many predecided votes. They tell us: 'Take all the time you want, but we have the votes.' This will beat them in the next election. The public doesn't want any three people to run anything."

Because of the element of subjectivity involved in coding the three governing styles by the imputational method, a systematic effort was made to err on the conservative side—on the assumption that, given the tradition of manager government and nonpartisanship, the political style would be least likely to occur, the pragmatic style somewhat more frequently, and the benevolent style most often. In other words, a council was coded as having a political or pragmatic style only if the evidence was strong and cumulative. While, as Table 5.3 shows, 48 of the 82 councils seemed to be primarily characterized by the benevolent style, the political style was slightly more prevalent (in 19 councils) than the pragmatic style (in 15 councils).

Table 5.3   Relationship between Governing Styles and
Decisional Structures in 82 Councils (in %)

	Decisional Structure		
	Harmonious ←⎯⎯⎯⎯→		Conflictual
	Unipolar	Nonpolar	Bipolar
Governing Style	$N = 33$	$N = 29$	$N = 20$
Benevolent ($N = 48$)	64	59	50
Pragmatic ($N = 15$)	30	17	0
Political ($N = 19$)	6	24	50
Total	100	100	100

Table 5.3 offers an initial opportunity to speculate about the problem of how governing styles may aid in overcoming possible rigidities in the decisional structure—be it the rigidity of a unipolar council that is compulsively harmonious or the rigidity of a bipolar council obsessively conflictual. While majorities of councils with unipolar and nonpolar structures have benevolent styles, half of the bipolar councils have this style as well, surprisingly more than one might expect. It might at first appear that in these bipolar councils a benevolent governing style is conducive to effective council functioning in an otherwise conflictual situation. And the fact that as many as 30 percent of the unipolar councils have a pragmatic governing style might suggest that whatever rigidity is introduced into the legislative process by unipolarity is offset in these councils by their pragmatism.

These speculations make sense, but they are subject to doubt. It may well be that governing styles are less responses to structural conditions than to those interpersonal circumstances that give rise to the council's legislative atmosphere. Table 5.4 relates governing styles to legislative atmosphere. Three aspects of the table are noteworthy. First, the distribution of governing styles in collegial councils is almost identical with their distribution in unipolar councils. One might infer that unipolarity and a collegial legislative atmosphere reinforce each other, calling forth a governing style that seems congenial to both. As Table 5.5 shows, this inference is wrong. Second, the political style appears to be associated with a tense atmosphere. Fifty-nine percent of the tense councils, as against only five percent and twenty percent, respectively, of the councils with other types of atmosphere, are characterized by the political style of decision-making.

Table 5.4   Relationship between Legislative Atmosphere and Governing Styles (in %)

| | Legislative Atmosphere | | |
	Collegial $N = 40$	Neither Collegial Nor Tense $N = 20$	Tense $N = 22$
Governing Style			
Benevolent	63	70	41
Pragmatic	32	10	0
Political	5	20	59
Total	100	100	100

In order to disentangle the relationships between decisional structure, legislative atmosphere and governing styles, Table 5.5 presents these multivariate relationships. Although a table of this sort, based on only 82 cases, is at best a very inelegant analytic tool, it is likely to give more insight into the behavioral complexities involved in legislative decision-making than would a sophisticated summary statistic.

In the first place, then, it appears that benevolence as a governing style is less a response to possible rigidities inherent in the unipolar structure as such than to difficulties arising out of the legislative atmosphere. If the atmosphere is neutral or tense, all unipolar councils are characterized by the benevolent style. On the other hand, only unipolar councils with a collegial atmosphere possess a pragmatic governing style. In other words, a benevolent style is a congenial response of unipolar groups to situations of stress or strain, and a pragmatic style is evidently feasible only if such stress and strain is absent.

Table 5.5   Decisional Structures, Legislative Atmosphere and
Governing Styles

Governing Style	Collegial $N = 40$	Neither Collegial nor Tense $N = 20$	Tense $N = 22$
Decisional structure: unipolar (harmonious)	$N = 23$	$N = 8$	$N = 2$
Benevolent	48	100	100
Pragmatic	43	0	0
Political	9	0	0
Total	100	100	100
Decisional structure: nonpolar	$N = 12$	$N = 10$	$N = 7$
Benevolent	75	50	43
Pragmatic	25	20	0
Political	0	30	57
Total	100	100	100
Decisional structure: bipolar (conflictual)	$N = 5$	$N = 2$	$N = 13$
Benevolent	100	50	31
Pragmatic	0	0	0
Political	0	50	69
Total	100	100	100

Second, and by way of contrast, benevolence as a governing style does not serve to alleviate stress or strain and possible rigidities in councils with a bipolar or nonpolar structure. The more bipolar and nonpolar councils are characterized by tension in the legislative atmosphere, the more do these councils give evidence of a political governing style. Fifty-seven percent of the nonpolar and sixty-nine percent of the bipolar councils with a tense legislative atmosphere possess a political governing style. In other words, it would seem that a political governing style is a normal response to highly conflictual structural and interpersonal relations. Moreover, in neither of these situations does a pragmatic style seem clearly to commend itself to the decision-making group. Solutions to stresses or strain in governance are found by political rather than politically neutral governing styles.

One can read Table 5.5 in another way. In councils whose legislative atmosphere is collegial, the more conflictual the decisional structure, the more emphasis is placed on a benevolent style to cope with the problem of governance. On the other hand, in councils which are tense the opposite is the case. The more conflictual the decisional structure, the less is a benevolent and the more is a political governing style forthcoming.

The two readings of Table 5.5 are complementary. They suggest that in the operation of legislative bodies both legislative atmosphere and governing style may contribute significantly and systematically to the variance in legislative outcomes. Decisional structures, it appears, are both causes and consequences of interrelationships between personal factors, revealed by the legislative atmosphere and cultural factors, revealed by governing style.

Decisional Practices

Decisional practices are to governing style what tactics are to strategy, but the analogy should not be misunderstood. Governing style rather than strategy has been used in order to distinguish our conception from that of writers concerned with such strategic problems as whether majority voting is rational,[19] whether rationality maximizes or satisfices utilities,[20] or whether decision-making is incremental or synoptic.[21] We assume that in the councils such strategic problems have been "solved." A decision is not only thought to be legitimate if it has been reached by a majority or unanimous vote, but is also considered as the "best possible" outcome from the perspective of the council as a whole. Voting strategies as plans of action to obtain goals are here assumed to be given.

For very much the same reason the notion of decisional practices rather than tactics is used. The task here is not to assess the rationality or optimality of the political process in decision-making but to discover under what conditions what practices are being adopted.[22] In small, face-to-face legislative groups little calculated risk-taking characterizes the decision-making process. The individual is particularly subject to structural constraints and social pressures for conformity that, his protestations to the contrary notwithstanding, obstruct individual rationality and irrationality. Not only is he under pressure to abide by the "rules of the game,"[23] but he is likely to adapt himself to prevailing practices. As a result, one would expect different decisional practices to be followed in different decisional structures under different conditions of legislative atmosphere or governing style.

Five practices were identified as characteristic council properties. Before

[19] See James M. Buchanan and Gordon Tullock, *The Calculus of Consent: Logical Foundations of Constitutional Democracy* (Ann Arbor, Michigan, 1962).

[20] See Herbert A. Simon, "A Behavioral Model of Rational Choice," in *Models of Man* (New York, 1957), pp. 241–60.

[21] See David Braybrooke and Charles E. Lindblom, *A Strategy of Decision: Policy Evaluation as a Social Process* (New York, 1963).

[22] In subsequent publications we shall analyze the consequences of governing styles and decisional practices for other aspects of council functioning and policy outcomes, as well as analyze unanimity as a strategic and tactical problem.

[23] Although data are available on these rules, they are not treated here.

proceeding with the analysis, we must explicate the concepts used to describe them.

Exchange. Involved in this practice is the frank transmission of attitudes, views, or opinions of a private nature that cannot be transmitted in public. Exchange therefore tends to establish mutual trust and confidence in the group as a whole or, where the group is split, among the members of a faction.[24] Exchange may be practiced among all or most members or only among some members. It is possible to distinguish between general exchange and limited exchange, and to classify the councils accordingly.

What is exchanged, then, is not factual information but information about feelings, doubts, or convictions. If it were a matter of factual information, it could be exchanged in public session. Rather, the practice is designed to find out where another member stands on an issue or to clarify one's own stand before a public commitment is made. It contributes to the unity of the group as a whole or that of a faction. The cost of such private exchange is low because, if exchange is not reciprocated, it is likely to cease.[25] The following illustrations of exchange negotiations from the interview protocols are highly selective and do not give a full picture of the great variety of particular exchanges that can take place:[26]

"I like to discuss a problem beforehand if possible, and it's hard to discuss it freely in a meeting. I like to talk about it with individuals and the councilmen beforehand so we can look into doubtful areas before the meeting."

"On some problems you cannot state your position publicly. You can go to individual councilmen—one at a time. You can get their opinions and their line of thought, so when it comes before the council as a whole. you can see whether it will survive."

"I don't wait for our council meeting. I talk with the mayor on the train, or have lunch with him or other councilmen in S.F. We get a feel of the

[24] For a theoretical discussion of "social exchange" as used here, see Peter M. Blau, *Exchange and Power in Social Life* (New York, 1964), pp. 88–114. See also George C. Homans, *Social Behavior: Its Elementary Forms* (New York, 1961), pp. 30–50.

[25] See Alvin W. Gouldner, "The Norm of Reciprocity," *American Sociological Review,* **25** (1960), pp. 161–78.

[26] Decisional practices were coded for each council from responses to a variety of questions concerned with the council's internal operations, but especially from these two: (1); "We just spoke about *what* you should do as a councilman. Now I would like to ask you whether there are particular strategies that you employ to accomplish what you want to do as a councilman? Just what's the best way of doing what you want to do?" (2) "City councilmen sometimes talk about decisions in terms of bargaining—do you think this goes on in your council?" If yes: "Could you explain a bit what this bargaining implies? Just what does one do in bargaining?" If no: "If there is no bargaining, what other ways are there to make decisions?"

views, so when you meet you know how they feel about various matters that are coming up."

"We have study sessions, both open and private. In private sessions we pre-discuss what we want to do or talk about. You don't throw anything out cold. You'll see a councilman at golf or Chamber of Commerce and you approach him and see what he thinks about it. If they don't support it, you usually give up. Or if you feel strong about it, make a motion. You usually wait until you get support."

Bargaining. This practice involves trading off things more valued by one legislator but less by another for other things more valued by the latter but less by the former. Bargaining implies that every one of the bargaining group will gain something. Although councilmen were often reluctant to admit that bargaining goes on in their council, they would give evidence of implicit log-rolling in "going along" with a proposal in expectation of reciprocal support at a later time. For instance:

"There might be a little bit. Not as a result of one going to the other, but a couple of councilmen are getting sophisticated, and I think there is a little reciprocation. I don't see anything too wrong with it. Traditionally from what I've heard and read, this is what makes the wheels go round. At first blush, it may seem wrong, but I think it is a necessary part of the mechanics."

"There can be implicit agreements, I guess. You're prone to support someone who supported your measure. You can't bargain effectively in public; therefore, little goes on since there's little informal contact. But you remember someone deferring to you."

In general, there seems to be more approval of tacit trading than of explicit bargaining where the terms of the deal call for tangible *quids* and *quos*. An explicit example of the latter:

"You know what's coming up from the agenda. You talk to people, get phone calls, you try to compromise—you scratch my back, I scratch yours. I tell them (council) the little guy pays the bill. The Arts Council, the Symphony, always get donations from the city because they have the backing. The other night, the Filippinos came up and wanted a $200 donation for their festival which they have held for two years without asking for any help. The council was against it; they said let them wait till budget time. So I put my light on at the right time—the little Filippino was practically in tears—and I said "the Filippino people are the least trouble of anybody, they are good citizens and they deserve this donation." This way I put them on the spot and they voted in favor. Only Toledano stuck to his guns. I told them to go along with me and I'd support the symphony and their things. If I make up my mind, I won't go with the gang. I have voted with the mayor many times when they asked me not to."

In this case as in the following example the respondents used the word "compromise," but it is quite clear from the context that the practice referred to is bargaining:

"Bargaining at council session does take place—but not behind the scenes. An example? If a councilman wants a stop sign in a certain place, but the police chief says it should be on a different corner, let's say a block away, the council might split—some with you and some with the police chief. But if another proposal is coming up with a similar problem, you can usually make a compromise and get some to go along with you in exchange for your going along with his request. You have to give a little."

If bargaining does not take place, it is not because of disapproval of the practice but because the stakes are not high or clear enough for bargaining to occur:

"There isn't too much bargaining we can do. It isn't like Congress where they say: If you vote for this bill for me, I'll vote for yours. We don't have this in our city. If it were a bigger city, then you would get this sort of thing happening according to each district. Like a man from one district who wanted something for his district would say he would back a man from another district in something he wanted . . . Horsetrading, that is, but you can't do it in a small city."

Compromise. Although the words "bargaining" and "compromise" were often used interchangeably by respondents, in coding the councils into one or the other category as sharp a distinction as possible is made between them.[27] The task of distinguishing is somewhat eased by the fact that compromise was almost universally approved as a practice while bargaining was either disapproved or denied. For instance:

"Occasionally, but not to a large extent. I have one or two on the council ask to trade votes. I have not agreed. I don't like vote trading. Compromise should be done by looking at one issue at a time. Give in on a point on one issue. I've considered doing it myself on a couple I wanted *very* strongly, but you don't actually know if they really would vote your

---

[27] Not all analysts make this sharp distinction which, in our view, is necessary to achieve analytical clarity. Lewis Froman, Jr., for instance, in *The Congressional Process* (Boston, 1967), p. 23, classifies compromise, along with logrolling and side-payments, as "negotiated bargaining." As we see it, bargaining may *involve* compromising as an activity, but it need not do so. A "bargain" is, by definition, not a "compromise." Ordinary language is helpful: in a "bargain sale," for instance, there is no compromising: the seller surrenders surplus stock of little value to him as stock for something he values more—dollars; the buyer gives up dollars that he can afford to give up for some good that he values more than his dollars. By way of contrast, the kind of higgling or haggling over price on a flea market is a form of compromising behavior.

way. What if you voted the way they wanted, what's to guarantee that they will vote your way? Are they going to give you a slip of paper saying so?"

Compromise, as interpreted here, means exchanging a part of a valued thing in order to safeguard another part. It means settling a disagreement over two alternatives in terms of a third: A wants x and B wants y. The settlement is z. Neither side gets all it wants, but it also does not lose all that might be lost if there were a stalemate. Compromise means avoiding a stalemate by searching for a mutually satisfactory middle ground or finding a common solution which a majority or all can support. For instance:

"You supposedly have five intelligent people and you think something should be accomplished. If you can't get the whole cake, you take what you can get. Same in Congress and State Assembly. I personally would like a golf course, and I personally feel we should plan and zone the surrounding areas to avoid a hodge-podge. There is a lot of opposition to that, so I settle for just a golf course. I aim at a high plateau, but have to settle for something less because otherwise I can't get it through."

In the case where two sides are evenly matched, an uncommitted member may serve as the catalyst of compromise. For instance:

"To a limited extent it probably does. On some issues, somebody will say—I'll go for this but not for that; it has the effect of setting up ranges, limits of action. This can be done for harmony . . . or for power reasons, I suppose. Take the Bridgeway widening. (2 in favor, 2 against). Irish was in the middle. A compromise was proposed which he voted for (one lane in the middle of the street for emergency vehicles only). Sometimes your vote is contrary to your intention. We recently considered the bond issue for parks (which would provide the city with $11,000). The Recreation and Planning Commissions hadn't taken a stand—I wanted them to consider it and take a stand before we voted (on endorsing the bond issue). Two city councilmen called for a vote, so rather than vote no, against parks, I voted yes."

Sensitivity to the position or opinions of opponents as a requisite for successful compromise was articulated as follows:

"Small strategies include finding out what and how intensely other councilmen feel and figuring out and watching how they are moved: logically or emotionally. I'm more logical and level than most. This is my strategy. It's the best one to figure out what's best for the city as a whole and not just what's best for a group or a few individuals that you're interested in or that make the most noise."

A compromise, then, may be negotiated by the parties themselves, or it may be negotiated by an uncommitted member. He will vote with one side or another only if it is willing to make concessions to the other side. In this case the compromise will lead to a majority vote or unanimity.[28] One of two conditions seems necessary for a successful compromise: both sides must be flexible in their approach to decision-making, or both sides must assume that each side has asked for more than it really wants. Both of these conditions, behavioral flexibility and reciprocal expectations, are among the rules of the game that facilitate the legislative process.[29]

Coalition Formation. Coalition is a characteristic of any whole council or faction that is basically united, but as a decisional practice it may be more or less consciously and persistently pursued. A distinction must therefore be made between coalitions that result inadvertently from exchange bargaining, or compromise and coalition formation as a deliberately pursued practice to build a winning majority. Coalition is here defined therefore as a "purposive or goal-oriented alliance between two or more members of a group for some indeterminate period of time."[30] The crucial element in this definition is that the activity involved in coalition formation be purposive and goal oriented.

In coding councils in terms of coalition formation, therefore, a council is characterized as a coalition-forming group only when there is strong and direct evidence that members made deliberate efforts to attract sufficient votes to win for a legislative purpose. Bipolar councils with highly stable cliques or factions may therefore not engage in coalition building as a purposive practice because there is no need for it.[31] Minority factions in stable bipolar situations may attempt coalition building in order to attract a member of the majority and win, or a majority faction may engage in coalitional activity in order to maintain the loyalty of a marginal member. But it does not follow that coalition formation is the only feasible practice to win in these cases.

In general, the evidence of coalition formation in the interviews is unambiguous and strong. A variety of procedures seem to be involved—getting others involved in a proposal, persuasion through reasoned argument

---

[28] This is of course not the only possible outcome. One side may offer side-payments to the uncommitted voter in exchange for his support without making any concessions to the other side. But this strategy may not work if the minority is intense.

[29] As Aaron Wildavsky shows in *The Politics of the Budgetary Process* (Boston, 1964), reciprocal expectations of this sort are often entertained in budget-making.

[30] See Eulau and Lupsha, *op. cit.*, p. 153. This definition is a composite of definitions in William Riker, *The Theory of Political Coalitions* (New Haven, 1962), p. 12, and William Gamson, "A Theory of Coalition-Formation," *American Sociological Review*, 26 (June 1961), pp. 373–82.

[31] A faction is defined as "a stable subgroup whose members are closely related to each other over a long period of time." *Ibid.*, p. 153.

or presentation of facts, taking care of their needs, making promises, and so on. The following examples are anything but exhaustive:

"I plant seeds all the time. If I trust people, I give them the word to get it accomplished. I get someone else to get a job started, to present an idea. I get someone else to pick up the ball. If I got their vote, I got two votes. If I do it myself, I only have one vote. I talk to people in business, industry, etc. to spread word of necessary projects. I feel the pulse of the community at large, and the members of the community."

"Keep the majority of the councilmen with you. Take care of their needs and make them feel important. Appoint their favorite people to positions as long as they aren't complete jackasses. Keeping the four councilmen with me, we four compromise among ourselves."

"We have a five-man board, we need three votes. You have to convince your colleagues it's a good idea. For example, we wanted to build a new city hall. As Mayor, I formed a citizens' committee to go around and feel the public pulse. Have a group with you, not against you, that's the way to get things done."

"If you want to be effective you have to have support. At least two other guys on that council, or things die aborning. A great deal of time is spent trying to convince others. I try to see if I can get support. If I think it is worthwhile and will enjoy the support of the people I try to take it to the council chamber where there will be newspapers, so if it is defeated—somebody has to pay. I try not to embarras my colleagues."

Ministration. The practice called for lack of a better term "ministration" is difficult to define and illustrate. It refers to the formal process of government, the invocation of the council's authority, reliance on law or statute as guidelines in policy-making. The council is seen as having a clear-cut mission or mandate defined for it by legal prescription or electoral approval, and it goes about its work in a formal and businesslike manner. Ministration is a practice that may replace other, more political practices when politics is of low salience, but it may also be associated with other practices. For instance:

"It's simply that we discuss the problem as a group, as a board of directors, and arrive at a decision of the majority. We don't hold an axe over somebody's head and say, 'If you don't vote for this, we don't vote for that.' That's what you mean. We try to operate as a business board of directors. We hire a city manager to run things. If he doesn't, we get someone who does. We make the policy, he takes care of the administering. There is no bargaining, no petty politics."

"You notify the councilmen by letter what a problem is and the facts concerning it, with a very logical conclusion, and try to get a determination of the way they think it should go. If not my way, why? If they don't go along, I take it before the council at a meeting to the people there, if there are enough people there to approve or disapprove. If enough people are told what the problem is and the solution, there should be enough support."

Table 5.6   Decisional Structures and Decisional Practices (in %)

	Decisional Structures[a]		
Decisional Practice	Harmonious ←——————→ Conflictual Unipolar $N = 33$	Nonpolar $N = 29$	Bipolar $N = 20$
General exchange ($N = 39$)	67	45	20
Limited exchange ($N = 24$)	6	31	65
Compromising ($N = 20$)	24	24	25
Bargaining ($N = 24$)	12	35	50
Coalition formation ($N = 21$)	9	38	35
Ministration ($N = 33$)	61	35	15

[a] Percentages total more than 100 since councils may have more than one practice.

Table 5.6 relates decisional practices to decisional structures. The decisional practices seem to be meaningfully associated with the decisional structures. Just as general exchange is practiced in two-thirds of the unipolar, so limited exchange is practiced by an equal proportion of the bipolar structures. The relationship is linear, with the nonpolar councils in the middle of the continuum. Clearly, trust and confidence are widely distributed among the membership of the harmonious unipolar councils. In the bipolar councils, on the other hand, trust and confidence are clustered—everyone may trust someone, but no one trusts everybody.

It is interesting to compare the different patterns for compromise and bargaining. Compromise appears as a dominant mode of decision-making in one-fourth of the councils irrespective of their decisional structures. As noted in the earlier explication of compromise, it is a highly approved form of political conduct; it is not surprising, therefore, that it should be as common among unipolar as among nonpolar and especially bipolar structures, although it may perform different functions from one structure to the other. In unipolar councils compromise probably serves to reinforce the group's basic unity when there are occasional disagreements; by way of contrast, in bipolar councils it may serve as a *modus operandi,* not so much to resolve conflict as to keep it within bounds.

Similarly, we noted that bargaining or trading of votes or favors is not widely approved in the city council culture. It is evidently accepted without reluctance only in those politically charged situations represented by bipolar structures in which it may be conducive to conflict resolution. Bargaining is of course dependent on the presence of fairly well-defined actors or sides in order to serve as a viable practice. Where there are no sides, as in unipolar structures, it should not really occur at all (but 4 of the 33 unipolar councils apparently had some bargaining going on). Similarly, bargaining may be relatively difficult in structures like the nonpolar, where lines of cleavage are unclear and shifting.

With regard to coalition formation, it is rather astounding that more of the nonpolar councils do not engage in this practice, for one might expect it to be most needed in just this kind of unstable and fluid structure. In bipolar councils one should expect coalitional activity only in those with swing voters who from time to time disturb the basic bifurcated pattern. As Table 5.6 shows, only one-third of the bipolar councils practice coalitional politics. In unipolar councils coalitional activity is unnecessary and, as the table also indicates, is practiced in only three councils (possibly to maintain the cohesion of groups at the verge of transformation into another structural type). All of these interpretations are in the nature of speculations that require further investigation.

Ministration—the invocation of the council's formal mandate and authority—is practiced by a clear majority of the unipolar but only by 3 out of the 20 bipolar councils, again with the nonpolar councils in the middle position. Although ministration can serve in all councils as a residual practice on which the council may fall back when other practices do not seem feasible or promising, in some councils it may be purposefully cultivated as the only practice appropriate in decision-making.

Relationships among Practices

Some preliminary comment is needed before the data about associations between decisional practices and other variables are presented. In coding council practices, the components of two sets are treated as mutually exclusive: general and limited exchange as one pair and compromising and bargaining as another. While general and limited exchange are mutually exclusive in logic, the dichotomy of compromise versus bargaining is dictated by the data. Councils emphasing compromise as a practice invariably disavowed bargaining. In other words, while compromise-practicing councils do not bargain, bargaining councils may yet compromise. We assumed that all bargaining councils would also compromise and therefore opted for the mutually exclusive classification. If all bargaining councils are also practicing compromise, coding the latter would not yield any additional information.

Table 5.7 cross-tabulates the three possible types of exchange with the remaining decisional practices. The table provides some interesting insights. In the first place, ministration is predominantly a practice in councils in which neither all or most members, on the one hand, nor some members, on the other hand, exchange views in private. Moreover, few other practices are common in the nonexchange councils. The data support our interpretation of the formal nature of ministration as a legislative practice.

Table 5.7　Exchange Practices and Other Decisional Practices (in %)

| Other Decisional Practices | Exchange[a] | | |
	General $N = 39$	Limited $N = 24$	None $N = 19$
Compromising	33	21	11
Bargaining	21	63	5
Coalition formation	26	38	11
Ministration	36	17	79
No other practice	8	0	5

[a] Percentages total more than 100 since councils may have more than one other practice.

Second Table 5.7 shows some other tendencies which are suggestive. Bargaining, it appears, is quite strongly related to limited exchange. But limited exchange, as noted in Table 5.6, is likely to be a property of bipolar councils. We might infer that bipolar councils with this property are more likely to practice bargaining than bipolar councils which do not have it. Or, more generally, the more conflictual and fractionated the decisional structure, the more it will rely on bargaining as a mode of decision-making.

Although the number of cases becomes increasingly small, we can deepen the analysis by examining the relationships among three property sets—exchange, compromise or bargaining, and coalition formation. Table 5.8 is revealing. While in councils practicing general exchange it makes no difference whether bargaining or compromising intervene in shaping the formation of coalitions, in limited exchange councils the tendency to practice coalition formation noted in Table 5.7 (38%) is measurably increased when bargaining is also practiced (53%). In other words, it seems that the syndrome already partially identified—bipolarity, limited exchange, and coalition formation—is reinforced by the occurrence of bargaining but not by the occurrence of compromising.

The tables are suggestive of the interdetermination of decisional structures and legislative atmosphere, confirming in many respects the assumptions made about the pervasiveness of harmony and conflict in different councils. A collegial atmosphere, as found in the unipolar structure, is associated with general exchange and ministration as decisional practices, although compromising now seems to also be part of the cluster of harmony-producing properties. A tense atmosphere, as found in the bipolar structure, is linked with limited exchange practices and bargaining, somewhat more strongly than in the case of biopolarity with coalition formation.

Table 5.8 Exchange Practices, Compromise-Bargaining, and Coalition Formation (in %)

| | Exchange | | | |
| | General | | Limited | |
Coalition Formation	Bargaining $N = 8$	Compromise $N = 13$	Bargaining $N = 15$	Compromise $N = 5$
Present	37	38	53	20
Absent	63	62	47	80
Total	100	100	100	100

Table 5.9 introduces the decisional structures directly into the analysis. This is done reluctantly because the number of cases is quickly exhausted in a table of this size. However, as inspection of the table shows, enough cases are clustered in the critical cells to justify the procedure. Because interest is in the clustering, raw numbers rather than percentages are employed.

As can be seen, the cases are most conspicuously clustered in the two extreme situations—the unipolar, collegial structures that are characterized by general exchange, compromise, and ministration, and the bipolar, tense structures that are associated with limited exchange, bargaining, and coalition formation. Note might also be taken of the nonpolar, collegial structures with a clustering similar to that of the unipolar, though in weakened form, due perhaps to the ambiguities inherent in the nonpolar situation. Similarly, nonpolar structures that are neither collegial nor tense are more characterized by bargaining and coalition formation than any other practice, suggesting perhaps the adaptive qualities of these practices in this circumstance.

Table 5.9 Council Atmosphere, Decisional Structures, and Council Practices[a]

Council Practices	Collegial			Neither Collegial nor Tense			Tense		
	Unipolar $N = 23$	Nonpolar $N = 12$	Bipolar $N = 5$	Unipolar $N = 8$	Nonpolar $N = 10$	Bipolar $N = 2$	Unipolar $N = 2$	Nonpolar $N = 7$	Bipolar $N = 13$
General exchange	**15**	6	2	7	3	1	0	4	1
Limited exchange	0	3	1	1	4	1	1	2	**11**
Compromising	**6**	5	2	1	1	0	1	1	3
Bargaining	1	2	1	3	5	1	0	3	**8**
Coalition forming	1	3	1	1	5	0	1	3	**6**
Ministration	**16**	6	2	4	3	0	0	1	1

[a] The cases in each cell are numbers and not percentages. Bold numbers represent the critical cells.

It remains to link council decisional practices with governing styles in order to complete the picture. Table 5.10 presents the distributions. The benevolent and pragmatic styles are mainly associated with general excange and ministration—the same properties that are associated with a collegial atmosphere and unipolarity. The political style, on the other hand, is connected with limited exchange, bargaining, and coalition formation, all of which are also associated with bipolar structures.

Table 5.10   Council Governing Styles and Practices
(in %)[a]

	Governing Styles		
Decisional Practices	Benevolent $N = 48$	Pragmatic $N = 15$	Political $N = 19$
General exchange	58	47	21
Limited exchange	15	27	68
Compromising	27	20	21
Bargaining	13	27	74
Coalition building	25	7	42
Ministration	46	67	5

[a] Percentages total more than 100 since councils may have more than one practice.

Conclusion: Configurations of Properties

We have traced in some detail the complex interrelationships among a variety of group properties that are characteristic of legislative bodies. Three types of decisional structure—unipolar, nonpolar, and bipolar—serve as initial organizing foci. It is assumed that each type of decisional structure represents an institutionalization of more or less harmony or conflict in the behavioral system of the legislative group. We see that each decisional structure seems to have associated group properties that tend to be more or less conducive to legislative functioning under varying conditions of harmony or conflict. It is important to reemphasize, therefore, that the decisional structures are technically derived from data totally independent of the data out of which the associated properties are obtained. Moreover, we find that these properties are themselves more or less interdependent. Our purpose here is to show that the decisional structures and their associated properties are related in rather distinct and identifiable configurations.

Ideally, one would want to demonstrate the existence of a configuration

Decisional Structures

Table 5.11   Degree of Association between Decisional
Structures and Related Council Group Properties,
As Measured by Yule's Q

| Council Properties | Decisional Structures | | |
| | Harmonious ⟵—————⟶ | | Conflictual |
	Unipolar	Nonpolar	Bipolar
Collegial atmosphere	+.62	−.23	−.59
Ministration	+.62	−.19	−.68
Pragmatic style	+.59	−.05	−1.00
General exchange	+.59	−.08	−.68
Benevolent style	+.18	.00	−.23
Mixed atmosphere	.00	+.39	−.57
Compromise	−.16	−.01	.02
Bargaining	−.67	+.19	+.52
Coalition formation	−.70	+.45	+.30
Limited exchange	−.75	+.07	+.38
Political style	−.78	+.04	+.71
Tense atmosphere	−.83	−.11	+.83

by multivariate analysis. Unfortunately, the number of cases is much too small and the number of variables much too large to permit this procedure. However, we can summarize the bivariate relationships among all the variables in a manner that makes it possible to observe different configurations of group properties. Yule's Q serves as the measure of association.[32]

Table 5.11 presents the relationships between each type of decisional structure and every one of the associated group properties. The associated properties have been so ordered that the patterns can be easily observed.

[32] The measure Q especially recommends itself for the kind of analysis pursued here. It summarizes the results of a pairwise comparison of all entries (cells) in the table with all other entries. The measure's virtues include that it is unchanged from comparison to comparison by change in marginal frequencies, and it varies between −1 and +1. Finally, as a symmetric measure of one-way association, Q is conceptually clear: it is a measure of the proportionate preponderance of a property in association with another property over all other properties. Put differently, Q is the probability that for every pair of units drawn at random from a population of units, the order of A to Not-A and of B to Not-B will be the same. For instance, in Table 5.11 the $Q = .62$ for the association between unipolar structure and collegial atmosphere derives from comparison of all units in the unipolar category with all other units (those in the nonpolar plus bipolar) and of all units in the collegial category with all units in the other two atmosphere categories. The formula is simple to compute:

$$Q = \frac{ad - bc}{ad + bc}.$$

Unipolarity is strongly associated with a collegial atmosphere, ministration as decisional practice, a pragmatic governing style and general exchange among council members. These are the properties which show the strongest negative association with the bipolar structure. On the other hand, the properties strongly negatively related to unipolarity—bargaining, coalition formation, limited exchange, political style, and a tense atmosphere—are invariably strongly associated with bipolarity. The pattern for the nonpolar structures is much less distinct. In general, the directions of the coefficients are similar to those obtained for the bipolar structures, but in most instances much weaker, in some cases zero. The most notable exceptions are the presence of coalition formation and a mixed legislative atmosphere that is not collegial but also not tense.

The results obtained in Table 5.11 suggest that it might be feasible to inspect the correlation coefficients for all the associated group properties in a correlation matrix that orders them in the same way as the ordering in Table 5.11. Even a quick glance at Table 5.12 shows that the particular properties associated with one or another decisional structure are also more or less strongly associated with each other—in other words, that each submatrix (in a given box) constitutes a configuration of its own that is distinct and unmistakable. In the submatrix that corresponds to the unipolar configuration, all but two of the relationships among the associated group properties are positive, although some are low; in the submatrix corresponding to the bipolar configuration, all the relationships are positive, and none is really weak. The submatrix of property relationships that corresponds to the nonpolar configuration has all the earmarks of ambiguity already noted in connection with Table 5.11.

In general, then, we conclude that the ways in which legislative groups like city councils handle decisions are implicated in a variety of internal structural and behavioral patterns that constitute fairly clearly identifiable configurations. The analysis has been correlational rather than causal because group properties are probably interdetermined rather than causally linked. Moreover, interdetermination should not be confused with multiple or reciprocal causation. It is more than likely that, from a causal point of view, all the properties that constitute a particular configuration are dependent on some extraneous factor that this analysis has not identified. The properties associated with each other in a typical configuration seem to represent patterns of interaction in the council's behavioral system in which it is impossible to distinguish between cause and effect.[33]

[33] As so often, this standpoint is indebted to the insights of Harold D. Lasswell. See Harold D. Lasswell and Abraham Kaplan, *Power and Society* (New Haven, 1950), p. xvii, for a succinct statement of the standpoint. Also see Heinz Eulau, "The Maddening Methods of Harold D. Lasswell: Some Philosophical Underpinnings," *Journal of Politics,* **30** (February 1968), pp. 3–24.

Table 5.12 Degree of Association between Related Council Group Properties, As Measured by Yule's Q

	Collegial Atmosphere	Ministration Practice	Pragmatic Style	General Exchange	Benevolent Style	Mixed Atmosphere	Compromise Practice	Bargaining Practice	Coalition Formation	Limited Exchange	Political Style	Tense Atmosphere
Collegial		.69	.81	.37	.16	—	.41	−.73	−.62	−.78	−.86	−.83
Ministration			.59	−.17	.28	−.08	−.80	.00	.00	−.67	−.90	−.83
Pragmatic Style				−.02	—	−.41	−.15	−.08	−.71	−.08	—	−1.0
General Exchange				Unipolar	.49	.19	.44	−.39	.00	—	−.65	−.63
Benevolent Style						.32	.18	−.77	−.04	−.71	—	−.46
Mixed Atmosphere							−.57	.40	.14	.02	−.12	—
Compromise						Nonpolar		—	.30	−.14	−.12	−.06
Bargaining									.60	.82	.87	.53
Coalition										.39	.47	.58
Limited Exchange											.82	.79
Political Style										Bipolar		.86
Tense Atmosphere												

PART THREE

Legislators' Parties and Constituencies

Introductory Note

The effects of party and constituency influences on the behavior of legislators has been of interest for quite a long time. In this part we have assembled analyses of the impact of partisan orientations on legislators in The Netherlands and Finland, a comparison of the political attitudes of local councillors in Scottish cities and the views of their constituents, and an investigation of environmental feedback from the legislative outputs of state legislatures in the United States.

Hans Daalder and Jerrold Rusk show that the impact of political party in the Dutch parliament is very great, but that the legislative context intervenes powerfully between individual legislator and the extra-parliamentary party. The authors believe that the norms of the legislative institution and the composition of the membership contribute to the existence of trustee or politico role orientations among Dutch MPs within the framework of strong party attachments. Thus parliamentary party discipline exists on the basis of mutual solidarity rather than on the basis of discipline imposed by party organizations or leaders. Then, going beyond Dutch legislators' perceptions of their own party, Daalder and Rusk manipulate their data from interviews with legislators so as to expose legislators' "gestalt" of the legislative party structure.

Pertti Pesonon draws upon a variety of kinds of research on the parliament of Finland to focus upon the function of political parties in linking representatives and the represented. His research points to the role of Finnish parties in structuring the vote for parliamentary candidates where the list system of proportional representation has been used, in recruiting members of the legislature, and in structuring the voting behavior of legislators in the parliamentary setting.

Attitudes toward political issues held by Scottish local councillors and their electors are analyzed by John A. Brand. First, he shows that councillors are distinctively different from their constituents in the strata of society from which they come. Second, he analyzes the degree of aggregate agreement between councillors in each of three communities and their constituents on a set of relevant political issues. Third, he shows the relationships between councillors' own opinions on political issues and their appraisals of the opinions of their constituents. Finally, he shows the degree of agreement among voters and councillors with the position of their own party of the issues. The evidence documents in the Scottish cities the very great distance, both in terms of social origins and political opinions, which may exist between representatives and the represented. Interestingly enough, Labourite legislators appear in these data to be less attuned to constituent opinion than the more conservative party councillors in spite of their more "democratic" doctrine, perhaps largely because they constituted the majority party.

John G. Grumm analyzes the effects of "feedback" on the legislature. Using political system-level indicators for the United States, Grumm attempts to discover linkages between legislative outputs and environmental demands for future legislative decision-making. The analysis suggests the relatively low profile of "tension management" functions required to be performed in the United States legislative systems and leads Grumm to speculate that a more important function of the United States legislature is that of political integration.

CHAPTER SIX

Perceptions of Party in the Dutch Parliament*

HANS DAALDER, LEIDEN UNIVERSITY

and

JERROLD G. RUSK, PURDUE UNIVERSITY

Introduction

Comparative legislative behavior research inevitably meets with a fundamental problem of all studies in comparative politics: differences in political and social context are bound to affect the perceptions and behavior of actors in a political arena that forms only a part of a larger system. Two basic institutional features distinguish the Dutch political system[1] from the United States one, the system on which legislative behavior research has largely focused so far. First, The Netherlands like many other European

---

* This paper is an interim report from a larger study on the Dutch Parliament, undertaken with the assistance of the Netherlands Foundation for the Advancement of Basic Research (ZWO). We received valuable advice from Richard A. Brody, John P. van de Geer, Galen Irwin, Jan de Leeuw, E. E. Roskam, and Herbert F. Weisberg. We are indebted to W. G. A. Hazewindus for computer assistance, and to the Centraal Rekeninstituut of the University of Leiden for the use of their computer facilities.

[1] The two most readily available analyses of Dutch politics in English are Arend Lijphart, *The Politics of Accommodation: Pluralism and Democracy in the Netherlands* (Berkeley, Calif., 1968), and Hans Daalder, "The Netherlands: Opposition in a Segmented Society," in Robert A. Dahl, Ed., *Political Oppositions in Western Democracies* (New Haven, 1966), pp. 188–236. For a full bibliography of foreign language material on Dutch politics, see P. A. Vuurens and R. E. van der Land, "Bibliography of Foreign-Language Literature on The Netherlands of Interest for Political Scientists," in the Dutch political science journal *Acta Politica,* 5 (1969–1970), pp. 476–481.

states has a parliamentary system. The cabinet as the chief political executive organ has no independent electoral mandate, but must be formed on the basis of the strength of parliamentary parties. As no single party in The Netherlands has come even near the majority point for over half a century, this has meant coalition-building among numerous groups.[2] Second, an extreme form of national proportional representation does away with any direct electoral link between individual members of parliament and individual constituencies. Voters choose from a large number of rival parties each of which carries on separate national campaigns. Seats are apportioned to parties on the basis of their national percentage of the valid votes. Within parties, candidates are elected largely according to their predetermined rank-order on the party list.

Both the need to sustain cabinets and the absence of direct ties with distinct groups of voters make party loom large in the perception and behavior of individual legislators. Two fundamental questions arise: What is the relation between the individual member of parliament and his party? How do members of parliament perceive the party system—the "spacing" of parties in relation to one another—which, in turn, determines vital coalition-building processes in the making or unmaking of governments, or in the more incidental voting on legislative actions?

The Dutch case seems to offer an example of a political system in which parties have potentially a very high control over the behavior and perceptions of individual legislators. The dependence of nomination and renomination on internal party processes could give central party organs a strong weapon with which to discipline deviant behavior. The electorate gives a mandate to party, not to individual members of parliament: defiant members cannot bring their case to individual constituents but must satisfy themselves with such hearing as they can get within the party or leave.

The need to sustain cabinets further restrains the freedom of individual members to go against party, at least as far as representatives of "governing" parties are concerned: one need not subscribe to Leon Epstein's thesis that party cohesion is a necessary consequence of a parliamentary system to agree that it is at least a minimal condition.[3] But how is cohesion achieved? Does this imply imposition of discipline, and if so where does power to discipline lie within the party? How do legislators chart the party world? Should decisive power lie with the leadership or the plenary meeting of the parliamentary party? Who should prevail in case of conflict, the parliamentary party or the national executive of the larger party orga-

---

[2] See the detailed table listing all Dutch Cabinets as well as the strength of the chief political parties in the Lower House since 1888, in Robert A. Dahl, Ed., *Political Oppositions in Western Democracies*, pp. 418–422.

[3] Leon D. Epstein, *Political Parties in Western Democracies* (New York, 1967), passim.

nization outside parliament? Is Maurice Duverger correct in saying that the extra-parliamentary party is more likely to dominate the parliamentary group in mass parties than in cadre parties?[4] Or should one rather agree with Robert T. McKenzie's analysis that in a parliamentary system of government effective control *must* lie with the parliamentary party rather than any party body outside it, whatever the institutional or social structure of the parties concerned?[5]

The issue of party cohesion and discipline raises important questions about the role conceptions of legislators. Do they regard themselves as party delegates, or do they claim freedom from party directives, in order to live up to trusteeship concepts of representation? What cues should legislators follow in case they perceive a conflict: party will, electoral will, or their own conviction? And how do members assess the weight of party decision-making organs relative to other forces in the political system, such as the government, the bureaucracy, or interest groups?

A legislator does not look only to forces inside his own party but also across party boundary lines to other parties. He must weigh the chances of forming relatively enduring coalitions among various parties to make and sustain a cabinet or to promote specific legislation. Within the same party, different members may have different preferences that may cause strains in existing coalition patterns. One must therefore seek to understand the different ways members perceive the party system and the location of parties within it, as well as the feeling of nearness or distance between one party and another that different groups of legislators have.

In studying problems such as these, we rely chiefly on data from an extensive oral survey conducted among members of the Dutch Parliament in the spring of 1968. All in all, 141 out of 150 members of the Dutch Lower House cooperated in this inquiry. As refusals came almost exclusively from a few members at the extreme ends of Parliament, our findings are based on a 100% response among the members of the parties which are the leading actors in the system.[6]

We concentrate on questions of general, comparative interest. But a true

[4] Maurice Duverger, *Political Parties: Their Organization and Activity in the Modern State* (New York, 1963), pp. 182 ff.

[5] Robert T. McKenzie, *British Political Parties: the Distribution of Power within the Conservative and Labour Parties* (London, 1967), passim.

[6] This study, originally conceived by Hans Daalder, Nico Cramer, and Sonja Hubée-Boonzaaijer, comprises an oral survey among all members of the Lower and Upper House sitting in February 1968 as well as a number of former members of Parliament; the establishment of a biographical data archive of all members of Parliament since 1848; and an analysis of parliamentary records between 1963 and 1971. Interview refusals came only from the five members of the Communist Party, three members of the Peasant Party, and one member of a dissident Calvinist Party.

understanding of the political background against which these data must be interpreted requires some elementary information on the Dutch political system. This refers, in particular, to the electoral system, the prevailing nomination practices within political parties, and the outlines of the party system as a whole.

The Electoral System. The Dutch Lower House, composed of 150 members, is elected every 4 years or, occasionally, after a shorter interval when a Parliament is dissolved before its constitutional term is over. The electoral law provides for a party-list system of proportional representation, in which votes are aggregated nationally, Seats are divided among numerous contesting parties according to the d'Hondt system of the largest average. There is a very low threshold, since a party qualifies for entry if it secures at least a minimum of $\frac{1}{150}$ of the total national vote.

Technically there are 18 districts which coincide largely with the boundaries of the 11 provinces (the four most populous provinces being subdivided, and the three large cities of Amsterdam, Rotterdam, and The Hague forming separate districts). Parties present individual lists within each district, but they may combine these district lists across the country for seat allocation purposes. Each voter may mark only one candidate. His vote accrues first to the national party and then to the district list. He can effect the election of a given candidate only if this candidate by himself obtains one-half the district list quotient (which is slightly below $\frac{1}{150}$ of the total national vote). But in practice, the overwhelming majority of the electorate tends to vote for the top candidate on the party list. The rank-ordering of individual candidates on these lists, therefore, virtually decides a candidate's chances of election to Parliament. This system makes party rather than individual candidates the chief actors in political campaigns. Individual politicians depend for election much less on special appeal to distinct groups of the electorate than on their personal or group leverage in internal party nomination processes.

Internal Party Nomination Processes. The only stipulation of the electoral law with regard to party elective practices is that parties must register a given name for their exclusive use and that 25 signatures plus a financial deposit are necessary to submit a party list in any district. The law is silent on nomination processes within parties.

Different parties employ different nomination procedures.[7] Most often

---

[7] The subject of nomination has been little studied in The Netherlands. The best single article is I. Lipschits, "De Politieke Partij en de Selectie van Candidaten," in *Sociologische Gids,* 10 (1963), pp. 273–281. Some data on factors in nomination and Sonja Hubée-Boonzaaijer, "Sociale Herkomst en Politieke Recrutering van Neder- to the Lower and Upper House in 1968 have been published in Hans Daalder

the initiative for nominating candidates lies with local party branches, which may submit the names of candidates to regional and/or central party organs. Either the central party executive or some ad hoc nominating body looks over the suggested nominations, possibly adding candidates of its own, and then proposes a rank-order. This proposal is then subject to approval by a larger party parliament, regional assemblies, or a mail ballot of individual party members within each electoral district.

In practice, these formal procedures are shot through with complex political processes. Electioneering considerations may result in the appointment of one top candidate for all 18 district lists or to a spread of top positions among different candidates. The existing parliamentary groups seek to influence the composition of the party list by indicating the desire for a continuation of sitting members, or by emphasizing the need for certain specialists to ensure the quality of future parliamentary work. In many parties there is a built-in tension between regional groups pressing for favorite local candidates and the central leadership circle striving to obtain a balanced list on other than regional criteria. Various stratagems are used to secure the representation of candidates with links to special groups in the electorate (whether women, young voters, or specific interest groups) or with certain expert skills. The jockeying for positions on any or all of the 18 district lists is a complex process far from clear even to insiders in the parties, let alone to the voters at large. We shall presently see to what extent sitting members of parliament approve of the existing practices.

The Main Outlines of the Dutch Party System.[8] Traditionally, five political parties have dominated the Dutch political system. Three religious parties—one Catholic (KVP), and two Orthodox-Protestant, Antirevolutionaries (ARP) and Christian-Historicals (CHU)—have contested or shared power with two nonconfessional parties—the Liberals (VVD) and the Socialists, organized in the Labor Party (PvdA). Of these five parties, the Catholics and the Socialists have been the two largest (occupying one-quarter to one-third of the seats in the Lower House since 1918). The other three parties are much smaller, generally fluctuating around 10 percent of the House. For a long period, the three religious parties together

---

landse Kamerleden in 1968," *Acta Politica,* **5** (1969–1970), pp. 292–333 and 371–416, especially pp. 401 ff.

[8] The most recent information in English on the Dutch party system is in Peter R. Baehr, "The Netherlands," in Stanley Henig and John Pinder, Eds., *European Political Parties* (London, 1969), pp. 256–81, and Arend Lijphart's chapter on The Netherlands in Richard Rose, Ed., *Comparative Electoral Behavior* (New York, in press).

controlled over half the seats. But as their combined strength dwindled, they have formed coalitions since the 1930s either with the Liberals or with the Socialists, while generally maintaining cooperation among themselves. Two other parties have been present in the Dutch Parliament for some 50 years, the Communist Party (with five seats in 1971) and a dissident Calvinist Party (SGP, with three seats in 1971). But they have never affected the operation of the coalition system.

In recent years, the party system has witnessed considerable fragmentation. A new Pacifist-Socialist Party (PSP) has offered a home since 1959 for the non-Communist left with strong anti-NATO sentiments. A new Calvinist party (GPV) emerged at the wings of the Antirevolutionary Party with one seat in 1963. A Poujadist-type of protest party, called the *Boerenpartij* (BP, Peasant Party, called Peasants in this chapter even though their electoral following has tended to be strong in cities as well), made fairly heavy electoral inroads on the existing parties between 1963 and 1967. But it has now lost its momentum because of internal quarrels and lack of voting interest on the part of its one-time clientele.

In 1966 a new party, Democrats '66, was formed that posed a much more forceful challenge to the existing political system. Originating mainly among younger intellectuals, it successfully mobilized younger voters and disillusioned one-time partisans of the older parties behind a program of institutional reform—notably the introduction of a directly elected Prime Minister and the replacement of proportional representation by some type of district system. More recently, left-Catholic dissenters staged a walkout from the Catholic Party and established the Radical Party (PPR). This attempt proved abortive; only a small part of the electorate of the religious parties has tended to follow the three dissident members of Parliament. The party has therefore become little more than a satellite of the Socialist Party with which it formed a temporary electoral alliance in the 1970 provincial elections.

This process of fragmentation resulted in twelve independent political parties in the Dutch Lower House at the time of our survey. None of the newcomers has yet succeeded in forcing entry into government, and each one singly has tended to represent only a small part of the political spectrum. But collectively, they have weakened the hold of the five main system parties. It will be part of our inquiry to determine empirically the political dimensions on which Dutch members of Parliament envisage the resulting relationship of these 12 parties to one another. In order to reduce the complex picture of the Dutch party system to some semblance of order, we have classified the parties in Figure 6.1 according to relatively formal criteria: seniority in the system, size, experience in cabinet office, and the presence or absence of specific denominational ties.

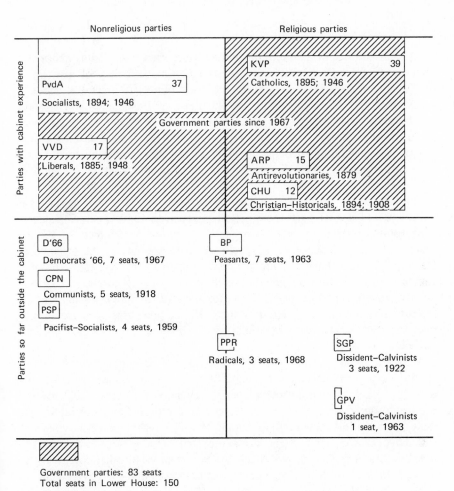

Figure 6.1. A Classification of Dutch political parties by size, seniority, experience in office, and religious base. Number of seats: seats obtained in the election of 1967, or in the case of PPR, number of members of Parliament who seceded from the KVP in 1968, leaving that party with 38 members in our sample (though it actually retained 39 seats, as one PPR member immediately resigned his mandate and was then replaced by a new KVP member from the KVP list). The dates following party names in the upper two quadrants refer to the years of official establishment of these parties; for parties in the lower two quadrants, to the years they first entered Parliament.

The Party and the Legislator

In legal writings of another era, parties were often regarded as abhorrent phenomena bound to destroy the unfettered right and duty of a member of Parliament to vote as his conscience bade him. The arrival of modern party organizations, active both on the floor of Parliament and outside the parliamentary arena, was greeted as a breach of constitutional propriety. Many thought "the rule of parties," the *Parteienstaat* or *Partitocrazia,* a degeneration of democracy. Were not members henceforth to be mere automatons being directed from irresponsible centers of political power?

We have seen that the Dutch electoral system—and the absence of legal control over internal party nomination procedures—give "party" a seemingly total control over the election and re-election of members of Parliament. Members of one party generally do vote together in the legislature. Do members then have any independence left to them? Are they not controlled by forces from outside, compelling them at will to support or oppose a government coalition? Must not men of an independent bent of mind feel restless in these circumstances, either preferring to leave Parliament or else to seek ways by which to regain their freedom even against party?

We seek some answers to such questions by presenting interview data from a survey among Dutch legislators on three main issues: (1) on attitudes of Dutch legislators toward party nomination processes and toward proposals aimed at increasing the element of electoral choice outside immediate party control for individual candidates; (2) on the perception legislators have of the party decision-making structures in day-to-day parliamentary life; and (3) on the effect of party relative to other forces in the system: the electorate, regional and group interests, and the government.

Party and the Nomination Process. If the legislator perceives himself as extremely dependent on internal party forces for renomination, one might hypothesize that he would welcome certain safeguards against central party controls. These might be found in various directions: some degree of tenure security; the possibility of appeal to forces independent of the central party executive, such as the party membership or the wider party electorate; and increased possibilities of carrying an independent campaign to the electorate by an easing of the present fairly rigid control of preference voting. Our survey among sitting members of parliament gives the following results on these general issues.

Little confirmation is found for the hypothesis that members demanded guarantees of greater tenure security. Only 3.5 percent of the members of the Lower House thought there was too little certainty about renomination; 68.1 percent thought existing chances adequate; and 16.3 percent felt that existing securities were if anything too great (some 12.1 percent did not answer this question). Of all members of the Lower House, only 10.6 percent indicated agreement with the statement that parties should renominate sitting members automatically at the time of a new election; 61.7 percent thought renomination should not be automatic; and about a quarter (27.7 percent) argued that a claim for continued tenure should be judged in the light of prevailing circumstances. Clear majorities subscribed to the view that membership in parliament should not develop into a professional career to be held until retirement at 65 years of age and endorsed the statement that "it would be a healthy development if members were to sit less securely in their seats than is true at present."[9] Members failed to claim a particularly strong voice for the parliamentary group in such matters as renomination; when asked where in their view the chief influence should lie in determining renomination—the parliamentary group, the party executive, the party membership, or the electorate-at-large—only 9.2 percent would give absolute priority to the parliamentary party, while only a further 15.6 percent demanded a strong voice for it, suggesting that it share power with the party executive.

If the parliamentary group was not singled out as a decisive prop, neither did members particularly desire central party organs to control renomination. When asked to state their preference between nomination by some central organ alone and a drawing-up of party lists based on a mail-ballot among all regular party members, only 14.2 percent of the members of the Lower House expressed themselves in favor of a decision by central party organizations alone; 44.7 percent of the members—heavily concentrated among the smaller Protestant and liberal parties—preferred the mail-ballot; an almost equal number, 39.0 percent (chiefly Catholics and Socialists), wished to see a combination of both procedures worked out; and 2.1 percent gave no answer. This result tallies with another finding that many more members prefer decisions about renomination to lie with the membership-at-large than with the central party executive. Does this desire for a possible appeal to the party membership also extend to the wider party electorate?

[9] In the course of our study, we also interviewed 50 members who had sat in the Lower House between 1963 and 1967 but were no longer members. Of these 50 members 12 gave up membership because they would not or could not combine their mandate with other political functions (e.g., Cabinet Minister, Mayor, membership of a local executive, or an official post). Fifteen members resigned for reasons of age or health; six for family or other personal reasons. Seventeen members saw their mandate terminated involuntarily: their party lost seats, they were not renominated, or they received too low a place on the party list to get reelected.

The concept of "primary" elections is not familiar to the political culture of The Netherlands, and their introduction has rarely been advocated. We received a broadly negative response to the theoretical proposition itself, phrased in the following manner: "Sometimes people suggest that non-members, sympathizers of the party, should also share in decisions on the composition of the list of candidates, via a system of prior elections or 'primaries.'" In order to allow various shades of opinion to be expressed, respondents were given a card which read: "I am absolutely in favor," "I have some sympathy for that idea," "I have no particular feelings about that," "Actually, I am absolutely against." The responses are shown in Table 6.1.

Table 6.1 Attitudes Toward the
Desirability of Primaries ($N = 141$)

Attitude	%
Absolutely in favor	5.7
Some sympathy for idea	19.1
No particular feeling	1.4
Not so happy with suggestion	12.1
Absolutely against	44.0
No reply; not codable	17.7
Total	100.0

A breakdown by the respondents' party revealed only one party with a strong majority in favor of primaries, Democrats '66. Liberals and Ortho-dox-Protestants were heavily against. Some sympathy was expressed by Catholic members, possibly because within the larger Catholic Party some form of quasi-primary election has long been practiced; although only party members were allowed to participate in nomination ballots, the definition of party membership tended to be so loose that many subgroups in the Catholic subculture could force entry without strong membership credentials.

Judging from these responses, Dutch members of Parliament prefer nomination to rest with internal party mechanisms. They do not claim a prescriptive right to continued tenure, nor do they feel that the parliamentary group should have a strong voice relative to the party membership at large; they react negatively to the idea of widening the choice of candidates outside the circle of paying party members, but at the same time they wish to retain the possibility of appeal to the party membership vis-à-vis central party bodies, however representative in character.

Attitudes toward Individual Preference Votes. Another possibility of appeal against party nomination decisions is provided in the electoral law
concerning individual preference votes. As mentioned earlier, voters may
in theory influence the election of particular candidates placed too low
on the party list to win election otherwise, but they have rarely done so
in practice. Sitting members attribute little importance to personality as
a factor in actual electoral behavior. When asked to choose between three
possible interpretations of electoral motivation: "(1) voters vote mainly
for a party; (2) voters vote mainly for a party but also pay definite attention to the composition of party lists; and (3) voters vote above all for
the person of the party leader," members tended strongly to endorse the
view that the electoral vote is above all a party vote (see Table 6.2).

This makes the possibility of an independent campaign in behalf of a
particular candidate largely an academic matter as far as Dutch politicians
are concerned. Only in the case of one party, the loosely structured
Catholic Party, have such campaigns occurred at all frequently (just as
in this same party, regional interests and various socioeconomic groups
have also made for the most lively group conflict during internal party
nomination balloting). To counteract what it felt was an unwarranted di-
visiveness, the Catholic Party has increasingly resorted to certain controls.
It has reduced the influence of internal party ballots by keeping an increasing number of candidacies outside party ballot procedures, and prior to
an election it has asked for written assurances from candidates that they
will not accept election if chosen by preference vote, thus removing even
the last traces of a direct link between a representative and an individual
group of voters.

This action has caused political debate in The Netherlands on the desirability and constitutionality of such measures. We elicited the views of
the members of the Lower House on this point in a series of three questions: we asked first whether a member chosen by preference votes should
accept election; second, whether respondents approved of internal party
regulations limiting the effect of such preference votes; and finally, whether
they wished to see legislation passed declaring such party regulations illegal. The replies are summarized in Table 6.3.

Clearly, large majorities in all parties outside the Catholic Party are of
the opinion that persons elected by preference votes should unconditionally
accept their mandate. Equally impressive majorities (again outside the
Catholic Party) disapprove of party regulations in this matter. But respondents differ greatly on the question of whether the legislature should
declare such internal party regulations illegal; only members of the Left
Opposition parties are in majority agreement on such action. This leaves
the question of whether members would like to enlarge the possibility of

Table 6.2 Views on Determinants of Voting Behavior—Members of Lower House (in %)

	Nonconfessional Parties			Confessional Parties			% of Lower House (N = 141)
	Socialists (PvdA) (N = 37)	Liberals (VVD) (N = 17)	Democrats '66 (D'66) (N = 7)	Catholics (KVP) (N = 38)	Antirevolutionaries (ARP) (N = 15)	Christian-Historicals (CHU) (N = 12)	
Voters vote mainly for a party	81.1	70.6	85.7	54.8	46.7	41.7	63.8
Voters vote mainly for a party but also pay definite attention to the composition of party lists	8.1	5.9	14.3	31.0	40.0	41.7	22.7
Voters vote above all for the person of the party leader	5.4	17.6	—	2.4	6.7	16.6	6.4
No opinion	5.4	5.9	—	11.8	6.6	—	7.1
Total	100.0	100.0	100.0	100.0	100.0	100.0	100.0

Table 6.3   Attitudes about Preference Votes (in %)

	A Member Elected by Preference Votes Should Accept Election as a Matter of Course	Party Regulations Should Not Tamper with the Effects of Preference Votes	Such Party Regulations Should Be Declared Illegal	N
Socialists (PvdA)	86.5	89.2	56.8	37
Democrats '66				
(D'66)	85.7	85.7	71.4	7
Catholics (KVP)	57.1	35.7	16.7	38
Antirevolutionaries				
(ARP)	80.0	80.0	13.3	15
Christian Historicals				
(CHU)	100.0	83.3	16.7	12
Liberals (VVD)	88.2	94.1	29.4	17
All members of the				
Lower House	78.0	71.6	31.9	141

independent campaigns on behalf of individual candidates. We asked respondents whether they thought the existing legal procedures for the casting of individual preference votes too flexible, adequate, or too rigid. Only 2.8 percent thought the existing regulations too easy, and some 5 percent gave no answer. A majority of the members (51.8 percent) endorsed the existing system, a further 6.4 percent adding that they agreed to the existing system but that it was too little known or used by the voters. Roughly one-third (34.0 percent), on the other hand, thought the prevailing system too difficult. A cross-tabulation by parties reveals that this latter opinion is found considerably more often among the members of the three main nonreligious parties than among the members of the three important religious parties.

This leads to an interesting conclusion. According to Table 6.2, many *more* members of the religious parties than of the nonconfessional parties are of the opinion that personalities count in electoral behavior. But they are less anxious to expand the possibilities of direct personal choice by easing the conditions under which lower-placed candidates can jump ahead of higher-placed candidates on party lists. And they frown substantially more on the idea that the legislator would interfere with existing party rights to control the effect of preference votes. This seemingly ambivalent attitude is probably best explained by the very special political composition of the religious parties. These parties seek to combine voters from very different social groups under the banner of a common religious interest. This requires a very careful balancing of these varied social groups in the determination of party policies and party representations. These delicate balancing acts might be readily upset if at the time of balloting on nominations, or during the election itself, special groups carried on independent campaigns in order to increase their own influence beyond the agreed party compromises. The nonconfessional parties—more program-oriented and socially less heterogeneous—are not faced with such strong centrifugal pressures. They tend therefore to be more permissive about individual preference voting, possibly judging this a somewhat academic issue in view of the actual dominance of party in nomination processes and electoral behavior.

The Legislator and the Party. In view of the strong control of the party over nominations, the perception of the internal structure of party in the day-to-day operation of political decision-making assumes vital importance. To what extent does the individual legislator feel that he should subordinate his own view to party in performing his tasks? And insofar as he does, where in his view should the decisive influence lie within the party?

In actual politics, power relations will undoubtedly differ depending on the type of political party a member represents, on personalities, on the general political situation of the moment, and on particular decisions taken. The policy process itself is best studied by a series of detailed case studies that would probably reveal highly complex and undoubtedly shifting relationships. In this chapter, we are more interested in role concepts, however, and in the perceptions members have of the internal balance of power in their party and their own position within and towards it. In an admittedly somewhat formal model of the decision-making process within party groups, one can distinguish four potential foci of influence: the party leader or party leadership, the recognized specialist within the parliamentary party for a particular field of policy, the plenary meeting of the parliamentary group as a whole, and the national executive in charge of the extra-parliamentary organization. In order to trace the attitudes of members toward these four possible centers of political influence, we inserted a series of questions inquiring where in their view final authority should lie. We paired in successive order the party specialist against the leader of the parliamentary group, the leadership of the parliamentary party against the plenary meeting of the parliamentary group, and the plenary meeting of the parliamentary party against the national executive. In each case we asked what person or body in the respondent's opinion should normally have the decisive voice in case of conflict. Although we offered straight pairs, we noted all comments and introduced recoding categories to refine results where appropriate. The overall results are given in Table 6.4.

Table 6.4　Focus of Authority within Party Groups:
"Who should have the decisive voice?" ($N = 141$; in %)[a]

	Party Specialist vis-a-vis Party Leader[b]	Party Leadership vis-a-vis Plenary Meeting of Parliamentary Party[b]	Parliamentary Party vis-à-vis National Executive
No answer	2.8	—	2.1
Party leader/party leadership	24.8	8.5	—
Depends on circumstances	29.1[a]	2.8[a]	7.1[a]
Party specialist	12.8	—	—
Plenary meeting of parliamentary party	28.4[a]	88.7	74.4
National executive	—	—	5.0
Division of duties between national executive *and* parliamentary group	—	—	10.6[a]
Other	2.1	—	0.8
Total	100.0	100.0	100.0

[a] These alternatives were not offered to respondents, but resulted from recoding afterwards.
[b] In view of the relatively unassuming position of the party leader in Dutch politics, we spoke of the party *leadership group* rather than the party *leader* in the second of our paired questions.

Table 6.4 makes clear that a great many respondents refused to decide on whether the party specialist or the party leader should have a decisive vote. More than half of our respondents introduced new elements like "that depends on the circumstances" or "that is really a matter for the plenary meeting to decide."

Opinions were much more clearcut on the relative role of the party leadership group vis-à-vis the parliamentary meeting. An overwhelming majority rejected any idea of front benchers' politics and put the plenary meeting above the party leadership. We followed this question with a further probe on where, *in fact,* the focus of decision-making authority tended to lie, with the party meeting or the party leadership. This resulted in somewhat greater nuances, even though a large majority still mentioned the plenary meeting; only in the case of the Catholic Party, and to a lesser extent in the Labour Party and the Liberal Party, did any number of respondents regard the party leadership as more powerful than the party meeting.

Pairing the parliamentary group against the national executive resulted in strong endorsement of the principle of autonomy of the parliamentary party vis-à-vis extra-parliamentary pressures even from the national executive. Only 5 percent of the members of the Lower House granted supremacy to party organs outside the parliamentary arena; a further 18 percent offered somewhat equivocal answers, suggesting that this should depend on circumstances or that a division of labor should be arranged, extraparliamentary party organs being responsible for long-term planning and policy, the parliamentary group for short-run political decisions. Overall support for the predominance of the parliamentary party over the party executive was so strong in *all* parties that little confirmation was found for Duverger's thesis that the parliamentary party groups of mass parties are more dependent on extra-parliamentary party organs than those of cadre parties. The data indicate that most Dutch legislators underwrite the thesis of Robert T. McKenzie that a parliamentary system of government requires effective political power to lie with the parliamentary groups.[10]

If these are the perceptions members use to chart the legitimate distribution of power within party organizations, what is their view about the importance of their own convictions in relation to party directives? To test normative views of Dutch legislators on this point, we used an open-ended question. We first asked respondents whether they had ever found themselves in a position in which their party decided to vote one way while they themselves wanted to vote differently: 113 out of the 141 respondents indicated that this situation had occurred in reality.[11] We then asked what in their opinion should be done in such a situation. Coding the various open-ended answers gives the results shown in Table 6.5.

Clearly, there exists a fairly wide spectrum of opinion on this issue. Only a very small number of respondents consider themselves to be the absolute

---

[10] See footnotes 4 and 5.

[11] Peter Gerlich and Helmut Kramer have attempted to investigate this same issue with a slightly different question in the Vienna City Council Study: "Is it conceivable that you might get into a conflict with the party in facing certain problems in the municipal council?" They found a much lower percentage of people who recognized this as possible or probable than we did in our study. This may be the consequence of the far tighter forms of party organization prevailing in Austria. But it could also be the result of differences in phrasing: the term "conflict with the party" has a more ominous ring than the question used in the Dutch study. We have extended the triad "trustee—politico—delegate" beyond the original meaning in *The Legislative System,* to characterize relations not only between representatives and voters but also between the representative and other political forces, such as party, interest groups, etc. Gerlich and Kramer use the terms "individualists" and "loyalists" for the relations between individual representative and party; see Peter Gerlich and Helmut Kramer, *Abgeordnete in der Parteiendemokratie* (Vienna, 1969), Chap. 5.

Table 6.5 Attitude to Take in Case a Conflict Is Perceived between the Will of the Representative and the Will of the Party Group (in %)

	Socialists (PvdA) (N = 37)	Democrats '66 (D'66) (N = 7)	Catholics (KVP) (N = 38)	Anti-revolutionaries (ARP) (N = 15)	Christian-Historicals (CHU) (N = 12)	Liberals (VVD) (N = 17)	% of Lower House (N = 141)
No answer	2.8	—	7.0	—	—	11.8	5.7
Follow own opinion	18.9	28.6	31.0	26.7	66.7	23.5	29.8
Follow in principle own opinion, unless highly important issue	5.4	14.3	14.3	—	8.3	23.5	9.9
Depends on circumstances or issue	35.1	14.2	28.6	33.3	8.3	11.8	24.1
Follow decision of party, unless a matter of conscience	29.7	42.9	16.7	33.3	16.7	23.5	24.8
Follow party decision	8.1	—	2.4	6.7	—	5.9	5.7
Total	100.0	100.0	100.0	100.0	100.0	100.0	100.0

delegates of party organs. On the other hand, only about one-third are inclined to claim an absolute trustee position vis-à-vis party. Some members, though inclined to follow their own convictions, will still qualify this by saying that on really vital political matters they might follow the party ticket. Other members, generally convinced that they should follow party decisions, do make an exception for situations where a matter of conscience is at stake. A majority of the members therefore wish to judge ad hoc, in the light of the issue presented, or the general political situation prevailing.

The party breakdown on this question reveals some interesting differences between parties. Members of the more tightly organized mass parties (Socialists and Antirevolutionaries) tend to attach greater importance to the decisions of the plenary meeting than do Catholics or Christian-Historicals. This need not imply that Catholics or Christian-Historicals show more attachment to trustee concepts than others. We know from other data (not presented in this chapter) that the political prestige of the ARP and Socialist parliamentary parties among all members of Parliament is much higher than that of Catholics or Christian-Historicals. The greater willingness of Antirevolutionaries and Socialists to abide by party decisions may be a result of the feeling that existing decision-making processes in their parties offer adequate guarantees for the due weighing of individual opinions before final decisions are made. On the other hand, individual Christian-Historicals or Catholics may stress the importance of the individual vote, because group meeting procedures leave many of them in a state of some dissatisfaction. Numerous members of these parties expressed the view that their party groups should meet more often.[12]

The Legislator, the Party, and the Electorate. The pervasiveness of "party"—not only in the nomination and election process, but also in the day-to-day actions of the individual members of parliament—cannot help but influence their perceptions of other stimuli in the political system. Many of the standard probes of American legislative research that seek, for instance, to relate the perception and behavior of individual legislators to that of their constituents, cannot be repeated for that reason in The Netherlands. Pretests of such questions with former members of parliament confirmed that respondents could not disentangle a vote for themselves from a party vote. The very notion of constituents is diffuse, and comparisons are only possible on the level of the party group and the party electorate taken as a whole.[13]

[12] This argument is not conclusive, however, as a similar sentiment was expressed by the Antirevolutionaries.

[13] At the initiative of Warren Miller, an elaborate study of representation is underway in The Netherlands by a collaborative research team of the Catholic

We nevertheless hoped to get some idea about the role conception which Dutch legislators have in their relation to the mass electorate. We therefore included in our questionnaire an open-ended item based on our earlier question about possible conflicts between legislators and party groups. We first asked "Did it ever happen to you that you wanted to vote in a particular manner, but that you were convinced that the majority of your voters wanted you to vote differently?" Typically, only a little over half of the respondents (51.8 percent, disproportionately found among Antirevolutionaries and Socialists) recognized this as a situation which had actually occurred, 39.1 percent said it had not, and close to 10 percent refused to answer or thought the question irrelevant. When we followed up with our open-ended question "What would you regard as the right attitude to take if such a situation were to occur?" we obtained highly qualified responses. Many members felt that a deviation between voters and legislators should be a reason for second thought. Some held that they should at least account to the electorate afterwards; others said that they wished to see the party settle the affair, or that they should follow electoral opinion unless a matter of principle or general interest were at stake.

Coding such ambivalent answers is not an easy task. We have attempted to rank respondents in six categories ranging from those who stated that members of Parliament should always follow the will of the voters, via four intermediate steps, to those who unhesitatingly affirmed that their own conviction should always predominate.

We present the results of this grouping in Table 6.6. However hesitantly expressed, an overwhelming majority of Dutch members clearly embrace a Burkean concept of representation in their relation towards the electorate. It is clear from our data that this relationship holds firmly across all parties in our study.

In order to compare the effect of party will and electoral will on the role conception of Dutch legislators, we cross-tabulated the replies to both the party-legislator conflict question and the voter-legislator conflict question. We have collapsed the answers somewhat to make for greater clarity of presentation (even if this meant bracketing those who felt that they should in principle follow the will of the voters, unless the general interest or principle required differently, with the few members who have a more outspoken delegate concept of their role towards the electorate).

Table 6.7 shows the greater emphasis placed on party than on the elec-

University of Tilburg (headed by Philip Stouthard) and the Department of Political Science at Leiden University. Data are being collected on the concept of representation in the Dutch electorate, on the one hand, and two levels of political elites (members of Parliament and a sample of local political leaders), on the other.

Perceptions of Party in the Dutch Parliament

Table 6.6   Attitude to Take in Case a Conflict Is Perceived between a
Representative's Own Will and the Will of the Voters ($N = 141$)

Attitude To Be Taken	Percentage of All Respondents
Follow will of voters	2.1
Follow will of voters unless general interest or principle requires differently	11.3
Follow party program or party decision	4.3
Vote according to own conviction, principle, or insight, but account to voters afterwards	9.2
Vote according to own conviction or conscience, but only after due thought	23.4
Follow own will, opinion	40.4
No answer	9.3
Total	100.0

torate in members' role conceptions. Only 12 members chose a position
that might be described as that of *party-plus-voter* delegate; only 7 members attributed a greater role to the electorate than to the party. Contrasted
to this, 48 members, or about a third of the respondents, advanced a
trustee concept to both electorate and party. A slightly larger number (52)
felt themselves free agents in their relation to the electorate but took much
less definite positions in their relation to the party, either tending to yield

Table 6.7   Trustee—Politico—Delegate Roles in Relation to
(a) Party (b) Electorate (in frequencies)

	Case of Conflict with Party				
Case of Conflict with Electorate	Follow Own Opinion in Principle	Depends on Circumstances	Follow Party in Principle	No Answer	Total
Follow own opinion	48	27	25	3	103
Follow party decision in case of conflict with electorate	4	—	2	—	6
Follow electorate in principle	2	5	12	—	19
No answer	2	2	4	5	13
Total	56	34	43	8	141

Table 6.8   Qualities Deemed Important for Successful Candidates
for Membership in Parliament (N = 141; in %)

Specific Quality	Very Important	Somewhat Important	Of Little or No Importance	No Answer	Total
General political experience and insight	69.5	21.3	5.0	3.5	0.7	100.0
General ability/expertness	56.0	31.9	10.7	1.4	—	100.0
Solidarity with party ideas	53.2	31.2	9.2	5.7	0.7	100.0
Active party membership	32.6	37.6	15.6	14.2	—	100.0
Technical ability/expertness	19.9	44.7	26.9	8.5	—	100.0
Personal reputation in the country at large	10.6	36.2	25.5	24.8	2.9	100.0
Regional representation	12.1	29.8	28.4	27.7	2.0	100.0
Popularity with the voters	4.3	33.3	28.4	31.9	2.1	100.0
Representation of particular social groups	3.5	17.0	28.4	48.9	2.2	100.0

to party or at least taking a qualified stand, not undeserving of the name "politico."[14]

Qualities Required of Good Parliamentary Candidates. To investigate further the role conceptions of members, we confronted them with a series of possible qualities a parliamentary candidate might possess and asked them to grade the importance of each of these in a simple scale ranging from highly important to unimportant. We have rank-ordered these various attributes in Table 6.8 according to the relative importance attached to each of them.

Table 6.8 neatly confirms the earlier finding that party factors loom

[14] Our findings based on responses from the parliamentary elite may be compared with the preliminary findings of a cross-section survey carried out in the spring of 1970 in the context of the representation study discussed in footnote 13. When faced with a similar set of questions, 44.9% of the sample of Dutch voters thought that the opinion of party should prevail as against 38.3% giving priority to the personal opinion of the deputy (15.9% having no opinion and 0.9% not replying). A larger percentage (59.5%) thought electoral will should prevail over the personal opinions of the representative; 21.3% preferred the deputy to follow his own convictions; while 19.2% had no opinion or did not reply. In case of a conflict between party will on the one hand and the will of the voters for that party on the other, about half (49.7%) wished electoral opinion to predominate, a quarter thought the will of party more important (25.9%), while another quarter (24.4%) did not answer or had no opinion. (Data from a national cross-section survey, made available by the Katholieke Hogeschool, Tilburg).

larger than electoral cues. Members may attach greatest importance to such factors as overall ability, but following almost immediately is a general sense of solidarity with party ideas and (to a somewhat lesser extent) experience in active party work. Technical skills come next. Only then follow more electoral qualities, like a legislator's personal reputation, popularity with the voters, regional roots, or special links with certain social groupings. The picture is one of experienced, able men standing well with the party rather than of persons who should be able to draw above all on their personal reputation and popularity or on their role as representatives of particular regions or social groups.

The findings of Table 6.8 reflect ideal role conceptions, not necessarily realities. Our questionnaire also contained an open-ended question asking each legislator how he or she was first nominated to Parliament. We found eight different factors which had played a role, either singularly or in combination. Table 6.9 lists these eight factors and the percentage of members mentioning each of them as having been important in their nomination to Parliament.

When comparing the factors which have played a role in actual nomination (Table 6.9) with the earlier opinions about attributes a legislator should possess (Table 6.8), one finds both agreements and contrasts. In both cases general party activity ranks high. Technical skills are also greatly valued in both instances. But effective ties to social groups (whether organized or not) and regional factors seem to have played a

Table 6.9   Factors Leading to Nomination of Dutch Legislators
(N = 141)

Attribute	% of Members Mentioning Factor[a]	Absolute Number of Members
Special expert skills	35.5	50
Political activity within party	34.0	48
Representativeness for a particular social group (not organized)	24.8	35
Special ties with social organizations	21.9	30
Regional roots	18.4	26
Previous experience in political office	9.9	14
Personal acquaintance with party leaders	7.8	11
Former employee of party organization (research unit, secretariat, etc.)	6.4	9
Other	13.5	19

[a] Percentages represent the proportion of members who mention this factor as having played a role in their own nomination; some respondents gave more than one codable answer.

greater role in actual nomination than in the normative assessment of valuable qualities.

The Legislator, Party, and Group Links. In order to probe further the role attitudes of members in connection with regional and group pressures, we inserted a direct question: "Do you regard yourself, apart from being a representative of a political party, also as a representative of a particular region?" and "as a representative of a particular group in Dutch society?" Almost two-fifths of the members of the Lower House did not regard themselves as in any way a representative of a particular region. A much greater percentage (70.2 percent) denied any representative role in connection with particular social groups.

A more detailed inspection of these figures reveals that members tended to reject any assumption of ties which might be construed as a direct mandate on behalf of regional or group interests. In the case of regional factors, respondents referred vaguely to their region of residence or particular parts of the country to which central party organs assigned them for political work. As for social groups, not only did more than two-thirds of the members of the Lower House disown any representative role here, but even the remainder referred very little to important socioeconomic groups. Nine mentioned ties with the agricultural community, seven with labor, six with small businesses or shopkeepers, two with employer groups. The rest pointed to less-structured groups for which they regard themselves as self-appointed guardians—sports interests, intellectuals, a particular denomination, the poor, the old, and so on. This general attitude stands in considerable contrast to known associational ties that have not only played an important role at the time of nomination (see Table 6.9), but which continue to exist through overlapping memberships between executive functions in interest groups and legislative roles. Typically, only one Socialist mentioned workers' organizations, and not a single Liberal referred to employers' organizations, even though a close reading of the parliamentary record would easily reveal where effective sympathies go.

Should one conclude from this widespread rejection of a specific representative role that Dutch members of Parliament regard the activities of interest groups as of little importance to parliamentary work? Far from it—a very large majority (85.5 percent) were of the opinion that interest groups have a great or fairly great influence on legislative decision-making in Parliament. Only a slightly smaller number said the same about the decisions of the government. But when asked this question about political parties, responses were less clearcut; about half of the respondents thought the influence of interest groups on parties great or fairly great; others deemed it small or said that this depends on individual parties (other parties presumably being more subject to such pressures than their own). Party, then, stands between the individual member and other political groups. Although members readily agree that interest groups influence legislative work, they attribute a greater role to party and reject the assumption that individual members fulfill direct representative roles in behalf of other groups than party. In this field, too, members deem themselves trustees for the *bonum commune,* rather than spokesmen for specific interests.

This implicit placement of party above interest groups and other stimuli can be further buttressed by the results of another question. We asked members of parliament to specify where in their opinion chief power tends to lie in the Dutch political process: with the central government, the parliamentary parties, the national executive in charge of the extra-parliamentary party organization, interest groups, or permanent officials. Each respondent was requested to order these five choices from the most to the least powerful. The answers are shown in Table 6.10.

Table 6.10   Perceived Influence of Five Political Actors
(rank-order, $N = 141$; in %)

	First Choice	Second Choice	Third Choice	Fourth Choice	Fifth Choice	Other or No Answer	Total
Government	56.7	22.7	9.9	3.5	2.8	4.4	100.0
Parliamentary party	17.7	38.3	19.9	12.8	2.1	9.2	100.0
High civil servants	9.9	15.6	16.3	20.6	26.2	11.4	100.0
Interest groups	5.7	12.8	18.4	31.2	27.0	9.9	100.0
Party executives	2.8	2.8	26.2	21.3	39.7	7.2	100.0

Clearly, Dutch members of Parliament put the cabinet first, and the parliamentary groups a close second. Both permanent officials and interest groups receive a much lower average score, with the party executives trailing even further behind. Respondents may judge the role of officials and interest groups highly important, but they have little difficulty in stating that the cabinet and the parties in Parliament play a more important role, not only in the normative world but also in the actual exercise of power.

Conclusions. The general impression that "party" looms large in the daily life of Dutch legislators is amply corroborated by the data discussed in this chapter. A Dutch member of Parliament cannot disentangle an individual electoral constituency from a party constituency; nomination is party-controlled; decision-making in Parliament depends on party-group action; the parliamentary party is deemed a more important center of political power than are interest groups or permanent officials; party also predominates over other stimuli such as electoral will. If members feel themselves free to assume a position of trustee towards voters or interest groups, this may well be because, in their view, party shields legislators from any direct political pressure from these directions.

Does this predominant role of party make the individual legislator feel directly dependent on party? Findings on this point are much more ambivalent. A majority regard their own convictions as ultimately a more decisive determinant in conflict situations than party directives. Practically all members squarely put the plenary meeting of the parliamentary party (in which they have a voice) above the national executive of the extra-parliamentary party, both as a normative ideal and in their assessment of actual power relations. Most members show little anxiety over their chances of renomination; they do not advocate stronger guarantees for tenure security and are well satisfied to leave the decision about renomination to internal party procedures. Most members reject the assumption that the parliamentary party should have a decisive voice in renomination. Many look askance at the proposal that the decisions about nomination should be given to a wider group by the introduction of some form of primary election. There is little active desire to ease the effect of direct preference voting for individual candidates. Large majorities honor the principle that a candidate elected by preference votes should always accept this mandate, and disapprove of party regulations tampering with the effect of electoral preference votes; but the idea of declaring such party regulations illegal finds support only with two opposition parties. In the assessment of desirable qualities for prospective members of Parliament, the possession of political and technical skills, active party identification, and party work rank higher than attributes often more particularly valuable for representative and electoral roles.

In sum, most Dutch legislators orient themselves toward party but do not show that they feel themselves unduly harnessed by party ties. They reject any notion of themselves as party *delegates*. They are thoroughly convinced of the need to keep the parliamentary party free from extra-parliamentary party intervention in day-to-day legislative work. And they do *not* feel themselves implicitly controlled by their dependence on the extra-parliamentary party for renomination.

How do we account for these findings, for they run counter to the views of those who see European parties as typically "ideological parties," and they suggest that particular institutional arrangements in force for nominations and elections need not lead to an excessively strong sense of dependence on party?[15]

[15] According to Duverger: "When there is proportional representation with fixed lists and the presentation of candidates in a strict order the power of the caucuses reaches its zenith." See *Political Parties,* pp. 193–94.

One easy answer would be that the existing system secures the nomination of sedate party faithfuls; hence the assumption of potential conflict between party cues and individual convictions would assume an air of unreality because of the very respondents from whom we drew our findings. Such a simple conclusion would do insufficient justice to the fact that a great many respondents did regard the possibility of conflict between individual and party as a very real issue and that much the larger group saw their role towards party to be one of trustee or politico, not one of delegate.

A more telling explanation might lie in the effect of constitutional norms. Dutch political life has been strongly affected by ancient legal traditions which emphasize trustee concepts of representation. Such norms have become strong "operative ideals," not least because of the traditional presence of numerous persons with a legal training in Parliament which has given debates about political affairs a predominantly legal tone.[16] But such legal doctrines would ultimately be ineffective were it not for the parallel working of political forces.

One such factor is that political parties do not operate in a vacuum. Fear of criticism by its rivals might make a party honor constitutional tenets that it would otherwise be inclined to dismiss.

More importantly, parties must at all times be prepared to adjust their daily actions to the activities of other parties. The need for constant coalition-building—not only at the time of the formation of cabinets but also in a variety of other legislative actions—demands wide discretion of parliamentary parties vis-à-vis extra-parliamentary party organs. Powerful politicians reinforce this tendency by shifting their main activities to the floor of Parliament. A study of the relations between parliamentary parties and national party executives reveals that there are many overlapping memberships in Dutch parties, but it concludes that this tends to strengthen the hands of the political leaders in Parliament rather than to make parliamentary politicians dependent on extra-parliamentary controls.[17] The very multiplicity of political parties in the Dutch system—and the concomitant need for flexible policies on the part of the major parties in the

---

[16] The percentage of members in the Dutch Parliament with legal backgrounds has varied between 20 and 30 percent since 1930. See F. G. Moquette, "Het Nederlandse Parlement: gegevens over leeftijd, lidmaatschapsduur, opleiding, beroep, wetgevende ervaring en bestuurspraktijk," *Acta Politica*, 1 (1965–1966), pp. 112–153, in particular pp. 131 ff. See also the articles by Daalder and Hubée-Boonzaaijer mentioned in footnote 7, pp. 299 ff. Most persons with legal training were not practicing lawyers but former government officials or executives of interest groups.

[17] I. Lipschits, "Partijbestuur en Fractie," *Acta Politica*, 1 (1965–1966), pp. 154–171 and Idem, "De Organisatorische Structuur der Nederlandse Partijen," *Acta Politica*, 2 (1966–1967), pp. 265–296.

system—tend therefore to shift the locus of power within parties towards their parliamentary wings.

A concentration of power in the parliamentary groups might still imply strong disciplinary control over individual legislators. Little evidence is found of this in The Netherlands. Parties are fairly cohesive, but they are so more by mutual solidarity than by imposed discipline. Various factors may explain this fact. Small size makes for collegial rather than hierarchical relationships: not a single party group in the Dutch Parliament has more than 40 members, and all but two have less than 20. Even within such small party groups, one finds a deliberate balancing of diverse subcultural interests. This makes daily decision-making within the party a matter of careful adjustments among relatively autonomous actors. Dutch parliamentary life is characterized by a tendency to leave matters to recognized specialists within each party. Specialists across parties often find each other in common policies that other members of the Chamber do not readily challenge. Party specialists thus develop a fairly wide discretionary field, which is reinforced by the willingness of specialized members of Parliament to respect the specialism of colleagues in other fields.

This may help explain, then, our finding that Dutch deputies honor party *and* demand at the same time a position of considerable independence from it. It also makes one understand why most legislators are not very anxious to expand the role of electoral choice—this might increase the element of personality in politics at the expense of destroying the careful "politics of accommodation" which is characteristic of intra-party as well as of inter-party relations.[18]

The Legislator and the Party System

Our focus thus far has been on the way legislators perceive their own party, and on the effects these perceptions have on role conceptions and power images. But the political domain of legislators extends beyond the confines of their own party to the relations among parties. In the absence of single-party majorities, these relations assume vital importance; they determine the composition of cabinets and the passing or blocking of particular legislative actions. How then do legislators perceive the relations of parties to each other and to their own party? What "maps" do they use to interpret the party system?

The Basic Data: Rank-Order Preferences. As a basis for ascertaining the empirical dimensions used, we asked Dutch members of Parliament the following question:

[18] The reference is to Arend Lijphart's well-chosen title for his book on Dutch politics. (See footnote 1.)

"In foreign studies a good deal of attention has been paid to the question of what distances exist among different parties. We have been asked to investigate this problem for The Netherlands and we would very much appreciate your help. Here are some cards. Each card has the name of a party which is now represented in Parliament. Would you please arrange these cards in such order that the party on top is the party to which you yourself feel closest, the next one the second-closest, and so on?"

Each respondent was given cards of all 12 parties sitting in the Parliament at the time of the 1968 survey except his own. As is evident from the question wording, we asked the legislators to rank the parties without imposing a frame of reference on the rating system they used. Hence individual legislators may have used different criteria in expressing their preferences. Our task is to uncover the dimensions or "mappings" used to rank the parties from the preference orders given.

Before doing this, it is useful to survey some of the descriptive features of the data. Central tendency and dispersion figures can give us an overview of the assessments accorded to various parties. By integer scoring the preferences given, from 11 (party most preferred after one's own party) to 1 (party least preferred), we obtained the mean and standard deviation figures shown in Table 6.11[19] Also included in this table are the percentage distributions of first, second, next-to-last, and last place choices across the set of parties.

From an inspection of the mean values in Table 6.11, one can easily detect that the traditional system parties (the three religious parties —ARP, CHU, and KVP—as well as the Socialist PvdA and the Liberal VVD) rank relatively high. So do two minor parties, the radical PPR and the Democrats '66. All other minor parties—the Pacifist (PSP), the two minor Calvinist parties (GPV and SGP), the Peasants (BP), and the Communists (CPN) rank very much lower. This is especially true for the Communists, who collect 56 percent, and the Peasants, who collect as much as 80 percent of the two lowest ratings members of Parliament could give.[20]

---

[19] We did not include the score of "12" (the legislator's own party) in these computations since it would bias the average preference value of each party by the number of members it has in the Lower House. However, the score of "12" denoting one's own party is a vital piece of information in each legislator's preference ordering of parties, so we have retained it in the important correlational and dimensional analyses to be presented later in this paper.

[20] The somewhat higher rank given to the Communist Party as opposed to the Peasant Party may be partly a result of the very high popularity of the leader of the Communist Party in the Lower House, Marcus Bakker. He in fact obtained the highest score when we asked members of the Dutch Parliament in 1968 to name fellow members who did particularly good work in the Parliament.

Party	Mean Preference[a] (N = 186–189)	Standard Deviation[a] (N = 186–189)	First Preferred Party After Own[b] (N = 138)	Second Preferred Party After Own[b] (N = 137)	Next to Most Disliked Party[b] (N = 114)	Most Disliked Party[b] (N = 121)	Number of Respondents in Sample (N = 141)	Number of Seats in Parliament (N = 150)
Antirevolutionary Party (ARP)	9.2	1.7	29%	15%	0%	0%	15	15
Socialist Party (PvdA)	8.2	2.1	9	11	0	0	37	37
Christian-Historical Union (CHU)	8.0	2.4	17	24	1	1	12	12
Radical Party (PPR)	7.8	3.0	28	8	3	2	4	3
Catholic Party (KVP)	7.6	2.0	4	15	0	0	38	39
Democrats '66 (D'66)	7.6	2.2	6	17	2	0	7	7
Liberal Party (VVD)	6.9	1.9	3	3	1	1	17	17
Pacifist Party (PSP)	5.2	2.6	1	5	12	2	4	4
Dissident Calvinist Party (GPV)	4.3	2.0	1	1	12	2	1	1
Dissident Calvinist Party (SGP)	4.0	2.0	1	0	25	0	2	3
Communist Party (CPN)	2.9	1.8	1	1	25	31	—	5
Peasant Party (BP)	2.0	1.4	0	0	19	61	4	7
Total			100%	100%	100%	100%		

[a] These values are computed from an integer scoring of the legislators' party preference orders—assigning the numbers 1 through 11 to indicate the rank ordering of parties from the party least preferred (1) to the party most preferred after one's own party (11). We could also have used a converse scoring system, from 1 (party most preferred after one's own party) to 11 (party most disliked). For reasons of graphical presentation in Figure 2, where a long bar expresses closeness and a short bar distance, we have preferred scoring first preferences as a high figure and last preferences as a low figure. Average rankings on the reversed scoring system can be calculated by subtracting the mean scores in this table from the constant "12".

[b] Cases with ties are excluded.

The standard deviation figures (column 2 of Table 6.11) suggest stronger agreement on the placement of some parties than on others.[21] Apart from the consistently low rankings given to the Communists and Peasants, members tend to agree on giving a very high place to the Anti-revolutionaries and a somewhat low placement (at the bottom of all the main system parties) to the Liberal Party. There is no such overall agreement on the placement of some of the left-oriented parties (PSP and, above all, PPR) and of the Christian-Historicals. For a closer insight, we have broken down these average rankings into separate ratings given by members of the five largest parties (the three confessional parties, the socialists, and the liberals); the average rankings of all parties as given by the memberships of these five parties are represented in the bar graphs of Figure 6.2.

Figure 6.2 confirms the relatively low rank given to the VVD by members of most parties (except the CHU); it shows that the scores for the Radicals (PPR), and to a somewhat lesser extent Democrats '66, are strongly influenced by the high scores given to these parties by members of the Socialist PvdA, and it suggests differences among party memberships in their preferences of some smaller parties over others. While the Socialists give relatively high scores to Pacifists and Communists, members of the other parties tend to rank these parties even below the smaller dissident Calvinist parties SGP and GPV. (Christian-Historicals and Liberals also put the Peasants slightly above the Communists.) But at the same time, Figure 6.2 reconfirms the fact that effective sympathies of the party memberships go mainly to the five traditional parties, and to a lesser degree (but notably so for the Socialists) to the two newer opposition movements of Democrats '66 and the Radicals (PPR).

A Refinement of the Analysis: The Kruskal Preference Similarity Space. For a more refined representation of the data, we have calculated Pearson correlations on the rankings given to the parties by our legislative respondents. These correlations look at the preference order data in a certain way—noting the covariation in rank scores given to each pair of parties. We interpret the results as follows: parties having substantial positive correlations are being perceived in a similar fashion by legislators; pairs of parties having negative values are being viewed as quite dissimilar from one another; and correlation values close to zero indicate an absence of shared perceptions of the parties concerned.

By scanning the correlation matrix in Table 6.12, one readily discovers definite patterns of shared variance. If one draws a line by column and

---

[21] These standard deviations should be compared not only to each other but also to the value of 5.0—the maximum value possible for a party on our 11-point scale.

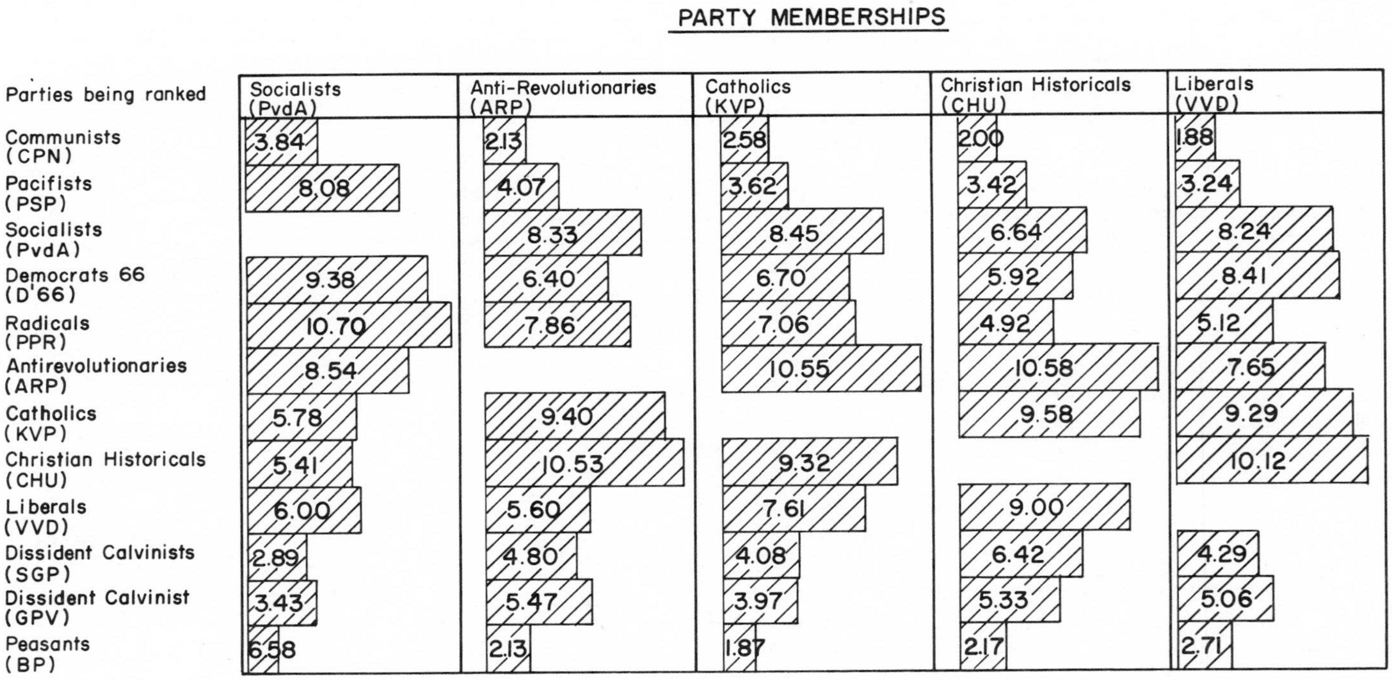

PARTY MEMBERSHIPS

Parties being ranked	Socialists (PvdA)	Anti-Revolutionaries (ARP)	Catholics (KVP)	Christian Historicals (CHU)	Liberals (VVD)
Communists (CPN)	3.84	2.13	2.58	2.00	1.88
Pacifists (PSP)	8.08	4.07	3.62	3.42	3.24
Socialists (PvdA)		8.33	8.45	6.64	8.24
Democrats 66 (D'66)	9.38	6.40	6.70	5.92	8.41
Radicals (PPR)	10.70	7.86	7.06	4.92	5.12
Antirevolutionaries (ARP)	8.54		10.55	10.58	7.65
Catholics (KVP)	5.78	9.40		9.58	9.29
Christian Historicals (CHU)	5.41	10.53	9.32		10.12
Liberals (VVD)	6.00	5.60	7.61	9.00	
Dissident Calvinists (SGP)	2.89	4.80	4.08	6.42	4.29
Dissident Calvinist (GPV)	3.43	5.47	3.97	5.33	5.06
Peasants (BP)	6.58	2.13	1.87	2.17	2.71

Figure 6.2. Average preferences of the members of five main parties for all other parties in the Dutch system, Dutch Lower House, 1968. These mean values are computed from the same integer scoring system as described in footnote 1 to table XI. High values indicate high average rankings and low values the converse.

Table 6.12 Correlations of Party Preferences[a]

	CPN	PSP	PvdA	D'66	PPR	ARP	KVP	CHU	VVD	BP	SGP	GPV
Communists (CPN)		.53	.35	.20	.29	−.19	−.40	−.52	−.32	−.22	−.33	−.41
Pacifists (PSP)			.65	.53	.61	−.28	−.59	−.77	−.49	−.37	−.58	−.54
Socialists (PvdA)				.56	.69	−.26	−.48	−.73	−.46	−.47	−.64	−.60
Democrats '66 (D'66)					.53	−.38	−.45	−.63	−.16	−.36	−.65	−.49
Radicals (PPR)						−.12	−.44	−.71	−.59	−.43	−.65	−.57
Antirevolutionaries (ARP)							.49	.40	−.23	−.23	.07	.04
Catholics (KVP)								.62	.30	−.07	.15	.05
Christian-Historicals (CHU)									.46	.20	.52	.45
Liberals (VVD)										.21	.21	.21
Peasants (BP)											.51	.49
Dissident Calvinists (SGP)												.77
Dissident Calvinists (GPV)												

[a] All correlations are Pearson *r*'s. They are computed for pairs of parties from the ranks given to these parties by the legislators. These ranks are integer scored from 1 (party least preferred) to 12 (party most preferred, the respondent's own party) for each legislator's preference ordering of parties.

row separating the Radicals (PPR) and the Antirevolutionaries (ARP), one can see that the positive correlations appear in the upper left and lower right quadrants of the matrix and the negative values in the upper right quadrant of the matrix. Three definite clusters appear, consisting of (1) a left cluster composed of Communists, Socialists, Pacifists, Radicals, and D'66; (2) a cluster of the three religious parties composed of Catholics, Antirevolutionaries, and Christian-Historicals (one may note that the Liberals have negative correlations with the Antirevolutionaries but positive correlations with the Catholics and the Christian-Historicals); and (3) a small cluster of the minor dissident Calvinist parties and the Christian-Historicals (with which Liberals and Peasants also show a low positive correlation). The consistently negative signs in the upper right corner of the matrix as contrasted with the positive signs in the upper left corner underline the existence of a significant cleavage between a left bloc and the other parties.

To get a clearer visual representation of possible dimensions in these correlations, we have employed a multidimensional scaling technique first developed by Shepard and later improved by Kruskal. Generally referred to as "Kruskal scaling," this technique uses the correlation information contained in Table 6.12, interpreting the correlations as monotonic with distances—the closer to +1.0 the correlation between two parties, the closer together should be their corresponding points in a geometric representation.[22] Hence this nonmetric technique makes weaker assumptions than factor analysis; it only requires that the ordering of the correlation values be regarded as meaningful data and not the exact values themselves. As our data are derived from rank-order information in the first place, this makes the Kruskal technique particularly suitable for our purposes.[23]

To see whether a simple left-right ordering could explain the correlations found, we first attempted a one-dimensional solution. Figure 6.3 does show

[22] A description of the Kruskal scaling method is contained in the following: J. B. Kruskal, "Multidimensional Scaling by Optimizing Goodness of Fit to a Nonmetric Hypothesis," *Psychometrika* (March 1964), pp. 1–27; J. B. Kruskal, "Nonmetric Multidimensional Scaling: A Numerical Method," *Psychometrika* (June 1964), pp. 115–130. We have used for our analysis the computer program Professor Kruskal developed from the Shepard-Kruskal theory on scaling analysis.

[23] Even though only the rank-order of the correlation values is being considered, it is, nevertheless, true that we have used an interval-level coefficient, the Pearson correlation (r), as input to the Kruskal program. To check this procedure, we inputed a Kendall tau b (rank-order) correlation matrix of the parties into the it is, nevertheless, true that we have used an interval-level coefficient, the Pearson r matrix. The reason for this is that the rank-order of correlation values (tau b and r) for pairs of parties is very close—the Spearman's rho value for such ranks being .98.

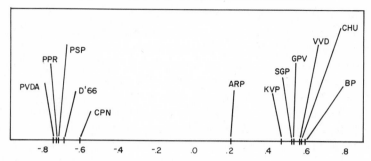

Figure 6.3. A unidimensional view of the Kruskal party space, Dutch Lower House, 1968.

a definite split between a left cluster and the other parties. The ordering of parties from left to right also has some correspondence to a political scientist's view of the situation, but, nevertheless, discrepancies do exist in the placement of parties within each cluster (e.g., the Communist Party should be to the left of the Socialist PvdA). Moreover, a high stress value for this figure indicates that a one-dimensional solution is not the best representation of the data—prompting us to try more dimensions.[24]

The two-dimensional solution provides additional discrimination among the parties, while still retaining the basic split between a left cluster and the other parties. The upper right quadrant of Figure 6.4[25] contrasts the religious parties with the left cluster, and the lower right quadrant contains two parties which share a negative characteristic in belonging neither to the left cluster nor to the world of the religious parties—the liberal VVD

[24] The Kruskal program computes a "goodness of fit" statistic called "stress" which measures the degree of monotonic fit between the data (the correlation values) and the distances between the parties in a given dimensional space. For this and other analyses in this paper, we encountered high stress values in the one-dimensional solutions, which necessitated our trying two- and three-dimensional solutions for a better fit to the data. The two-dimensional solutions gave low stress values—rated "good" to "excellent" in Roskam's terminology when using "stress formula two"; see E. E. Roskam, *Metric Analysis of Ordinal Data in Psychology* (Voorschoten, 1968) p. 41; the three-dimensional solutions hardly improved on this. For these reasons and because of the interpretability of the results, we show only two-dimensional spaces in the rest of this chapter.

[25] A few technical features of Figure 6.4 should be noted for a proper understanding of this space. The final positioning of the axes was determined by hand rotation. A varimax rotation yielded a fairly similar result. This procedure of hand rotation, comparing it with the corresponding varimax rotation, was also followed for the other figures to be discussed below. One should also be aware that the origin of such figures is arbitrary, in this case being the centroid of the coordinate axes involved. Hence, the main interpretation of the points (parties) in space should be with regard to their relative positioning and order vis-à-vis one another.

and the Peasant Party (BP). We have confidence in this positioning of the parties since the solution has a low stress value and, at the same time, fits well with "a priori" notions of the traditional typology of Dutch parties. The solution also agrees reasonably well with common-sense notions of the location of individual parties on each of the two dimensions underlying Figure 6.4—a left-right dimension on the horizontal axis and a secular-religious dimension on the vertical axis.[26]

Essentially, then, the Kruskal technique allows us to construct a preference similarity space as a composite result of the preference data derived from the large majority of Dutch legislators sitting in 1968. Starting from computed correlations between pairs of parties, this technique sorts parties according to their perceived similarity, using two dimensions for an adequate representation of the data. It thus offers an insight into the way Dutch members tend to classify parties in relation to each other.

But the Kruskal technique has its limitations, as all techniques do, in only being able to look at certain aspects of the data. The Kruskal tech-

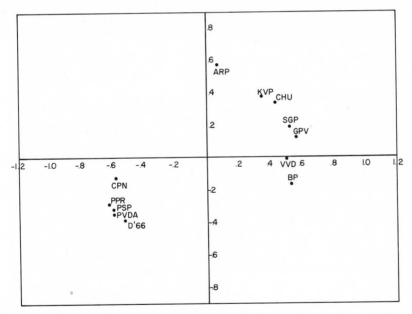

Figure 6.4. A two-Dimensional view of the Kruskal party space, Dutch Lower House, 1968.

[26] In order to check our findings, we also ran the Kruskal program on comparable data from 70 members of the Dutch Upper House. The result was virtually the same as that for the members of the Lower House, which gave us considerable confidence in our findings.

nique focuses on correlations—condensing individual preference orders into a series of correlation values measuring the covariation in ranks between pairs of parties. It does not deal with the individual preference orders per se, and for that reason we next concentrate on the actual preference order data—just as the legislator gave them to us—and employ a scaling technique which uses these data in this form.

A Second Map of the Preference Space: Coombs' Multidimensional Scaling. To treat the individual preference orders in their own right, we have employed a multidimensional scaling technique developed by Clyde Coombs for the type of preference data we have here. The Coombs' scaling technique assumes that each individual legislator has a point of maximum preference in a given dimensional space (his "ideal point") and that he ranks the parties in terms of their increasing distance from that ideal, attempting to locate the parties in space so as to fit this assumption as closely as possible for all legislators.[27] Operating in this basic fashion, the Coombsean technique obtains a very satisfactory two-dimensional solution for our data. (See Figure 6.5.)

The picture resulting from the Coombsean technique shows both points of congruence and dissimilarity with the corresponding picture of the 12 parties originating from the Kruskal technique. Basically, the left-right dimension shown in the Kruskal preference similarity space reappears (with some of the extreme parties moving further to the left—see the placement of PSP—or to the right, e.g., the Peasant Party). There is also a marked clustering on the left between Socialists, Radicals, and Democrats '66 who form the main opposition parties, but this is now balanced on the right with an equally clear cluster of the government parties—the three religious parties and the Liberal Party. This movement of the main religious parties nearer to one another and to the Liberal Party illustrates the effect of looking at the actual preference orders as distinct from similarity correlations. Dutch members of Parliament may perceive substantial differences between the religious parties and a secular party like the Liberal Party, but their actual preference rankings pull these parties closer together. Phrasing the same point differently: when one takes the actual preference orders for particular parties into account, the earlier cleavage between religious and

---

[27] A description of this technique can be found in Clyde H. Coombs, *A Theory of Data* (New York, 1964), pp. 80–121. In this chapter, we have used a computer program developed by E. E. Roskam that adapts Coombsean scaling to the multidimensional case. It also calculates a "stress" statistic which measures the monotonic fit between a person's rank-ordering of parties and the distance between his "ideal point" and these parties in a given dimensional space. As indicated in footnote 24, the two-dimensional solution showed a low stress value and hence is included in this paper.

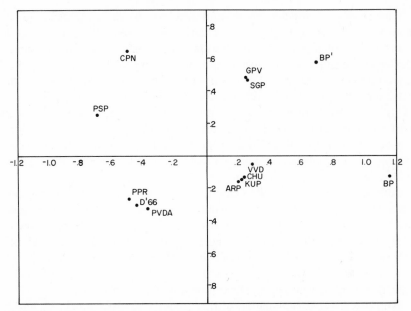

Figure 6.5.   A two-Dimensional view of the Coombsean party space, Dutch Lower House, 1968.

nonreligious parties (found in the preference similarity space) is replaced by a new dimension which separates the major government *and* the major opposition parties from five minor parties: Communists, Pacifists, Peasants,[28] and the two dissident Calvinist parties. This is a point of vital importance.[29]

[28] There is some ambiguity about the placement of the Peasant Party (BP) in the Coombsean space. Our original computer runs tended to locate this party at the far side of the lower right quadrant, although at a considerable distance from the cluster of government parties. This position is indicated in Figure 6.5 as BP. We assumed that the intense dislike of this party (having received 61% of the last-place choices of all respondents) worked in a unique fashion to push it off the side of the space, disrupting its expected flow to the upper right quadrant of the picture. We had hoped to confirm this notion by finding a "pro-anti BP factor" in the three-dimensional solution of the space, but the slight explanatory power the third dimension provided did not indicate the presence of any such factor. As a further test, we calculated the stress value with the Peasant Party located at the position indicated in Figure 6.5 as BP′, keeping all other party points in their previous place. We found that the stress value went up from .119 to .121, a trivial difference. We are inclined to regard this latter location, BP′, as politically more relevant than the somewhat curious placement of BP.

[29] See the methodological note at the end of the chapter concerning comparison of Coombsean and Kruskal techniques.

The results of Figure 6.5 depend heavily on the preferences of the deputies of the *major* parties. They agree on differentiating parties along a left-right dimension, clearly marking the existence of a government cluster and an opposition cluster. But in addition to this left-right dimension, they use a second dimension that definitely separates seven "in" parties on the one hand from five "out" parties on the other. Whatever extra sympathy there might exist in the Protestant parties for the two dissident Calvinist parties, or, in the Socialist Party for the Pacifist Party, does not really pull the main system parties apart. Their members prefer *crossing* traditional ideological lines to hugging the minor dissident parties in their own ideological subculture.

Although the effect of the second dimension is very readily apparent, its nature is less immediately obvious. The distribution of parties along this dimension corresponds rather closely to the average rank-order preferences accorded to them, so that suggestions of a "popularity-unpopularity" dimension come to mind. Speaking in a little more elegant fashion, this dimension could be labeled a "system-nonsystem" dimension, an "eligible-noneligible" dimension, or a "player-nonplayer" dimension.

Another possible explanation of this second dimension might be an "intensity of ideology" factor. One could argue that at least four of the five small parties in the upper two quadrants of Figure 6.5 are heavily ideological in nature, denoting a type of party elsewhere dubbed "integralist" (i.e., a party which prefers the surety of ideological position above the potentiality of office).[30] The fifth party, BP, is more a general "protest" party; its ideology is less developed and less restricted to any one subculture than is true of the ideologies of the other minor parties. In contrast, the major parties in the lower quadrants would appear as parties more pragmatically concerned with policies and the possibility of entry into the cabinet than with intense ideological concerns.

The Coombsean solution, then, reflects, more than the Kruskal picture presented in Figure 6.4, a clear "mapping" of the dimensions which seem relevant to the actual interaction of parties with one another. Giving full scope to differences in rank-ordered preferences between parties, it shows the distances which are thought to exist among parties, revealing meaningful clusters of parties. It portrays a clear differentiation between parties regarded as potentially *in* the system of day-to-day parliamentary politics, and parties *outside* the system. Within the main system, the Coombsean

---

[30] See Hans Daalder, in Robert A. Dahl, Ed., *Political Oppositions in Western Democracies*, pp. 225 ff. A somewhat fuller treatment is given in H. Daalder, "De Kleine Politieke Partijen—een voorlopige poging tot inventarisatie," *Acta Politica*, **1** (1965–1966), pp. 190–196.

picture presents a realistic differentiation between leftist parties in opposition to the government and the parties forming the government.

The Coombsean Preference Space for the Five to Seven Main Dutch Parties. Figure 6.5 is a composite picture of the party system: it tells us the location of parties in relation to one another in a two-dimensional space on the basis of the scaled preferences of all deputies who responded to our request to rank-order parties in terms of their closeness to or distance from themselves. Therefore it offers an overview of the distances thought to exist among parties on the basis of judgments expressed by all respondents on all parties.

This figure raises a problem of some importance, however. It is based on the assumption that Dutch legislators discriminated among parties with equal precision, regardless of whether they ranked parties high, low, or in the middle of their preference scale. We know from our actual interviewing experience that this assumption is not completely valid. Most members of the major parties have a much more definite opinion about their relative preferences for the other major parties in the system than for some of the minor parties (even though the very lowest places given must be regarded as possibly more relevant than particular distinctions made in seventh, eighth, or ninth choices, for example). By treating all parties presented as rank-order stimuli as though they were equal, the Coombsean technique may have given too much importance to marginal differences in preferences expressed for the lower-ranking, less important parties in the system.

In order to correct for this effect, we have made new computer runs using as stimuli not all 12 parties, but only the parties we know from Figure 6.5 to be the main actors in the actual system of coalition politics. We have thus eliminated Communists, Pacifists, Peasants, and the two dissident Calvinist Parties as possible stimuli. Three separate runs were made—a five-party run using the chief system parties as the only stimuli (Figure 6.6*a*), a six-party run adding Democrats '66 as a stimulus point (Figure 6.6*b*), and a seven-party run including Democrats '66 *and* Radicals with the five major system parties (Figure 6.6*c*). In each case, we have confined the evaluation of parties to just the party memberships involved; hence the five-party run reflects the preferences of the party memberships of the five main parties only, the six-party picture adds the preferences of six D'66 members, and the seven-party picture comprises the preferences from an additional four Radical members. This simultaneous inclusion of (1) more party stimuli and (2) the preferences of the party memberships concerned was deliberate. It reflects our aim to construct the party spaces which are most meaningful to the decisive actors in the Dutch system. Figure 6.6*a* portrays the party preference space of the five main

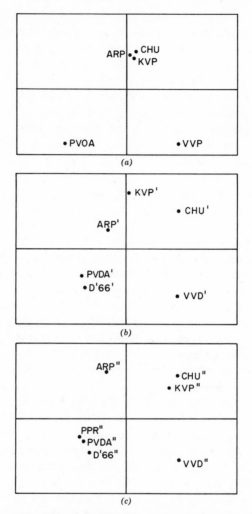

Figure 6.6 Party preference space for five, six, and seven parties, Dutch Lower House, 1968. 6(*a*) Party preference space for *five* parties. 6(*b*) Party preference space for six parties. 6(**c**) Party preference space for seven parties.

parties for one another, thus limiting the analysis to those legislators and parties who traditionally preempted the formation of cabinet coalitions in Dutch politics. The addition of Democrats '66 and later of the PPR-Radicals to the space corresponds to the arrival of new forces in Dutch politics, which forced the legislators of the five system parties to determine their own attitude toward these new parties, while at the same time including these latter party members as possible new actors in coalition politics.

What conclusions can we draw from the three different pictures in Figure 6.6? In all three pictures the close identification of the Liberals with the religious cluster of Catholics, Antirevolutionaries, and Christian-Historicals found in the 12-party space of Figure 6.5 has been broken up. Notably, the five-party picture (Figure 6.6a) reflects in a very clear way the traditional three-cornered contest of Dutch politics in which Socialists and Liberals compete for the favors of the three religious parties who themselves would much prefer to keep both suitors at arm's length.[31] Figure 6.6a has a very low stress figure, moreover, suggesting that the members of the five main system parties substantially agree on the relative positioning of their parties vis-à-vis one another.

The stress values of Figure 6.6b and c are somewhat higher. Although they continue to meet the standards for a "good" representation of the data according to Coombsean scaling requirements, the introduction of two new parties (Democrats '66 and Radicals) in the system makes it more difficult to arrive at a consistent representation of all preferences in the same two-dimensional space. But at the same time, the increase in the number of stimuli would seem to reveal properties of the political world that were not so easily seen in the simpler five-party picture (Figure 6.6a). Although there are certain methodological problems in comparing the movement of party stimulus points in Figure 6.6,[32] two properties of the

---

[31] See Hans Daalder in Robert A. Dahl, Ed., *Political Oppositions in Western Democracies*, pp. 220–225 and *Idem, The Relations between Cabinet and Parliament in The Netherlands*, a report delivered to the International Political Science Association (Rome, 1958), passim.

[32] The following methodological reservations should be made in comparing Figures 6.6a, b and c with one another. In the first place, one must remember that we are, in fact, working with a single data set in which respondents were asked to rank order all 12 parties in the Dutch system, not some lesser number per se. Hence, Figures 6.6a, b and c do not represent an actual simulation of the "party world" in the Dutch legislature, but rather a simple manipulation of key subsets of the data, subsets which we as investigators have defined and assume to be politically important. In the second place, though these figures show the best obtainable two-dimensional solution for the five, six, and seven party subsets, respectively, the planes representing each of these two-dimensional spaces need not be projected the same way through the actual *n*-dimensional space. Hence the movement of particular party stimulus points from one figure to the other may be the result of different angles of projection as well as of substantive properties inherent in the data. Also, the location of individual party points in Figures 6.6b and c need not be perfect, as is clear from the higher stress values these figures have compared to Figure 6.6a. We nevertheless feel that the differences among the three figures reveal interpretable political properties of the data because we found definite confirmation of our conclusions when we looked at the actual rank order preferences of individual members of different parties.

data are so clearly evident that we are inclined to attribute considerable political importance to them.

In the first place, the six- and seven-party preference spaces reveal that members of the Dutch Parliament regard the two newcomers in Dutch political life, Democrats '66 and the Radicals, in fact as close partners of the Socialist Opposition. This finding is interesting, as it foreshadowed political developments that came about only 3 years after our interviews were held. In 1968 the D'66 party still tended to treat all other parties indifferently as representatives of outdated ideological traditions. But after some disappointing election results in the provincial elections of 1970, the party decided in March 1971 to join in an alliance with the Socialists and the Radicals, forming one shadow cabinet with them to fight the 1971 elections.

In the second place, the inclusion in the data of Democrats '66 and the Radicals as stimulus points and as party memberships causes the original tight cluster of the three religious parties to break up. The Antirevolutionary Party moves closer to the left opposition parties, separating from both the Catholic Party and the Christian-Historical Union. Actual inspection of the preference orders makes us believe that two forces are at work: (1) Members of all three left-oriented parties show definite selective preferences for the Antirevolutionary as distinct from the Catholic and Christian-Historical Union parties. The addition of ten new members of left parties, therefore, pulls the ARP nearer to the left cluster. (2) The addition of D'66 and the Radicals (PPR) as stimulus points tends to force Christian-Historical and Catholic members away from the left parties; the Catholic and Christian-Historical Union parties not only tend to be the last choices of the left cluster, but their party memberships, in turn, reciprocate such negative feelings, especially toward D'66 and the Radicals. The presence of two new left parties in the system thus widens the gulf between the left opposition and two of the three religious parties. Here again, the 1968 data foreshadowed later events. One year after our survey, the Socialist Party Congress (partly from old grudges over the Catholic dismissal of a cabinet in 1966, partly in a deliberate attempt to polarize Dutch politics for electoral reasons) declared itself unwilling to enter into a future government coalition with the Catholics. The Socialists professed greater sympathy for the Antirevolutionary Party. But as the Antirevolutionaries and the Christian-Historicals retained their strong preferences for the Catholic Party, this Socialist decision had as its net effect to make the governing coalition of the three religious parties with the Liberal Party an inevitable choice. Figure 6.6c still continues to have definite political reality, however; the Antirevolutionaries and Catholics (in contrast to the

Christian-Historicals) have tended to keep as aloof from the Liberal embrace as the political constraints of an inevitable coalition permitted.

Actual Preferences: Individual "Ideal Points" Compared with the Location of Parties in the Preference Space. Even a restriction of the stimuli to the main parties in the system does not fully reveal the actual political preferences involved. The various Coombsean spaces show only the result of the combined preferences of all individuals, without specifying the preferences of individual deputies or indicating the special direction of sympathies of one party for another. Yet politics is not a mechanical weighting game but a tugging of forces among individuals in elite positions and among parties consisting of groups of deputies. Individuals within the same party may have divergent preferences for other parties, in some cases leading to definite internal party strains. The aggregated preferences of members of one party may show strong sympathies for another party, without these sentiments being reciprocated. And the preferred location of members for their party in the preference space need not coincide with the place assigned that party on the basis of the judgments of all members of Parliament; for the latter, after all, are in the majority members of other parties.

For a better insight into individual preferences, we have made separate plots of the "ideal" points of each member of Parliament for each of the various preference spaces shown in Figures 6.5 and 6.6. As is to be expected, the increase or decrease in the number of parties serving as stimuli affects individual preference points. The twelve-party picture, by giving a strong weight to differences in preferences for the more extreme parties, tends to cluster the "ideal points" of the many members who have given their first preferences to the main parties in the system. In contrast, a plotting of individual preference points in a five-party picture makes the location of individuals entirely dependent on their rank-ordering of the traditional parties in the system, without considering the impact of newer political forces. The seven-party picture does give full scope to attitudes expressed toward Radicals and Democrats '66. But by offering as many as three potentially left stimuli (to which members may systematically react positively, negatively, *or* with more mixed emotions), this picture tends to somewhat doubtful results. It leads for instance to a clustering of all Catholic members whose declared sympathies for the Socialist Party tend to be nullified by equally strong negative reactions to the dissident Radicals (who had split off from the Catholic Party at the time of our interviews) or to Democrats '66, or to both. On balance, we have therefore decided to include the six-party picture as giving full importance to the five traditional coalition pretenders, plus the one party which has proved the most

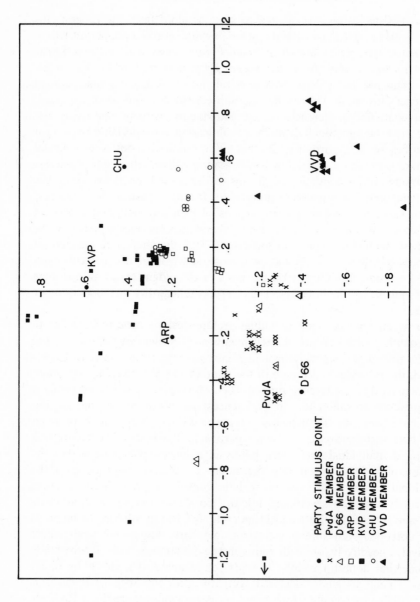

Figure 6.7 Party preference space for six Dutch parties and their members, Dutch Lower House, 1968. ● = party stimulus point, × = PvdA member, △ = D'66 member, □ = ARP member, + = KVP member, ○ = CHU member, ▲ = VVD member.

successful challenger to date in the old game of coalition politics in The Netherlands—Democrats '66.

The location of individual party members in Figure 6.7 tells an interesting political story.[33] It shows that for the Socialists and Liberals there is on the whole a fairly good coincidence between their locations in space and the location of their parties as determined by the combined membership of all six parties. Both Socialists and Liberals may have a moderate spread in scores, but they tend to agree on a basic left-right positioning between themselves. The scatter of the few members of D'66 reveals that these deputies also agreed to the leftward location assigned to their party, even though at the time of our interviews in 1968 the party still professed a "pragmatic" orientation that allegedly aimed at the equal destruction of all ideological divisions.

Members of the religious parties seem to have a somewhat greater discrepancy between their own locations in space and that of their parties. Roughly speaking, members of the Antirevolutionary Party tend to lie to the right of their assigned party point, while Christian-Historical Union members lie to the left of their party point. The spread in scores for each party's membership is quite low (i.e., regardless of where the party point lies, the members of the ARP, for example, show little spread in their locations in space vis-à-vis one another). Catholic members tend to scatter somewhat to the right of the place where the collective judgment of all six-party memberships locates their party, though a sizable minority lie to the left of their party point. Mutual sympathies of the members of the three religious parties for each other's parties would work towards a clustering of these three party points. But the selective preferences of the Socialists and D'66 for the ARP work against this trend and draw the ARP to the left in the party space, while concurrently the Socialist and D'66 dislike of and the Liberal preference for the Catholic Party and the Christian-Historical Union move these two parties away from the left cluster. At the same time, the individual plots reveal that a fair number of Catholics and Antirevolutionaries, but only very few Christian-Historicals, prefer the Socialist Party over the Liberal Party, even though the three religious parties were members of the governing coalition with the Liberals. This paradox of Dutch politics receives our attention shortly.

---

[33] We call the locations of these individuals in the preference space "ideal points" although they are only best-fitting approximations to this. The Coombsean program developed by Roskam attempts to accommodate all individuals in the space, "perfect" data and "imperfect" data alike, giving each individual the same weight in the scaling process. The program, therefore, approximates the actual preference orders of individuals, attempting to reproduce these preference orders as if each individual's preference order had been equally perfect.

sumption that variances within parties reveal the parties' degrees of internal cohesion. We present these quasi-cohesion scores in Table 6.13, Finally, we have attempted to calculate variance figures for all the parties from the coordinates of individual preference points, on the as- although with considerable hesitancy. As we have seen, a reduction or increase in the number of party stimuli has a substantial effect on the degree

Table 6.13   Cohesion Scores for the Party
Memberships in Figure 6.7[a]

Party Memberships	Standard Deviations for the Two Dimensions	N
Antirevolutionaries (ARP)	.13	15
Christian-Historicals (CHU)	.15	12
Socialists (PvdA)	.20	37
Liberals (VVD)	.22	17
Democrats '66 (D'66)	.35	6
Catholics (KVP)	.47	38
Total		125

[a] Low values indicate high party cohesion; high values, low party cohesion. Party cohesion has been operationalized as the standard deviation of the individual coordinates (in Figure 6.7) of a given party's membership. An example will make this clearer. If one had a two-member party represented in two dimensions, the first member located in space at .5, .6 (dimension 1, dimension 2) and the second member located at .2, .4, then one would get the party averages of .35 and .5 on the two dimensions, and the resulting variance would be $(.5 - .35)^2 + (.6 - .5)^2 + (.2 - .35)^2 + (.4 - .5)^2$ divided by the number of members in the party (2). The square root of this result is the standard deviation for this party's membership on the two dimensions.

of scatter of individual preference points, and hence on relative variance figures among parties. These quasi-cohesion scores should therefore only be considered *within* the assumption that a six-party preference space reveals the party distances most meaningful for an understanding of the dimensions of contemporary Dutch politics.

Interparty Preferences and Potential Government Coalitions. The location of individual "ideal" points within a given party space, more than the placement of the parties themselves, reflects feelings of personal nearness to or distance from parties. But, as noted in the preceding part of this chapter, the effective actors, at least in the making of cabinets, are not isolated individuals but politicians grouped and voting in parties. For a more accurate explanation of coalition potentialities, we must therefore convert individual preferences of members of a party into a composite party preference. We have attempted a solution for this problem in two ways: by an analysis of the party spaces of the members of the major party groups separately, and by drawing up a matrix showing the rank-order in the preferences of each party for all other parties that might conceivably enter into a realistic government coalition.

To trace the composite preferences of the individuals of each of the five major parties, we have run the Coombsean scaling program separately on each of these party memberships. Limiting our analytic interest to just the memberships of these five parties is politically acceptable because their relative size makes them certain actors in future coalition situations. It is also technically necessary, since the Coombsean program should have populations to work with that are at least as large as each of these parties provides. In our analysis of the preference spaces for each of the party memberships, we have used all 12 parties as stimuli. But the unfolding of such preference spaces for each separate party membership leads to a technical problem. In cases where the first several preferences of a given party membership are very similar, this will exaggerate the clustering of these higher-ranked parties, at the same time leading to disproportionate movements in the more peripheral choices. For that reason, we do not present the actual preference spaces for each of the party memberships, but instead concentrate on which parties are being drawn into the central cluster of preferred parties. As coalitions actually require such clustering, we regard differences in such clustering between one party membership and another as in fact meaningful.[34]

The five separate runs for the chief parties in the system gave the results shown in Table 6.14. Table 6.14 presents a very realistic political picture. Scaling the individual preferences of the Socialists clearly reveals a preference for a left coalition reinforced by the Antirevolutionaries. The antirevolutionaries themselves are more strongly oriented to the traditional coalition of the religious parties (but in the actual ARP preference space the Socialists and D'66 figure nearer than the Liberals). The Catholics prefer the straddling of dividing lines, balancing a religious coalition with both a Socialist *and* a Liberal wing. The Christian-Historicals and the

---

[34] This is an unorthodox use of Coombsean scaling. The technique was developed to unfold preference spaces for heterogeneous groups of people, not fairly homogeneous sets such as our separate party memberships. But because of our unique purpose here, we have used it on homogeneous sets—wanting to look at the clustering effect induced by the algorithm to see which parties a given party membership clustered with itself. It goes without saying that such findings should be interpreted with caution.

Liberals appear as the staunchest supporters of the governing coalition of the three religious parties and the Liberals. Such findings are close to the actual behavior of these parties in past coalition situations.[35]

Table 6.14 does, therefore, indicate meaningful political preferences for certain coalitions, but it does not differentiate among the parties drawn

Table 6.14   Parties Drawn into Central Cluster in Coombsean Preference Scaling as Applied to the Preferences of the Memberships of Each of the Five Main Potential Governing Parties

	Parties Drawn into Coalition Cluster							
Party Memberships Naming Preferences	PSP	PvdA	PPR	D'66	ARP	KVP	CHU	VVD	Total Seats in Coalition for Lower House
Socialists (PvdA)	+	+	+	+	+				66
Antirevolutionaries (ARP)					+	+	+		66
Catholics (KVP)		+			+	+	+	+	120
Christian-Historicals (CHU)					+	+	+	+	83
Liberals (VVD)					+	+	+	+	83
Number of seats in Lower House	4	37	3	7	15	39	12	17	150

into each cluster. As the distribution of preferences set out in Table 6.14 is such as to rule out a majority coalition equally preferred by all participants who should be in it, one needs to obtain actual preference orders for each of the potential actors in a coalition game.

One possible way to construct such preference rankings would be to use the mean values given in Figure 6.2. But, particularly for the smaller parties, these averages might be distorted by idiosyncratic preferences on the part of one or two individual members. We have instead chosen to use a simple majority principle—whenever a majority of the members of

[35] Material for studying past coalition situations in The Netherlands is provided in two books: G. Puchinger, *Colijn en het Einde van de Coalitie—de geschiedenis van de kabinetsformaties 1918–1924* (Kampen, 1969), and F. J. F. M. Duynstee, *De Kabinetsformaties 1946–1965* (Deventer, 1966).

a given party preferred one party over another, we have ranked that party above the other party, repeating this procedure for each pair of parties. We have thus arrived at a matrix of rank-ordered preferences for the eight possible coalition contestants, as shown in Table 6.15.

Table 6.15   Ranks of Majority Preferences in Paired Party
Comparisons for Members of Eight Dutch Parties,
Dutch Lower House, 1968[a]

Preferences from Party Members	Parties Being Ranked								
	PSP	PvdA	PPR	D'66	ARP	KVP	CHU	VVD	*N*
Pacifist-Socialists (PSP)	1	2	3	4	5	6	7	8	4
Socialists (PvdA)	4	1	2	3	5	6	8	7	37
Radicals (PPR)	6	2	1	3.5[b]	3.5[b]	5	8	7	4
Democrats '66 (D'66)	5	3.5[b]	2	1	3.5[b]	6	8	7	6
Antirevolutionaries (ARP)	8	4	5	6	1	3	2	7	15
Catholics (KVP)	8	4	5	7	2	1	3	6	38
Christian-Historicals (CHU)	8	5	7	6	2	3	1	4	12
Liberals (VVD)	8	5	7	4	6	3	2	1	17

[a] The procedure for obtaining these party ranks is as follows. For the members of a given party A, all paired party comparisons are made, and a score of 1 is assigned to the party in each paired comparison that is favored by the majority of party A's membership. After all paired comparisons have been observed, the rank for each party being rated is based on the number of 1 scores assigned to it. The party with the most 1's will be given the rank of 1 (this is always the legislator's own party), the party with the next most 1's will be given the rank of 2, and so on.

[b] Cases of ties.

The matrix in Table 6.15 provides a vivid illustration of the complexity of the Dutch party scene. As described elsewhere, "difficult party relations" have made for extraordinarily long processes of cabinet formation.[36] Even a cursory glance at the rank-ordered preferences of Table 6.15 suggests a possible explanation. The three religious parties readily find one another, but they lack a majority, as do the combined left parties. A combination

[36] See Hans Daalder, "Parties and Politics in The Netherlands," *Political Studies*, 3 (1955), pp. 1–16. For specific data on past cabinet formations, see Georg Geismann, *Politische Struktur und Regierungssystem in den Niederlanden* (Frankfurt, 1964), appendix, p. 289.

of Socialists plus the religious parties encounters strong opposition from two of the four parties—the Socialists, who have low preferences for the Catholics and Christian-Historicals, and the Christian-Historicals, who heartily reciprocate. The alternative coalition of Liberals and the three religious parties sits uneasily with the Liberals and the Antirevolutionaries who might prefer other partners to one another. Even if Catholics and Antirevolutionaries could surmount the negative feelings Socialists harbor for the Catholics, they are still hardly likely to forego cooperation with the Christian-Historicals, whose personal preferences would indicate alliance with the Liberals.

The great variety of possible actors in a coalition situation, and the lack of agreement on individual party preferences, would seem to make Dutch politics a haven for "coalition theorists"![37]

Conclusions. Before offering our data to the theorists, however, we should pause and review our findings.

We have used two kinds of scaling techniques on different aspects of the preference ratings that Parliament members gave for each others' parties in order to derive some insight into the empirical dimensioning of the Dutch party system. Using the Kruskal multidimensional scaling program on correlations computed from these party preference ratings, we find that members of the Dutch Parliament clearly structure their perceptions of the 12 parties in the system along two basic dimensions: a left-right dimension and a secular-religious dimension. Ancient cleavages in the Dutch political system are thus shown to retain considerable importance for the perception of the contemporary party system. Using the Coombsean scaling technique on the party preference orders of individuals results in a different preference space from that of the Kruskal technique. In this space, even though a left-right dimension again appears, a new second dimension emerges, which separates the parties eligible for a government coalition ("in" parties) from those who were not ("out" parties). It appears from the solution space that a majority of the Dutch Parliament were turning their backs on some of the more ideologically oriented fringe parties in the system, preferring to cross old cleavage lines for the sake of government by mutual accommodation. We then investigate in greater detail the relationships among the five to seven main legitimate actors in the system, constructing further Coombsean spaces for just these sets of five, six, and seven parties. We plot individual preference points in one

---

[37] A Dutch political scientist, Abraham de Swaan, is preparing an elaborate theoretical study on the applicability of various theories of coalition behavior to the political experience of The Netherlands and other European countries. He uses, among other sources, data on cabinet formation and on the election of executive boards of municipal councils in The Netherlands.

of these spaces and compare such points with the location of the parties in that space, the latter being determined by the combined preferences of all the party members involved in that space. Finally, we seek to delineate the subjective distances separating Dutch political parties from one another as seen by each party membership separately, by analyzing the preference spaces of each of the five major parties, and by constructing a matrix showing the majority preferences of the members of eight potential governing parties for each other.

Our findings show a good correspondence with the known behavior of Dutch political parties in relation to one another, thus revealing the importance of elite dimensionality perceptions as a potential explanatory variable.[38] But so far our findings are based only on the responses to a single rank-order question asked at one particular point in time in the context of a much larger survey. To substantiate our findings, we should possess answers to questions that probe the same similarity and distance phenomena in a different manner. And we should also repeat our questions

[38] Our findings also show a good correspondence with those uncovered in other countries using similar techniques on mass samples. In a 1958 mass survey in France, Philip Converse discovered the identical two dimensions evident in our Kruskal solution. Obviously, left-right thinking and religious-secular cleavages are important aspects in the perception of French parties as well. See Philip E. Converse, "The Problem of Party Distances in Models of Voting Change," in M. Kent Jennings and L. Harmon Zeigler, Eds., *The Electoral Process* (Englewood Cliffs, N.J., 1966), pp. 175–207. Bo Särlvik, in his 1964 Swedish data, also found the left-right dimension prominently centered in the masses' evaluations of the parties in that country. See Bo Särlvik, "Partibyten som Mått på Avstånd och Dimensioner i Partisystemet" ("Party Change as a Measure of Distances and Dimensions in the Swedish Party System"), *Sociologisk Forskning,* 1 (1968), pp. 35–80. As a slight twist on these research procedures, two American scholars asked their country's electorate to rate a multiple set of possible presidential candidates in 1968 (using candidates rather than parties, since the United States has only two major parties, an insufficient number for dimensional analysis) and found that the candidates were evaluated on two different dimensions: the left-right distinction apparent in concepts of social welfarism and the social welfare state, and a left-right dimension associated with the current issues of the day (civil rights, law and order, urban unrest, Vietnam). See Herbert F. Weisberg and Jerrold G. Rusk, "Dimensions of Candidate Evaluation," *American Political Science Review* (December 1970), pp. 1167–1185. Also, as a final note, a preliminary analysis of *mass data* on party perceptions in The Netherlands has begun and in a future publication Jerrold Rusk will detail the points of congruence and divergence in the party belief systems of these two sets of political actors. In this early stage of analysis, one can tentatively say that the masses show a similar structuring of the parties to that of the elite—revealing both a left-right and a system-nonsystem dimensioning in the data. However, the relative positioning of the parties on these dimensions is not as "accurate" as that seen in our elite data for The Netherlands.

in future research to see whether the dimensions found are more or less stable over time, or transient phenomena, disproportionately influenced by the political situation prevailing at the time of our survey.

We should enter a second caveat. We have mainly used our data to investigate potential coalition relationships in the Dutch party system, using the Coombsean technique as an analytical tool. But the question from which our data were derived was not originally intended to elicit coalition preferences. We did not ask Dutch legislators to rank-order parties in terms of their eligibility as a partner in actual coalitions, but in terms of personal closeness or distance. The two need not coincide. Party members may easily work with politicians from other parties without feeling personally close to them. This may be particularly true in The Netherlands where ancient ideological differences continue to structure party alignments without necessarily affecting day-to-day politics.[39] This one factor alone may explain our finding that a majority of Antirevolutionaries and Catholics feel closer to the Socialists than to the Liberals, even though they formed a coalition with the Liberals at the time of our survey. Memories of parallel struggles against a long-time Liberal dominance in Dutch politics may explain why Catholics or Calvinists have greater empathy with the Socialists, though they prefer governing with the Liberals.[40] As we have seen, the use of dimensionality analysis for explaining actual coalition behavior is further complicated by the fact that preferences may not be reciprocal between parties.

In actual politics, even shared dimensionality is not necessarily the decisive factor in all political situations. In the formation of real government coalitions, other factors may enter, such as possible pay-offs in policies or in political offices.[41] Our analysis, moreover, has so far proceeded from the somewhat unrealistic assumption that the preferences of all members of a given party are weighted equally in determining coalitions, thus neglecting the more realistic proposition that the preferences of leaders within

---

[39] See the article by Daalder mentioned in footnote 36.

[40] See the general analysis in Daalder, "The Netherlands: Opposition in a Segmented Society," in Robert A. Dahl, Ed., *Political Oppositions in Western Democracies, passim.*

[41] Although not otherwise very applicable to Dutch Cabinet experience, the Riker minimum-size principle may have been one factor in persuading Antirevolutionaries and Christian-Historicals to form a Cabinet with the smaller Liberal Party in preference to a Cabinet with the larger Socialist PvdA: the number of ministerial offices available to these two parties is larger in the first than in the latter coalition. See William H. Riker, *The Theory of Political Coalitions* (New Haven, 1962), *passim.*

parties may have a more fundamental political importance. A coalition choice will rarely be the outcome of an exact calculus of consent, but rather will be the result of complex processes of political negotiation in which many ad hoc factors will play an important role.

Once formed, the existence of specific multiparty coalitions will itself become an intervening variable in legislative behavior, for in crucial matters, members of governing parties must support the government whatever their personal preferences (unless they deem these sufficiently important to risk destroying a specific cabinet). The importance of the coalition factor for the behavior of legislators explains why we have put such great emphasis on the potential value of Coombsean dimensionality analysis for an understanding of relations in the Dutch Parliament. But at the same time, the existence of clearly different individual preferences should sensitize one to the fact that coalition relations do not exhaust the energies of individual legislators, for they participate in policy-making within their parties. Although the specific composition of the government is a most powerful restraint on the freedom of action of at least members of governing parties, there yet remains a definite scope for individual initiative. As we saw in the beginning of this chapter, specialization of labor allows individual members a not inconsiderable autonomy, which they value highly. If the Coombsean dimensions might be the most important for an explanation of political coalitions, the dimensions found in the Kruskal analysis might be more important for a study of such individual actions. By scoring individual members of Parliament on the most important dimensions found in our Kruskal analysis, one could attempt to account for the political behavior of individual deputies. The relative unimportance of individual roll calls in which most parties tend to vote as a bloc might discourage traditional methods of roll call analysis. But one could test the value of scoring individual deputies on certain dimensions by an analysis of other individual actions:[42] parliamentary questions, committee memberships, internal party positions (as checked by a panel of qualified observers, like lobby correspondents), and so on. One could seek to use these individual scores as one variable to explain responses to a large number of other questions in our 1968 survey.

One final warning should be made. As the Kruskal analysis has shown, old dimensions continue to have an important effect on current percep-

---

[42] Data for this kind of analysis are being collected in the context of the Dutch Parliament Project. For fuller data on this project, see Hans Daalder, *Research on Legislative Behavior in The Netherlands—A Preliminary Report,* a paper presented at the Comparative Legislative Behavior Conference, Iowa City, May 1969.

tions. But these dimensions are not necessarily stable over time. New dimensions may arise as new issues come to challenge old cleavages. The relations among parties may change as new personalities or political groups come to dominate particular parties or as new party platforms are established in a deliberate attempt to turn a given party in new directions.

One should, therefore, continue to study elite perceptions over time in order to trace possible changes in effective political dimensions. And one should simultaneously investigate possible changes in the actual interaction of parties with one another. A study of cabinet-making processes would be an important key to an understanding of a party system at a given moment. But such inquiries should be supplemented by a close analysis of actual parliamentary voting of parties in relation to one another, along the lines of such promising analyses as those on Danish parliamentary politics pioneered by Mogens Pedersen and Erik Damgaard.[43]

Methodological Note

Considerable speculation has ensued as to why the Coombsean and Kruskal techniques often produce different solutions. Obviously, they operate on different aspects of the data—preference orders versus correlations—and this has something to do with their producing different solution spaces. But this is hardly a complete explanation. Experimentation with our data seemed to yield further suggestive guidelines for closing the circle of explanation. For one thing, we noted that the two techniques could converge to a somewhat similar solution space when appropriate transformations were made on the preference order data imputed into the Coombsean computer program. When computing "normal" or "z" scores on each individual's preference order, we saw a resemblance to the Kruskal solution when the Coombsean program worked on these "corrected" data. The reason for this seems apparent—when such transformations on the preference order data are made, they can be seen as correcting the data for the average preferences (popularity or unpopularity) of the parties in much the same fashion as the correlational computations are doing, since the correlations also subtract out the mean value for each party from each legislator's score for that party (in the process of measuring the covariation in scores between pairs of parties). (See the definitional formula for Pearson correla-

[43] See, for instance, Mogens N. Pedersen, "Consensus and Conflict in the Danish Folketing, 1945–66," *Scandinavian Political Studies*, 2 (1967), pp. 143–166; Erik Damgaard, "The Parliamentary Basis of Danish Governments: The Patterns of Coalition Formation," *ibid.*, 4 (1969), pp. 30–57; and Mogens N. Pedersen, Erik Damgaard and P. Nannestad Olsen, "Party Distances in the Danish Folketing," *Scandinavian Political Studies*, 6 (forthcoming), pp. 87–106.

tion.) If there are considerable differences between the parties in their mean preference values (their popularity or unpopularity), this correction has an important effect in adjusting the data before they are treated by the Coombsean or Kruskal computer programs. But since the Coombsean technique most usually works on "uncorrected" data—raw preference orders of individuals—it is necessarily affected by popularity/unpopularity notions in the data, since, in this case, the mean popularity or unpopularity of each party has not been subtracted from each legislator's score for that party.

The Kruskal technique is not affected by the varying popularity of the parties, since it corrects for this when using correlations as input to its algorithm. If the parties of concern do not vary much in their relative popularity (their mean values), then the Coombsean and Kruskal techniques should produce similar solutions even if the data are not "corrected" for the Coombseam algorithm. This is so because, in this case, there is little variation in the popularity of parties to correct for. A strong case for this point was made when we obtained virtually identical solution spaces for the six main parties in the Dutch system (the four government parties, PvdA, and D'66) when using both Coombsean and Kruskal methods. These six parties were all relatively popular parties which varied little among one another in their mean values—hence, the corrections the correlations were making for the Kruskal algorithm had little effect since there was very little, if anything, to correct for. But when we added six relatively unpopular parties to the solution space with the six popular parties, then differences did appear between the two scaling techniques as Figures 6.4 and 6.5 show.

Note that in Figure 6.5, the CPN and PSP move out in the periphery of the space, as well as SGP, GPV, and BP. This is obviously a function of the Coombsean technique being affected by the unpopularity notions in the data as well as by the substantive dimensions by which the legislators viewed these parties. Also note the effect the popular notions of the data have on the Coombsean technique—the relatively popular parties (on the government side) move closer together into a cluster than was true in the Kruskal picture when their relative popularities were being corrected for. The Kruskal technique is only interested in the covariation in scores given to these parties, unhampered by popularity notions in the data, while the Coombsean technique, in moving these parties closer together, seems to be partially affected by variation unique to each party—its popularity—as well as by the relations between the parties (as seen from the perspective of each individual's "ideal point"). The Kruskal technique also does not seem affected by the unpopularity notions in the data since it draws CPN, PSP, SGP, GPV, and BP—the smaller, more disliked parties—closer in towards the center of the picture, something the Coombsean technique is unable to do.

At this point, our conclusions as to when and why Coombsean and Kruskal solutions differ must be stated in very tentative fashion, since only preliminary tests have been made on the propositions set forth. The methodology in this area is unsettled, although we hope that our experience with these data in The Netherlands suggests useful guidelines for future methodological inquiries.

CHAPTER SEVEN

Political Parties in the Finnish Eduskunta*

PERTTI PESONEN

UNIVERSITY OF HELSINKI, FINLAND

and

STATE UNIVERSITY OF NEW YORK AT STONY BROOK

Introduction

For a long time political scientists have noted a decline in the status of national legislatures. As governmental functions have grown broader and more numerous in the twentieth century, the laymen legislators apparently have lost some of their previous powers to the more knowledgeable experts of the executive branch of government. Yet it is not altogether clear whether a possible decline in relative importance justifies the notion that the importance of legislatures has also declined in an absolute sense. One does find nowadays busy and professional fulltime legislators acting out their inherited role of the amateurish representative of the people.

Even fewer doubts exist about the increased importance of the modern political party, the extra-legal by-product of systems of democratic representation. That "association that activates and mobilizes the people, represents interests, provides for compromise among competing point of view, and becomes the proving ground for political leadership, appears to be the rule today."[1] Analysts of the growing importance of parties usually speak in absolute rather than relative terms, not comparing parties with pressure groups or other extra-governmental forces in the political system; moreover, they most often speak of the period following soon after the introduction of universal suffrage.

---

* The author wishes to thank Vernon Van Dyke of the University of Iowa for very helpful criticism.

[1] Roy C. Macridis, Ed., *Political Parties: Contemporary Trends and Ideas* (New York, 1967), p. 9.

The legislators, and especially the constitution makers, remained for a long time officially silent about the emergence of powerful political parties. Even now, parties are not formally recognized in many countries, or when they are, not always in all connections in which they serve a crucial purpose. British laws provide a well-known example: parliamentary candidates are supposedly nominated by any two individual voters who can demonstrate the support of eight additional people (and deposit £150), and the official ballot contains only the names of the individual candidates without party labels. The 1936 constitution of the Soviet Union was distinctive in this respect, as its Article 126 expressed juridically the monopoly position of the Communist Party of the USSR. The party occupies the formally recognized place of "the leading core of all organizations of the working people, both public and state." The West German Basic Law of 1949 "followed suit" and recognized officially the existence of political parties. The Germans were less harsh than the Russians, though, in imposing restrictions on political opposition: the Electoral Law excludes only those minor parties that receive less than 5 percent of the valid votes cast in a national election.

In Finland, the law had totally failed to recognize political parties until their legal status became an important political issue in the late 1960s. The Constitution Act of 1919 defines the basic function of the country's parliament, the *eduskunta,* as follows (Article 2):

"The sovereign power in Finland rests with the people, represented by the Parliament convened in session."

"Legislative power shall be exercised by Parliament in conjunction with the President of the Republic."

The 200 legislators, in turn, have been assigned a highly individualistic mandate. Another constitutional law, the Parliament Act of 1928, defines their role in following terms (Article 11):

"Every Member of Parliament is obliged to act according to justice and truth in the exercise of his mandate. He should observe the Constitutional Laws and is not bound by any other instructions."

This act makes Finland one of those representative democracies where the official norms firmly reject the idea of the instructed delegate. There is no "imperative mandate"; Finnish legal analysts offer unanimously the interpretation that the representative has no duty to obey instructions from his voters or to report to them about his activities. Over the years, some jurists and countless public speakers have also been concerned about the claims that the political parties may have over their representatives. There has been a fairly high consensus that political parties should have no right to interfere with the legislative decisions of any individual members of Parliament.

It is not surprising that the above quotations of Finnish constitutional law do not refer to political parties as a necessary link between the "sovereign power," that is, the people, and their elected representatives. However, one might have expected to find political parties mentioned in some legislation, at least in Finland's previous Election Laws (1906, 1935, 1955). But whatever legislation there was to guide party activity, its purpose was always accomplished either by equating the parties with all other civic associations or by inventing legal terms that made explicit reference to political parties unnecessary.

However, very recently the *de facto* acceptance of political parties reached a point where the parties could no longer operate without a formal juridical definition. The first legal recognition came, unexpectedly, in the state budget for 1967 which appropriated 10 million marks to support Finland's political parties. This caused an urgent need of a "party law," and such a bill was introduced by the government in late 1966. Similar state support was again appropriated for 1968 and for the succeeding years, and the "party law" bill finally became a law in February 1969. Another urgent need for legally distinguishing political parties from other types of civic organizations concerned new election legislation. An amendment of the Parliament Act to lower the voting age to 20 passed its second reading on May 13, 1969; on the agenda the same day was the new Election Law bill which obviously intended to limit the right to nominate parliamentary candidates to officially registered parties only. These reforms became effective legislation in July 1969. In order to prevent or to handicap the birth of new competitors by these means, the established political parties needed to take successfully the first step, that of defining juridically what a political party is.

In Finland, as elsewhere, political parties have several functions in the political process. This chapter does not deal with all of them. The intention is to describe Finnish parties only as they relate to the legislature. More specifically, the interrelationships of political parties and the *eduskunta* are viewed for three levels in the Finnish political system: that of the mass electorate, that of the party activists, and that of the legislators. Because one needs to admit an embarrassing lack of research on both topics, the parties as well as the legislature, this paper cannot attempt anything more comprehensive than a modest review of the relevant phenomena that have been subjected to research. The underlying conviction, however, is that political analysis needs to emphasize increasingly the interactions of various components in the political system.

The Institutional Setting

In late 1905, an obsolete four-chamber legislature was still elected in Finland. The Diet Act of 1869 extended the suffrage to no more than about 20 percent of the country's adult male population, and the legislature, consisting of the estates of nobility, clergy, burgesses, and peasants, was structured in accordance with the Swedish Parliament Act of 1617. But, although the Diet of four estates was obsolete structurally, it demonstrated a modern spirit when it decided on the new Parliament Act in 1906. The estates (three quite unanimously) replaced themselves with the unicameral *eduskunta,* and furthermore, they adopted a proportional system of representation and enfranchised both sexes. For so early a year the reform of 1906 was indeed far-reaching. There were unicameral parliaments nowhere but in Bulgaria, Greece, and Serbia; Norway then fell between the uni- and bicameral classification. Proportional representation was used in Belgium, Serbia, and Denmark (upper chamber), in six Swiss cantons, and in two Argentina provinces. Universal male suffrage had been introduced, at least for one of two chambers, in Norway, Denmark, Switzerland, the German Reich, Baden, France, the United States, Greece, and Bulgaria. But universal suffrage equally for men and women existed only in New Zealand, four states in the United States, and five Australian provinces.[2]

The 200 members of Finland's unicameral legislature were elected for the first time in March 1907. Both the electoral system and the structure of the *eduskunta* have remained basically unaltered ever since, as later reforms have concerned practical matters that leave the principles unaffected. The Parliament Act of 1928 is currently in force with some amendments, such as those lowering the voting age from 24 to 21 in 1944 and to 20 years in 1969 and lengthening the term of office from 3 to 4 years in 1954. The Election Act of 1906 was replaced by new ones in 1935 and 1955, and by a fourth one in 1969. So far 25 *eduskunta* elections have been held: eight from 1907 to 1917, nine from 1919 to 1939, and eight from 1945 to 1970. The total number of multimember constituencies (electoral districts) has always been either 14 or 15. In addition, Åland has since 1948 consituted a single-member constituency, as Lapland did from 1907 to 1936. In the most recent election of 1970, the 14 constituencies returned from 8 to 22 members each. Consequently, the average number of seats for one multi-member constituency has been either 13.3 (in 1907–1945, 1953–1958) or 14.2 (1948–1951 and 1962–to date). To use Douglas Rae's terminology, Finland is characterized by a large district P.R. system and by d'Hondt's highest average formula.[3]

---

[2] Klaus Törnudd, *The Electoral System of Finland* (London, 1968), p. 30.
[3] Douglas Rae, *The Political Consequences of Electoral Laws* (New Haven, 1967), pp. 41–42.

The reform of 1906 responded to a strong popular demand. All four political parties, the Swedes, the Old Finns, the constitutionalist Young Finns, and the Social Democrats, also felt that broad popular support for the new legislature was essential in Finland's resistance to Russian pressures; therefore, the principle of universal and equal suffrage was not questioned. An overwhelming majority preferred unicameralism to bicameralism. Only the electoral system caused some differences among the parties, and here parties or individual legislators did take stances which were motivated by their particular interests. The Swedish Party was the best example; it strongly favored proportional representation in order to guarantee the Swedish minority's influence in the new legislature. The Old Finns were the main opposition on that issue, preferring either very small or single-member constituencies. The Social Democrats had meager representation in the old Diet, but they were a well-organized outside group and created strong political pressure. Actually, they obtained all the representational reforms that they sought except for a voting age of 21.

No less than 70.7 percent of the universally enfranchised population voted in 1907. The outcome of this election was a surprising socialist victory; the SDP polled 37.0 percent of the votes and gained 80 of the 200 seats in the first *eduskunta*. That made it the relatively strongest socialist party in the world, and its share rose to 47.3 percent in 1916, making it Finland's only party ever to hold a majority of the seats (103); that situation lasted only until the election of 1917. Since 1944 the SDP has had an almost equally strong and a more radical competitor, the Finnish People's Democratic Union. In 1958 a social democratic splinter party, the Social Democratic League, appeared for the first time. The largest and at times quite dominating nonsocialist group has been the Center Party, until 1965 called the Agrarian Union. It is followed in size by the conservatives (the National Coalition), founded in 1918. There are also two People's Parties, the Swedish one (founded in 1906 to succeed the Swedish party), and the Liberal one, founded in 1965 to succeed to Finnish People's Party (1951–1965) and the National Progressive Party (1918–1951). The fifth nonsocialist party which rose from only one representative in the 1966 *eduskunta* to 18 in 1970 is called the Finnish Rural Party, former Smallholders' Party. The representation of political parties in the legislature is summarized in Table 7.1.

Parliamentary seats are not the only immediate prize for political competition. Finland has municipal elections every 4 years; the president of the republic is elected every 6 years by 300 electors, themselves elected like the 200 members of Parliament. The size of the parties' parliamentary groups is also of considerable importance for the formation of the cabinet. Generally there is an attempt to form majority cabinet coalitions (and in

Table 7.1   Parliamentary Elections in Finland, 1919 to 1970

					Party			Con-serva-		
Year	FPDU	SDL	SDP	FRP	Center	LPP	Swedish	tives	PPM	Others
Vote %										
1919	—	1.5	38.0	—	19.7	12.8	12.1	15.7	—	0.2
1922	14.8	—	25.1	—	20.3	9.2	12.4	18.1	—	0.1
1924	10.4	—	29.0	—	20.3	9.1	12.0	19.0	—	0.2
1927	12.1	—	28.3	—	22.5	6.8	12.2	17.7	—	0.4
1929	13.5	—	27.4	1.1	26.1	5.6	11.4	14.5	—	0.4
1930	1.0	—	34.2	1.8	27.3	5.8	10.0	18.1	—	1.8
1933	—	—	37.3	3.4	22.6	7.4	10.4	16.9	—	2.0
1936	—	—	38.6	2.0	22.4	6.3	11.2	10.4	8.3	0.8
1939	—	—	39.8	2.1	22.9	4.8	9.6	13.6	6.3	0.6
1945	23.5	—	25.1	1.2	21.3	5.2	7.9	15.0	—	0.8
1948	20.0	—	26.3	0.3	24.2	3.9	7.7	17.1	—	0.5
1951	21.6	—	26.5	0.3	23.2	5.7	7.6	14.6	—	0.5
1954	21.6	—	26.2	—	24.1	7.9	7.0	12.8	—	0.4
1958	23.2	1.7	23.2	—	23.1	5.9	6.7	15.3	—	0.9
1962	22.0	4.4	19.5	2.2	23.0	6.3	6.4	15.0	—	1.2
1966	21.2	2.6	27.2	1.0	21.2	6.5	6.0	13.8	—	0.5
1970	16.6	1.4	23.4	10.5	17.1	6.0	5.7	18.0	—	1.2
Elected Members										
1919	—	2	80	—	42	26	22	28	—	—
1922	27	—	53	—	45	15	25	35	—	—
1924	18	—	60	—	44	17	23	38	—	—
1927	20	—	60	—	52	10	24	34	—	—
1929	23	—	59	—	60	7	23	28	—	—
1930	—	—	66	2	59	11	20	42	—	—
1933	—	—	78	—	53	11	21	18	14	5
1936	—	—	83	1	53	7	21	20	14	—
1939	—	—	85	2	56	6	18	25	8	—
1945	49	—	50	—	49	9	14	28	—	1
1948	38	—	54	—	56	5	14	33	—	—
1951	43	—	53	—	51	10	15	28	—	—
1954	43	—	54	—	53	13	13	24	—	—
1958	50	3	48	—	48	8	14	29	—	—
1962	47	2	38	—	53	13	14	32	—	1
1966	41	7	55	1	49	9	12	26	—	—
1970	36	—	52	18	36	8	12	37	—	—

FPDU = Communist groups (1922–30); Finnish People's Democratic Union (SKDL)
SDL = Christian Labor (1919); Socialist Democratic Opposition 1958, Social Democratic League 1959–to date.
SDP = Social Democratic Party
FRP = Small Farmer's Party, Smallholders' Party (1959–to date), Finnish Rural Party (1962–to date)
Center = Agrarian Union; Center Party (1965–to date)
LPP = Progressive Party, Finnish People's Party (1951–1965); Liberal People's Party
Swedish = Swedish People's Party
Cons. = National Coalition (Conservative Party)
PPM = Patriotic People's Movement (allied with Conservatives in 1933)

204

any case the cabinet needs the confidence of a parliamentary majority). For example, after the nonsocialist electoral success in 1962, the political base for the cabinets was a coalition of four nonsocialist parties, with Agrarian (Center Party) leadership; during the period of the leftist majority between 1966 and 1970 the Cabinet was based on a large "popular front" coalition, mainly of the SDP, Center Party, and the FPDU, with a Social Democratic Prime Minister. The socialist parties have usually been less visible in the executive branch than in Parliament, none of the eight presidents has belonged to the left, and only seven of the 53 Cabinets since 1917 have been led by a Socialist Prime Minister.

It would seem sensible to define Finland's organizational parties more broadly than Leon D. Epstein does when speaking of democratic parties in democratic times as "any groups, however loosely organized, seeking to elect governmental office-holders under a given label."[4] For example, that definition leaves out of consideration the early years of the Social Democratic Party during which the SDP mainly sought to educate workers to class consciousness, and it neglects the underground years of the Finnish Communist Party which was founded in Moscow in 1918. In general, the party organizations have developed through four stages in Finland. The SDP created its organizational network over the entire country before the reform of 1906, while the others still operated as loose parliamentary parties only. When all had to face the need to appeal to the mass electorate, they established party organizations. Yet those were quite reminiscent of what Maurice Duverger calls cadre parties. The third stage, one of establishing large mass organizations, followed soon after World War II. The reported membership of the Agrarian Union rose from 37,000 in 1938 and 30,000 in 1945 to 300,000 in 1957; the SDP climbed from 33,000 members in 1939 to 62,000 in 1945 and some 108,000 in 1951; the party organization of the conservatives grew from 14,000 members in 1945 to 62,000 in 1947.[5] In the 1950s the membership figures became rather stabilized. A total of some 700,000 people (about 28 percent of the electorate) were then reported as the rank-and-file membership of Finland's political parties. Currently it seems that these mass organizations are shifting to another stage of development, one of increasingly secure and routinized bureaucratization, possibly with less-active participation by volunteer militants. One might hypothesize that the recent state subsidies have speeded such a development while also transferring additional organiza-

[4] Leon D. Epstein, *Political Parties in Western Democracies* (New York, 1967), p. 9.
[5] Jaakko Nousiainen, "The Structure of the Finnish Political Parties," in *Democracy in Finland* (Helsinki, 1960), pp. 28–32.

tional power to the national party leadership. Still there remains considerable vertical decentralization in most party organizations. The lower levels are those of the district or constituency organization and the primary units. Between them may function two additional levels, the regional and the communal.

The Finnish *eduskunta* can boast a record of an increasing work load. For example, 515 items of business were on its agenda during the 1937 legislative session, but there were 1566 items during 1954 and 3917 during the 1965 legislative session. Whereas only 8 percent of these items were not finished in 1937, no less than 52 percent remained unfinished after the 1965 session. Most of this increase has been caused by private members' motions.[6] The 200 members elected in 1970 again scored a new record by initiating a total of 2718 items during their first two weeks of legislative work.

In 1954, the term of the *eduskunta* was increased from 3 to 4 years, partly to provide legislators with additional "peaceful" working time before their immediate worry about the next election. During the terms, each annual session forms a significant unit in itself. For example, the speaker and the two deputy speakers are elected annually, as is the Grand Committee. This body of 45 members reviews all bills before their second reading and, consequently, reminds one somewhat of a second legislative chamber. The special committees are appointed each year by the 45 electors (whom the Parliament chooses for the entire 4-year term). Until 1918, no unfinished business was transferred to the succeeding session, but since then only a new election terminates the unfinished items once initiated in Parliament. The members may present bills and other motions in the beginning of each legislative session but not later, unless particular events (such as a government proposal) justify later private initiatives. But the government may propose legislation at any time during the session. The parliamentary procedure includes, in a customary fashion, a report from the relevant special committee and three hearings. The president can not only initiate but also veto legislation; his veto may be overridden by a new Parliament after an election. The president can also dissolve the Parliament and order new elections. The cabinet, which he appoints, does not ask for a vote of confidence in Parliament before taking office, but it must resign whenever it gets a vote of nonconfidence.[7]

---

[6] Nousiainen, *Suomen poliittinen järjestelmä,* 3rd ed. (Helsinki, 1967), p. 247.

[7] Nousiainen (*ibid.,* p. 313) classifies the reasons for the fall of 49 cabinets between 1918–1966. Of these, only 4 resigned due to an interpellation resulting in a vote of nonconfidence, and 8 others resigned because Parliament did not accept their political position. Other reasons include, e.g., 18 elections, 2 conflicts with the presidents, and 5 cases of a lack of cohesion within the cabinet.

The Structuring of the Vote

In his book on western political parties Epstein considers vote-structuring the "essential minimum modern function" of parties and therefore "a democratic necessity." By the term structuring he means simply "the imposition of an order or pattern enabling voters to choose candidates according to their labels."[8] Parties are the one most important basis on which voters make up their minds; therefore vote-structuring by the parties, as modified by the electoral system, not only determines the strength of parliamentary parties for a given term but also provides long-range continuity and predictability in the legislature. The linkages which political parties constitute between the legislators and their popular power base are of major importance in a political system.

One can view vote-structuring from several angles. Relevant questions would seem to include at least the following: what are the important correlates of party support; how durable and habitual is vote-structuring in the system; how do the individual electors' perceptions of all parties structure the dimensions and distances within the party system; what are the dynamics of the restructuring which takes place in deeply reorienting critical situations; what are the parties' appeals and negative images in addition to their "labels" as such; and what are their actual means to the electoral end, that is, what methods and techniques do and can they apply when attempting to influence voters in parliamentary elections?

A review of Finland's aggregate election statistics (Table 7.2) suggests long periods of remarkable stability in the electorate's political structuring. The election of 1954 is a good example. Using his power to dissolve the *eduskunta,* the president ordered new elections to be held 100 days prior to the normal election time; he did this hoping that enough political change would occur to bring some solution to the then current deadlock in coalition formation. Yet the election solved nothing because the political composition of the Parliament remained almost unaltered. Over the years, there have been some genuine election victories, though, and one does find steady trends in the vote structuring. For example, both the Rural Party and the Conservatives scored striking victories in March 1970. Longer trends include the increasing support of the Agrarians between 1907 and 1930; the decline of the Progressives between 1919 and 1948; and the consistent weakening of the Swedish People's Party since 1936. If one calls the socialist parties and the Agrarians jointly the "populist" party grouping—in contrast to the more traditional "gentlemen's" parties—, one finds a long range trend towards the "populist" direction in the *eduskunta.*

---

[8] Epstein, *op. cit.,* p. 77.

Table 7.2 A Comparison of the Party Choice of Finnish Electors in 1966 with Their Voting Behavior in 1962[a]

| | Parties in the 1966 Election | | | | | | | | |
1962	FPDU	SDL	SDP	FRP	Center	LPP	Cons.	Swedish	Total in 1962
Nonvoters, no answer	59,000	5,500	89,000	—	25,400	13,700	22,500	16,900	232,500
Age 21–24	37,200	1,800	47,600	—	36,300	10,700	18,100	14,500	166,200
FPDU	391,000	—	8,300	—	—	—	—	—	399,300
SDL	—	47,900	5,400	—	—	1,900	1,700	—	56,900
SDP	12,400	4,600	449,000	4,000	9,100	10,700	6,600	—	496,400
SFP	—	—	—	17,800	—	—	—	2,500	20,300
Agrarian	2,900	—	23,300	1,200	413,900	13,300	16,400	—	471,000
FPP	—	—	8,300	1,400	3,700	72,700	6,800	3,600	96,500
Conservative	—	1,500	11,600	—	14,600	30,200	251,600	3,600	313,100
Swedish	—	—	2,500	—	—	—	3,400	100,700	106,600
Total in 1966	502,500	61,300	645,500	24,400	503,000	153,200	327,100	141,800	2,358,800
Number of cases	185	35	427	18	272	86	196	65	

[a] The actual party vote in 1966 has been distributed, according to the recalled behavior in 1962, separately in each party in proportion to the survey responses. This table summarizes two tables thus estimated separately for the south-west and for the north-east.
SOURCE: The 1966 Election Study by P. Pesonen (in preparation).

That grouping held 90 seats in 1907, but 123 seats in 1919, 143 in 1939, and 153 seats in 1966.

It is obvious that aggregate statistics do not reveal the actual number of individual voters who are exchanged between the parties. In a two-party system the parties are separated by just one borderline that the voters may cross in either direction. But a third party raises the number of borders to three, and Finland's system of eight political parties would provide the total of 28 crossable borders, as the supporters of each party are offered seven possible directions to change to. One might presume that such a multiplicity of "temptations" causes a much higher frequency of party change than one finds in two-party systems. However, available research evidence does not support such a notion. For example, there were three parliamentary elections and one local election in Sweden between 1956 and 1960; of those electors who were enfranchised through the period and voted at least once, 64 percent reported participation in all four elections, voting consistently for the same party, and additional sometime nonvoters were also true to one party, while only 13 percent reported voting for two or more of the five parties.[9] According to a panel survey, 68 percent of Sweden's electorate were consistent voters in the 1964 and 1968 parliamentary elections; 15 percent changed parties and 17 percent did not participate in both of the two elections.[10] In Norway (with seven parties), 86 percent of those who voted both in 1961 and 1965 favored the same party at the two *Storting* elections.[11] In Finland, a comparison of the 1962 and 1966 parliamentary elections indicates about equal constancy: 89 percent (Table 7.2). The Norwegian and Finnish figures are again based on the respondents' recollections and may, therefore, somewhat underestimate the actual frequency of changes in party choice.

Those 11 percent of the Finnish sample who reported voting for different parties in 1962 and 1966 indicated "traffic" across 18 of the 28 "borders." Table 7.3 summarizes this information. It shows how many voters the parties exchanged and what the resultant net gains or losses were. Here one should be warned against both the possible unreliability of recollections and the illusion of more accurate measurement than the data actually provide.

The eight parties received in 1966 a total of 2,359,000 votes. In other words, 11,795 ballots were cast per seat in the *eduskunta*. Thus our

[9] Bo Särlvik, "Political Stability and Change in the Swedish Electorate," *Scandinavian Political Studies*, **1** (1966), pp. 194–195.

[10] Särlvik, *Electoral Behavior in the Swedish Multiparty System* (mimeo, 1970), Table I:6.

[11] Henry Valen, "Partiforskyvninger ved stortingsvalget i 1965," *Tidsskrift for samfunnsforskning*, 1967, p. 132.

Table 7.3   A Summary of Recollected Changes in
Party Choice, 1962 to 1966

Parties Exchanging Voters	Total Conversions	Net Effect
Intersocialist		
FPDU/SDP	20,700	4,100
SDL/SDP	10,000	800
Total	30,700	4,900
Socialist/nonsocialist		
FPDU/Center	2,900	2,900
SDL/LPP	1,900	1,900
SDL/Conservative	3,200	200
SDP/FRP	4,000	4,000
SDP/Center	32,400	14,200
SDP/LPP	19,000	2,400
SDP/Conservative	18,200	5,000
SDP/SWEDISH	2,500	2,500
Total	84,100	33,100
Nonsocialist		
FRP/Center	1,200	1,200
FRP/LPP	1,400	1,400
FRP/Swedish	2,500	2,500
Center/LPP	17,500	9,600
Center/Conservative	31,000	1,800
LPP/Conservative	37,000	23,400
LPP/Swedish	3,600	3,600
Conservative/Swedish	7,000	200
Total	100,700	43,700

215,500 mobile voters represented, theoretically, the power to transfer 18 of the 200 parliamentary seats from one party to another. But mutual cancellations reduced the net effect of the changes to 81,700 votes and consequently reduced to seven the number of seats that the mobile voters could theoretically transfer. For an equally theoretical comparison, Table 7.2 would tell that about ten seats were in 1966 "controlled" by the young first-time voters and some twenty seats by the newly activated group of previous nonvoters. But it tells also that these votes were actually structured in proportions that did not dramatically differ from the hard core of the stable votes.

According to a Gallup poll taken in 1958 of a smallish national sample, 81 percent of Finnish workers who indicated a party preference favored either the FPDU or the SDP, whereas only 15 percent of the combined group of farmers and members of the middle class had a leftist preference.[12] This gives for Finland the "index of class voting" value of +66, which is relatively high, since the corresponding index values for Great Britain ranged in the 1950s between only +36 and +44.[13] Other data support the conclusion of a high incidence of class voting in Finland. For example, an urban sample interviewed in 1958 had an index value of $84 - 33 = +51;$[14] and the national sample of the 1966 election study provided the value $83 - 19 = +64$. However, this particular measure demonstrates only one social correlate in the structuring of the vote. Excluded are the ethnic background of the Swedish People's Party and the farming support of the Center Party. Neither does the index intend to measure or show such within-class and intrablock structuring as appears to be more directly due to the influence of political parties per se. The liberal-conservative cleavage in the middle class and, especially, the communist-social democratic cleavage within the working class have been good examples of such vote-structuring.

Although the votes are generally structured durably and in an immobile fashion, the parties on their part concentrate mainly on isolated short-term efforts to enable voters to choose candidates according to their labels. It is during the election campaigns that parties attempt to reach as many potential voters as possible. Furthermore, while doing so they need to stress the identity of their labels. The politics of compromise and coalition may be characteristic of governmental parties, but electoral parties want to keep their labels not only appealing but also clearly distinct from others. A content analysis of campaigning in Finnish party newspapers showed that while the campaign increased the volume of political material, it also changed the relative emphasis given to the various targets of partisan critique. More than average attention was paid to the parties' closest rivals. Obviously the attempt to prevent erosion and to scare away support from the competitors was focused increasingly along those party boundaries that were potentially the easiest to cross.[15] The pre-election negotiations to form joint electoral alliances are also at times a test of the parties' attempt to safeguard or improve their identity. Because the d'Hondt system of proportional representation is a bit unfair to small parties, they have sometimes

---

[12] See Erik Allardt and Pertti Pesonen, "Cleavages in Finnish Politics," in Seymour M. Lipset and Stein Rokkan, Eds., *Party Systems and Voter Alignments* (New York, 1967), p. 342.

[13] Robert R. Alford, *Party and Society* (Chicago, 1963).

[14] Pesonen, *An Election in Finland: Party Activities and Voter Reactions* (New Haven, 1968), p. 42.

[15] *Ibid.*, p. 213.

won legislative seats from their more distant antagonists through mutual cooperation by forming joint electoral alliances (party lists) with each other. But often one finds cases where a party has been more willing to keep its label clean and to risk losing representation in a constituency than to cooperate electorally with a "neighboring" political party.

Several methods can be used to analyze which parties are close and which ones far apart in the party system. Legislative voting records provide good information, of course, but the perceptions of the electorate may also be revealing. One sort of party sociogram is seen in the directions and the frequencies of actual changes in party preference. We notice in Tables 7.2 and 7.3 that five out of the seven FPDU borders remained shut from one election to the other, whereas the SDP exchanged voters with every other party in the system. Some lines are easy and some are hard to cross. The red/white cleavage was for a long time a very important factor in Finnish society, but that border became less of a barrier in the late 1950s;[16] the FPDU remained quite isolated longer. Survey responses may provide more refined information on the existing likes and dislikes. When Finnish and French voters were asked to rank in order all parties, the results in terms of party distances proved largely alike. Forced on a single continuum, the parties become ordered in the customary left-right sequence, and the communist end of the spectrum remains far apart from the other parties.[17] The communist/noncommunist cleavage was again very salient in 1966. According to that year's election study, 80 percent of the electorate was willing to name one party for which they "could not vote under any circumstances," and 62 percent of those mentioned the FPDU. The extreme left was also highly disliked by the social democrats (57 percent), although 64 percent of the FPDU voters (only 38 percent of all) in their turn named SDP as the number two party they "might consider voting for." Such perceptions of party distances relate to the *eduskunta* in two ways. They may influence its composition by predicting potential directions in vote-structuring and by determining some party tactics; they are reflected higher up in the legislative voting patterns.

There is an additional way to determine how durably the parties structure the electorate in parliamentary elections. One can compare the voters' parliamentary party preference with their choice in those elections involving less emphasis on the party label and more on the personal appeal of the candidate. Presidential elections provide such comparisons, and Fin-

---

[16] *Ibid.,* p. 289.

[17] Philip E. Converse, "The Problem of Party Distances in Models of Voting Change," in M. Kent Jennings and L. Harmon Zeigler, Eds., *The Electoral Process* (Englewood Cliffs, N.J., 1966), pp. 175–207.

land is particularly useful here because parliamentary elections mobilize higher turnouts in Finland than do presidential elections.[18] According to a panel study of university students who voted in the 1956 presidential election, there was more deviation from their party's nominee for president before the campaign than in its final days. Earlier party affiliation thus tended to draw deviants back toward the party label. Obviously this was caused by two interconnected factors: the strength of the party itself as a psychological reference group and the additional need, due to the electoral system, to vote for any one politician running for the Electoral College, many of whom had become familiar as the parties' candidates for Parliament.[19]

An Additional Vote Decision: The Choice of Individual Candidates

The Finnish variant of the list system of proportional representation gives the voters a very decisive word in determining which individual candidates are to be elected to Parliament. Grouped in an electoral alliance (party list) may be as many candidates as there are seats to be filled in the constituency (or fewer), and each candidate is assigned an individual number; the voter is to pick just one candidate and write his/her number on the ballot. Thus the ballots serve a double purpose—not only do they determine the distribution of seats among the parties, but they also rank-order the candidates within the party lists. Election campaigns tend to have a corresponding dual character. They are contests between political parties, but in addition, they constitute individual competition, especially more-or-less open competition among those candidates who were nominated by the same party.

In a country where the electoral system emphasizes individual candidates to such a high degree it is a natural question whether the voters want to give their legislative mandate primarily to individual legislators or to political parties. The answer is political parties. First, it is clear that voters do not entertain any thoughts about sending individuals to Parliament who have not been backed by a party nomination. Finnish voters have had the option of writing on the ballot the name of any eligible person who does not appear on the official lists, but only 161 (0.007 percent)

---

[18] Turnout percentage in parliamentary elections varied between 55.6 and 58.5 in the 1920s and was 85.1 in 1962; in presidential elections it was 39.7 in 1925 and 81.5 in 1962.

[19] Pesonen, *Valitsijamiesvaalien ylioppilasäänestäjät* (Student Voters in the Election of Presidential Electors), (Helsinki, 1958), pp. 180–183.

wrote a name in 1966. Second, when faced with the lists, most voters indeed think of parliamentary elections mainly as a choice between the parties and not between the individual nominees.

This is evidenced by the fact that many voters have no more than a slight familiarity with the candidates. Before the nominations in 1958, only 26 percent of the electors were able to name a person whom they wanted to elect to the Parliament, and soon after the election as many as 35 percent did not mention which candidate they had voted for. When asked directly, "Did you first choose the party and then the candidate, or did you primarily choose a person without regard to the party?" 80 percent of the voters mentioned the party and 15 percent the candidate.[20] In 1966 the result was basically the same, only with less difference: 67 percent said that the party, and 31 percent that the person "is more important to vote for in national elections." The reverse was found true of comparable attitudes toward local elections (37 and 61 percent).

Some differences have been found between the voters for the party and the voters for the candidate. In 1958, the new splinter group, the social democratic opposition, eroded some support from its mother party through the personal following of its candidates, and even generally the voters for the candidate tended to make up their minds later than did the party voters. Female voters seemed to become motivated to party work in a peculiar fashion—like the men, the women who were active in the campaign were strong party identifiers, yet they voted primarily for an individual candidate. It thus seems that an attachment to individual candidates activated partisan women to the extent that when voting they actually perceived the person as more important in the election than the party they identified with.[21]

It would be erroneous to conclude here that the majority who voted for the party did not care about individual representatives. Although generally secondary to the vote-structuring by the parties, the candidates obviously did matter to far more than one-half of the voters. As many as 60 percent of the interviewed voters gave reasons for their choice of candidate. Such reasons coincided often with the themes which had been used in the candidate's personal campaign. The voters thus paid attention to local representation, group representation, experiences, potential, and, to a lesser extent, the familiarity of the candidates.[22]

Women might be used as an example of a group that is offered and does obtain representation in the *eduskunta*. Most of the votes cast for

[20] Pesonen, 1968, *op. cit.*, pp. 325, 331.
[21] *Ibid.*, pp. 332–335.
[22] *Ibid.*, pp. 327–328.

women candidates really seem to be influenced by the sexual consideration. For example, in the Finnish city analyzed in 1958, about one-half of the women voters but only few men (7 percent) cast their ballot for a female.[23] Finland's large district magnitude, in turn, leaves room for long distances and considerable local variations within each multimember constituency, except Helsinki. And local interests are an important factor in the electors' choice of individual candidates. Recent data come from a study on four constituencies in 1966. That study shows how most candidates ranked either on top or in second place in their own place of residence, when compared with the other candidates of the same party—from 76 to 92 percent of all candidates in each constituency were such home-town favorites. Even neighboring communes gave above-average personal support to the local candidates.[24] There is no residence requirement in Finnish candidate selection, and outside candidates are often nominated. Their lack of a local power base is seen in that they tend to receive votes in even proportions from all corners of the constituency.[25]

Political Parties and the Recruitment of Legislators

The linkage function of political parties between the people and their representatives shows up in several ways. Some are the result of analytic theorizing, while others are directly observable in concrete events. In elections, political parties have a mediating role of a quite concrete type. A remarkable division of labor takes place as parties ignore or reject most people as potential legislators and give support to only a tiny fraction of those theoretically eligible (in Finland 0.04 percent). Correspondingly, in order to analyze the process, it seems useful to conceptualize recruitment as a sequence of eliminations through increasingly demanding "screens" or "thresholds." Only those very few citizens get the power to legislate who become (1) eligible, (2) certified, (3) willing, (4) selected, and (5) elected.

Eligibility is a legal concept and seldom becomes a political issue. Yet it is conceivable that parties eliminate their political opponents from eligibility through legislation. Finnish examples of this are the outlawry of communist activity in 1929 and of the extreme right-wing Patriotic People's Movement in 1945.

[23] *Ibid.*, p. 330. Among the students who voted in 1956, no man but 24 percent of the women cast a ballot for a female candidate for the Electoral College: Pesonen, 1958, p. 169.

[24] Esko Juppi, draft manuscript on "Regional distribution of the support of parliamentary candidates."

[25] Pesonen, 1968, *op. cit.*, pp. 328–329.

Certification has been defined as "the social screening and political channeling that results in eligibility for candidacy" (eligibility used here in a nonjuridical sense).[26] For research purposes certification could also be given more narrow and precise definitions; for example, we might here call those people certified who are considered or may be considered for candidacy in a political party organization. This definition leaves the parties or party members as our operational judges of the more general "social screening" for potential candidacy.

Willingness to run for the legislature needs to be assured before the process continues. All certified persons do not agree to accept a nomination, even when urged to do so by the party.

The selection of candidates is a very concrete affair; its end result is the list of names on official ballots. In Finland the candidates are selected in the district conventions of political parties. Some parties also poll their rank-and-file membership in order to get advice for the assembled district delegates, and the SDP makes its membership "primary" a necessary and decisive part of candidate selection. The safe seats of single-member constituencies would be actually decided at this stage.

Election is the final stage calling for the electorate to determine the composition of the legislature. To a certain extent it is a party affair, too. The partisan structuring of the vote is discussed above. Where rigid list systems of proportional representation are used, nominating parties may actually decide the success of individual candidates, and even elsewhere the parties may help to channel votes to some of their candidates.

Political parties relate to the recruitment of legislators in two different ways—they act, and they are a forum. We might ask, accordingly, what do the parties do through the elimination stages and how do they influence the process, and second, what do the potential legislators, in their turn, do in the parties? The third relevant research problem would be to describe those nominated and to determine how well the list reflects the electorate's desires.

According to our definition of certification, all those (and possibly many more) people are certified for candidacy who are openly suggested for nomination within the party organization. We have data which provide an opportunity to follow the progress of people thus certified in the SDP in 1966.[27] In that party, each basic unit was permitted to suggest names of party members to be submitted to a vote of the members of the dis-

---

[26] Henry Valen, "The Recruitment of Parliamentary Nominees in Norway," in *Scandinavian Political Studies, 1* (1966), p. 123.

[27] Information on the SDP nominations was obtained from Pertti Timonen, draft manuscript on "The 1966 Membership Poll in the Social Democratic Party."

trict organization, that is, to something like a party primary. A total of 527 persons were both suggested and willing to be considered; their number was 96 in Helsinki and varied from 22 to 58 in the 13 other constituencies. In a very obvious sense, these persons had passed the threshold of certification. Of them, 199 were selected for candidacy by the rank-and-file members. In one district (Vaasa), 80 percent of the dues-paying party members participated, in the 9 others where turnout is available, the number varied between 41 and 62 percent; it thus seems that, on the average, about 52 percent of members voted in the SDP "primary." The district conventions had a right to raise the maximum of 25 percent (since 1969, 20 percent) from lower-ranking positions up to candidacy, and in 1966 they did thus help 32 lower-ranking persons (17 percent) to the party lists. Of the 199 candidates, 55 were successful in the election and gained membership in the *eduskunta*.

Table 7.4 compares those only certified, only selected, and those elected for their physical age and their "party age." The physical age structure of the three groups was rather similar. However, the youngest eligible age group did not pass through all the stages. Although youth did not prevent certification for candidacy, the young had difficulty in getting selected and thereby lost their chance of gaining election. Most favored by the party organization were those between 40 and 59; but the electorate preferred even more maturity and tended to vote for those in their fifties. Possibly the electorate also had a tendency to level out age differences by unwillingness to support the oldest certified and nominated persons.

A comparison of the partisan records of the three groups reveals more differences. According to Table 7.4, the local units of the SDP organization certify willingly even new party members, and the new ones do not have too much difficulty in getting nominated, either. But the SDP voter, not the party, wants to send old-timers to the *eduskunta*. Although both the local units and the party membership in general may seem anxious to launch their new comrades to responsible political careers, the electorate is too traditional to follow the attempt. The SDP voters seem to prefer candidates who have accumulated political experience through a long career in the party. Furthermore, two-thirds of the elected members had joined the party before they were 30 years of age (Table 7.4). They had been the youngest when joining. But here we find a difference between the certified and the selected, too. The local party units did not mind suggesting late converts for the party primary, but it was more difficult to become selected for candidacy unless one had entered the party ranks when young.

A true test of the congruence between the selection by the relatively few partisans and the election by all party voters would be the coefficients of

Parties in the Finnish Eduskunta

Table 7.4   The Success of Persons Suggested for Candidacy
in the SDP Party Primaries in 1966 (in %)

	Suggested, Not Nominated (N = 336)	Nominated, Not Elected (N = 144)	Elected Members (N = 55)	Total (N = 535)
Age				
21–29	6	1	—	4
30–39	16	13	16	15
40–49	36	42	36	38
50–59	26	25	40	28
60 and over	11	11	8	10
No information	5	8	—	5
Total	100	100	100	100
Years of Membership				
0–6 (1960–)	22	19	9	20
7–11 (1955–)	15	12	4	13
12–16 (1950–)	12	9	9	11
17–26 (1940–)	26	24	31	26
27–36 (1930–)	8	14	21	11
37–46 (1920–)	5	7	13	6
47 and over	2	1	—	2
No information	10	14	13	11
Total	100	100	100	100
Age when Joining Party				
20	14	17	20	15
21–29	21	36	44	34
30–39	25	20	16	23
40–49	15	9	5	12
50 and over	4	3	2	4
No information	11	15	13	12
Total	100	100	100	100

correlation between actual vote distributions. Unfortunately the measures of popularity are somewhat lacking in comparability, because several names could be voted for in the "party primary," whereas in the election each voter can support one candidate only. Nevertheless, there were striking similarities. In thirteen constituencies, the Pearson coefficient ranged from .63 to .98. In only one was there a lower correlation (.41). That was the only constituency (Southern Häme) where any candidate who was elected had been placed by the party in a rank higher than he had gained in the "primary."[28]

[28] Calculated for the whole country, the Pearson coefficient was .72 (the Spearman rank-order correlation was .77), Pertti Timonen, "Sosiaalidemokraattisen puolueen kansanedustajaehdokkaiden menestyminen jäsenäänestyksessä ja varsin-

This analysis of the social democrats in the election of 1966 suggests four generalizations: (1) one needs to be a party member to be certified for candidacy; (2) generally only members of long standing gain election to the *eduskunta,* at least to its SDP group; (3) the more thresholds of elimination one crosses, the more essential a consideration becomes one's party career; and (4) the popularity of the certified and selected persons among active party members is a rather good predictor of their electoral success as well. What seems to be an unexpected finding here is the fact that ordinary voters are in effect even more partisan than are the party members. The lack of a long record of services for the party handicaps election more than it handicaps certification or selection.

The importance of party activity for election to the *eduskunta* has been demonstrated more generally, too. For example, of those 717 different persons who were elected in the nine elections between 1919 and 1939, two-thirds had been active in the party organization before gaining their first election (Table 7.5). But the parties differed from each other in this respect. After "explaining away" two exceptional cases, the short-lived communist groups of the 1920s and the 21 representatives of the Patriotic People's Movement who were mostly recruited through the party organization, we find a considerable difference between the SDP and the four nonsocialist parties. Specifically, 93 percent of the SDP legislators but only 46 to 58 percent of the nonsocialist members had belonged to the leading party echelons before their election to the *eduskunta.* Party organization seems even more important for the social democrats if we consider the fact that 40 percent of the SDP members had been employed by the party machine before gaining election to the legislature.[29] Party was the normal start of a socialist legislative career. It was less important for the nonsocialists, as one-half of them could enter the parliamentary party before distinguishing themselves in the party organization. However, this was in a sense compensated for by the visibility that the nonsocialist legislators had gained in local self-government (Table 7.5). At least 82 percent of all the legislators had been in some trustee position in their municipality before being elected to Parliament, and 44 percent had held the chairmanship of the

---

aisissa vaaleissa vuonna 1966" (The Success of the Parliamentary Candidates of the Soc. Dem. Party in the Membership Balloting and in the Actual Election in 1966), Research Reports, Institute of Political Science, University of Tampere, No. 11 (1969). According to a new draft manuscript by Timonen, the correlations were remarkably similar in 1970; there was one low $r_p = .42$; the other constituencies ranged from .63 to .97, and for the whole country $r_p = .71$, $r_s = .77$.

[29] Martti Noponen and Pertti Pesonen, "The Legislative Career in Finland," in Erik Allardt and Yrjö Littunen, Eds., *Cleavages, Ideologies and Party Systems* (Turku, 1964), pp. 456–457.

Parties in the Finnish Eduskunta

Table 7.5   Members of the Eduskunta Elected in 1919–1939 by Party and by Level of Trustee Position in Municipal Government, Level of Position in Party Organization, and Leading Position in Other Organizations, Held Prior to Their First Election to the Eduskunta (in %)

	Socialist Labor (69)	SDP (210)	Agr. (154)	Progressive (56)	Conservative (131)	Swedish (69)	PPM (21)	Total (717)
Municipal government								
Chairman of council	7	15	37	23	35	38	19	25
Council member	45	49	29	34	34	38	24	38
Chairman of board	4	9	34	25	23	22	4	19
Member of board, etc.	24	32	18	18	11	6	24	20
No position, no information	46	23	10	8	10	14	24	18
Party								
National level	9	31	22	52	22	27	43	27
District or affiliated organization	15	49	25	2	36	7	19	29
Local level	14	13	6	4	—	12	10	8
No position, no information	62	7	47	42	42	54	28	36
Other organizations								
Cooperatives and/or trade unions	48	63	60	50	36	28	19	50
Farmers, producers, and/or business	—	13	74	70	53	57	43	42

SOURCE: Martti Noponen, "Riksdagsmännens sociala backgrund," in Jans-Magnus Jansson, Ed., *Studier i finländsk politik* (Falkenberg, 1968), p. 97.

municipal council or of some municipal board. But the latter percentage was only 24 for the social democrats, and varied between 48 and 71 percent for the nonsocialist groups. Chairmanships in local government were simply more accessible in the numerous nonsocialist rural communes than they were in the fewer large cities.

Table 7.6 presents additional data for the 1966 parliamentary election. Here, too, all the parties are represented, and we can compare the successful and unsuccessful candidates within each party. But unlike the case in Table 7.4, the party activity variable is here the level of national leadership, not the duration of party membership, and unlike the case in Table 7.5, the information is current and not "frozen" at the time of the members' first election to the *eduskunta*.

We find a high degree of overlap between the parliamentary parties and

Table 7.6 Level of Leadership Position in National Party Organization for Candidates in the 1966 Parliamentary Election (in %)

	FPDU	SDL	SDP	FRP	Center	LPP	Conservative	Swedish	All
Nonelected									
Highest level[a]	13	27	8	9	10	17	8	24	12
Party council	10	7	19	5	24	12	9	15	14
Party convention	12	7	15	18	4	2	2	5	8
None	53	53	52	51	53	65	75	49	58
No information	12	6	6	17	9	4	6	7	8
Total	100	100	100	100	100	100	100	100	100
N	(137)	(15)	(144)	(57)	(135)	(113)	(160)	(41)	(802)
Elected									
Highest level[a]	32	71	20	(100)	20	78	27	42	29.5
Party council	15	—	20	—	43	22	27	33	25.5
Party convention	7	—	14	—	2	—	—	—	6
None	44	29	44	—	29	—	38	25	35.5
No information	2	—	2	—	6	—	8	—	3.5
Total	100	100	100	100	100	100	100	100	100
N	(41)	(7)	(55)	(1)	(49)	(9)	(26)	(12)	(200)

[a] Party Chairman, Deputy Chairman, Party Secretary, or member of Executive Committee.

SOURCE: Data provided by Tapio Koskiaho.

the national leadership of the party organizations; 55 percent of the legislators (i.e., 110 members) took part in the between-convention decision-making of their party on a national level, either as members of the party council or as higher leaders. Only 26 percent of the nonelected candidates had the same distinction. This seems, at the first sight, to support some conclusions made above. But an analysis by party seems to suggest some inconsistencies. Now the nonsocialist members are the ones with the most partisan background; besides, the voters for the SDP were the least prone to pick national party leaders from among the candidates. However, the partisanship of the nonsocialist members does not contradict Table 7.5 if it is true that many nonsocialist legislators were recruited to party leadership from the Parliament, whereas the tendency in the SDP was in the opposite direction—to recruit parliamentarians from the party organization. Party leadership via the *eduskunta* is suggested by the fact that the percentages of nonsocialist members in national party leadership were much higher in 1966 than were the percentages with such a background when elected for the first time between 1919 and 1939. One consistency in the two tables is also the heavy reliance on the parliamentarians for organizational leadership in the weakly organized liberal parties, the Progressives, and the Liberal People's Party.

The social democrats are an unexpected exception on the district level, too. Table 7.7 gives the percentages of the only-selected and the elected

Table 7.7   Percentage of Candidates in the 1966 Parliamentary Election
Holding a Leadership Position in their Party's District Organization[a]

	FPDU	SDL	SDP	FRP	Center	LPP	Con-serva-tive	Swedish	All
Nonelected candidates	66	60	56	54	41	42	43	27	49
Elected candidates	80	86	56	(0)	55	67	69	58	64

[a] Included are Chairmen, Deputy Chairmen, Secretaries, and members of Executive Committee of District Organizations.
SOURCE: Data provided by Tapio Koskiaho.

candidates holding a leading position in the district organization of their party in 1966. The general pattern is clear: the members of Parliament were more likely to lead their district organizations than were the unsuccessful candidates. But further analysis is needed in order to explain why the attachment of SDP voters to party members with a long "tenure" did not appear as an equally clear attachment to such party members who occupied positions of leadership. One element of exceptionality was the high turnover of SP legislators in 1966, as the party's parliamentary group grew from 38 to 55. However, in many other parties it would also seem quite plausible again that several legislators were elected to organizational leadership in their constituencies after they had proven themselves in successful elections.

It is a well-known generalization that voters send to the legislature representatives of a higher status, although it has not been established as frequently whether this is a result of their choice or of the preceding elimination of possibly more favored eligibles from the race. For an example, Table 7.8 reviews how the educational level of Finland's *eduskunta* has

Table 7.8   Development of the Education of Finnish Legislators from 1905 to 1966, and the Education of Unelected Candidates in 1966 (in %)

Level of Education	The Estates, 1905–1906 ($N = 415$)	Parliaments, 1907–1917 ($N = 580$)	Parliaments, 1919–1939 ($N = 717$)	Parliament, 1958 ($N = 200$)	Parliament, 1966 ($N = 200$)	Unelected, 1966 ($N = 802$)
Academic degree	68	30	33	34	37	31
Secondary or vocational education	16	14	14	18	20.5	26
Lower technical school, etc.	4	12	28	30	31	23
Primary school	4	12	15	17	11	15
No school	2	12	6	—	0.5	0
No information[a]	6	20	4	1	—	5
Total	100	100	100	100	100	100

[a] For 1907–1917, most cases are probably with low or no formal education.

SOURCE: Noponen, *op. cit.* (1968), p. 95; and data provided by Tapio Koskiaho.

developed. Although the breakthrough of democratic representation lowered the educational level of the legislature dramatically in 1907, it was still far above that of the population at large.[30] The six decades of the

[30] According to the 1960 Census, only 4 percent of the population over 25 years had matriculated from high school; 1.3 percent had an academic degree. Secondary (middle school) education was held by 8 percent of those over 15 years of age.

eduskunta have witnessed a slow trend toward an increased level of education among the legislators, despite the long-range increase in the "populist"
party grouping. But what is most relevant here is the comparison of elected
and defeated candidates. Obviously Finnish voters did not give their mandate in 1966 to persons with a higher education because of any lack of
other choices. Rather, they even tended to support candidates with an
above-average education and thus to bias more the already biased selection
of candidates.

The study of the recent SDP "primary" included additional information
that helps us with the question What do the parties do? The district secretaries of the party explained why the party leadership in some cases
changed the rank-ordering of suggested candidates from the order obtained
in the membership poll. They gave the following kinds of reasons: (1) to
balance geographic representation on the ballot, (2) to balance the representation of various internal groups (e.g., small farmers, union labor, the
young, the women, the sports organizations), (3) to make adjustments
in the light of some last-minute refusals to run, (4) for a circumstantial
reason, the desire of some SDL candidates to return to the SDP, and (5)
in some cases because other responsibilities or old age were considered
a handicap in legislative performance. Such changes might be initiated
either by the national leadership or by the district convention. Contrary
to a popular belief, it seems that the national SDP leadership did not propose changes in an oligarchic fashion. The changes in candidate selection
were generally wanted by the district conventions for one specific purpose:
to maximize the list's appeal to the voters in the constituency.[31] This very
point is a potential reason for conflict between the party leadership and
some internal groups in Finnish parties. Because the voters rank-order the
individual candidates, one candidate only for the women, the young, the
locale, or the occupational group might have a secure election in a constituency; whereas several candidates with the same characteristic, although
likely to bring in more votes for the party, might divide the votes and
thus prevent each other from gaining election.

The Parties in the Legislature

When the *eduskunta* assembles after an election, its newly elected members are seated alphabetically and its oldest member chairs the meeting.
But in all other plenary meetings the members occupy their named seats,
first assigned as a block to their party and then by the party to the members individually. The extreme left is occupied by the FPDU and the ex-

---

[31] Timonen, the 1966 manuscript, *op. cit.*

treme right by the Swedish People's Party (not necessarily because of the Swedes' location on some left-right continuum but because it is handy to sit there for the interpreter's services). Although nonexistent juridically, the parties have been thus recognized *de facto* since 1907. The party groups also have their own meeting rooms and internal organization. Proportionality has been followed within the *eduskunta* in dividing the committee posts and chairmanships among the parties. Another traditional *de facto* recognition of parties is demonstrated when negotiations are opened for a new cabinet coalition: the president meets then with the chairman of each party's parliament group. Partisanship is so pervasive in the *eduskunta* that the legislature can be better conceived of as the sum total of its party groups than as an aggregate of its 200 individual members.

Because there are eight party groups, none can make decisions alone. Furthermore, each party group (except the only member of the Finnish Rural Party in 1966–1970) might sometimes be in the position where it holds the balance of power between two committed blocks. This idea has led to the theoretical conception of parliamentary voting power, which does not necessarily equal the group's actual size. A good reminder is the famous vote of confidence in the Norwegian *Storting* in 1963, when the Socialist Party with two members broke a 74–74 tie, decided to side with the opposition, and defeated the Labor government after its 28 years in power; in that situation the voting power of the two representatives equalled that of 74. Table 7.9 gives the theoretical voting power of party groups in the *eduskunta* during five legislative terms. In the table, the power of parliamentary parties is thus not determined by the group's actual size but by the number of possible combinations in which that party would determine which side gets the majority. We notice that in three out of five Parliaments, the conservatives with 24–29 seats had no more voting power than did the small people's parties with 8–14 seats, and again in 1966 the 26 conservative members as a group were no more powerful than were the 12 Swedish members. Party groups with more than about 42 members gain increasing strength, and a party with more than 100 seats would alone have enough of the voting power to assure its control (the SDP in 1916 is the only Finnish example). The Center Party, which the electoral system has given some overrepresentation, has also received the most increased theoretical advantage due to its "surplus" voting power. That surplus, however, has not been as large as the conservative disadvantage.[32]

The analysis of unweighted theoretical voting power would be realistic

---

[32] Risto Sänkiaho, "Äänestysvoimakkuudesta eduskunnassa v. 1951–66" (On the Voting Power in the Finnish Parliament in 1951–66), *Politiikka,* **4** (1966), pp. 179–189, 214–215.

Table 7.9   Theoretical Voting Power of Party Groups in the *Eduskunta* from 1951 to 1966, Compared with the Parties' Share of Parliamentary Seats and of Popular Vote

		FPDU	SDL	SDP	Center	Other	LPP	Conservative	Swedish
	VP	.200	—	.302	.302	—	.066	.066	.066
1951	A	−.015	—	+.037	+.047	—	+.016	−.074	+.009
	B	−.016	—	+.037	+.070	—	+.009	−.080	+.010
	VP	.200	—	.302	.302	—	.066	.066	.066
1954	A	−.015	—	+.032	+.037	—	+.001	−.054	+.001
	B	−.016	—	+.040	+.061	—	−.013	−.062	−.004
	VP	.273	.038	.238	.238	—	.071	.071	.071
1958	A	+.023	+.023	−.002	−.002	—	+.031	−.074	+.001
	B	+.041	+.021	+.006	+.007	—	+.012	−.082	+.004
	VP	.249	.016	.179	.323	—	.055	.106	.072
1962	A	+.014	.006	−.011	+.058	−.005	−.010	−.054	+.002
	B	+.029	−.028	−.016	+.093	−.005	−.008	−.044	+.008
	VP	.209	.020	.325	.287	—	.031	.066	.006
1966	A	+.004	−.015	+.050	+.042	−.005	−.014	−.064	+.006
	B	−.003	−.006	+.053	+.075	−.010	−.034	−.071	+.006
	VP	1.131	.074	1.344	1.452	—	.289	.375	.341
Total	A	+.011	+.014	+.106	+.182	−.010	+.024	−.320	+.019
	B	+.035	−.013	+.120	+.306	−.015	−.034	−.339	+.024

VP = voting power according to the formula

$$VP_i = \sum \frac{(s-1)!(n-s)!}{n!};$$

see Irwin Mann and L. S. Shapley, "The A priori Voting Strength of the Electoral College," in Martin Shubik, Ed., *Game Theory and Related Approaches to Social Behavior* (New York, 1964) p. 159.
A   = difference from share of seats
B   = difference from share of popular vote
SOURCE: Risto Sänkiaho, "Äänestysvoimakkuudesta eduskunnassa v. 1951–66," *Politiikka* 4 (1966), p. 186.

only if each party group would always vote as a unanimous block and if all possible combinations of party groups would be equally likely to occur in actual legislative voting. The latter is obviously not true in any multiparty system. How unanimously the groups vote has been measured on the basis of roll calls in the legislatures of several countries.

During the three legislative sessions in 1948–1951, 2286 votes were taken in the Finnish *eduskunta*. Of them, 745 (32.6 percent) were by the show of hands. Any member could demand a vote by the machine, and 1144 (50.5 percent) votes were thus taken by pushing buttons. After that, 20 members could demand a recorded roll-call vote, of which there were 397 (7.4 percent). Only the last-mentioned votes are available for analysis. In them the party groups demonstrated high internal consistency. Stuart Rice's index of cohesion ranges from 0.0 to 100.0, but the mean of such indexes calculated for the Finnish party groups varied between 74.5 for the Swedish People's Party and 95.1 for the FPDU. Even on this generally high level there were three distinguishable intensities of party uniformity. Between the Swedes and the extreme left there was an intermediate group of other parties, which ranged from the Progressive Party's 82.0 to the Agrarian Union's 87.3. We might mention for comparison that the French Chamber of Deputies had party groups in the 1930s which scored index averages below 50. In the *eduskunta* 1948–1951, the number of open votes in which the entire party group was unanimous varied between 191 votes (48 percent) by the SDP, and 332 votes (84 percent) by the FPDU.[33]

From this kind of summary measurement of relative party cohesion an analyst can proceed in two directions. He may study the development of party cohesion over time, or he may look for the types of issues or other causes that strengthen or loosen "party discipline." A comparison between the three annual sessions, 1948 to 1951, did not show much difference nor very consistent development while the *eduskunta* "matured," except perhaps the tendency to have less cohesion during the first year after election.[34] Table 7.10 summarizes the time series of the average index of cohesion calculated for each electoral term, 1930 to 1954. These indexes lead to several observations: (1) there is, in general, considerable consistency over time within each party group; (2) the nonsocialist parties show a general trend toward increased internal cohesion; (3) the FPDU, after its arrival in the *eduskunta*, has been without exception the most cohesive group; (4) on the other hand, the SDP lost some of its high cohesion when it was no longer the most leftist group, and thus shows a trend toward decreasing cohesion; and (5) the change in the quality of the voting data in 1951, when all machine votes became recorded individually, does not seem to change greatly the measures of cohesion from the earlier infrequent roll-call voting. One might hypothesize here that the strength of growing party organizations accounts for the apparent growing cohesion

[33] Pekka Nyholm, "Riksdagsgruppernas sammanhållning under 1948–1951 års mandatperiod" (The Cohesion of Parliamentary Groups during the Electoral Term of 1948–1951), in Jansson, *op. cit.;* esp. pp. 213–219.

[34] *Ibid.*, p. 220.

in some nonsocialist parliamentary groups; yet such a relationship can be verified for the conservatives only. Actually a partial reason for the increasing cohesion after World War II, especially after 1951, may have been the general tendency of nonsocialists to vote against communist proposals; these became even more numerous in 1951 because earlier they had been often decided by machine votes that were not individually recorded. At the same time the lowering Agrarian and SDP cohesion might be seen as the result of the difficult position of these parties between two "fires": opposition to communist proposals and competition for the same voters with the FPDU.[35]

Table 7.10   Average Indexes of Party Cohesion in the *Eduskunta*

Years	(*N*)	FPDU	SDP	Agrarian	Progressive	Conservative	Swedish	PPM
(All Open Votes, 1930–1954)								
1930–1933	(157)	—	87.4	72.4	73.0	73.3	63.7	—
1933–1936	(244)	—	86.2	79.7	74.3	79.5	73.0	81.3
1936–1949	(154)	—	89.4	76.1	73.0	92.1	67.4	84.7
1939–1945	(136)	—	89.5	82.0	74.4	71.7	74.7	81.9
1945–1948	(282)	92.1	76.6	81.9	83.3	85.7	75.5	—
1948–1951	(397)	95.1	86.6	87.3	82.0	84.0	74.5	—
1951–1954	(1026)	94.9	81.7	82.6	86.2	85.5	81.3	—
(FPDU Proposals, 1945–1954)								
1945–1948		95.7	55.0	79.8	82.9	85.4	77.4	—
1948–1951		99.2	82.0	84.3	91.8	93.6	90.2	—
1951–1954		97.1	84.8	88.7	91.6	92.7	93.9	—

source: Pekka Nyholm and Carl Hagfors, *Ryhmäyhtenäisyyden kehityksestä eduskunnassa,* Research Reports, Institute of Political Science, University of Helsinki, No. 14/1968.

When the FPDU was on the scene for the first time in 1945–1948, the social democrats reacted with an exceptional ambivalence to proposals by the new extreme left; the cohesion of the SDP in these open votes averaged only 55.0. But after 1951 the pattern became consistent in all party groups; whenever FPDU made a motion, all party groups reacted with an above-

[35] Nyholm and Carl Hagfors, *Ryhmäyhtenäisyyden kehityksestä eduskunnassa 1930–1954* (On the Development of Party Cohesion in the *Eduskunta* between 1930–54), Research Reports, Institute of Political Science, University of Helsinki, No. 14 (1968); esp. pp. 4–12.

average internal uniformity. This is shown in Table 7.10 by a comparison between the average indexes with the averages for the FPDU initiatives only. An analysis of the 1948–1951 period also indicated that the political content of the votes had an impact on group cohesion. First of all, the greater the political stakes the more intense was the cohesion—in the votes of confidence all party groups tended toward unanimity. But the issue content was influential also. In general the easiest votes seemed to be those in which parties followed the traditional left/nonsocialist division; in them an above-average cohesion was observed. Special cases of high cohesion included votes where the interests of agriculture or the communist/noncommunist cleavage were present; whereas groups tended to lose cohesion in certain cases when the urban-rural cleavage formed the voting coalitions.[36] One might generalize that no political party was supported by such a uniform or monolithic segment of the electorate that it would have been always wise or possible to vote with maximum party cohesion. Even in a multiparty system and even in a socially homogeneous party, the political competition for pluralistic voter groups forces legislative parties to an occasional incohesiveness, as well as individual legislators to deviations from their party line. We may conclude that three general factors are related to the cohesion or the amount of discipline applied in the party groups: the initiator of the matter, the general political importance of the matter, and its specialized substantive importance to particular political groups.

Patterns of legislative voting not only reveal the intensities of party discipline and cohesion which militate against legislative individuality; they are a major source of information about the basic dimensions of a country's party system. The three most obvious Finnish dimensions are actually mentioned above. When the four largest party groups (i.e. majorities within the groups) are used as the behaving entities in the study of the 397 roll-call votes in 1948–1951, they formed four typical combinations. The communists voted against all others 83 times (21 percent); the left/nonsocialist cleavage was the most pervasive (194 votes, 49 percent); and two other groupings reflected either the producer/consumer or the more general rural/urban cleavage. The Agrarian Union was alone against the three others 46 times (12 percent), and together with the FPDU against the SDP and conservatives 47 times (12 percent). The three other combinations were very rare; the conservatives voted alone 15 times and with the FPDU six times, the SDP alone only five times. Once the four groups voted in unison.[37]

Although highly important, the political party is not the only factor that

---

[36] Nyholm, *op. cit.*, 1968, pp. 231–234.
[37] *Ibid.*, p. 224.

influences Finnish legislative behavior. Regional, occupational, and moral considerations cut across party lines; at times, it seems that even attitudes toward the President of the Republic have divided party groups. But we will not review those studies that have been made of individual voting records in Finland, nor do we attempt to summarize those few data that have been collected through interviews of the legislators. We might, however, refer to an experimental attempt to measure the party distances by means of individual voting records. Of the 474 recorded votes during the 1960 legislative session, a sample of 100 was taken. The members were forced onto a presumed left-right dimension by giving to each member −1 point when he voted with the majority of the FPDU and +1 point when voting with the majority of the conservative party. There were, indeed, two communist members who scored the full −100 points. The most extreme conservative member scored +65 points. Generally, the results are quite reminiscent of those conclusions about party distances that were based on survey evidence. Out of the 199 members (the Speaker not voting), one-third (68 members) were located on the dimension's "center range," from the SDP median +18 to the Swedish People's Party median +40. This range was dominated by the 38 Agrarian members located there (also, SDP 19, Swedish 7, FPP 3, and Conservative 1). To the right from the central range (from +40 to +65) were 47 members. Only two party groups, the FPDU and the Social Democratic League, were located on the left side of the dimension. Furthermore, the study showed the young deviating more from their party line than the old members. An illustrative finding about the impact of the party was that especially the chairmen of the groups tended toward their traditional party identity—left from the party median in the FPDU and the SDL, right from the median in the conservative and FPP groups, and toward each other in the SDP and Agrarian groups. There was an Agrarian minority cabinet in Finland in 1960, and its ministers were concentrated on a very narrow range of this left-right dimension of legislative voting. They were just slightly right of the Agrarian party median.[38]

When changes over time in the distances between parliamentary parties constitute the research problem, the high degree of internal party cohesion typical of multiparty systems obviously justifies the use of party groups rather than individuals as the units of analysis. Mogens N. Pedersen has thus shown in Denmark the usefulness of his simple index of party dis-

---

[38] Tapani Saukkonen, "Äänestysulottuvuudet vuoden 1960 valtiopäivillä" (Voting Dimensions during the 1960 Legislative Session), Master's Thesis, University of Helsinki, 1965.

tances (ranging from 0 to 100).[39] Applied to the parties of Finland's *eduskunta* during the three cabinets of 1962–1966, similar index scores illustrate distinctly the cleavage between the left and the nonsocialist parties. Moreover, inside the left the SDP and the FPDU were moving toward each other during this 4-year legislative term (the index scores were 39, 30, and 16.5). The nonsocialist party groups tended to vote very much alike (with scores as low as 3). The most distant parties in the system were the FPDU and the conservatives (93, 96, and 89.5), although during the second period, that of a nonparty cabinet, the Finnish and the Swedish People's Parties also differed almost regularly from the FPDU (index scores 97 and 95).[40] The author of the analysis, Risto Sänkiaho, also correlated with each other individual votes cast by a 45-member sample of legislators. Here party labels were not the a priori starting point of legislative behavior analysis, but once again the focal impact of the party was illustrated. For each period a varimax rotation produced five factors, almost all of which were characterized by one single party group. Only the more general left-right dimension was an exception in this factor analysis of parliamentary voting in Finland.[41]

An overlap of the parliamentary parties and of the national leadership of party organizations is noted before. But, formally, each party tries to keep its parliamentary group separate from the party organization. Party rules mention the parliamentarians only rarely or not at all. The Center Party is the only one that has entitled its parliamentary group as such to representation in the party executive and the party council. Others only allow legislators to be present at such meetings, and they do require parliamentary groups to present their reports to the party conventions. In practice, however, the legislators frequently have leading positions in the membership organization, and the further left one proceeds on the left-right dimension, the less do the parliamentarians usually emphasize their

[39] The distance between two parliamentary parties a and b is defined as:

$$\frac{(0 \cdot X_{ab} + 0.5 \cdot Y_{ab} + 1 \cdot Z_{ab}) \cdot 100}{N}$$

in which N = the total number of divisions; X_{ab} = the number of divisions where (majorities within) a and b voted the same way, Y_{ab} = the number of divisions where either a or b abstained, and Z_{ab} = the number of divisions, where one voted for, the other against. Mogens N. Pedersen, "Consensus and Conflict in the Danish Folketing 1945–65," *Scandinavian Political Studies,* 2 (1967), pp. 152, 164–165.

[40] Risto Sänkiaho, "Eduskunnan äänestysdimensioista vaalikaudella 1962–1966" (On Voting Dimensions in the *Eduskunta* during the 1962–66 Legislative Term), Research Reports of the Institute of Political Science, University of Helsinki, No. 17 (1969), pp. 33–35.

[41] *Ibid.*, pp. 4–13.

independence from the party organization. Sometimes, when the party organization functions as a pressure group, one may even encounter a genuine conflict of interests. It seems that the state subsidies to the parties were an exceptionally large-scale case of this sort. It was in the interests of the party organizations to pressure for public money, but all parliamentarians were not exactly delighted to be forced into the position where they had to assume the responsibility for the decision and to defend it to the voters, both immediately and during the campaign of 1970.

Conclusion

Democratic representation has been practiced in Finland since the radical reform of 1906. All the law and formal terminology have viewed representation as the mutual relationship between the people and the legislators. Moreover, official norms characterize legislation as the product of the work done by 200 independent, totally uninstructed individuals. Such conceptions do not easily fit in with the equally prevailing norm of proportionality in representation, and are quite empty of empirical content.

Political parties have constituted a *de facto* link between the people and the legislature. They structure the vote, they train and select the candidates for the legislature, and they again structure the legislative vote in the *eduskunta*. For each of the three levels in the system, various kinds of research evidence bear on the essential function which the parties serve in popular representation. The general legitimacy of party activity, an increasing politicization in several previously unpoliticized areas of social life, and the general trend toward an increased division of labor and specialization in the society have led to a situation in which political parties could no more function without *de jure* as well as *de facto* recognition as components of the Finnish political system. At the same time the parties seem to feel secure enough to attempt to prevent new competitors from arising in the future and to grasp for open material benefits from the state. A semi-official status was first reached, and a Party Law was enacted in 1969.

The Finnish electorate may react after some time lag to certain recent developments. According to a survey in 1968, the people were, in general, satisfied with the performance of various public institutions. The governing of administrative provinces and the work of the courts were approved of with some *laude;* the average citizen was critical only of the *eduskunta* and of the offices working for taxation.[42] The legislature attracts criticism,

[42] Raimo Blom, "Kansa katselee laitoksiaan" (The People Look at Their Institutions), Mimeograph series of the Institute of Legal Studies, University of Tampere, No. 2 (1968), p. 3.

it seems, because the old suspicion of parties and partisanship still exists. Only 15 percent of the people found it a good idea in 1966 to support political parties with public money. Although such suspicion may originate largely outside the legislative system, even the legislative parties seem unable to gain full public support. One basic reason might be the large number of political parties. In mass media and other public debate each party is constantly blamed by an overwhelming majority of others. In the legislature the parties are caught between two mutually inconsistent fires. Since compromise is always necessary, no party satisfies its clientele so as to fulfill its specific promises; even the sweetest rhetoric cannot cover how the partisan realities fail to harmonize with the widely shared Burkean expectations of legislative nonpartisanship.

CHAPTER EIGHT

Councillors, Activists, and Electors: Democratic Relationships in Scottish Cities*

JOHN A. BRAND

UNIVERSITY OF STRATHCLYDE

The relationship between electors and their representatives in the legislature is ambiguous and controversial. In Britain, the argument is particularly acute within the Labour Party, where there have been many examples of the extra-parliamentary policy conference passing a resolution that has been ignored, and indeed sometimes actively opposed, by the parliamentary leadership. In the debate over capital punishment, for example, there is no doubt that the majority of the electors would vote for the retention and even the extension of hanging, but their MPs are in opposition to the practice. One prominent abolitionist held a seat in which it was known that 80 percent of the voters were for hanging. In general, therefore, the autonomy of the representative and the rights of the elector in influencing what the representative does in the legislature are real issues.

This chapter first describes the relationship between city councillors and their electors in three of the largest towns in Scotland, in terms of familiar conceptions of representation. It then examines two hypotheses that attempt to account for differences in the relationships. Specifically, it is suggested that two factors are important: the character of the community, and the type of party that the councillors and their constituents support.

* The study described in this research was funded for Aberdeen and Edinburgh by a grant from the Social Science Research Council. In Glasgow it was funded by the University of Strathclyde. The data in Aberdeen were collected by a team under the supervision of Professor Frank Bealy and in Edinburgh by Professor James Cornford. In Glasgow the author organized the collection of the data.

Alternative Conceptions of Representation

The "models" sketched out here are essentially the same as those discussed in the well-known article by Miller and Stokes.[1] The first, which might be called the microcosm conception, considers one set of individuals to represent another insofar as the first group is a replication in miniature of the second. Thus, for an assembly truly to represent the nation it must have proportionally the same characteristics as the nation. This view is akin to the "descriptive" view of representation discussed by Hannah Pitkin,[2] who cites as an example John Adams's claim that a representative legislature "should be an exact portrait in miniature of the people at large, as it should think, feel, reason and act like them."[3] Many theorists holding this view maintain that such matching of feeling and opinion can occur only if the social composition of the legislature also matches that of the nation at large. On such grounds, for example, Sidney and Beatrice Webb regarded the House of Lords as "the worst representative assembly ever created, in that it contains absolutely no members of the manual working class; none of the great class of shopkeepers, clerks, and teachers; none of the half of all citizens who are of the female sex."[4]

The two principal elements comprising this model—correspondence of opinion or feelings and correspondence of social or demographic structure between representative body and represented citizenry—are fairly simple to operationalize. But the model does present several conceptual problems. One concerns the mechanisms linking the elements. The process by which microcosmic representation produces correspondence of opinions is not specified at all, nor is the process by which correspondence of feeling or opinion between representatives and represented that automatically leads the representative body to make decisions which are in the interest of the public at large. Equally unspecified is the rule by which we determine *which* opinions and feelings or which demographic or social characteristics of a population are important enough to be mirrored in the legislative microcosm. Presumably it makes little difference whether legislators' views on the validity of structuralist theory in anthropology match the distribution of popular views on that topic. Presumably it makes equally little difference whether the weight distribution of legislators matches that of the general population in mean, median, mode, skewness, kurtosis, class

---

[1] Warren E. Miller and Donald E. Stokes, "Constituency Influence in Congress," *American Political Science Review*, **57** (1963), pp. 45–56.

[2] Hannah Pitkin, *The Concept of Representation* (Berkeley, Calif., 1967).

[3] John Adams, *Works* (Boston, 1852–1866), Vol. IV, p. 205.

[4] Cited by Carl J. Friedrich, *Constitutional Government and Democracy* (Boston, 1950), pp. 304–305.

interval groups, and so on. While we assume in the following argument that social class is an important variable in this respect, we must yet recognize that theorists gives us little guidance in understanding why.

A second possible conception, which may be called the Burkean model, is concerned not with demographic similarity but much more with opinion. The representative gains status by some legitimating procedures (such as election or appointment by some legitimate authority), but this carries no necessary implications concerning the opinions he holds or the actions he takes. The model outlines a legitimate, perhaps contractual relationship between representative and represented, but one in which similarity of opinion between the two is irrelevant. It assumes a representative who is more knowledgeable than his constituents because of the time he has given to considering public problems, especially in deliberation with his fellow representatives, but perhaps also, as suggested by Burke, because persons chosen to be representatives are likely to be of a type superior to the average. Constituents may well choose not a common man but one who has uncommon qualities whom they choose because of them. In any case, the distinctive feature of this model is that it posits no necessary correspondence between the views of the legislator and those of his constituents. The important implication of this for representative behavior, as argued by Edmund Burke, for example, is the view that the representative should not be "mandated," that is, bound by instructions, by those who vote him into office. He is not to be told how to vote, not only because membership in the Parliament, if not personal capacity, makes his judgment superior to theirs, but also because electors see only their own interest, whereas it is the duty of the representative, while forwarding the legitimate interests of his constituency, to determine and enact the interest of the community as a whole.

Something very like this view is often expressed in Britain and is written into the constitution in many other countries:

"The members of the Reichstag are the representatives of the people as a whole and shall not be bound by orders or instructions."

"The members of Congress are representatives of the nation and not of the colleges which elect them."

"The members of the two Houses shall represent the nation, and not the province alone nor the subdivision of the province which elects them."

"Deputies shall represent the nation as a whole and not the several provinces from which they are chosen."

The particularities of political and legislative structure introduce complexities and refinements into conceptualization of representation, although they do not vitiate the basic distinction between microcosmic and Burkean conceptions briefly described before. Thus the microcosmic conceptions of representation may concern themselves not with the total legislative body's collective mirroring of the community it collectively represents but with the match between individual representatives' opinions and socioeconomic or other characteristics and those of the small segment of the community, the small district or constituency which each represents (assuming the mode of selection relies on such district-by-district representation). If the legislators individually mirror their constituencies in that fashion, of course, then the legislature collectively would also be reasonably reflective of the community as an aggregate of those constituencies. But the converse is not necessarily the case; that is, the legislature collectively might well be a microcosmic representation of the community at the same time as individual legislators did not very well match their own individual constituencies.

Finally, the development of modern party systems introduces questions about the representative's mirroring or fiduciary representation of his political party, or, to keep our conceptual classification uniform, the citizens and voters of his own political party. The relationships between legislators and the party organizations and officials (precinct, election district, parliamentary, etc.), and how these relationships affect the basic representative relationship between legislators and citizens (in this case, citizens of their party) is, of course, a special problem within the larger conceptual scheme.

In this chapter we examine some of the key relationships and perceptual linkages—between constituents, voters, party, and so on—in several local representative situations in Great Britain in the light of these alternative conceptions of representation.

The Research Setting

Current interest in local government reform, as well as a general neglect of that level of government in previous research on representation, suggested that the links between local government voters and their city councillors should be a fruitful area in which to explore these conceptions of representation. The three largest towns in Scotland were selected for this purpose—Glasgow, with an electorate of 636,432, Aberdeen, with 121,363, and Edinburgh, with 329,906.

Political Parties in Scottish Local Government. Understanding of local politics in Scotland can best begin with some understanding of the political parties involved. Whereas in national affairs it is the Conservative and Labour parties which play the key roles, supported in varying degrees and various ways by the Liberals, in Scottish local affairs the chief political parties are Labour and the Progressive Party.

The Labour Party is a wing of the national Labour movement. It has an association in the vast majority of the wards in the big towns. (There are 37 wards in Glasgow, 23 in Edinburgh, and 12 in Aberdeen.) These bodies, most of which meet monthly, are responsible for the nomination of municipal candidates from a panel that has been approved by the executive of the City Labour Party concerned. This latter organization is made up of people nominated to it by the party organizations themselves, by the trades unions, by the Co-operative Movement, and by the Socialist societies (such as the Fabian Society or the Society of Labour Teachers). If a ward association chooses not to name a candidate, it is possible for the City Party to put in a candidate of its own, but this is the exception rather than the rule.

It is often said that Progressives are simply the local government wing of the Conservative Party. This is not correct, although it is true that the majority of Progressive electors and councillors vote Conservative at elections for Parliament and that many Progressive associations have agreements with the local Conservative Party, either for help during elections or for cash. Not all Progressives are Conservatives—they may be Liberals or Scottish Nationalists. Most of the Progressive parties were set up as antisocialist coalitions in the 1930s, in response to the entry of Labour into local government. One of their principles was that national parties should have no part whatever in local government. For this reason, they were intensely local, even to the extent of having no contact among different Progressive Associations in different towns. In the last 10 years, a strong feeling has developed among officials of the Conservative party that the day of the Progressives is done and that the job of opposing Labour should be taken over entirely by the Conservatives. This point of view has made great headway among the Conservative party workers. For many Progressive Councillors, however, this constitutes unwelcome central interference, and they have fought it with varying success. Opposition to a takeover by the Conservatives has been common even among Progressives who are staunch Tories. Among most Progressives there is the feeling that this latest initiative is another assault by the Centralisers on local (and healthy) public life.

Strictly speaking, the Progressive Party is an organization only among the city councillors. In each city, there is a Progressive Association that generally meets only once a year to hear a report from the Councillors. The meeting is usually a very formal affair. In fact, the Association is made up of people who have made donations to the election funds of the party, and the annual meeting is about finance. There is little or no Progressive organization in the wards. In Aberdeen, for example, three of the marginal wards have such a body, but meetings are very intermittent and concern themselves only with the organization of elections. This means that the Progressive councillors are more or less a self-selecting group. When there is a vacancy for a Progressive candidate, Progressive councillors make informal contacts with people whom they know may be interested in standing. The potential candidate then has a meeting, which is invariably informal, with the sitting councillors, or a small group of them. In many cases, it takes place over a meal. If the candidate is suitable, arrangements will be made for the candidate to be nominated by a group of electors in a ward, and the councillors have their contacts within each ward who can be relied upon to run an election campaign.

One main reason for the difference in organization between Labour and Progressives arises from the philosophy and background of the parties. For Labour, the local parties are simply extensions of the working-class movement as a whole. Historically, members of the Labour Party started fighting local government elections before they were able to win seats in Parliament, because they believed that much could be done by town councils to improve the quality of working-class life.

The Progressives follow a much older pattern. The tradition of urban local government in Scotland, as in England, was rule by a group of local notables who regard this task as their prerogative, and sometimes as their duty. This tradition largely explains the self-selecting quality of the Progressives. When the Labour Party started contesting elections at the beginning of the twentieth century, it was precisely this group that complained that there was nothing "political" about local government. It could be best accomplished by a joint effort of the "best men." For this group, the aim was the businesslike management of town affairs, with no waste of the ratepayers money.

Provision of services for the worse-off members of the community hardly bulked large in this philosophy. On the other hand, notables often had support because of a general feeling that the rates should be kept down, as well as because local government electors have often tended to look to the business interest for leadership in local affairs. Local businesses are, after all, very visible local institutions; people who run them are locals in a sense that does not apply to other members of the middle class who can be geographically more mobile in their jobs and their social lives. Local businessmen are committed to a community.

The fact that chain stores have taken over many local businesses has meant the end of this kind of pattern in a pure form. It has also meant that the intensely local Progressives are now being replaced by the Conservatives. The Progressive candidate or councillor traditionally paid his own way and often made substantial contributions to the central fighting fund of the party. To do this, he had to be moderately well off. For candidates standing as Conservatives, however, to whom large central funds of the Conservative Party are available, individual independent financing is not as important. In areas where the old businesses are now on their knees, Conservatives are successful, and their success means that a new type of anti-Labour councillor is appearing, one who is not as affluent as his predecessor. Instead of a substantial businessman, he is typically a professional or semiprofessional or an executive in a larger firm, or perhaps even has a rather humble job, such as an insurance agent or salesman. Thus the character of local government in Scotland is changing and with it, perhaps, the basis of representation.

Politics in the Three Cities. Glasgow, the first of our cities, is by far the largest city in Scotland. Within the city boundaries there are just under 1 million people; in the Glasgow metropolitan region there is a population of 2 million. In other words, two of every five people living in Scotland live in a community centered on Glasgow. Until very recently Glasgow had the highest housing density in Europe, and its density is still the highest in Britain. It has an enormous slum problem, slums of a degradation unparalleled in Britain. Until the interwar years, much of its industrial base was in heavy engineering and shipbuilding. Now that these are in decline there is a great deal of unemployment.

Despite the city's poverty, unemployment, and consequent violence, there is no local pride like that of a Glaswegian. It is a pride in the people more than just the place, not in the aristocratic patrons or the merchant princes but in the very ordinary people. That is to say, Glasgow's is a distinctive working-class culture, which embodies pride in the very size of their city, pride in the traditions of skill which made "Clyde-built" a synonym for excellence in shipbuilding, and—perhaps symbolizing it all, but surely central for most of the working-class male population—pride in football (soccer) prowess.

It is impossible to live in Glasgow more than a few days and not realize the centrality of football. It seems likely that football rivalry in Glasgow is a ritualization of religious conflict. About a quarter of the population of Glasgow is Catholic, the vast majority of these of Irish descent. When the Irish first came (in the nineteenth century), many atrocities were committed in the name of "The Protestant Cause." Between the wars there were gangs loosely based on these religious or ethnic loyalties that were able to pin down an entire police force for about 10 years. The Shamrocks and the Billy boys fought pitched battles in the main squares of the city and proceeded to them like medieval knights to the tilting yard.[5] It is true

[5] For a fictionalized account of this time see, A. McArthur and H. K. Long, *No Mean City* (London, 1966).

that old hatreds have now somewhat abated. For the mass of Glaswegians, the Catholic-Protestant rivalry is expressed in the efforts of their two football teams, Celtics and Rangers.

While the struggle has become ritualized, it has by no means been eliminated. For Glasgow, "The Football Game" still expresses the cleavage between the two religious communities. And this rigid division does not begin with the game, of course. From the age of 5 until 15, Protestant and Catholic children are segregated with a thoroughness unknown in the rest of Scotland. It might be said that Glasgow, while it is geographically in Scotland, is really the largest city of Northern Ireland.

What does this mean for politics? The working-class character of the city implies an almost built-in Labour majority. Labour took power in 1933 and, with a gap from 1949 to 1952, controlled the city in an uninterrupted reign until it was defeated in 1968, the year after our research was completed. The Labour administration did a great deal for Glasgow. At the same time, its long period of office confirmed it in the prejudice that it could do nothing wrong.

The factionalism of Labour politics in Glasgow, however, has been notorious. This feature appears to be based largely on personalities and arguments over seemingly trivial issues. But behind what so often seems pointless name calling is, in fact, the religious division: the Labour party in Glasgow comprises a Protestant and a Catholic faction. They are seldom referred to openly, but their effect upon nomination for office or support in debate is often evident.

The character of the city, then, has produced an inward-looking working class elite, itself torn by quasi-religious factionalism. When the fortunes of Labour in Britain as a whole have been high, the party has done well in Glasgow. When Labour has slipped nationally, it has failed nowhere as completely as in Glasgow.

Assured of their predominance, fascinated by their intramural problems, Labour politicians have all too often tended to ignore the demands of their rank-and-file members. At the beginning of 1969, when a number of councillors were arrested on bribery charges, the National executive of the Labour party ordered an official enquiry that found, among other things, that six of the twelve Labour-held Parliamentary seats in the city were in districts with less than 30 party members; only one had more than 300 members. In light of the requirement that Labour constituency associations have 1000 members or more in order to affiliate with the National Labour Party, the forlorn state of Labour organization in Glasgow is plain. A city that, in terms of its class structure, would be expected to produce a permanent Labour majority, in fact presents a Labour movement broken by religious factionalism and personal bickering.

In Glasgow, as in most Scottish cities, the Labour Party is opposed by the Progressives. Progressives regularly claim in their election literature that they represent "the business interest" and that local government is a "business" and should therefore be run on businesslike lines by business-men. In earlier times, Progressive Councillors in Glasgow were often prominent businessmen, but, because of the rather hopeless electoral prospects for Progressives since the 1930s, no really important names in the business world have appeared on the Council roster. Rather, Progres-sive Councillors have been directors of relatively small businesses or sec-ondary figures in larger businesses. As previously noted, there have re-cently been repeated appeals from the Conservative Central Office that Progressives stand as Conservatives. Since this has been bitterly fought by many Progressives, who see power slipping from their hands to those of Edinburgh and London, Progressive candidates have been opposed in many wards by Conservatives, and Conservatives have begun in some places to replace the Progressives. The more recent trend, however, is to-ward greater cooperation between the two. Progressives and Conservatives now meet in the same caucus before Corporation meetings, and they reach agreements about the contesting of seats. The fortunes of the Glasgow Progressive Party have for so long been at such low ebb that they have really been unable to resist the advances of a very affluent suitor.

In Edinburgh, by contrast, local politics have meant Progressive politics since ever Progressives were a party. We are dealing, of course, with a part of the world where there are still many old, family-owned businesses and in which there was no really important industrial development in the nineteenth century to shape the politics of the region for the twentieth cen-tury. In all of Scotland, the Edinburgh region is the only one specifically excluded from special government economic help. It is by far the most prosperous. It is small wonder that local politics in Edinburgh differ mark-edly from local politics in Glasgow.

We have noted that, while Glasgow councillors tend to be rather unim-portant figures in the social or business life of the city, "representation of the business interest" is regularly mentioned in their election literature. In Edinburgh, local politics has for long been dominated by the business interest and by very considerable representatives of it. One former Lord Provost of Edinburgh, head of a nationally known firm of builders, went on to become Lord Mayor of London. Along Princes Street there is a line of very large department stores, more than one of which has, within recent years, had a senior member of the family on the Corporation. In Edin-burgh, membership on the Council is still prestigious. In Edinburgh, people whose prestige antedates and is independent of their political status have been able to represent their privileged group on the Council through the long-established Progressive Party.

The Edinburgh Labour Party, too, differs from its Glasgow counterpart.

There is, of course, no intraparty religious rivalry. A further difference stemming from the differing industrial base of Edinburgh is well symbolized by comparison of the party chairmen. In Glasgow, the chairman of the City Labour Party is a trades unionist and a Corporation employee; his counterpart in Edinburgh is a distinguished lawyer, who is a Queen's Counsel and chairman of the Scottish Fabian Society. In brief, the influence of middle-class radicalism is much clearer in the Edinburgh than in the Glasgow Labour Party.

This difference has its effect upon the character and work of the city party. As we saw, the quarterly meeting of the Glasgow City Labour Party is an occasion for the transaction of business and discussion of organization, but never for discussion of policy matters. Although there is a standing order that requires the meeting to move onto consideration of a report from the Council group, this is often suspended. Resolutions on aspects of city affairs that are sent by constituencies and wards are discussed by the executive, but, despite frequent efforts, never raised at the general meeting. In Edinburgh, by contrast, the City Labour Party meets monthly. There is regular provision for debate on policy, and there is little of the bitterness of the Glasgow meetings. So concerned with the discussion of policy is the Edinburgh Labour party that it has set up a number of working groups composed of its own members, in addition to outside people, some of them not from Edinburgh or even members of the party. These groups discuss topics that are remitted to them and report for a full discussion in the city party. On virtually all counts, the Edinburgh City Labour Party is held in much higher esteem than is that in Glasgow. It is also notable that, as a result, the relationships between Edinburgh Labour Councillors and their party is much closer, happier, and more informed.

The discussion so far has emphasized the unity and consensus in both major parties in Edinburgh. There is, however, one issue which tends to split both parties. Edinburgh, quite unlike Glasgow, is a cosmopolitan city. At the heart of its position as a center of culture and tourism is the Festival. But there is a certain politically relevant division of opinion concerning this event. Both Labour and Progressives contain factions which want minimum involvement in the Festival, and this attitude extends to a wider difference of attitude toward the work of the Council. On the Labour side, there is a substantial wing of trades unionists that views the Festival as an overwhelmingly middle-class event, little deserving of working-class support or participation, that feels that money would be better spent on houses and schools than on Festivals. On the Progressive side there are also councillors opposed to the Festival. These are largely the older members, for whom Edinburgh was good enough before the Festival was instituted. In their eyes, Councillors are elected to see that ratepayers' money is not wasted. In short, across the lines of right and left, there lies a factional split on the question of whether Edinburgh is to be a cosmopolitan center of art, sport, and tourism, or whether it is to be a sort of 1930s backwater.

The "backwater brigade" also has its platoons in Aberdeen. In the early 1960s, at a time when Aberdeen had one of the highest unemployment rates in Scotland, an official statement included the sentiment that no new industry should be attracted to Aberdeen, because that would change the character of the town. Aberdeen is the smallest of the three cities we are examining, with a population of just over 200,000. It is an ancient city, with a medieval cathedral and University, and at the same time it is very much a county town. Since its foundation, it has been an *entrepot* for some of the riches farming land in Britain and, as such, has been somewhat cut off from the rest of Scotland. In the first place, it is geographically far from any other settlement of comparable size. This isolation has contributed to the fact that the speech, customs, and history of that North East corner are altogether distinctive. Furthermore, a large proportion of the population has close family links with the surrounding countryside. Thus Aberdeen, unlike Glasgow and Edinburgh, is very much a "small town," with an intimate style of social life where everybody is interested in everybody else's business.

The political consequences of this could be either endless bitterness or a rather close political consensus. It is the latter that is the case in Aberdeen. For example, not only is there greater agreement on policy within each party than in the other two cities, but there is also a great deal of agreement across party lines.

The rather old-fashioned nature of politics in Aberdeen is evidenced by the complete absence of a Conservative challenge to the Progressives. For example, one Progressive councillor was a prominent Conservative in local government before he moved to Aberdeen. On the other hand, it is not true that there have been no changes in the Progressive ranks in Aberdeen. Before 1956, when Labour captured control of the Council, there were many substantial businessmen on the Council as Progressive members. Since that date, Progressive councillors have tended to be smaller businessmen or employees. This has made for a rather sharper contest between the parties.

For Labour also the story is different in Aberdeen. Politics in Aberdeen is generally a much more social affair than in the other two cities. Conservatives or Progressives here, as elsewhere, usually have social gatherings associated with their political activities. Such social affairs are generally unusual for Labour in Scotland. In Aberdeen, however, not only does the local Labour Party sponsor a remarkable number of dances, whist drives, socials, and so on, but in a sense, every meeting, whether to discuss policy or to organize canvassing, becomes a social occasion.

Since the late 1960s, the organization of the City Labour Party has become increasingly democratic. In a small town, it is always possible to obtain good relations between the various wings of the party, and there has always been a great deal of overlap between the membership of the Council Labour group and the City Labour Party. The last three chairmen of the City Party, for example, have been Councillors, a fact that may in part be explained by the sheer shortage of personnel in this smaller community. On the other hand, in recent years there has developed a relationship between the Labour Group and the City Labour Party that is unique in Scotland; any member of the City Party can attend caucus meetings of the Labour Group and speak there. While they cannot vote, of course, the very fact that they are invited to attend is remarkable.

Summary. Glasgow, Edinburgh, and Aberdeen, then, with their different community characteristics, their different party balances, and the differences from one city to another in local party organization and practice in both major parties, provide a useful basis for comparative analysis of the relationship beween representatives (in this case, city councillors) and those whom they represent. The analysis involves examination of the views, perspectives, and attitudes of both electors and councillors, as well as socioeconomic and political characteristics of both Councils, constituencies, and cities.

The Data

Since the electoral register is a fairly accurate record in Britain, the electoral registers of the three cities were utilized to draw a sample of 700 names. These samples were effectively stratified by wards at the same time, since the register is maintained by wards. In Glasgow, interviews with 563 voters out of the sample of 700 were completed in March of 1966; interviews with 562 in Aberdeen and 613 in Edinburgh were completed in March of 1967.

At the same time the interviews were under way with the electoral samples, contact was made with all city councillors in their respective cities. (Each city is divided into words—37 in Glasgow, 12 in Aberdeen and 23 in Edinburgh. Each ward is represented by three councillors, besides whom there are one or two councillors nominated by the historical business organizations—in Glasgow, the Merchants' House and the Trades House; in the other two cities, the Trades Houses.) A total of 82 out of 113 councillors were interviewed in Glasgow; in Aberdeen, 32 out of 36, and in Edinburgh 49 out of 60.

Preliminary study in each city determined what political issues were salient in the town at the time. At first it was thought that Councillors and their constituents might themselves identify the issues that they felt were most important and that comparison of these answers might illuminate the linkages between political strata. Pilot surveys showed, however, that most local government electors could not mention more than one or two issues that they felt were important. Moreover, they often named issues which were not within the province of the local authority at all. It was found that this open-ended method of comparing opinions allowed comparison on only the most general sort of issues named. It seemed preferable to identify issues on which there were identifiable points of view so that these points of view, rather than merely estimates of an issue's importance, could be compared. The idea of asking Councillors to name the important issues was rejected because it was felt that they might name issues too complex or too remote for ordinary electors. Finally, panels of all local newspapermen concerned with local government in each city were asked to name four issues—two on which there were interparty controversy and two on which there was controversy but not between the political parties—that they thought were the most important of the current issues being discussed by the Council and to judge their importance in terms of the impact that they felt a decision would have on the lives of people in the area. No claim is made, of course, that these issues were the most important in any absolute sense, or even that they were the most widely discussed. It can be said only that the issues chosen were considered to be important by well-qualified observers and that subjectively it is possible to see that decisions upon them would have important consequences for the lives of people in the cities.

In Glasgow, the two "party issues" were increasing the local rate (tax) and the abolition of fees in Corporation schools. The Labour Party group (in theory at any rate) was in favor of both these courses of action, which were opposed by the Progressives. For Labour, fees were seen as a device for making the schools privileged-class institutions; the Progressives believed that fee-paying was a way of encouraging quality in these schools. The two nonparty issues in Glasgow were the introduction of parking meters throughout the whole of the city center and the introduction of public houses (selling beer, wines, and spirits) into Corporation Housing Estates. (Most cities in Britain have large public housing developments, in which tenants usually pay a rent well below that in the private sector. Since the beginning of the century, thanks to the temperance movement, it has been the policy of Glasgow Corporation to forbid the building of pubs in these areas. It is this policy which is at issue.)

In Aberdeen, the party issues were a proposal by Labour to make all secondary schools comprehensive and a proposal by the Progressives that

Council Houses be sold to their tenants. It is the policy position of the national Labour Party that examinations at age 11 be scrapped and that pupils not be sent to different schools according to whether they pass or fail this examination. Many educationalists besides those who are socialists feel that this selection is made too early and that, in any case, the system favors the child from a middle-class background. The issue of selling Corporation houses arises from the Progressives' feeling that ratepayers might be saved money by such sale, thus ending the subsidy which ratepayers in private accommodations make to council tenants. The nonparty issues in Aberdeen were, first, the question of selling corporation land, and, second, the question of bringing more industry to Aberdeen.

Finally, in Edinburgh, the party issues were the question of fee paying in Corporation schools, which Labour opposed and Progressives supported, and the raising of rents for Corporation (Council) houses. There was no clear party line on the issue of subsidising the Edinburgh Festival or that of building an inner ring road.

In each city, on each issue, a series of identical questions was put to Councillors and electors:

"Have you heard of the proposal to . . . ?" "Would you say that you personally agreed or disagreed with this proposal?" "What would you say was the position of the Labour Party on this proposal?" "What would you say was the position of the Progressives on this proposal?" The Councillors were asked, in addition, "How would you say that your own constituents felt about this issue? Would you say that they agreed, or disagreed, or what?"

Results

Let us consider first the extent to which the City Council in the three cities can legitimately be considered a microcosm of the people it represents. Table 8.1 shows the data relevant to the socioeconomic version of this conception.[6]

In Glasgow figures, it is clear that the council is not at all a microcosm of the society. Given the philosophy and methods of recruitment used by

[6] The classification used here is basically that used by the Registrar General (*Classification of Occupations, 1966,* Her Majesty's Stationary Office, 1961, p. x), the origins of which are discussed by T. H. C. Stevenson in the *Journal of the Royal Statistical Society,* XCI (1928), 207–230. The first, second, third, and fourth categories in Table 8.1 are equivalent to Categories I, II, IV, and and V in that list, but Category III ("Skilled Occupations") has been split into two categories (the third and fourth) here. In a very general way these categories are ranked in order of social prestige.

Table 8.1   Social Class of Councillors and
Electors in Three Scottish Cities (in %)

| | Councillors | | |
Social Class	Labour	Progressive	Electors
Glasgow			
Professional and Company Directors	19.0	40.0	3.0
Intermediate occupations	23.0	34.0	12.0
Nonmanual unskilled occupations	40.0	16.0	15.0
Manual skilled occupations	5.0	—	40.0
Partly skilled occupations	2.0	3.0	15.0
Unskilled occupations	—	—	11.0
Total	89.0ª	93.0	96.0
Number of cases	43	39	563
Edinburgh			
Professional and Company Directors	26.0	39.0	4.0
Intermediate occupations	22.0	35.0	17.0
Nonmanual unskilled occupations	22.0	26.0	18.0
Manual skilled occupations	30.0	—	31.0
Partly skilled occupations	—	—	18.0
Unskilled occupations	—	—	9.0
Total	100.0	100.0	97.0
Number of cases	23	26	613
Aberdeen			
Professional and Company Directors	—	14.0	3.0
Intermediate occupations	33.0	78.0	17.0
Nonmanual unskilled occupations	33.0	—	12.0
Manual skilled occupations	28.0	7.0	31.0
Partly skilled occupations	6.0	—	21.0
Unskilled occupations	—	—	11.0
Total	100.0	99.0	95.0
Number of cases	18	14	562

ª The percentages here, and in some other cases, do not total to 100 because of the respondents in each group who had no occupation or whose occupations were insufficiently described.

the Progressive Party, it is not surprising that theirs should be so "unrepresentative" a group of councillors, but it is interesting that the Labour councillors are in this respect only a few steps behind. While the vast majority of their electors are members of the manual working classes, less than 10 percent of the councillors are manual workers. There are several reasons for this, but perhaps the most obvious is that the business of being a councillor, especially in Glasgow, is very time consuming. The meetings are in the middle of the day, and most manual workers simply cannot get the permission of their employers to leave work. This is not to say that there are not people among the Labour councillors who have working class backgrounds. Such councillors, however, have either become trades union officials, or they have taken up a job in which they could more easily be masters of their own time. (Being an insurance agent is a favorite retreat.) Even such people fall in the third category, however; there are still over 40 percent who are from the professional or managerial sections of Glasgow society. Thus we cannot explain the high social status of most Glasgow councillors in terms of the demands of their political work.

The pattern in Aberdeen is almost the same as in Glasgow. Once more the Progressives are overwhelmingly drawn from the upper social classes. Although the Labour group on the Council contains a larger proportion of manual workers than that in Glasgow, the proportion is still small in comparison with its counterpart among the electors.

In Edinburgh, as Table 8.1 shows, the Councillors of both parties are even more clearly drawn from the upper classes.

As suggested in our initial discussion, however, a more important aspect of representation than the question of whether or not the representatives come from different social backgrounds than their constituents is whether they look after the interests of their constituents and whether they voice the same opinions as their constituents when it comes to the resolution of issues in the Council. The remainder of this chapter compares the opinions of Councillors and electors on issues.

Table 8.2 presents the distribution of opinion among City Councillors and among the general public on the four issues presented in the Glasgow interviews. The data show that opinions are similarly divided among Councillors and electors in three of the four issues. It was perhaps predictable that electors would be generally opposed to increase in the rates and Councillors more equally divided. It should also be noticed, however, that on the highly political issue of fee-paying schools it was the Councillors who tended more than electors to be opposed. But on the whole, Councillors' and electors' opinions do not appear to be in conflict with one another over the four issues. In terms of majority attitudes on issues among Councillors as compared with citizenry, the microcosm model appears to be somewhat descriptive of the Glasgow situation, although the differences in proportions favoring a given option indicates that the Council is hardly a perfect mirror. It is worth noting there that the proportion who "don't know" is substantially greater among electors than among Councillors.

The picture is not substantially changed when we compare the issue opinions of each party group in the Glasgow City Council with the views of their supporters in the electorate. Table 8.3 presents these data.

Perhaps the most interesting finding revealed here is that the match be-

Table 8.2   Attitudes on Issues in Glasgow

	Councillors	Electors
Party issues		
Pubs on housing estates		
For	**85**[a]	**56**
Against	12	36
Don't know	3	8
Total	100	100
Fees in corporation schools		
For	42	44
Against	**56**	**45**
Don't know	2	11
Total	100	100
Nonparty issues		
Motors in the city center		
For	**72**	**48**
Against	23	32
Don't know	2	20
Total	100	100
Increase rates		
For	**45**	7
Against	43	**87**
Don't know	12	6
Total	100	100

[a] The modal category in each group for each issue is in bold-face type in this and subsequent similar tables.

tween Councillors' and electors' opinion distributions is closer among Glasgow Progressives than among Glasgow Labourites. In every one of the four issues, the modal class for Progressive electors is the same as for Progressive Councillors. In the Labour party, on the other hand, electors are opposed to Councillors on the rates issues, and the differences between the percentages of Councillors in the modal class and the percentages of electors are, on the whole, larger. This finding is especially interesting in view of the fact that a very large proportion, if not a majority, of Labour supporters in Glasgow are municipal tenants, who would presumably benefit if a high rate is levied, and that rate used to subsidize the rent in Corporation houses. Despite this presumed interest, Labour electors do not support Labour Councillors in their demand for a higher rate.

Tables 8.4 and 8.5 present the data concerning attitudes on issues in Edinburgh and Aberdeen, respectively. In Edinburgh we again find one issue (that of increasing the Corporation subsidy to the Festival) on

Table 8.3   Attitudes on Issues in Glasgow (in %)

	Progressive		Labour	
	Councillors	Electors	Councillors	Electors
Party issues				
Pubs on housing estates				
For	76	52	93	58
Against	21	40	5	35
Don't know	3	8	2	7
Total	100	100	100	100
Fees in corporation schools				
For	13	32	68	51
Against	84	60	30	37
Don't know	3	8	2	11
Total	100	100	100	100
Nonparty issues				
Motors in city center				
For	58	48	84	49
Against	34	36	14	30
Don't know	8	16	2	21
Total	100	100	100	100
Increase rates				
For	5	2	81	10
Against	84	93	5	82
Don't know	11	5	14	8
Total	100	100	100	100

which Councillors' and Electors' opinion distributions differ. But the differences between the two are not as great as was the case in Glasgow.

Once again when we control for party, a rather different picture emerges. This time it is the Progressive councillors whose opinion distribution differs from that of Progressive electors on two of the four issues, but only a hair's breadth separates them in both cases. The majority of Labour councillors share the same opinions as the majority of Labour electors in all four issues, but in every issue except the building of the ring road there are quite substantial differences in the sizes of these percentages.

In Aberdeen we find two issues, the proposal to sell Corporation-owned land and the proposal to sell Council Houses to Council House tenants, over which there is quite a marked divergence between the electors and the councillors as a whole. Once again, when party is controlled, we see a difference. The Progressive councillors seem to be out of tune with their electors over the question of changing the school system to a comprehensive one. On the Labour side there is a disagreement on the question of

Table 8.4   Attitudes on Issues in Edinburgh (in %)

	All		Progressive		Labour	
	Council-lors	Elec-tors	Council-lors	Elec-tors	Council-lors	Elec-tors
Party issues						
Increase council house rents						
For	**47**	**58**	**89**	**75**	2	34
Against	32	32	—	12	**74**	**54**
Don't know	11	10	11	13	24	12
Total	100	100	100	100	100	100
Fees in corporation schools						
For	39	30	—	26	**88**	27
Against	**47**	**38**	82	47	8	26
Don't know	14	32	18	27	4	**47**
Total	100	100	100	100	100	100
Nonparty issues						
Increase Corporation subsidy to Festival						
For	**64**	29	**82**	38	48	19
Against	28	**58**	11	**44**	**52**	**70**
Don't know	8	13	7	18	—	11
Total	100	100	100	100	100	100
Build an inner-ring road						
For	**55**	**45**	32	**41**	**61**	**55**
Against	30	33	**54**	39	39	27
Don't know	15	22	14	20	—	18
Total	100	100	100	100	100	100

selling Corporation land and in relation to the sale of Corporation Houses. The latter of these two was a clear party issue debated at a national level. Labour electors, many of them Council House tenants, are opposed to the party line.

Tables 8.3–8.5 bring out several general points. First, it is clear that Councillors have more definite opinions than do electors, in the sense that there are fewer Councillors than electors who are unable to answer the questions. It is also true that the opinions of Councillors polarize party versus party more than those of the electors. The contrast between political contention in the Council and difference of opinion in the electorate is indicated in Table 8.6, which presents the correlations between opposing party groups in the Council and in the electorate for all three cities. The high negative figures for Councillors in Edinburgh and Aberdeen and the near-zero correlation for Councillors in Glasgow demonstrate still more

Table 8.5   Attitudes on Issues in Aberdeen (in %)

	All		Progressive		Labour	
	Council-lors	Elec-tors	Council-lors	Elec-tors	Council-lors	Elec-tors
Party issues						
Bring more industry to Aberdeen						
For	94	87	86	87	100	91
Against	6	3	—	3	—	2
Don't know	—	10	14	10	—	7
Total	100	100	100	100	100	100
Change school system to comprehensive						
For	65	54	21	54	100	57
Against	32	20	79	20	—	19
Don't know	3	26	—	26	—	24
Total	100	100	100	100	100	100
Nonparty issues						
Sell Corporation land for use of private builders						
For	44	61	93	61	5	48
Against	53	26	7	26	89	30
Don't know	3	13	—	13	6	22
Total	100	100	100	100	100	100
Sell Corporation houses to their tenants						
For	34	67	79	67	—	60
Against	66	20	21	20	100	26
Don't know	—	13	11	13	—	14
Total	100	100	100	100	100	100

Table 8.6   Correlations between Progressives' and Labourites'
Attitudes on Political Issues in Council and in Electorate

	Glasgow		Edinburgh		Aberdeen	
	Council-lors	Electors	Council-lors	Electors	Council-lors	Electors
Councillors	0.12	—	−0.89	—	−0.56	—
Electors	—	0.88	—	0.15	—	0.69

clearly than the earlier figures the polarization of opinions in Council. Only in Edinburgh, however, is there very much disagreement between Progressive and Labour supporters in the electorate.

Table 8.7 utilises a slightly different measure to examine more specifically the relationship between party and electoral views on issues. The varying effect of party becomes more clear here. The Progressives, in each city, display greater agreement between the two groups than Labour. In Edinburgh and Glasgow, the Labour party does very badly indeed. In Aberdeen, although the two strata of Labour groups do not seem as close in their opinions as are the Progressives, there is still a relatively high correlation.

Table 8.7   Agreement between Councillors
and Electors (correlation coefficients)

Group	Glasgow	Edinburgh	Aberdeen
All	+0.44	+0.38	+0.69
Progressive	+0.92	+0.74	+0.83
Labour	−0.08	−0.003	+0.61

The figures for Labour are, of course, quite anomalous, especially in view of the Progressives' historic insistence on the autonomy of representatives from constituent instructions and Labour's historic insistence, particularly in the national party, on their representatives' obligations to be guided by official party policy resolutions. It is hardly likely that the explanation lies in party responsibility for government as opposed to the party's being in opposition since, at the time of the surveys, Glasgow had been firmly in Labour hands since 1951, Aberdeen had changed party hands several times, and Edinburgh had always been a Progressive stronghold. Most likely the divergence on issues between Labour Councillors and Labour electors is closely related to the well-known difference on many policy matters between Labour voters and Labour politicians at the national level. It may also be related to a difference in degree of politicisation between Labour and Conservative politicians. For Labour activists there are numerous party schools, voluminous party literature to be absorbed, and other politicising activities to occupy the budding politician. There is little comparable political activity for the budding Progressive politician. Indeed, as we have seen, the recruitment process is quite different for Progressives than for Labour politicians. Many Progressives have had no experience of politics at all before standing for the Council. One might therefore argue that the Progressives are most like their electors not in their social composition but in the fact that, like the electors, they are unpolitical. Conversely, Labour councillors are usually less like the voters of their own party in that they *are* political. All such reasoning is at this point purely speculative, of course.

So far we have been considering representation of the cities as a whole, by Councillors as a collective body, and examined the influence of Councillors' and electors' political party affiliations and loyalties on it. We turn now to examine Councillors' views in relation to political attitudes of electors in their own electoral districts, that is, wards.

Table 8.8 Comparison of Councillors' Views with Views of Constituents in Their Own Wards, Selected Issues in Three Cities (in %)

	Party Issues		Nonparty Issues	
Glasgow	Build Pubs in Housing Estates	Scrap Fees in Corporation Schools	Put Meters in City Center	Raise Rates
Agree	61	51	46	41
Disagree	23	48	25	48
Indeterminate	16	5	29	10
Total	100	100	100	100
Edinburgh	Raise Council House Rents	Scrap Fees in Corporation Schools	Pay Subsidy to Festival	Build Inner Ring Road
Agree	60	60	51	53
Disagree	23	25	42	42
Indeterminate	17	15	8	6
Total	100	100	100	100
Aberdeen	Bring in More Industry	Make Schools Comprehensive	Sell Corporation Land	Sell Council Houses
Agree	94	63	47	34
Disagree	6	36	50	66
Indeterminate	—	—	3	—
Total	100	100	100	100

Table 8.8 presents data concerning the extent of match between Councillors' views on the various issues and those of constituents in their own wards for each of the three cities. These data suggest slightly greater agreement between representatives and constituents in Glasgow and Edinburgh than did the citywide data just cited but generally less in Aberdeen. On the whole, however, they do not substantially alter the picture already de-

rived. It might be thought that there would be substantial variation between wards in this respect according to the size of the district, the party controlling it (Labour or Progressive), the degree of marginality or competitiveness of the seat, or the extent of voter involvement and turnout in it. In a very small district, for example, it might be easier for electors to form homogeneous opinions, easier for Councillors to know what the opinions are, and easier for constituents to impose those opinions on their representatives. In apathetic (low turnout) districts one would expect constituents to have fewer opinions on issues and representatives to feel less concern with the opinions they might have. None of these factors affected the agreement between Councillors and constituents in any significant way, however (data not shown).

Whatever constituents' opinions may be, a crucial question is, what does the representative think they are? For it is his perceptions of reality that guide his political behavior, and not the "objective" facts that analysts or observers may see. Tables 8.9–8.11 show the Councillors' opinions about the extent of agreement between their own and their constituents' views on the various policies studied in each of the three cities.

Perhaps the most striking feature of these tables is the extent to which Councillors in all three cities, but spectacularly so in Edinburgh, are unable to attribute an opinion to their constituents (the percentages in "Don't Know, No Answer," in the tables). It is also interesting to note the differences among the patterns for the three cities in this respect, Glasgow Councillors tend more to attribute opinions of one kind or another to their constituents than do Councillors in Aberdeen or Edinburgh. Edinburgh Councillors not only tend to attribute opinions to far fewer, but to a greater extent than either Glasgow or Aberdeen Councillors, tend to see all those constituents whom they think have opinions as in agreement with their own.

Another interesting finding, perhaps less predictable, is that there are greater differences among Councillors of different cities, regardless of party, than between Councillors of different party in any given city. Aberdeen Councillors, both Progressive and Labourite, generally perceive much greater agreement between themselves and their constituents than Councillors in Glasgow or Edinburgh. Note, however, that, as already suggested, there are also interesting differences in perceptions of disagreement between Councillors' own and constituents' views which are not the mere inverse of perceived agreement. Glasgow and Edinburgh Councillors perceive about the same extent of agreement with their views among their constituents, but Edinburgh Councillors perceive almost no disagreement, whereas Glasgow Councillors perceive almost as much disagreement as agreement with them.

Table 8.9   Glasgow Councillors' Perceptions of Their Constituents' Agreement with Them on Selected Issues (in %)

	Appraisal Same as Own Opinion	Appraisal Different from Own Opinion	Don't Know No Answer	Total
All				
Party issues				
Build pubs in				
housing estates	43	38	18	100
Scrap fees in				
Corporation schools	32	44	24	100
Nonparty issues				
Put meters in				
city center	30	52	18	100
Raise rates	48	41	10	100
Labour only				
Party issues				
Build pubs in				
housing estates	51	23	16	100
Scrap fees in				
Corporation schools	29	53	18	100
Nonparty issues				
Put meters in				
city center	32	32	16	100
Raise rates	16	72	12	100
Progressive only				
Party issues				
Build pubs in				
housing estates	44	36	20	100
Scrap fees in				
Corporation schools	38	38	24	100
Nonparty issues				
Put meters in				
city center	33	47	20	100
Raise rates	78	22	—	100

What is the relationship between the Councillors *perceptions* of constituents' views just described and the constituents' self-descriptions of those views (as discussed earlier). That is, to what extent are Councillors bringing accurate perceptions of their constituents' views into the Council chamber? Table 8.12 presents the data on this question—considering a Councillor's estimate of constituency opinion "accurate" if he attributes to them the same views that the majority of electors in his ward claimed as their own. These data will strike many believers in populist democracy as a

Table 8.10   Edinburgh Councillors' Perceptions of Their Constituents' Agreement with Them on Selected Issues (in %)

	Appraisal Same as Own Opinion	Appraisal Different from Own Opinion	Don't Know No Answer	Total
All				
Party issues				
Raise council house rents	53	—	49	100
Scrap fees in Corporation schools	35	6	59	100
Nonparty issues				
Pay subsidy to Festival	29	12	59	100
Build inner ring road	22	—	78	100
Progressive only				
Party issues				
Raise council house rents	57	—	43	100
Scrap fees in Corporation schools	43	7	50	100
Nonparty issues				
Pay subsidy to Festival	21	11	68	100
Build inner ring road	35	—	69	100
Labour only				
Party issues				
Raise council house rents	48	—	52	100
Scrap fees in Corporation schools	26	4	70	100
Nonparty issues				
Pay subsidy to Festival	39	—	61	100
Build inner ring road	—	—	100	100

shocking revelation of irresponsible perception by representatives. Almost always, in all three cities, a fourth or more of the Councillors are inaccurate in their descriptions of constituency opinion; in a third of the possible cases, less than half are accurate. Considering that the issues in almost all cases were issues that had been highly publicised over relatively long periods of time, these figures on first hearing sound scandalously low. A

Table 8.11   Aberdeen Councillors' Perceptions of Their Constituents' Agreement with Them on Selected Issues (in %)

	Appraisal Same as Own Opinion	Appraisal Different from Own Opinion	Don't Know No Answer	Total
All				
Party issues				
Bring in				
more industry	87	—	13	100
Make schools				
comprehensive	63	6	31	100
Nonparty issues				
Sell Corporation land	56	13	31	100
Sell Council houses	66	—	34	100
Progressive only				
Party issues				
Bring in				
more industry	72	—	28	100
Make schools				
comprehensive	64	22	14	100
Nonparty issues				
Sell Corporation land	72	21	7	100
Sell Council houses	64	—	36	100
Labour only				
Party issues				
Bring in				
more industry	100	—	—	100
Make schools				
comprehensive	67	—	33	100
Nonparty issues				
Sell Corporation land	50	17	33	100
Sell Council houses	67	—	33	100

moment's reflection, however, suggests that the data are reflecting not so much any perceptual incapacity or arrogant disinterest on the part of Councillors as a characteristic of "public opinion" on the issues concerned. We have already seen that large numbers of voters simply have neither information nor opinions on seemingly overpowering issues. Analysis of survey research in other places has suggested that even those "opinions" ventured by respondents who claim to have them may, in many instances, be ritualistic, "nonopinion" responses.[7] Indeed, it is quite likely that the

[7] Philip E. Converse, "New Dimensions of Meaning for Cross-Section Sample Surveys in Politics," *International Social Science Journal*, **XVI** (1964), pp. 19–34.

figures in Table 8.12 for "percent indeterminate" reflect the most accurate perceptions of all. On the bare question of accuracy and inaccuracy, therefore, the general picture presented in Table 8.12 is in no wise surprising.

What is more interesting is the light the table sheds on the function of political parties in linking constituency and Councillor opinions on the

Table 8.12 Accuracy of Councillors' Appraisals of Constituents' Opinions on Selected Issues in Three Cities (in %)

	Party Issues		Nonparty Issues	
Glasglow	Build Pubs in Housing Estates	Scrap Fees in Corporation Schools	Put Meters in City Center	Raise Rates
Accurate	40	28	24	79
Inaccurate	44	50	55	18
Indeterminate	16	22	21	3
Total	100	100	100	100
Edinburgh	Raise Council House Rents	Scrap Fees in Corporation Schools	Pay Subsidy to Festival	Build Inner Ring Road
Accurate	60	60	51	53
Inaccurate	23	25	42	42
Indeterminate	17	15	7	5
Total	100	100	100	100
Aberdeen	Bring in More Industry	Make Schools Comprehensive	Sell Corporation Land	Sell Council Houses
Accurate	93	63	47	35
Inaccurate	7	37	50	65
Indeterminate	—	—	3	—
Total	100	100	100	100

issues. In only one city (Glasgow) is there so much as one issue (raising rates) for which Councillors' perceptions of constituency opinion is higher for a nonparty than a party-related issue. On the other hand, the capacity of parties to focus and mobilize opinion is by no means spectacularly great. Only in Aberdeen and only on one issue (bringing in more industry) has party conflict appeared to sharpen issues to the point where Councillors almost universally know where constituents stand (93 percent correct). Even on party-related issues, usually only about 60 percent of Councillors' estimates are correct. And once again, there are some interesting differences among the cities in this respect. The accuracy of Councillors' perceptions is greater on both party-related issues in Aberdeen than on any party-related issue in either of the other two cities, and it is less on both party-related issues in Glasgow than in either Aberdeen or Edinburgh.

The reverse side of the coin of Councillors' perceptions of constituency opinion is the question, How do constituents perceive the policy opinions of their representatives? In this case, we go directly to examining their views on the policy stands of their own party on the issues in question. Table 8.13 presents the data concerning electors' agreement with what they perceive to be their party's stand on those issues.

As should be expected in light of all the earlier data relevant to the point, substantial proportions of electors do not know what position, if any, their party has taken, as indicated by the high percentage of "Indeterminate" answers. Once again interesting differences among the cities appear. Aberdeen electors appear to be surprisingly much more aware of how their parties stand (if at all) on the four issues probed there; the most claiming an "indeterminate" position amounts to more than 18 percent on only one issue in one party group, Labourites, on the nonparty-related issue of selling Council houses. This stands in striking contrast to the situation in Glasgow, where from 24 percent to 61 percent indicate unfamiliarity with their party's issue positions, and even more so to that in Edinburgh, where from 53 percent to 83 percent give such answers.

Once again, the function of party in focusing issues is suggested by the fact that in almost every instance agreement with party is greater than on nonparty-related issues, and agreement is greater than disagreement. There is, however, greater variation in both respects than was the case with Councillors' perceptions of constituency opinion, suggesting that party is much more salient for Councillors than for constituents, as one would naturally predict. And there are once again interesting differences among the cities. Electors in Aberdeen generally exhibit greater support for the issue positions of their parties than electors in either Glasgow or Edinburgh, where on no issue do a clear majority of constituents approve of their party's stand. Once again, the differences among cities are in all these respects more striking than the differences between parties. The most striking feature about the distributions viewed by party is that electors in neither party seem to agree very extensively with their party's position on issues.

Finally, a comparison of Councillors' agreement with their parties' positions with the comparable constituency figures reveals, as would be expected, that party is much more salient to Councillors (in terms of awarness of party positions) and more acceptable to them (in terms of agreement with it). (Table 8.14 presents these data.) They also exhibit perhaps greater variation among parties and, within parties, on issues, than one might expect. But once again we find that the differences among cities are,

Table 8.13 Electors' Perceptions of Their Own Party's
Position on Selected Issues in Three Cities (in %)

	Party Issues		Nonparty Issues	
Glasgow	Build Pubs in Housing Estates	Scrap Fees in Corporation Schools	Put Meters in City Center	Raise Rates
Labour				
Agree	25	48	28	11
Disagree	25	16	36	62
Indeterminate	50	36	48	27
Total	100	100	100	100
Progressive				
Agree	34	47	32	70
Disagree	28	18	7	6
Indeterminate	58	35	61	24
Total	100	100	100	100
Edinburgh	Raise Council House Rents	Scrap Fees in Corporation Schools	Pay Subsidy to Festival	Build Inner Ring Road
Labour				
Agree	37	30	36	26
Disagree	10	13	2	2
Indeterminate	53	57	62	72
Total	100	100	100	100
Progressive				
Agree	35	30	19	10
Disagree	12	13	10	7
Indeterminate	53	56	71	83
Total	100	100	100	100
Aberdeen	Bring in More Industry	Make Schools Comprehensive	Sell Corporation Land	Sell Council Houses
Labour				
Agree	60	49	31	30
Disagree	35	44	51	13
Indeterminate	5	7	18	57
Total	100	100	100	100
Progressive				
Agree	56	58	49	41
Disgreee	42	38	38	49
Indeterminate	2	4	13	10
Total	100	100	100	100

Table 8.14   Councillors' Agreement with Their Own Party's
Position on Selected Issues in Three Cities (in %)

	Party Issues		Nonparty Issues	
Glasgow	Build Pubs in Housing Estates	Scrap Fees in Corporation Schools	Put Meters in City Center	Raise Rates
Labour				
Agree	61	44	50	—
Disagree	22	28	44	78
Indeterminate	7	28	5	22
Total	100	100	100	100
Progressive				
Agree	58	58	100	100
Disagree	7	14	—	—
Indeterminate	35	28	—	—
Total	100	100	100	100
Edinburgh	Raise Council House Rents	Scrap Fees in Corporation Schools	Pay Subsidy to Festival	Build Inner Ring Road
Labour				
Agree	74	91	9	9
Disagree	—	—	4	—
Indeterminate	26	9	87	91
Total	100	100	100	100
Progressive				
Agree	100	79	67	15
Disagree	—	17	—	—
Indeterminate	—	4	23	86
Total	100	100	100	100
Aberdeen	Bring in More Industry	Make Schools Comprehensive	Corporation Land	Sell Council Houses
Labour				
Agree	100	100	61	89
Disagree	—	—	—	11
Indeterminate	—	—	39	—
Total	100	100	100	100
Progressive				
Agree	86	21	93	58
Disagree	7	21	—	14
Indeterminate	7	57	7	28
Total	100	100	100	100

on the whole, substantially greater than the differences between parties within cities.

Conclusion

This has been, of course, a very preliminary report. We can at this stage do little more than amplify a bit our descriptive understanding of representative relationships at the local level, a context in which they have to date been studied precious little.

It has shown that the microcosmic conception of representational relationships—both the socioeconomic and the attitudinal version of it—is as inappropriate to describe the situation in our three Scottish cities as it has been generally found to be for national legislative bodies. On the other hand, political parties enter into the picture, in one way or another, in all three of our cities, to make the traditional Burkean conception of representation equally inadequate as a description of what goes on in local representative systems. Even political parties, however, do not simplify the picture very much. The problem is not so much that there is great variety from one party to the next in electors' and Councillors' roles and their perceptions of them as that each city appears to have its own cultural and institutional patterns that impose themselves on politicians and laymen in all parties and that superimpose themselves on the representational relationships in ways which may vary from one local issue to another but which seem to stamp the relationships in every issue with a distinctive local character.

It is plain that considerable research is needed to extend our knowledge of representative processes at the local level. And until our knowledge does extend there we can hardly hope to establish firm knowledge about representation as a basic function in government in general.

CHAPTER NINE

A Test for the Existence of Feedback in State Legislative Systems

JOHN G. GRUMM

WESLEYAN UNIVERSITY

William James described democracy as a system in which you do something and then wait to see who "hollers." Then you go and relieve the cause of the "hollering" as best you can and wait again to see who "hollers" as a result of your remedying the first woes.[1] James's words also provide one of the most succinct descriptions of what some latterday political scientists would term the "feedback effect" in a political system.

The notion of feedback is an essential element in the so-called systems approach to political analysis, although operationalizing the concept for empirical research poses some difficulties. Briefly, it may be conceived as consisting of a three-stage process, the first of which involves the impact of outputs from the political system on the environment, then the flow of information about these effects back to the authorities in the political system, and finally, the adjustment of subsequent outputs based on what was "learned" from the data feedback. The function of the process is to produce stability in the system by providing for a self-adjustment of outputs based on information regarding the impacts of previous outputs.[2] The easiest analogy is that of an air-conditioning system controlled by a thermostat that continuously feeds back information on the environmental

---

[1] As quoted in T. V. Smith, *The Promise of American Politics,* 2nd ed. (Chicago, 1936), pp. 199–200.

[2] David Easton, *A Framework for Political Analysis* (Englewood Cliffs, N.J., 1965), pp. 128–29.

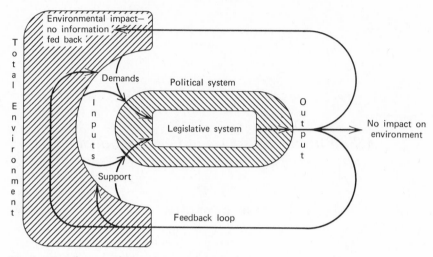

Figure 9.1. Response model of a political system.

temperature. As changes in the temperature are produced by the cold air output from the system, adjustments are thereby made so that new outputs conform to the changes, and the temperature is stabilized. Without this informational feedback and the ability of the system to respond to it, the system would "run wild."

A diagramatic representation of feedback in a political system is seen in Figure 9.1. What is labeled the "feedback loop" is really only the beginning of a process that could be depicted as a closed circle. This particular segment of the circle, however, is the unique feature that distinguishes a system in which there is feedback from one where there is none. The path from outputs *back* to inputs is essentially what we mean by *feedback*. But, again, the total process goes beyond the feedback loop itself. In Karl Deutsch's conception, it is "a communications network that produces action in response to an input of information, and includes the results of its own action in the new information by which it modifies its subsequent behavior."[3] The circle is closed, therefore, when the system responds to the information feedback.

The legislature can be viewed as the central institution in this whole process. It is the legislature that is theoretically the most sensitive to the feedback of information regarding changes in the environment produced by outputs of the political system. Individual legislative representatives are presumably the closest of all authorities in the system to the people and

[3] Karl W. Deutsch, *The Nerves of Government: Models of Political Communication and Control* (New York, 1966), p. 88.

can most easily detect the environmental effects of public policy. Most of the "hollering" will be directed at them. Legislative staff services—committee staff, legislative reference agencies, and legislative councils—are provided to enhance the information flow in this respect.

The functions of the legislature have been defined as the "management of tensions" and the "integration of the polity."[4] Now, if we may combine a little incentive theory with functional analysis, we can unearth a further theoretical foundation for the concept of feedback. One might ask: What are the incentives for legislators performing these functions? The answer must be that they wish to reduce the pressures and demands being made on them and to lower the tensions created in their own individual system. Their individual responses, to this extent, will be aimed at producing an institutional response designed to attack that part of the environment responsible for the stress that eventuated in the initial demands for a response. If the outputs produced thereby have the intended impacts, presumably this information will be fed back in the form of lower stress on the individual legislator. If they do not have the intended effects, the stress will be maintained or enhanced, but in any case subsequent responses and outputs will be adjusted to take into account the revised conditions of stress.

In this chapter we test a model of the feedback process that goes from outputs to environmental impact, from environment to inputs, and then through the conversion process to a subsequent output related to the intial one. The crucial stage of the model is that going from environment to inputs. The other parts of the model are either tautological or virtually axiomatic. If we define outputs as policy decisions or nondecisions of the political system (as Easton does), then we have pretty well established by the inclusiveness (or the exhaustiveness) of the definition that outputs are continuously emanating from the political system. If we define inputs (as is customary) as the immediate causes of the outputs, we establish by definition the causal link between the two. If outputs exist, their cause must exist; if we label these causes "inputs," then inputs exist and are the causes of outputs. That outputs have an impact on the environment should be self-evident. Policy decisions, or even nondecisions, must have some effects on some segment of the environment. The effects and the area affected may not coincide with intentions or design, and they may not readily be detected, but there surely must be a strong presumption that outputs have some impact somewhere.

Although most of the systems models assume a completed feedback

---

[4] Malcolm Jewell and Samuel Patterson, *The Legislative Process in the United States* (New York, 1966), p. 8.

loop, it is still an empirical question as to whether environmental impact is converted into inputs that have a self-adjusting effect on subsequent outputs. Again, it may be tautological that inputs are caused by factors in the environment (environment may be defined as the sources of inputs), but not all environmental forces cause inputs, and not all inputs eventuate in self-adjusting responses by the system. We surely cannot therefore take the feedback process for granted, and the major thrust of this chapter is to test for it empirically by means of comparative analysis.

For purposes of clarification let us take a concrete, though hypothetical, example. Suppose that after the passage of a voting rights law by the legislature, tensions were substantially reduced as intended, and objective indications were that only minor or implementing legislation was needed along these lines to maintain stress at a low level. If the lower stress in the environment were converted into corresponding inputs of reduced demands on the legislators, their reaction might then be to make the minor adjustments that seemed called for, and then turn their attention to other demands from other parts of the environment. It is conceivable, however, that minority group spokesmen on their own might continue unabated to press for further similar legislation, even though the previous act had the effects of reducing the demands among the rank-and-file of the minority groups for such legislation. The lobbyists for the minority groups may be simply out of touch with their membership, may be pursuing independent goals of their own, or may feel that strategic considerations indicate that pressure on legislators should be maintained. In any event, this communication defect in the system could bar the legislators and other authorities from perceiving the reduction in tensions, and they might continue by responding with outputs that would be quite dysfunctional from the standpoint of tension management.

It might be well to digress at this point and suggest that lobbyists and other interest groups spokesmen are crucial to this communication phase of the feedback process. They provide the major linkage between the legislators and the environment, at least in the absence of strong state party organizations. If they perform this function well by accurately reflecting changes in tensions within the polity, they can be extremely useful to the maintenance of the system. There are other ways, however, in which the information flow can be accomplished, such as by routine contact with constituents, through the staff agencies of the legislature, and by inputs from the executive branch and the state party organization. Nevertheless, the conversion of variations in environmental stress to inputs probably is most rapidly and effectively accomplished in most states by the interest group spokesmen.

Let us now return to the example of the enactment of voting rights legislation. It was noted that reduced tensions in the environment may or may not be reflected in a reduction of input pressures from that source; but a third possibility is that they are reflected in increased input pressures. This might be the result, for instance, if a lobbyist concluded that he did not want to lose the momentum created in the process of getting the first bill enacted, that even though his constituents were temporarily satisfied, his long-term position with the group required a continuous progression of victories, and that now was the time to apply increased pressure for further legislation of the same kind. A feedback condition such as this would appear to be even more dysfunctional than no feedback at all for the management of tensions.

What I have just described is often referred to as "positive" feedback, or by Karl Deutsch as "amplified" feedback.[5] Thus the more "normal" type, the type that leads to self-adjustment of the system, and the only type that David Easton considers, may be called "negative" feedback. These terms, which have been borrowed from the technology of electronic amplifiers, servomechanisms, and guidance systems, are rather unfortunate, since so-called "positive" feedback seems to lead to negative results in terms of stability of the system. There is, nevertheless, a certain logic to their use. Electronic and electromechanical systems require for self-regulation the feedback of a signal of the opposite polarity from that driving the mechanism. The feedback signal partially counteracts the drive signal and increases in intensity as the mechanism approaches a goal or an equilibrium state, thereby slowing down the operation to avoid overshooting. Finally, as the goal is reached, the inverted feedback signal completely counteracts the drive signal, and no further action takes place until stimulated by an outside force. In these mechanisms, if we were to feedback a signal of the same polarity as the drive signal, this would cause a great overshooting of the goal and then wide oscillation in most such systems between limits set by the energy available to the system or other system parameters.

Most system theorists would regard positive feedback as an aberration, and some might even deny it is a possibility in any existing system. The latter would reason that any surviving system could not contain a mechanism destructive of its survival, that positive feedback is destructive of survival, and therefore it is not and could not have been operating in any existing system.[6] Nevertheless, one needs to take a skeptical view of this sort of

[5] Karl W. Deutsch, *op. cit.,* pp. 192–195.

[6] Defects in this logic are discussed in Jerone Stephens, "The Logic of Functional and Systems Analysises in Political Science," *Midwest Journal of Political Science,* **XIII** (August, 1969), pp. 367–94.

reasoning and remain alert to the possibility of finding positive feedback. Systems surely can contain destructive elements within them and still survive. Furthermore, in political systems this kind of feedback may not turn out to be so destructive after all.

Despite some logical support for the use of the terms "positive" and "negative" feedback, I would like to propose some different terminology that is more consistent with political system effects. Let us refer to the "normal" kind of feedback that promotes system stability as "integrative" feedback instead of "negative," and to the unstabilizing or "positive" type as "disintegrative" feedback.[7]

Measurement of Inputs, Outputs, and Environment

Our model of the feedback process involves three basic elements: inputs, outputs, and environment. Our method requires the quantitative measure of each of these. Direct indicators of any of these are hard to come by, but probably the most serious difficulty is posed by the measurement of inputs. Boynton, *et al.* have successfully measured the input of support for the Iowa legislature.[8] There have been a few studies of local political systems which have approached this problem, but sufficient data for comparative analysis is unavailable and would be extremely expensive to produce. We cannot, however, resort to using environmental measures as surrogates for inputs, as has been done in previous studies of this type, since we are particularly interested in the segment of the feedback loop going from environment to inputs. It would be impossible to test for this if we could not distinguish between these two. A different expedient that might serve our purposes better would be to let outputs stand as surrogates for inputs. This is logically more defensible because every output has inputs by definition, while not every particular environmental measure that we may wish to examine is necessarily related to an input. This latter approach still leaves us in the same basic dilemma, however, because it also combines two elements that should be analytically separate. The only way out is to recognize that one must "skip over" the input stage of the process and take the consequences. These consequences are quite acceptable if one is able to establish a causal relationship going from environment to output. Thus, since inputs are defined as the mediating factors between the two, one could demonstrate that causal links exist between environment to in-

---

[7] I am indebted to Fred I. Greenstein of Wesleyan University for suggesting these terms.

[8] G. R. Boynton, et al., "The Structure of Public Support for Legislative Institutions," *Midwest Journal of Political Science*, **XII** (May 1968), pp. 163–80.

puts and thence to outputs. The consequences are not as acceptable if we have to reject the proposition of a causal link betweeen environment and output, because we then cannot pinpoint when the breakdown in feedback occurred—in the communication stage between environment and input or in the conversion process between input and output. Still, it should be useful to be able to identify feedback breakdown in general.

Reasonably satisfactory environmental measures are available, although they might not always be as comprehensive as we might wish. In this chapter I concentrate on the economic environment, since this seems the most closely related to many inputs and the most directly affected by measurable outputs. One of these measures is an index of general affluence or economic well-being. The other is a measure of income maldistribution. It is assumed that tensions will be higher when the former index is low and the latter index high than when the reverse condition exists.

The affluence index was constructed by factor analysis of 34 economic and demographic variables pertaining to 48 states.[9] The five variables with the highest positive loadings were as follows (with the factor loadings in parentheses):

1. Income per capita (.927)
2. Retail sales per capita (.907)
3. Federal income tax collections per capita (.827)
4. Sound housing as a percentage of total (.821)
5. Number of telephones per 1000 population (.821)

Percent of population with incomes under $2,000 was the only variable with a high negative loading (−.884).

Four other factors were produced, and all five accounted for 74 percent of the total variance. Two of these were identified as an "urban-industrial" factor and a "population-expansion" factor, but two were unidentifiable. All were used in the analysis as environmental measures in the same way as the economic factor, even though it was not anticipated that they would be related to any of the policy outputs. Generally, this expectation was confirmed, and no further use was made of them.

A Gini Index was constructed to measure income maldistribution. This was not used as a variable in the factor analysis because it was to be

[9] An "alpha" factor analysis was performed and five factors were rotated according to the "varimax" criterion. The "economic affluence" factor, which was the first factor, accounted for 30 percent of the total variance. The analysis incorporates measures of the variables from both 1950 and 1960 in a single factor matrix and treats both sets of measurements as if they constituted a single variable. Thus there are 96 observations for each variable instead of 48. Alaska and Hawaii are not employed in the analysis because neither was a state in 1950.

analyzed separately. It was also deemed to be a sufficiently direct indicator of the phenomenon that I wanted to be measured and did not need to be combined with other variables to produce an "income-maldistribution" factor. The index was constructed, according to a method suggested by Alker, from 1949 and 1959 census data on individual income.[10] Essentially, the index is a measure of the divergence of the actual income distribution from perfect income equality (where everyone has exactly the same income). Specifically, it involves the construction of a Lorenz curve which represents the cumulative proportions of aggregate income accruing to cumulative proportions of the population ranging from the lowest to the highest income earners. The area between this curve and a straight diagonal line connecting the origin with 100 percent of both axes—a line representing perfect income equality—is the basis for the Gini coefficient. The actual values of the coefficient are adjusted so that it ranges from zero (when the Lorenz curve coincides with the diagonal line of perfect equality) to 1.0 (a value which is approached but never reached as total income is concentrated in fewer and fewer hands). It seems reasonable that high values of the Gini index would be associated with high tensions in the polity and demands for measures to bring about greater income equalization.

The measurement of output presents somewhat fewer problems, although we again have to use indirect indicators. I have focused for the most part on financial policy as it was assumed that these would have the greatest impact on the economic environment. Fortunately it is relatively easy to obtain reasonably valid measures for these.

From an original list of 31 quantitative measures of policy output, a group of 15 was selected that showed the closest relationship to the economic environmental measures. The 15 were the following:

1. General revenue of the state government per capita
2. General sales and gross receipts tax revenue per capita
3. State debt outstanding per capita
4. Appropriation for public elementary and secondary education per capita
5. Average teachers salaries in public schools
6. Total public assistance expenditures per capita
7. Average monthly payment per recipient under old age assistance
8. Weekly payments per recipient under unemployment compensation
9. Appropriations to public higher education per capita
10. State aid to cities per capita

[10] Hayward Alker, *Mathematics and Politics* (New York, 1965), Ch. 3.

11. Health and hospital appropriations per capita
12. Average weekly earnings of full-time state employees
13. Number of full-time state employees per 1000 population
14. Appropriations for public safety per capita
15. Utility regulations score[11]

These 15 output variables were also factor analyzed, and both the variables and the factors scores were used in the ensuing analysis. Four factors, explaining 58 percent of the original variance, were rotated. The first factor was identified as a "welfare-liberalism" factor, the second as an "educational-support" factor, the third, a "health-expenditure" factor, and the fourth, a "scope-of-government" factor. Only the first and second turned out to have a very close relationship with the measures of economic environment, and so the other two were eliminated in the major part of the analysis.

Method of Analysis

The hypothesis that there is a feedback effect implies a causal relationship between outputs and inputs and succeeding outputs. This notion and our desire to identify linkages between various stages of the process suggest the application of some form of causal modeling. The data can readily be made to fit the major requirements of causal analysis, that is, that the variables form a recursive system. The demands of such a system are that the sequence of causation can be determined *a priori* and that reciprocal causation is ruled out. In the present study these demands can be met by "time-lagging" the measurement of the variables. Thus, if output is measured at time t, the environmental variable might be measured at $t + 5$ years, and subsequent output at $t + 10$ years. A hypothetical causal model of the feedback loop (with inputs eliminated since they cannot be measured) might look like this:

$$t \qquad\qquad t + 5 \qquad\quad t + 10$$
$$\text{output} \rightarrow \text{environment} \rightarrow \text{output}$$

Another requirement of this method of causal analysis is that no variable that has a substantial impact on two or more variables included in the analysis is excluded from the analysis. Such an exclusion is obvious in the model above. We need to add environmental conditions prior to the first

[11] This was supplied by Richard Hofferbert, now of the Inter-University Consortium for Political Research; it is an ordinal scale computed from statutory provisions relating to the regulation of public utilities.

output measurement at t. This environmental measure will be highly correlated, one can predict, with output at time t and environment at time $t + 5$. It is essential to include this in the present analysis in order to sort out the *independent* effects of output on environment. We proceed, in fact, by initially ruling out all combinations of outputs and environmental variables that show no independent impact of the former on the latter. We therefore go back one more step in time and pick up environmental influences 5 years prior to the initial output measurement. The resulting model of the total process therefore is as follows:

$$t - 5 \qquad t \qquad t + 5 \qquad t + 10$$
$$\text{environment} \rightarrow \text{output} \rightarrow \text{environment} \rightarrow \text{output}$$

In terms of the actual years for which the data were collected, time t is approximately 1954 (some of it is for 1953), $t - 5$ is 1949 or 1950, $t + 5$ is 1959 or 1960, and $t + 10$ is generally 1964. (Henceforth, the four time periods will be designated t_1, t_2, t_3, and t_4, respectively.)

The model, as drawn, is confirmed when the partial correlations between two variables connected by arrows are nonzero, and the partials for the other pairs of variables not connected by arrows are zero. In computing the partials, all variables preceding either of those involved are held constant. But for the present study the feedback theory will not necessarily be disconfirmed if there are some nonzero partial coefficients between variables not represented by arrows in the model. It is only necessary that the arrows shown in the model be confirmed by the analysis.

Findings

Since it was determined that there could be no feedback effect in situations where an output produced no environmental impact, it was first necessary to sort out those situations from the ones in which impact was detectable. The three-variable model of output at time t and of environment at $t - 5$ and $t + 5$ was tested for all combinations of the two economic environmental variables with the 15 output variables and two output factors. There were 34 models tested therefore. Of these, 26 were rejected. Table 9.1 presents the output variables and factor that appeared to have a significant impact (at $p < .05$) on economic affluence.

From this it appears that only the welfare programs of state governments have an important impact on state economies, and even this is not very great. There is some suggestion here that educational policy might have a slight impact but further examination of the data would seem to rule this out. Neither state expenditures for public elementary and secondary

Table 9.1 Relationships of Outputs to Economic Affluence Factor

	Simple Correlation	Holding Prior Economic Factor Constant	Beta Coefficient
Old age assistance payments	.692	.473	.161
Welfare-liberalism factor	.800	.322	.135
Average earnings state employees	.707	.348	.125
Average teachers' salaries	.668	.240[a]	.084[a]

[a] Partial correlation coefficient is significant at $\rho \geq .05$; beta coefficient is not.

education nor for higher education showed anything but the slightest partial correlation with the economic factor. Earnings of teachers and state employees show a partial relationship, probably because they tend to be high in states where welfare payments are high and low where welfare programs are minimal.

What is very striking in this analysis is the very high self-correlation between this environmental factor measured at t_1 and t_3. For the 48 states the product-moment correlation between the two time periods was .964! Statistically, this meant that there was very little variance left in the economic factor at t_3 to be explained by the outputs at t_2. It appeared that all of the states benefited from the general rise in the economy between 1950 and 1960, and they seemed, with very few exceptions, to have benefited almost equally. One is driven to the conclusion that no matter what policies the legislatures would have pursued, there was very little they could have done to either help or hinder the economy of the state.

Another possible reason for the paucity of a detectable relationship between outputs and the environment may be due to the small amount of variation in the outputs. Would it make any difference in a state's economic position, one would like to know, if the legislature decided to eliminate all welfare programs or, if it decided to triple the payments in the various welfare categories? A look at some of the extreme residuals from the regression analysis indicates there could be such an effect. Six states—Delaware, Maine, Mississippi, Pennsylvania, Vermont, and Virginia—showed negative residuals greater than one standard deviation from the regression line of 1954 old age assistance payments against the 1950 economic affluence factor. These states, in other words, fell the furthest short in 1954 of coming up to the level of payments based on expectations from 1950 economic conditions. Four of these states had high negative residuals in the regression of 1960 economic factor on the same factor for 1950, although the other two (Delaware and Vermont) fell just about on the regression line. On the positive side of the regression lines, Colorado and Louisiana had the highest residuals for old age assistance payments regressed against 1950 economic conditions, and these two states also showed two of the greatest gains from 1950 economic levels to 1960 (as measured by the residuals of the 1960 economic factor against the 1950). But the next two states in terms of the level of welfare payments versus 1950 economic conditions, North Dakota and Washington, showed only a slight economic gain and a slight loss, respectively. These are rather inclusive results. Although they do suggest that the limited variation in the output data and the possibility of a curvilinear relationship in which the partial regression slopes are steepest for extreme values of the output variable and are inhibiting us from making a more valid assessment of policy impact on the economic environment.

The analysis of policy impact on income distribution is, however, more conclusive. Possibly this is due to the slightly lower correlation (.829) between the environmental variable in 1950 and 1960, or perhaps the relationships are more linear than in the previous case. Table 9.2 lists those outputs that showed a significant impact on income maldistribution (the Gini coefficient):

Table 9.2   Relationships of Outputs to Income Maldistribution

	Simple Correlation	Holding Prior Gini Index Constant	Beta Coefficient
Average teachers' salaries	−.754	−.625	−.421
Welfare-liberalism factor	−.782	−.534	−.411
Old age assistance	−.657	−.430	−.287
Unemployment compensation	−.660	−.418	−.234

The first beta coefficients are significant at the .01 level, and the coefficient with unemployment compensation is significant at .05. This provides some evidence that liberal education and welfare policies tend to reduce inequalities in the distribution of personal income. Welfare programs, of course, are designed to do this, and it is conceivable that liberal educational policies might tend to bring up the earning capacity of individuals coming from the lowest economic classes and thereby narrow the gap between the poorer segments and the rest of society. The level of teachers' salaries would not in itself produce such an effect, but this level is perhaps indicative of the general policy of support for public education, and this may then ultimately account for some of the variations in income distribution among the states.

Before going on, let us note that all the correlations between the Gini coefficient and the output measures are negative. This does not fit the management-of-tensions theory very well, at least if our assumption is correct that a high Gini coefficient would indicate high tensions. According to the theory, the higher the coefficient, the greater the expenditures on programs designed to reduce the magnitude of the coefficient and thereby reduce tensions. Yet, our evidence suggests that a high Gini coefficient encourages less liberal education and welfare policies, and a low Gini coefficient appears to result in more liberal policies; while at the same time, we observe that the more liberal these policies are, the greater the subsequent reduction in the Gini coefficient. Thus the states that would seem to be the least in need of improving income distribution are doing the most toward that end, while those most in need are doing the least. These same tendencies were present, but to a lesser extent, in regard to the welfare outputs and the economic affluence factor. That is, the most affluent states (apparently because they were more able to afford them) tended to enact the more liberal policies, which tended further to increase (at least slightly so, it appeared) their already high affluence.

This first stage of the analysis, as we have seen, produced eight combinations of variables evidencing policy impact. Thus in these eight situations the minimum conditions for feedback were present. The final stage of the analysis, then, was to determine in which, if any, of these instances the impact of outputs on environment was fed back into the system and reflected in changes in subsequent outputs. Figure 9.2 depicts the total process for the three cases in which the evidence permitted us to reject the null hypothesis that there was no feedback.

Discussion

The major points to note in Figure 9.2 are the polarities of the beta coefficients. The signs remain the same as we proceed from t_2 to t_4. This means that in each of the three instances we have cases of positive or disintegrative feedback. For negative or integrative feedback it would be necessary to have a sign reversal in going from the impact coefficient ($\beta t_3 t_2 \cdot t_1$) to the feedback coefficient ($\beta t_4 t_3 \cdot t_1 t_2$). That is, the direct effects of output on the environment would have to be the inverse of the effects of the environment on output in order to produce the self-regulation postulated by the concept of integrative feedback. What we have in the first case (Fig. 9.2a) is a situation where states with high economic affluence (low tensions) are led to enact comparatively liberal welfare programs,

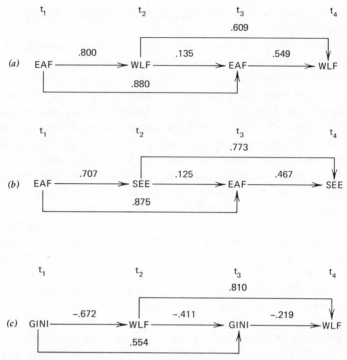

Figure 9.2. Causal models of the feedback process. (*a*) Economic affluence factor and welfare-liberalism factor. (*b*) Economic affluence and state employee earnings. (*c*) Gini index and welfare-liberalism factor.

which, in turn, have the effect of further increasing their affluence (reducing tension further), which results again in a further liberalization of the welfare programs, and so on. On the other hand, the states with the lowest relative affluence (highest tensions) will tend to have the most conservative welfare programs, and the impact of the latter will tend to further diminish their relative position of affluence among the states (possibly increasing tensions), which will result in further lowering of their relative position on the welfare-liberalism scale, and so on. This process would almost seem to provide a built-in "self-destruct mechanism" for the political system.

In analyzing the second model, we have to keep in mind that the variable "state employees' earnings" is somewhat like the welfare-liberalism index in that it is a summary indicator of a general policy of liberality in the state political system. This variable does, in fact, have a relatively high loading (.863) on the welfare-liberalism factor and is generally correlated at a fairly high level with most of the welfare indicator variables and with average teachers' salaries. We can see, actually, that there is not much difference between this and the previous model (Fig. 9.2*a* and *b*); so we cannot regard this second one as supplying additional information of any significance.

The third model represents another case of disintegrative feedback, but it is somewhat more interesting than the other two. In the first place, there is more empirical support for the notion that relative, rather than absolute, deprivation generates tensions in the polity; therefore income maldistribution ought to provide a better gauge of tensions than the average level of incomes. Furthermore, the impact of welfare programs seems to be much greater on income maldistribution than on the level of income; at least the statistical coefficient is higher. The third model, therefore, seems more convincing, and a little more startling, than the previous ones because the assumptions on which it is based seem sounder, and the statistical results seem to inspire more confidence. We have now quite clearly delineated a set of relationships where the conditions most likely to produce high tensions tend to produce responses least likely to reduce those tensions, and shown that after these seemingly dysfunctional responses have had their impact on the environment, the subsequent response is not to correct for the previous "mistaken" response, but to continue in the same direction as before.

One might question at this point whether we were destined to wind up with a finding of disintegrative feedback when we discovered in the first stage of the analysis that initial outputs tended to be in the wrong direction from what would have been predicted by the management-of-tensions theory. Certainly the conditions would be more conducive to integrative feedback if initial outputs tended to be corrective in this sense, but it is mathematically and actually possible to produce a sign reversal at this final stage of process even without these favorable conditions. This would be the case if the direct or net effect of the policy output on the environment were greater than the direct effects of environment on policy output. Translating this into the actual behavior of legislators, the policy impact would have to be great enough to break through their thresholds of perception and become a more influential factor in the decision process than consideration dealing with the financial resources of the state, estimates of what the taxpayers would stand for, or what legislators thought the state could "afford." In one sense, negative feedback could result under conditions like those in the first stages of the three models if the legislators simply could be influenced to take a longer-term orientation toward policy on the basis of perceived information on policy impact. Among the many reasons for their not behaving in this way are undoubtedly the short terms for most state legislators (generally 2 years) and the large turnover in the membership of state legislative bodies (almost 50 percent for the average).

Conclusions

The evidence presented here is concerned with only a portion of the vast arena of public policies and of the relevant environment of the state political system. One obviously cannot generalize very far from this. Nevertheless, our findings have been such as to cast serious doubt on the theory which generated the hypotheses on which the analysis was based. The theory had been formulated essentially to provide an explanation for stability and persistence of political systems. As I have interpreted it, it involves two major propositions. One is that the political system (primarily the legislature) reacts to stress in its environment by issuing policy outputs designed to lower that stress. The other is that a feedback of information about the effects of these outputs on the conditions of stress is necessary to perform this function effectively; otherwise the legislature may overreact, underreact, or continue in a policy direction that is ineffective or dysfunctional. This study has cast some doubt on both of these propositions, at least if they are assumed to be statements of the essential business of the legislature.

One need not deny that the legislature manages tensions, but perhaps this is not its main business. It appears to be aiming at other goals much of the time, and many of its inputs do not seem to be related to tensions at all. Let us first consider the effects on policy of economic affluence. It had been assumed that this variable would be inversely related to tensions in society which would precipitate demands for welfare spending. One might argue that the assumption is invalid and that economic affluence is not inversely related to such tension. Perhaps this is true, but it hardly makes sense to explain our findings by proposing that it is *directly* related to these kinds of tensions, that as the economy of a state improves, the tensions precipitating demands for welfare spending increase.

For a more satisfactory explanation of these findings one has to go beyond the management-of-tensions notion. It is stretching the meaning of "demands" too far to postulate that an input of this nature is responsible for the higher welfare spending in the more affluent states. On the basis of this study, I would propose an addition to the Eastonian framework. Mainly what is needed is an additional input that can account theoretically for environmental influences that are not readily incorporated under the categories of "demands" and "supports." The additional category might be called "resources." This is suggested by the resemblance of the political system model to an economic model, which leads one to the conclusion that if the political agencies of society are charged with allocating values for society, the total supply of allocatable values would constitute a discrete input to the system, along with the various demands for specific allocations of the values. Thus we might view the level of a state's economy not as an indicator of demands, but as a determinant of the parameters within which the legislatures perceive they must operate in reconciling conflicting demands.

To correspond with this formulation, I would also propose analytically to divide the relevant environment into a "sustaining environment" and a "tension-generating environment." Indicators of the former would be such things as the general economic level of the state, the total wealth contained within its boundaries, and other factors that could produce the resource input to the system. Indicators of the latter would be various distributive measures such as the Gini index for income and distribution of educational attainment, as well as measures of discrimination and segregation.

Thus the economic affluence factor would not be regarded under this conception as an indicator of tension, but would still be considered as a valid environmental measure related to inputs to the system. On the other hand, it is difficult to abandon the notion that income distribution is an aspect of the tension-generating environment and is related to demands for welfare spending, even though our findings force us again into the rather untenable proposition that states with the most inequitable distribution have a lower level of demand for liberal welfare legislation than states with more equitable distribution. To find our way through these paradoxes toward an explanation, let us note that there is a negative correlation between the income maldistribution index and the general economic level of the state (about $-.60$). So it is possible that demands in states with poor income distributions are higher than in other states but are not effective in producing the desired output because these states are also the ones with the fewest resources for liberal welfare programs. Here, the two separate inputs of resources and demands would be involved, but the influence of the former on policy outputs would be the greater.

On the basis of the above reasoning, one might expect that if we control for economic affluence, we would observe a tendency for states with the most inequitable distribution indexes to produce the most liberal policies. It does not quite work out this way, since all of the coefficients in the model become too small to provide any convincing evidence, but the evidence is on the side of tentative acceptance rather than rejection of this explanation. The effects of inequitable income distribution in this model on the liberality of welfare programs is not very great, but this may be laid to a failure of interest articulation rather than a failure of this variable as a valid indicator of tensions. The systems approach does not embody the notion that all tension in the environment are automatically translated into demands as input to the system. The most poverty-stricken segments of our population are not organized for political action and are quite difficult to organize, as the Office of Economic Opportunity has discovered. The states with the highest Gini coefficients are the states where there is widespread rural poverty, and it would be extremely difficult to organize these rural poor to exert political pressure. Thus strains and stress undoubtedly are great within the environment of these states, but they are contained by the social and political system and are not translated into effective inputs to the legislature.

Even if one is willing to accept these explanations, we are still faced with the finding that the feedback effect in important areas of state policy is nonequilibrating in its operation. How, then, can we account for the stability of our state governmental systems? There are a number of explanations that can be offered.

First, it would appear that political systems, like the individual, can survive under a good deal of tension. There are a number of constraints in the social and political system of the United States that keep the tensions contained. One would also expect, on the basis of this study, that tensions exist well below the level at which they threaten survival most of the time. It even appears that despite considerable interstate variation in these tensions, they most generally remain below a threshold level at which they become factors in policy decisions.

Secondly, the leveling effects of federal grants and federal programs undoubtedly contribute to social and political stability in the states. In the welfare field particularly, the influence of federal policy has considerably reduced interstate variation compared to what it might be if the states were strictly on their own in these matters. The federal leveling effect is also increasingly felt in the fields of education and health. The existence of these federal programs also suggests that some of the tensions within the state are projected upward and become inputs at the federal level, either because the policy area involved is not a state responsibility under the division of powers, or (more likely) the state legislature has been reluctant to assume responsibility. Most of the tensions that have been building up in our urban areas have not found relief at the state level, but have at the federal level. Now the channels of communication between the cities and Washington are so well developed that many of these urban tensions routinely become articulated as inputs to the federal system and do not impinge upon the state system at all.

Finally, the high degree of interstate population mobility must surely act as a "safety valve" for the relief of excessive tension. Migration rather than political action has been the chosen course of the poverty-stricken rural residents of the South. While relieving tensions in some states, this process undoubtedly increased them in others, but the overall effect would appear to be an equalizing one in terms of the relative tension levels among the states.

As a concluding observation it should be noted that, for most of the policy areas examined, no environmental impact was detectable, and therefore no feedback could be measured. In the normal course of events, the slight effects of outputs on the environment are not fed back as information about increased or reduced tensions to the legislature. In effect, the feedback process appears to be inoperative most of the time. Nevertheless, the state legislatures manage to maintain support for themselves and for the political system. Though quite imperfectly, they appear to be performing the function of political integration. Although these bodies may not be particularly effective in managing tensions, they seem to be satisfying the citizens that their views are represented in the policy-making process and that the system is generally working as it should. They are also the only agencies of government that provide a protected platform for the opposition, which helps to ensure that dissent will not be directed at the legislative institution itself or at the political system in general. They probably can continue to perform these functions passably, if not brilliantly, without the assistance of integrative feedback.

PART FOUR
Conclusion

CHAPTER TEN

Trends and Prospects in Legislative Behavior Research

SAMUEL C. PATTERSON, UNIVERSITY OF IOWA

and

JOHN C. WAHLKE, UNIVERSITY OF IOWA

The chapters in this volume constitute only a fraction of the materials presented and discussed at the Shambaugh Conference on Legislative Behavior Research. And the Conference itself, wide-ranging as were its discussions, was constrained by limitations of time to pursuit of the particular problems raised by the formal presentations and critiques and discussions of them. It may therefore be useful to conclude with a summary view of the implications for future research which seemed to emerge from the meetings.

Although the question was never formally discussed, there was general informal agreement among almost all participants at the conference that the techniques and technology of research are now as advanced and sophisticated as are found in use in any area of political research today. Indeed, the chapters in this book and the other papers presented at the conference hardly begin to illustrate the many different methods of data collection and data analysis now in common use among legislative behavior researchers. The discussions also demonstrated widespread consensus on what uses are appropriate and what are inappropriate for most of these methods, even the newest, most complex, and most innovative.

The point to which discussion returned again and again, however, and upon which there was also general agreement, was the lack of a common framework, common focus, and common agreement upon what problems are important, and what questions most need answering. Time and again

289

questions were raised, not about the validity or the intrinsic merits or interest of any given contribution or research finding, but about the bearing of findings in one area upon findings and questions in others. In short, it was generally agreed at this conference, as it has often been recognized in other contexts, that the greatest needs are not methodological but theoretical and conceptual.

The need is not so much for "the" theory, or even "a" theory of legislative behavior, although should genuine theory in the usual, scientific sense of that term be available it would no doubt represent landmark progress. It is necessary to settle for something considerably less at the present stage of research on legislative behavior and institutions, but it is possible to make considerable progress even with something less. What would seem, under the circumstances, to be attainable as well as useful is a conceptual map that would relate the various concerns to one another, thereby helping us to see more clearly where the investment of research energy is most needed and where it is most likely to yield substantial payoffs.

This is not the place, of course, to attempt to construct such a conceptual map. While there has been considerable theoretical and conceptual progress in the global mapping of research on mass political behavior, there has been no comparable schematicization which could bring some paradigmatic order to scientific analysis of political institutions such as the legislature.[1] To pursue the metaphor, despite an impressive amount of legislative research, mostly about legislatures in the United States and much of it characterized by considerable conceptual and methodological sophistication, we really do not know where we are on the map in comparative, analytic terms.[2] Indeed, we have hardly begun the research-

---

[1] The mapping efforts for comparative research on mass political behavior are reflected in: Stein Rokkan, "The Comparative Study of Political Participation: Notes Toward A Perspective on Current Research," in Austin Ranney, Ed., *Essays on the Behavioral Study of Politics* (Urbana, Illinois, 1962); Stein Rokkan, *Citizens, Elections, Parties* (Oslo, 1970); Seymour M. Lipset and Stein Rokkan, Eds., *Party Systems and Voter Alignments: Cross-National Perspectives* (New York, 1967); Erik Allardt and Yrjö Littunen, Eds., *Cleavages, Ideologies and Party Systems* (Helsinki, 1964); Erik Allardt and Stein Rokkan, Eds., *Mass Politics: Studies in Political Sociology* (New York, 1970); Richard Merritt and Stein Rokkan, Eds., *Comparing Nations* (New Haven, Connecticut, 1966); Stein Rokkan, Ed., *Comparative Research Across Cultures and Nations* (Paris, 1968); Stein Rokkan, Sidney Verba, Jean Viet and Elina Almasy, *Comparative Survey Analysis* (The Hague, 1969); Mattei Dogan and Stein Rokkan, Eds., *Quantitative Ecological Analysis in the Social Sciences* (Cambridge, Massachusetts, 1969); and "Data in Comparative Research," *International Social Science Journal,* **16** (1964), 7–97.

[2] Recent work in American legislative behavior research is reviewed in Heinz Eulau and Katherine Hinckley, "Legislative Institutions and Processes," in James A. Robinson Ed., *Political Science Annual, Vol. I* (Indianapolis, 1966), pp. 85–189. See also John C. Wahlke, "Behavioral Analyses of Representative Bodies," in Austin

mapping operation that would give us the map on which to try to locate the corpus of extant legislative research.

It could be argued that attempts at global mapping for legislative research, at constructing a paradigm for systematic, comparative investigation, are unnecessary or premature.[3] Gaps in knowledge about legislative institutions and behavior are enormous. For many countries, even elementary information about legislative organization, procedures, political powers, or legitimate authority is not available in a substantial or meaningfully comparable form. Even for highly developed political systems alone, the scope of existential statements available about legislative structures and processes is narrow, and the availability of systematic evidence is remarkably uneven. It could reasonably be contended that the major preoccupation for comparative legislative research, at least as a first step, should be to develop a monographic literature at the level of sophisticated descriptive, institutional analysis. We could, without resolving conceptual problems about what constitutes a legislature or how to assemble conceptually equivalent cross-national (or even comparative subcultural) evidence, simply pursue descriptive studies so that, hopefully for a wide range of systems, we would answer such questions as: "How is the institution called *legislature* organized in Country X? What formal and informal powers does it have? What tasks does it have to perform? How does it process its work? Who are the people who constitute it and run it?"

We could be ahead of the "knowledge game" if we had this kind of primitive, existential information about a wide range of operating legislative institutions. It seems clear that progress in legislative research is more likely to be made by mounting a range of descriptive studies of legislatures in countries where it is reasonably easy to identify such an institution than to proceed by the more circuitous and conceptually ambiguous strategy of attempting a precursory definition of legislative *functions* to be followed by potentially quixotic cross-national inventories of how and where these functions are performed. Little lessons about functional sensitivity need not be lost even though we may reject the field research imperatives of functional analysis.[4]

Ranney, Ed., *Essays on the Behavioral Study of Politics* (Urbana, Ill., 1962), pp. 173–190; and Samuel C. Patterson, "Comparative Legislative Behavior: A Review Essay," *Midwest Journal of Political Science,* **12** (November 1968), 599–616.

[3] See Joseph LaPalombara, "Parsimony and Empiricism in Comparative Politics: An Anti-Scholastic View," in Robert T. Holt and John E. Turner, Eds., *The Methodology of Comparative Research* (New York, 1970), pp. 123–149.

[4] As these imperatives may be implied, for instance, from someone like Gabriel Almond. See *Political Development: Essays in Heuristic Theory* (Boston, 1970). And see John C. Wahlke, "Policy Determinants and Legislative Decisions," in S. Sidney Ulmer, Ed., *Political Decision-Making* (New York, 1970), pp. 76–120.

Loewenberg's seminal work on the West German Bundestag could be taken as a model for the proliferation of monographic studies which is critically needed in legislative research.[5] Loewenberg adroitly sets the lower house of the German parliament into its historical and political setting, pointing to the relevant factors of institutionalization which have affected the viability of the institution in the post-World War II period and isolating the main constraints affecting the linkages between the German legislator and his constituents. His analysis elucidates the context of the parliament, showing the principal characteristics of legislative recruitment and the socioeconomic status of the Bundestag membership. He is able to suggest how the *status distinctiveness* of the German legislator both facilitates and inhibits political representation through the parliamentary institution in that political system.[6] His thorough description of the structural context in which the German legislator operates consciously attempts to relate the main structural features of the institution to its performance as a legislative body. He then analyzes the performance of the Bundestag with respect to its role in cabinet formation, lawmaking, and representation of constituents by carefully examining the instrumental and symbolic behavior of members, the activities of parliamentary committees, and the character of party cleavages and party leadership within the legislature. If a study of this caliber were available for a large number of political systems, theorizing, or at least empirically grounded mapping of comparative analysis, could proceed much more effectively.[7]

But the urge to look beyond an array of descriptive, institutional analyses is compelling if, however gropingly, we are to hope that we will have built the foundations for deductive theory in the comparative analysis of legislative systems. Some progress in the direction of operational mapping for comparative legislative research may be made if we attempt specification of three identifiable analytical problems: levels of analysis, system properties, and analysis of individual behavior.[8]

[5] Gerhard Loewenberg, *Parliament in the German Political System* (Ithaca, N.Y., 1967); the German edition, *Parliamentarismus im politischen System der Bundesrepublik Deutschland* (Tübingen, 1969), contains a more extensive bibliography on German parliamentary politics.

[6] See Heinz Eulau, "Changing Views of Representation," in Ithiel de Sola Pool, Ed., *Contemporary Political Science: Toward Empirical Theory* (New York, 1967), pp. 53–85.

[7] For a synthesis of work on legislative behavior in the United States, see Malcolm E. Jewell and Samuel C. Patterson, *The Legislative Process in the United States* (New York, 1966).

[8] These problems are, of course, matters of general discussion in comparative politics. See, for example, Adam Przeworski and Henry Teune, *The Logic of Comparative Social Inquiry* (New York, 1970).

Focus of Comparative Legislative Research

Levels of analysis problems are endemic to comparative political research in general, although they may have much greater complexity in institutional analysis than in research on mass political behavior. There, the main problems involve territorial considerations, concern with appropriate research strategies for analysis of electoral or other mass political behavior in different kinds of territorial units, or the methodological considerations involved in making reciprocal inferences between aggregate and individual data. In legislative research, there is great temptation to generalize from research at one territorial level of analysis to another, even though it cannot be said that conceptual, institutional, methodological, or other difficulties in generalizations across territorial levels of analysis have been much taken into account or even speculated about. In the United States experience, we simply have not dealt with the question of the idiosyncrasy of legislative institutions operating for different territorial units. Some persist in hoping for an analytic level-specific theory, such as a "theory of congressional behavior."[9] Much of the so-called behavioral research about legislative politics in the United States is grounded in studies of the state legislature, often as if no analytical difficulties attend inferring to a national parliament from research on the representative institution in one or more of its territorial subunits.

Quite apart from territorial levels of analysis, comparative legislative research will want to deal with different levels of analysis within the system of legislative behavior in whatever territorial unit.[10] The legislative system should be operationally defined so as to encompass not only the official legislative assembly, but also the components of political interest groups, the executive in his role as legislative leader, the bureaucracy when it seeks legislative representation or is supervised by legislative elites, extra-parliamentary party organizations, and so forth. The legislative system is a constellation of relevant components, and we may wish to analyze different components comparatively. For example, we may wish to investigate the structure and process of interest group legislative representation, as has been attempted across the United States.[11] The focus of research may, therefore, be on the legislative system as a whole, on one or more of its

---

[9] See, for instance, Robert L. Peabody, "Research on Congress: A Coming of Age," in Ralph K. Huitt and Robert L. Peabody, Eds., *Congress: Two Decades of Analysis* (New York, 1969), pp. 3–73.

[10] A very helpful discussion of levels of analysis problems is that of Heinz Eulau, *Macro-Micro Politics* (Chicago, 1969), pp. 1–19.

[11] Harmon Zeigler and Michael Baer, *Lobbying: Interaction and Influence in American State Legislatures* (Belmont, Calif., 1969).

subsystems, or on the individual participant in legislative politics. Here, some algorithm of the ecological fallacy may plague legislative research if we are not careful in making inferences about individual behavior from analyses of aggregate subsystem behavior. In the United States context, for instance, there has been difficulty for a long time in inferring about the behavior of lobbyists from the behavior of pressure groups.[12]

Again, insofar as comparative legislative research will want to focus heavily upon the legislative assembly itself, we can within it break out commonplace differences in analytical levels. The legislature is a nesting of these levels. We may focus on the parliament as a whole, on its separate houses in bicameral cases, on its party or fraction structure, on its committees or commissions, on friendship or subterritory delegation cliques, on pairs of legislators, or on the individual representative. Our understanding of a given legislative institution may depend upon how well we can account for the way in which these components are assembled, and our facility in comparative analysis will certainly depend upon working out ways to test the linkages among components of the parliamentary institution and to make comparisons across legislatures in terms of the organizational constraints which may be differentially operating at different levels of the institution.

Legislative System Properties

System or group properties are those attributes that, while they affect the behavior of individuals in the system, either characterize the system as a whole in such a way that they cannot be inferred from individual behavior, or are aggregates of individual properties to the system level. A high priority in comparative legislative research is to develop system-level indicators which can be used as variables in cross-national or comparative subnational research. A tentative inventory of the kinds of system properties relevant to comparative legislative research would include *settings, contexts, capacity, consequences,* and *diffusion patterns.*

Settings. Settings are made up of properties of the legislative system itself; they constitute major aspects of the institutional environment in which legislators and other participants in the legislative system behave. The environmental mapping necessary for comparative legislative research certainly would include such properties as the historical setting, the institutional matrix, external linkages, the behavioral environment, and the physical setting or ecology of legislative life. Each of these properties has been

[12] See Lester W. Milbrath, *The Washington Lobbyists* (Chicago, 1963), pp. 3–27, 328–358.

explored to some extent in some legislative system, although very little work is comparative. Polsby's work on the institutionalization of the United States House of Representatives illustrates the possibilities for comparative research on the historical settings of legislative institutions.[13] Probably the best analysis of the institutional matrix of a legislature is the work of Richard Fenno on the budgetary committees of the U.S. Congress.[14] External linkages have been examined in research on legislative apportionment and electoral laws.[15] In addition, some work has been done in the United States on support for legislatures in mass publics and among political elites.[16] The behavioral settings for legislatures are indicated in research on party cleavages, and especially inventive in this connection has been the work of Mogens Pedersen.[17] Similarly, the research of Heinz Eulau on the emergent decision-making properties of small legislative groups has been an important contribution.[18] While little has been done with the

[13] Nelson W. Polsby, "The Institutionalization of the U.S. House of Representatives," *American Political Science Review,* **62** (March 1968), 144–168; and Nelson W. Polsby, Miriam Gallaher, and Barry S. Rundquist, "The Growth of the Seniority System in the U.S. House of Representatives," *American Political Science Review,* **63** (September 1969), 787–807.

[14] Richard F. Fenno, Jr., *The Power of the Purse: Appropriations Politics in Congress* (Boston, 1966).

[15] See, for example, Jean-Marie Cotteret, Claude Emeri and Pierre Lalumiere, *Lois électorales et inégalités de représentation en France, 1936–1960* (Paris, 1960); and Douglas Rae, *The Political Consequences of Electoral Laws* (New Haven, Connecticut, 1967).

[16] See G. R. Boynton, Samuel C. Patterson, and Ronald D. Hedlund, "The Structure of Public Support for Legislative Institutions," *Midwest Journal of Political Science,* **12** (May 1968), 163–180; G. R. Boynton, Samuel C. Patterson and Ronald D. Hedlund, "The Missing Links in Legislative Politics: Attentive Constituents," *Journal of Politics,* **31** (August 1969), 700–721; Samuel C. Patterson, G. R. Boynton and Ronald D. Hedlund, "Perceptions and Expectations of the Legislature and Support for It," *American Journal of Sociology,* **75** (July 1969), 62–76; G. R. Boynton, Samuel C. Patterson and John C. Wahlke, "Dimensions of Support in Legislative Systems," in Allan Kornberg, Ed., *Legislatures in Comparative Perspective* (New York, 1972), forthcoming.

[17] Mogens N. Pedersen, "Consensus and Conflict in the Danish Folketing, 1945–1965," *Scandinavian Political Studies,* **2** (1967), 143–166. See also Duncan MacRae, Jr., *Dimensions of Congressional Voting* (Berkeley and Los Angeles, 1958); S. E. Finer, H. B. Berrington, and D. J. Bartholomew, *Backbench Opinion in the House of Commons, 1955–1959* (Oxford, 1961); Duncan MacRae, Jr., *Parliament, Parties, and Society in France, 1946–1958* (New York, 1967); Pekka Nyholm, *Suomen eduskuntaryhmien koheesio* (Helsinki, 1961); and William O. Aydelotte, "Voting Patterns in the British House of Commons in the 1840's," *Comparative Studies in Society and History,* **5** (January 1963), 134–163.

[18] Kenneth Prewitt and Heinz Eulau, "Political Matrix and Political Representation: Prolegomenon to a New Departure from an Old Problem," *American Political Science Review,* **63** (June 1969), 427–441.

physical setting in which legislative behavior occurs, some analyses have made reference to the importance of this property.[19]

Contexts. We may take the term contexts to refer to the aggregated attributes or properties of individuals behaving in the legislative system. Individual legislative behavior may vary in terms of the contextual climate of the legislative institution—the preponderance of lawyers, men of high status, adherents to a particular religious sect, working-class representatives, or members of particular political party can be expected to have an influence on the behavior of legislators. Dominant patterns of value or role expectations may constitute significant contextual effects. In legislative research, we do have a fairly extensive literature on the composition of legislative bodies, and particularly on the social background characteristics of members. The work of Canton in Argentina, Sartori in Italy, Hellevik in Norway, Daalder in The Netherlands, Dogan in France, Noponen in Finland, or Matthews in the United States illustrate the extent of work in individual countries on the social composition of legislative elites.[20]

Studies of legislators' role orientations, while they have not satisfactorily provided explanatory variables from which to account for the roll-call voting behavior of representatives, have greatly enriched our knowledge about the legislative context, and role analyses may ultimately serve as important providers of contextual variables in comparative analysis.[21] The original major work was done by Wahlke and his associates, whose research focused on four of the United States. Stemming from this work, Kornberg was able to use role analysis to reinterpret the context of the Canadian Parliament. Similar work has been done by Gerlich, who worked with the

---

[19] As in Samuel C. Patterson, "Patterns of Interpersonal Relations in a State Legislative Group: The Wisconsin Assembly, *Public Opinion Quarterly,* **23** (Spring 1959), 101–109.

[20] Dario Canton, *El Parlamento Argentino en epocas de cambio: 1890, 1916 y 1946* (Buenos Aires, 1966); Giovanni Sartori and associates, *Il Parlamento Italiano, 1946–1963* (Naples, 1963); Ottar Hellevik, *Stortinget—en sosial elite?* (Oslo, 1969); Hans Daalder and S. Hubee-Boonzaaijer, "Sociale Herkomst en Politieke Recrutering van Nederlandse Kamerleden in 1968," *Acta Politica,* **5** April (1970), I: 292–333, (July 1970), II: 371–416; Mattei Dogan, "Les filières de la carrière politique en France," *Revue Française de Sociologie,* **8** (1967), 468–492; Martti Noponen, *Kansanedustajien sosiaalinen tausta Suomessa* (Helsinki, 1964); Donald R. Matthews, *U.S. Senators and Their World* (Chapel Hill, N.C., 1960).

[21] A careful critique of American legislative role studies is provided by Malcolm E. Jewell, "Attitudinal Determinants of Legislative Behavior: The Utility of Role Analysis," in Allan Kornberg and Lloyd Musolf, Eds., *Legislatures in Developmental Perspective* (Durham, N.C., 1970), pp. 460–500.

Vienna Diet, and by Debuyst, who studied the Belgian House of Representatives.[22]

Capacity. Analysis of the capacity of legislative systems involves developing ways to gather evidence about the capabilities the legislative system has to perform effectively. Legislative tasks, goals, and functions vary in importance and emphasis across legislative systems, and ultimately, it will be necessary to delineate the varying statuses and functions of legislative systems in different polities. However, at least for the rather large subset of legislative systems in which the legislature has some political power—some role to play in substantive political decision-making—we could begin to make comparative estimates of legislative capacity by analysis of such components as:[23]

1. The *intelligence* capability of the legislature. Is substantial information relevant to substantive policy decisions available to legislators, and do legislators have sufficient expertise and expert staff support to use information effectively?

2. The *status* of legislators. Are legislators sufficiently prestigious in popular imagery and do they occupy adequate status within the political elite to play a viable role as influencers and makers of public policy?

3. *Support* for the legislature. Is the legislative institution supported in the critical constitutency; does it enjoy substantial social power, popularity, and legitimacy?

4. Legislative *leadership*. Is the leadership structure of the legislature well organized and sufficiently powerful to provide the steering for the legislature so that it can perform effectively within its terms of reference?

5. The *organization* of the legislature. Is the legislative institution organized so that it enjoys relative organizational autonomy and is characterized by procedural and structural complexity responsive to its tasks, functions, and goals?

6. The *formal power* of the legislative branch. Does the legislature have formal, legal power commensurate with its expected role in the polity?

7. The relative *importance* of the legislature as a policy-making entity. Does the legislative role in the polity carry substantial weight?

[22] See John C. Wahlke, Heinz Eulau, William Buchanan, and LeRoy C. Ferguson, *The Legislative System: Explorations* in *Legislative Behavior* (New York, 1962); Allan Kornberg, *Canadian Legislative Behavior: A Study of the 25th Parliament* (New York, 1967); Peter Gerlich and Helmut Kramer, *Abgeordnete in der Parteiendemokratie* (Vienna, 1969); Frederic Debuyst, *La fonction parlementaire en Belgique: mécanismes d'acces et images* (Brussels, 1966).

[23] Robert C. Fried, *Comparative Political Institutions* (New York, 1966), pp. 28–43.

As Blondel has said, the *viscosity* of the legislature in the processes of government varies among political systems.[24] What are the dimensions of these variations? How are these variations affected by the structural location of the legislative body in the polity—whether the legislature is largely part of the input machinery transmitting demands to policy-makers, whether the legislature is mainly involved in supervision of rule implementation, or whether the legislature is the principal rule-making agency in the governmental process?

Consequences. Hopefully, it will not seem irrelevant to assert that legislative systems have consequences. Their existence and their activities produce effects. In the case of highly-institutionalized, policy-making legislatures like that of the U.S. Congress, the tendency in research has been to take the consequences of legislative activity as self-evident. As a result, United States political scientists have not paid much attention to the policy or systemic impacts of legislative activity, especially beyond the point of accounting for the shape of legislative policy outputs. In a comparative framework, the saliency of analysis of the consequences of legislative activity ought to be clear. At the level of immediate legislative consequences, we would want comparative data on the differential outputs of legislative systems—the relative role of policy outputs, symbolic outputs, and services in different kinds of systems. We would want evidence about the relative short-run consequences of these differential outputs on social, political, or economic change in different kinds of polities. Packenham has tried to open the discussion of these kinds of effects in underdeveloped countries.[25] And we would want data about the longer-run consequences of legislative activity on the flow of demand inputs and support for the legislature (feedback effects). Loewenberg has begun to probe these long run consequences in his analysis of the effects of legislative behavior on regime stability.[26]

Diffusion Patterns. While it involves a general problem of comparative social research, analysis of patterns of diffusion of political structures or values may be especially critical in comparative research on highly institutionalized behavior such as we would expect to find exhibited in legislative settings.[27] It seems highly likely, for example, that research findings about

[24] Jean Blondel *et al.,* "Legislative Behaviour: Some Steps Towards a Cross-National Measurement," *Government and Opposition,* 5 (Winter 1969–70), 67–85.

[25] Robert A. Packenham, "Legislatures and Political Development," in Kornberg and Musolf, *op. cit.,* pp. 521–582.

[26] Gerhard Loewenberg, "The Influence of Parliamentary Behavior on Regime Stability," *Comparative Politics,* 3 (January 1971), 177–200.

[27] This is a problem of considerable complexity which cannot be elucidated here in any detail. It has been discussed most thoroughly in cultural anthropology, and especially by Raoul Naroll, "Some Thoughts on Comparative Method in Cultural

role expectations held by legislators or about specialized legislative structures may not indicate functional relationships to other individual attributes or system properties, but rather emerge because legislative conceptions and practices are often spread by diffusion. Little explicit research in political science has been given to the diffusion process.[28] Nonetheless, it does seem clear that, let us say, British and United States legislative models have been widely copied. Thus, the Indian Lok Sabha is patterned in many respects after the British House of Commons; the Philippine Congress bears many resemblances to the United States Congress; United States forms and practices very much influenced the development of the Congress of Micronesia.[29] In our analysis of functional linkages among variables or attributes in comparative legislative behavior research, we must be alert to the extent to which correlations may be largely artifacts of diffusional processes. If we were to discover, for instance, that 60 percent of the national legislators in Cambodia articulated Burkean expectations about their legislative role and that there was a high correlation between trustee role orientations and the marginality of elections in legislative constituencies in that political system, we may not be talking about a functional linkage at all. Anglo-American conceptions about what a legislator ought to do may be articulated widely in Third World settings without their having much meaning at all.[30] At the same time, patterns of diffusion may be of great interest in their own right. Intrinsically, mapping the diffusion of legislative structures and values on a cross-national basis may greatly illuminate the processes of institutionalization of legislative bodies, and provide an analytical device for plumbing in greater depth modes of cultural adaptation to innovations in institutions.

Individual Legislative Behavior

Although the individual behavior of representatives has been conceptualized and measured in a variety of ways, the predominant interest in

Anthropology," in Hubert M. Blalock, Jr. and Ann B. Blalock, Eds., *Methodology in Social Research* (New York, 1968), pp. 236–277.

[28] The most systematic work is Jack L. Walker, "The Diffusion of Innovations Among the American States," *American Political Science Review,* **63** (September 1969), 880–899.

[29] See L. M. Singhvi, "Parliament in the Indian Political System," and Robert B. Stauffer, "Congress in the Philippine Political System," in Kornberg and Musolf, *op. cit.,* pp. 179–227 and 334–365; and Norman Meller, *The Congress of Micronesia* (Honolulu, 1969).

[30] For a sophisticated analysis bearing on this point, see Raymond F. Hopkins, "The Role of the M. P. in Tanzania," *American Political Science Review,* **64** (September 1970), 754–771.

such behavior has been focused upon two kinds of dependent variables: role orientations and policy or issue attitudes. The study of legislators' conceptions of their jobs as representatives was opened by the seminal research of Wahlke, Eulau, Buchanan, and Ferguson and pursued by a host of investigators, including Gerlich, Debuyst, Kornberg, Barber, and Davidson.[31] Substantial research effort has been invested in identifying both the congeries of role orientations extant in different legislative bodies and the independent variables which help to account for variations in role conceptions held by legislators. Because of the interest of United States investigators in the representational linkages between legislators and their constituents clustered in territorial districts, much of the research in the United States has been concentrated on so-called "representational" roles; research outside the United States, in systems in which the impact of political parties appears to have, *prima facie,* the profoundest effect upon the perspectives of elected representatives, has given more attention to party-related role orientations. Although a large number of independent variables have been constructed to account for variations among legislators in their role orientations, most common have been those of legislators' social background characteristics, and attributes of the milieu from which legislators have been elected. In making an assessment of the outcomes of a number of these investigations, Jewell concluded that

"The evidence concerning possible sources of legislative roles is fragmentary and sometimes contradictory. For these reasons it would be hazardous to draw any firm conclusions about the sources of roles. The evidence does suggest that no single variable offers an adequate causal explanation and that characteristics of districts as well as personal qualities and experiences of legislators are associated with differences in roles. The fact that so many variables appear to have some effect on roles enhances the value of role as an analytical concept. It is doubtful that we could ever measure with great accuracy the impact that a combination of personal and district variables has on the attitudes and perceptions of an entire legislative body. Role provides a shortcut, a way of summarizing the total effect that these various forces have on legislators. An examination of the sources of role is useful because it can make us aware of the complexity of causal factors and point out those which are most likely to be important."[32]

[31] See Wahlke and associates, *op. cit.;* Gerlich and Kramer, *op. cit.,* Debuyst, *op. cit.,* Kornberg, *op. cit.,* James D. Barber, *The Lawmakers: Recruitment and Adaptation to Legislative Life* (New Haven, 1965), and Roger H. Davidson, *The Role of the Congressman* (New York, 1969).

[32] Jewell, "Attitudinal Determinants of Legislative Behavior," in Kornberg and Musolf, *op. cit.,* p. 483.

Analysis of the individual policy or issue attitudes of legislators has largely taken place where the roll-call voting behavior of representatives could provide the data necessary to construct a metric indicating legislators' relative location in regard to some issue domain (e.g. welfare support, internationalism, support for civil rights), or some generalized dimension of attitude (e.g. liberalism to conservatism). The methodological strategies and problems associated with constructing the appropriate dependent variable from roll-call voting data have been worked over pretty thoroughly.[33] Among the independent variables which have been investigated are those of political party, constituency factors, regionalism, legislators' personal predispositions and background characteristics, factors of legislative structure such as clique, committee or delegation, and legislative norms.[34] A finding of general importance has been that, even in the fluid partisan structure of United States legislatures, political party differentiation provides the independent variable of greatest importance in accounting for variations in the policy attitudes of representatives. Comparisons of different houses of bicameral legislatures, examination of different policy dimensions, analysis of voting dimensions over time, and analysis of voting behavior in multiparty legislatures have made it possible to specify the conditions under which party and constituency influences on roll-call voting have differential impacts on representatives.[35] The now-classic Miller-Stokes analysis illustrates the analytical potential of combining legislative roll-call data and data from systematic interviews with legislators and samples of legislators' constituents so as to make it possible to introduce as inde-

[33] See Duncan MacRae, Jr., *Issues and Parties in Legislative Voting: Methods of Statistical Analysis* (New York, 1970); Lee F. Anderson, Meredith W. Watts, Jr., and Allen R. Wilcox, *Legislative Roll-Call Analysis* (Evanston, Ill., 1966).

[34] An excellent summary and bibliography can be found in Cleo H. Cherryholmes and Michael J. Shapiro, *Representatives and Roll Calls* (Indianapolis, 1969). Major American studies would include: David B. Truman, *The Congressional Party: A Case Study* (New York, 1959); David R. Mayhew, *Party Loyalty Among Congressmen* (Cambridge, Mass., 1966); W. Wayne Shannon, *Party, Constituency and Congressional Voting* (Baton Rouge, La., 1968); Duncan MacRae, Jr., *Dimensions of Congressional Voting* (Berkeley and Los Angeles, 1958); Julius Turner, *Party and Constituency: Pressures on Congress*, revised by Edward V. Schneier, Jr. (Baltimore, 1970); and Leroy N. Rieselbach, *The Roots of Isolationism* (Indianapolis, 1966).

[35] Aage R. Clausen and Richard B. Cheney, "A Comparative Analysis of Senate-House Voting on Economic and Welfare Policy: 1953–1964," *American Political Science Review*, **64** (March 1970), 138–152; Duncan MacRae, Jr., *Parliament, Parties, and Society in France, 1946–1958* (New York, 1967), pp. 286–305; Howard Rosenthal, "The Electoral Politics of Gaullists in the Fourth French Republic: Ideology or Constituency Interest?" *American Political Science Review*, **63** (June 1969), 476–487.

pendent variables legislators' own perceptions of constituents' opinions, legislators' policy orientations measured independently from their voting behavior, and constituents' issue opinions.[36] Unfortunately, this very imaginatively designed analysis was based upon very small constituency samples and has not been replicated for elections beyond that of the 1956 congressional election in the United States.[37]

Ingenious attempts to construct dependent variables for legislators' policy attitudes where roll-call votes do not, in general, provide the basis for scaling nuances in issue attitudes have been made in research on the British House of Commons. The most imaginative effort of this kind has been that of Finer, Berrington, and Bartholomew, who analysed so-called "early day" motions in the House of Commons to array Labour and Conservative MPs on a number of issues dealing with foreign affairs, social welfare policy, civil liberties, European unity, and penal policy.[38] Variations in attitudinal positions within British parliamentary parties were investigated in terms of the independent variable of occupational background, education, trade union sponsorship, age, and type of constituency. In addition, attempts have been made at the analysis of the individual behavior of backbenchers in the House of Commons by selecting out for detailed analysis divisions on which significant rebellions occurred within one or both of the two major parliamentary parties, and this type of analysis is well-illustrated by the work of Jackson.[39] Finally, Richards has analyzed a fairly large number of "free votes," on which MPs voted without the benefit of party whips.[40] Richards' analysis involved an effort to assess the effects of occupation, education, age, religion, and region on voting on bills dealing with capital punishment, homosexuality, abortion, divorce, and Sunday entertainment. While his analysis is unnecessarily inconclusive, it does represent an illustration of the possibilities of analyzing the joint effects of party, constituency, and personal factors in legislators' policy attitudes, even in legislative institutions where most issues are decided purely along party lines.

The general task of mapping comparative legislative research strategy

[36] Warren E. Miller and Donald E. Stokes, "Constituency Influence in Congress," *American Political Science Review,* **57** (March 1963), 45–56.

[37] Some refinement of the Miller-Stokes model has been effected. See Charles F. Cnudde and Donald J. McCrone, "The Linkage Between Constituency Attitudes and Congressional Voting Behavior: A Causal Model," *American Political Science Review,* **60** (March 1966), 66–72.

[38] Finer, Berrington, and Bartholomew, *op. cit.,* pp. 15–121.

[39] Robert J. Jackson, *Rebels and Whips: An Analysis of Dissension, Discipline, and Cohesion in British Political Parties* (London, 1968).

[40] Peter G. Richards, *Parliament and Conscience* (London, 1970), pp. 179–196.

will require the time and effort of a large number of scholars in various countries who can refine and elaborate conceptual and strategic research problems and who can add bricks to the construction of comparative-based theory by persistent empirical research. The Shambaugh Conference and the book that grew out of it will, it is hoped, contribute toward such mobilization of scholars, energy, and resources.

Index